"Is there one morality for Christians and non-Christians? Is there a shared language between them? Andrew T. Walker gives rational articulation, not brute assertions, of the *reason* for the hope within us, of the morally ordered and intelligible reality created by God. Meet him on Mars Hill, introducing this fabric of reality in which we live and move and have our being called natural law. Walker goes a long way toward helping the evangelical church see reason and faith in harmony, the end of which is Jesus Christ—and thus be good witnesses to the truth."

—**Adeline A. Allen**, associate professor of law, Trinity Law School

"For a long time, natural law has been considered the exclusive province and preoccupation of Roman Catholic intellectuals. As a result, evangelicals have often approached the idea of natural law with suspicion that such reasoning either seeks to supplant revelation or is a distraction from it. Though other evangelical scholars have sought to generate greater interest in natural law by demonstrating its connection to the work of some of the Reformers, Andrew Walker's Christotelic approach takes the rapprochement between evangelicals and natural law thinking to a new level."

—**Hunter Baker**, provost and dean of faculty,
North Greenville University

"We are roughly two decades advanced into a period of significant retrieval of and re-engagement with natural law ethics by Protestants. Andrew Walker's volume represents a significant step forward in that necessary work as it seeks to articulate and apply the natural law for evangelicals today. While our culture becomes more and more disconnected from reality and a true understanding of God, humanity, and the created order, a rediscovery of the great Christian tradition of natural law thinking is urgently needed. Walker's work is a worthy entry in that broader conversation."

—**Jordan J. Ballor**, director of research, First Liberty Institute

"Some contemporary evangelicals have looked with suspicion upon the natural law, viewing it as either a Roman Catholic doctrine or as a rival to a more robust biblicism. This has been unfortunate because natural law remains a necessity for coherent Christian ethics. That is why I am so grateful for the appearance of Andrew Walker's *Faithful Reason*. This book is a clarion call for Christians—especially evangelicals—to embrace their

Christian inheritance, a part of which is the rich natural law tradition. I hope this book will be widely read."

—**Denny Burk**, professor of biblical studies,
The Southern Baptist Theological Seminary

"In *Faithful Reason,* Andrew Walker contributes to the growing project of retrieval in which Baptists are recovering their Reformed and Protestant theological roots. In a day when liberal Protestantism has abandoned its own patrimony in post-Reformation scholasticism, more and more evangelicals are awaking to the need to ground our confession in something older and deeper than revivalism. The recovery of natural law and its grounding in metaphysical realism is one exciting aspect of this project. While this work will not be the last word on the subject, it has the potential of being a door into a premodern world where reason and faith work harmoniously together to discern wisdom. It is to be hoped that many will enter this door and discover the intellectual and spiritual feast that awaits."

—**Craig A. Carter**, research professor of theology,
Tyndale University

"Many, if not most, pious Protestants would be amazed—perhaps even aghast—to learn that *all* of the magisterial Protestant Reformers affirmed the natural law. Given this witness of the church's history, Walker's book is part of a most encouraging trend. Walker joins a growing number of orthodox Protestants who have come to recognize both the inevitability of natural law and its utter necessity in the public sphere. For too long evangelically-minded Protestant types have divorced redemption from creation in their theological and ethical understanding. But because creation is ratified by redemption, moral reality, covenantally speaking, has not changed. 'Christian ethics' is in truth 'creation ethics,' as Walker properly and wonderfully reminds us. Christians shall need to acknowledge the law 'written on the heart' if they wish to engage the world around them responsibly."

—**J. Daryl Charles**, affiliate scholar, John Jay Institute

"Aiming to be an 'apologetic for the rational coherence and superiority of Christian ethics,' Andrew Walker's admirable and helpful book deftly explores and clarifies the bases and principles needed to achieve that aim philosophically as well as biblically; he does this by calmly critiquing misguided doubts and skepticisms whether theological, secularist, or simply crowd-following, and comprehensively getting beyond them."

—**John Finnis**, emeritus professor, Oxford University

"Can faith be reasoned and reasonable? Is a commitment to reasoned truth-seeking, especially in the quest for moral wisdom, compatible with faith? In *Faithful Reason*, Andrew Walker argues compellingly that faith and reason, far from being in conflict or even tension, are mutually supportive and, indeed, mutually required. A person of faith should hold reason and rational inquiry in high esteem. A person who prizes rational inquiry should understand faith as a reasonable response to truths that have been revealed."

—**Robert P. George**, McCormick Professor of Jurisprudence, Princeton University

"Andrew Walker argues that natural law thinking—sometimes dismissed as a tool of Catholic apologetics—is valuable in its own right, and for Protestants. That to affirm the integrity of human reason is not to challenge God's sovereignty, but to give him glory; not to spurn his gift of revelation, but to cultivate his gift of conscience; not to set aside his law, but to grasp its wisdom. And to those who already embrace natural law thinking, Walker urges that it allows for a wider theological frame and even finds its home there, in reflection on the humanity and reign of the man whom Christianity finds at the center of everything. In these ways, Walker's philosophical inquiry doubles as prophetic witness. Though born of recent cooperation between Catholics and Protestants, its value is broad and enduring."

—**Sherif Girgis**, associate professor of law, University of Notre Dame

"Andrew Walker has produced a masterful explanation and defense of classical natural law. He brings new insights and arguments to an ancient tradition. He exhibits the virtue of speaking the whole truth in season and out of season. This text skillfully combines subtle theological and philosophical analysis with an accessible style that speaks to any person of good will. The work skillfully balances necessary theoretical grounding and practical real-world applications."

—**Brian M. McCall**, Orpha and Maurice Merrill Chair in Law, University of Oklahoma

"Andrew Walker has done for all Christians, but particularly for evangelical Protestants, an enormous service with this book, by setting forward an understanding of natural law that is eminently compatible with their fundamental commitments. If the Christ of grace is no longer set in opposition to the Jesus of nature, but the two are understood as conjoined, it opens the way to think more cogently about the whole range of dilemmas facing us in such dispiriting times. At the same time, it reminds us that, at bottom, the Christian life is not about winning battles, or harvesting fruit, but in steadfastly witnessing to the truth for its own sake, whatever the outcome."

—**Wilfred McClay**, Victor Davis Hanson Chair in Classical History and Western Civilization, Hillsdale College

"*Faithful Reason* fills a gap that has long needed filling: a fully worked out theory of natural law from a Protestant perspective. Drawing on the historic Christian tradition as well as contemporary writings, Andrew Walker provides a satisfying account of natural law grounded in human nature and God's moral order, as well as examples of how to apply natural law reasoning in practice. This is an excellent volume which will give Christians greater confidence in the truths of God's word and the order of His world, and a robust framework for considering complex questions of ethics and policy."

—**Ben Saunders**, associate professor of law, Deakin University Law School, Australia

"If there is a renaissance of evangelical appreciation and practice of the natural law, grounded in biblical truths, and thoughtfully applied to contemporary challenges, Andrew Walker's work on these matters will be one of the reasons why. *Faithful Reason* is a comprehensive book that delves into the substance of natural law ethics with an eye toward accessibility and application. Newcomers to natural law thinking, veterans, and even skeptics will benefit from grappling with the themes herein."

—**Micah Watson**, Paul Henry Chair in Christianity and Politics, Calvin University

# Faithful
# Reason

FOREWORD BY CARL R. TRUEMAN

# Faithful Reason

## NATURAL LAW ETHICS FOR GOD'S GLORY AND OUR GOOD

### Andrew T. Walker

ACADEMIC
BRENTWOOD, TENNESSEE

Dedicated to my parents, Fred and Sue Walker,
who raised me in the Christian faith and love me as a son.

# CONTENTS

# ACKNOWLEDGMENTS

Every book is a labor of love. That is, a book is a work, hard work, that flows out of a love that one has for a subject. Doubtlessly is that the case for this book. It was in my early thirties that I realized it was natural law theory that tied together all my disparate interests—political theology, Christian ethics, and political philosophy. I pray that my passion for this topic is reflected in what ensues in the following pages.

Acknowledgment and gratitude are owed to several people and organizations in overseeing the development and writing of this book. I'm thankful to the administration of The Southern Baptist Theological Seminary for supporting me and encouraging me through this project, especially President R. Albert Mohler Jr., who on more than one occasion through conversation and debate sharpened, refined, and clarified my thinking about natural law theory as a Protestant and evangelical scholar. I'm also thankful for Boyce College Dean Dustin Bruce, who has been a forbearing friend listening to my ceaseless dronings about the natural law during neighborhood walks. Ryan T. Anderson, President of the Ethics and Public Policy Center, is a dear friend whose courage has fortified my own witness and whose intellectual sharpening as a mentor means the world. Alex Ward and Christopher Parr are owed appreciation for research assistance they provided. My friend Casey Hough was a great encouragement and helpful reader. My Spring 2023 Moral Theory class read the entire manuscript and provided helpful feedback. I also want to thank my doctoral students Marty Beamer, Josh Wester, Nick Spencer, Tyler Hurst, and John Simons, for reviewing the manuscript. My agent Andrew Wolgemuth is a helpful partner whose assistance I would be lost without. I'm also grateful to Madison Trammel and B&H Academic for working with me to see this book through from its proposal to publication. Lastly, Alliance Defending Freedom, an organization I highly respect and who I am thankful to serve as faculty for their Blackstone Legal Academy, provided a grant through the Ethics and Public Policy Center to provide additional resources to help see this book through to completion.

Of course, every endeavor is done in service to my Lord and Savior Jesus Christ and the gift of my family he has blessed me with. Christian, Caroline, Catherine, and Charlotte—I love you.

Andrew Walker
Louisville, KY
July 2023

# FOREWORD

As Christians, we live in strange times. To an extent, that is a truism. Christians have always lived in strange times: as citizens of the heavenly kingdom, we sojourn in the City of Man and therefore find that we are subject both to the division in our own hearts between our new nature in Christ and the remnants of our sin, and to the contradictions of living as Christians in a world that is at best indifferent, at worst hostile, to our faith. That was the same when Paul walked the earth as it is today. And yet each generation faces a world with its own distinctive strangeness and ours is marked both by the volatility and extremity of such. Perhaps never in human history have moral values been subject to such constant, rapid, and unpredictable change. And perhaps never have these changes been marked by such extreme rejection of things that were virtually unquestioned until what often feels like the day before yesterday. What is marriage? What is sex for? What is a woman? These are things that enjoyed broad social consensus until very recently and matters upon which the traditional teachings of the church and the broader views of society at large were largely in agreement.

Given that this consensus has collapsed, and collapsed with dramatic speed, Christians have been left scrambling to find ways of thinking about matters, particularly ethical matters, that in the past they could simply take for granted. Of course, Protestants love to quote the Bible and rightly so: the Bible is the final authority in matters of Christian faith and practice.

But with a generation rising whose minds are shaped by the therapeutic ethics and intuitions of the world around us, and where ghastly TikTok and Instagram "influencers" have emerged as a significant source for social and moral values, it is helpful to show not simply that the Bible is true but that it also makes sense. The young person who asks his pastor why homosexuality is wrong might well be convinced by a Bible verse; but he might also wonder if God wrote that simply because he wants gay people to be miserable. In that context, supplemental arguments can be hugely helpful. And what about those issues that arise today where there is no single Bible verse that addresses the issue: stem cell research, for example, or IVF or surrogacy? And what of the "next big thing" that, by definition, nobody can predict but everyone knows will be controversial and complicated?

In such a world, a return to the Protestant tradition of natural law is vital. Yes, Protestantism, under the influence of unfortunate strands of German and Dutch theology, abandoned this in the late nineteenth and twentieth centuries. But the price has been high and is set to go higher. This is why the recent renaissance in natural law among Protestant thinkers is to be welcomed. And it is why this book by my good friend Andrew Walker is so valuable. It is not a naïve presentation of natural law as the cure for all our ills, far less the assertion of an autonomous rationalism as many have (and no doubt will) suggest when the term "natural law" touches that reflexive nerve in their theological imaginations. It is rather an articulate argument both for the biblical authority of natural law and a reflection upon its utility both as a pastoral tool and as a resource for advocacy in the wider sphere. Neither a naïve optimist nor a myopic pessimist, Walker offers realism, practical realism, for Christians as they seek to develop the intellectual tools for tackling our current moral questions and whatever their next iteration might be.

Andrew is to be thanked for his work in this area. He has given us an important book on a subject that will only become more pressing in the coming years.

Carl R. Trueman
Grove City College
July 2023

"By reason I see a thing is so;
by faith I know it as it is."
—The Valley of Vision

# Introduction

# His Glory, Our Good

O ne of the most important moments in the history of ethics occurred on November 21, 1945, when Robert H. Jackson, Chief Counsel for the United States at the Nuremberg Trials, opened with the following speech before the International Military Tribunal. He had one objective: to prosecute Nazi war criminals for the unspeakable crimes they inflicted upon humanity. In Jackson's famous words:

> The privilege of opening the first trial in history for crimes against the peace of the world imposes a grave responsibility. The wrongs which we seek to condemn and punish have been so calculated, so malignant, and so devastating, that civilization cannot tolerate their being ignored, because it cannot survive their being repeated. That four great nations, flushed with victory and stung with injury stay the hand of vengeance and voluntarily submit their captive enemies to the judgment of the law is one of the most significant tributes that Power has ever paid to Reason.
>
> This Tribunal, while it is novel and experimental, is not the product of abstract speculations nor is it created to vindicate legalistic theories. This inquest represents the practical effort of four

of the most mighty of nations, with the support of 17 more, to utilize international law to meet the greatest menace of our times—aggressive war. The common sense of mankind demands that law shall not stop with the punishment of petty crimes by little people. It must also reach men who possess themselves of great power and make deliberate and concerted use of it to set in motion evils which leave no home in the world untouched. It is a cause of that magnitude that the United Nations will lay before Your Honors.

In the prisoners' dock sit twenty-odd broken men. Reproached by the humiliation of those they have led almost as bitterly as by the desolation of those they have attacked, their personal capacity for evil is forever past. It is hard now to perceive in these men as captives the power by which as Nazi leaders they once dominated much of the world and terrified most of it. Merely as individuals their fate is of little consequence to the world.

What makes this inquest significant is that these prisoners represent sinister influences that will lurk in the world long after their bodies have returned to dust. We will show them to be living symbols of racial hatreds, of terrorism and violence, and of the arrogance and cruelty of power. They are symbols of fierce nationalisms and of militarism, of intrigue and war-making which have embroiled Europe generation after generation, crushing its manhood, destroying its homes, and impoverishing its life. They have so identified themselves with the philosophies they conceived and with the forces they directed that any tenderness to them is a victory and an encouragement to all the evils which are attached to their names. Civilization can afford no compromise with the social forces which would gain renewed strength if we deal ambiguously or indecisively with the men in whom those forces now precariously survive.[1]

---

[1] Robert H. Jackson, Speech before the International Military Tribunal, November 21, 1945, Robert J. Jackson Center, available at https://www.robert

The Nuremberg Trials are one of the most infamous moments in world history. Never had barbarism of such scale been put on trial as were the Nazis who orchestrated the Holocaust. But according to Jackson, the very notion of morality itself was on trial. Were the Nazis to go free, we would be consigning ourselves to the reality that morality has no objective content and injustice can go unchecked. But suffused within Jackson's speech is an overture to a moral law that everyone knows the Nazis violated: the natural law. Its violation had to be answered for on a global stage. How to prosecute the Nazis in the absence of an international law code left the nations responsible for bringing them to "justice" in search of a standard to try them by. It is hard to see the Nuremberg Trials as anything less than the vindication of the existence of the natural law. The world's wrath against injustice and quest for satisfaction against an unspeakable moral evil was the *raison d'être* of Nuremberg. As one atheist public intellectual granted, secularism may have tried to eclipse its concepts of Satan and hell, but it merely replaced them with Hitler and Auschwitz. Our world is haunted by a moral quest that secularism cannot provide.[2]

While not all considerations of the natural law are as freighted and grandiose as topics like Nazism and Nuremberg, the topic of the natural law reminds us of one of the most important concepts not only to Christian ethics but to humankind in general—the need to live life well; to obtain an end to our existence that allows us to say with confidence and clarity, "This is the well-lived life." The idea that rational beings could direct themselves to necessary ends that complete them speaks to the very essence of what it means to be human. The very notion that God would implant within persons the ability to know right from wrong is the very foundation for meaningful interaction within the world. If there were no natural law, there

---

hjackson.org/speech-and-writing/opening-statement-before-the-international
-military-tribunal/.

[2] "Does God Exist? A Conversation with Tom Holland, Stephen Meyer, and Douglas Murray," Hoover Institution, January 9, 2023, https://www.hoover.org /research/does-god-exist-conversation-tom-holland-stephen-meyer-and-douglas -murray.

would be no personal morality or political morality to speak of. The very notion of Christians sharing in the same sort of moral agency as their non-believing neighbors is an invitation to consider how and whether people can live together in social harmony despite deep disagreement on many (though not all) important matters.

Questions immediately arise regarding the origin, knowability, content, and utility of the natural law. I submit that the natural law, being the very thing that the concepts says it is—"natural"—means that the natural law is all around us in 10,000 ways. Consider a few examples.

## The Everydayness of the Natural Law

A few years ago, when I had a longer commute to work, there was a snow-storm that hit the middle Tennessee area where my family was then living. The area was not accustomed to handling large amounts of snow, and it understandably snarls traffic and causes drivers to panic.

The Tennessee Department of Transportation had digital highway signs posted on overpasses that could communicate conditions and warn-ings to drivers. During this snowstorm, one sign over the highway read "Snow & Ice: Slow Down and Arrive Alive." The statement hardly needs explanation: everyone, it just seems, knows *intuitively* and *reflexively*, to exercise caution when conditions can deteriorate and endanger lives. We assume that no one in their right mind would wantonly seek to endanger themselves and their fellow travelers. This is hardly a controversial axiom. Whether to simply avoid the prospect of bodily harm or to avoid a costly insurance nuisance, did the Department of Transportation have to go about with prolonged analytical proofs to explain why individuals *ought* to drive safely? No. The oughtness of its directive presupposed axiomatic moral knowledge that requires no other ground for its justification than its own reflexive intelligibility. It would seem *self-evident* that individuals would order their behavior to protect their lives. The routine posting of a message in a snowstorm, however, is packed full of concepts integral to the philosophical contours of natural law and natural law theory, the topic this book seeks to rehabilitate for a Protestant audience. A routine situation like this invokes concepts such as moral goods (protecting life), norms (drive safely), and the means to apprehend both (practical reason). Natural law, in other words, is quotidian: We act upon its tenets every day without consciously declaring to ourselves, "I am conceiving of the natural law." It just *is*.

First, there is the most important concept of what the road sign is intending to communicate: life is intrinsically good, valuable, and worth protecting *for its own sake*. Every moment of our day, it seems, is consciously or unconsciously ordered for our safeguarding and self-preservation—from sleeping, bathing, eating, working. Tennessee's government wants to likewise protect the lives of its citizens by warning them of potential hazards. So according to the logic of the state of Tennessee's promulgating such a statement, the knowable fact of life's value has practical implication for one's conduct: drivers should drive with a higher degree of caution to protect their lives and the lives of their fellow citizens.

The state of Tennessee's warning has an implicit and explicit moral message: Harming yourself and others is a bad outcome—genuinely bad, not just an apparent bad. Basic categories of "good" and "bad" are pregnant with moral and philosophical meaning. Goodness and badness are moral properties human beings believe correspond to a state of affairs that is either truly and objectively good or bad. When something as horrific as a school shooting occurs, no one goes looking to moral philosophers to discern whether the death of innocent school children is truly bad. It is not just bad, but evil. Airy academic conversations about whether "good" or "bad" exists belies the reality that everyday living requires conformity to judgments that everyone, at their deepest levels, needs in order to live.

Back to our driving example. To prevent such an outcome as personal injury, drivers are encouraged to slow down and be mindful of their speed in order to bring about a situation where as few people as possible are harmed. But the issue of knowing life's value assumes a particular grasp of its value as an object worthy of ordering our behavior on behalf of. The fact that drivers can reason, grasp, and order their lives in response to the value of their life is how we understand the existence and operation of the natural law. Merely reflecting on the data of everyday experience gives us reasons to order our actions to obtain beneficial outcomes.

Let's break down the seemingly obvious into its constitutive parts. How do we know such a truth about life and what is required in response to that truth? Based on an innate, reflexive capacity and exercise of our practical reason and our reflective grasp of life's inherent (non-instrumental) value, people (ought to) desire not to harm themselves nor others. Therefore, to not harm others (which is a bad situation), people should drive cautiously. Thus, from the grasp of a good (life), a moral principle (drive safely) is derived. A basic moral good we should strive to achieve (life) established a norm (drive safely). That is all the natural law is at its essence—determining moral goods, moral duties, and moral norms as rational creatures and acting in harmony to obtain them. But the moral message of the snowstorm was no mere private moral law.

Telling passengers to slow down in a snowstorm is an attempt to convey or *promulgate* a message with a morally intelligible meaning. It isn't a statement of preference or condition. Rather, it was an imperative. You "ought" to do "X" in order that desired "Y" be the outcome. How do we know "Y" is desirable and what rule directs us to desire "Y" in the first place? Our capacity for reason. Why are humans reasoning creatures? Because God has implanted within our nature as human beings the ability to perceive and understand, through the capacity of reason, the basic goods that fulfill the nature of our being.

That this message to protect life was broadcast publicly, where thousands of drivers saw it, indicates even more how such a message was an exercise in public morality and public rulemaking. People *en masse* were the recipients of this message, meaning that for such a safe state of affairs to be realized, it would have to be followed by everyone. Such a reality speaks to the aspect of the natural law as *law*; that is, as a rule from which conformity to it applies to all, equally. This message by a political authority was coordinating all of the drivers' individual activities toward a common good—their continued livelihood and passable roadways. A single person who sees themselves as an exception to this rule and who drives too fast in order to harm those around them shows how one moral infraction can bring great harm to a large number of people. But a person who purposefully and wantonly endangers others and themselves is not only engaging in a criminal offense; they are acting outside of their rational mind, since action that thwarts the good is never truly choiceworthy as an end to be pursued. The common good of everyone's livelihood is at stake in people agreeing to follow principles of safe driving.

## Olympic Integrity and the Natural Law

Consider another example of the routine universality of natural law and moral norms. Since 1972, before the start of each Olympic games, coaches, athletes, and judges have all taken an oath. Each in their own respective capacity recites the following:

> We promise to take part in these Olympic Games, respecting and abiding by the rules and in the spirit of fair play, inclusion and equality. Together we stand in solidarity and commit ourselves to sport without doping, without cheating, without any form of discrimination. We do this for the honour of our teams, in respect for the Fundamental Principles of Olympism, and to make the world a better place through sport.[3]

Consider not only the words themselves, but the setting and participants making this pledge. Before a global audience, global participants who speak different languages from distinct cultures are all unified around the mutually-agreed-upon need for basic justice in their competition. There is a mutual assent to a principle which then entails a mutual commitment to

---

[3] "What is the Olympic oath?" International Olympic Committee, https://olympics.com/ioc/faq/games-ceremonies-and-protocol/what-is-the-olympic-oath.

standards of action. Three prongs of natural law are present: *Universality*, *Objectivity*, and *Intelligibility*. Universality is present by virtue of global participants before a global audience agreeing to set terms of competition, whereby each athlete is afforded equal standards of evaluation. Objectivity signifies the brute existence of a principle, whereby its recognized existence implies response and conformity to its standard. Intelligibility is present, wherein the propriety of "fair play" retains intelligible coherence. In other words, each person reciting the pledge knows what "fair play" conceptualizes and entails by their mouths uttering the words. The grasp of a particular good (skillful, competitive play) sets the conditions for action and the practical reason's grasp of particular goods establishes norms for rightly ordered conduct.

None of the examples above relied on any specific overture to divine revelation for their intelligibility. Regarding the Olympians, each may or may not believe that God exists, but the independent intelligibility of the norm of fair play—even if not perfectly obeyed or maybe even eventually violated—subsists within each athlete. No athlete was present who, in other words, failed to understand the terms of just competition. Of course, the reason such rules are necessary in the first place is because players are prone to cheat in order to perversely benefit themselves. A person may intend to cheat, but the knowledge of violating a standard is itself a testimony to true knowledge witnessed to by self-evident facts. Internal knowledge of one's own cheating is a function of practical reason's faculty of conscience setting off an alarm. But a pledge to fair play conditions the event to obtain a just outcome. The natural law does not deny disobedience to it. Rather, as offenses against the natural law take their toll, it is disobedience to standards of justice that make the tenets of the natural law most glaring.

## Awareness of Evil and the Natural Law

Consider yet another example: If I were to hold up images of the Auschwitz concentration camp alongside a picture of Mother Teresa and asked individuals to choose which image signifies wickedness and the other love, I would not need to engage in lengthy rhetorical back-and-forth to explain why Mother Teresa signifies love, charity, and compassion while Auschwitz signifies despair, revulsion, evil, and grief. Why? The response to these images does not call forth immediate action, but it elicits a moral judgment about prior historical circumstances and their outcomes. An internal faculty residing in each person awakens individuals to trigger the conscience to know that one is evil, the other good. The Holocaust stands as one of the evilest events in human history that everyone *just knows* is evil. An innate, seemingly underived moral law consisting of basic knowledge of good and evil seems a fact of human existence.

Are there individuals alive today who celebrate the Holocaust? There are. Racism, ethnic supremacy, and antisemitism are seemingly timeless pathologies locatable throughout human history. But everyone with a rightly calibrated mind believes that individuals who celebrate something as ghoulishly vile as the Holocaust are severely malformed persons. These individuals exist on the margins of society (justifiably so), and individuals of goodwill know that mainstreaming Holocaust defenses is beyond contemptible. Consider an irony, however, in that Holocaust defenders would not want *their* own children subjected to tortuous murder. What this tells us is that even individuals with morally perverted faculties retain some minimal moral knowledge, or else they would be unable to know what evil even is. More will be said later about inexplicable evil and how it is justified.

The fact that humans can be simultaneously capable of evil and capable of good reveals that wars of passion reside internally and socially, but the complete, exhaustive elimination of all knowledge of good and evil is impossible. How one can allow for another's child to be murdered as was the case in the Holocaust but act to spare their own testifies to the ways in which sadistic personality, deceitful reasoning, vicious habit, evil desire, barbaric custom, groupthink, cowardice, and philosophical error (about equality, for example) can obscure the response to the natural moral law inside of persons. Maniacal evil exists, but even maniacal evil exists because it thinks it is serving some desirable-though-evil end. The natural law tradition does not teach that every desire or perception welling up inside of persons is to be done. Rather, desires and perceptions must be subjected to the power of reason as an instrument to subordinate evil and disordered passions. Such is one reason why Christianity sees true knowledge of things as they ought to be as indicative of salvation (Rom 12:1–2; Col 3:10). As the natural law tradition insists, there are basic moral truths discernible by all, but that can err by way of judgment and application—especially the more remote the implications of natural law are when applied to more granular situations.

## Family and the Natural Law

Consider one final situation. My family enjoys going to our local pool over the summer. Several activities will ensue. I may pray quietly, listen to music, or read a book. I might even sit and simply enjoy the beauty of the sky on a cloudless summer day. I may take a nap or swim a few laps in the pool for exercise. I will play with my daughters and converse with my wife. We will eat a meal poolside, perhaps with friends from our neighborhood.

Why do I do any of these actions? Not only that, why do I not need to be convinced or coaxed into doing them? At the risk of being too obvious, the reason I pursue any of these actions is because they are worthwhile—or choiceworthy—things to do *for their own sake*. Resting, conversing with my wife, praying, playing with my children, chatting with a friend, enjoying a delicious Coca-Cola, attaining knowledge through a good book, and listening to good music are intrinsically beneficial activities pursued for their own sake that contribute to my fulfillment as a living person. Playing with my children, for example, is something I do because the fostering of a healthy relationship with my daughters is something beneficial and *good* for its own sake. The good of my family's well-being is not instrumental. It does not get me a greater good beyond the good of my family's own well-being. It, and other activities at the pool like I described above, are aspects of what the natural law tradition considers as "non-instrumental goods" that practical reason grasps as worthwhile activities to pursue that fulfill or complete what it means to flourish as a human being. These goods of my existence are grasped and inform what actions to take and what actions to avoid in order to obtain them. Moral principles are derived based on my understanding of these goods. I should never act, for example, to thwart any of the goods my mind understands as good. To do so would invite an injustice and a moral wrong.

## The Heartbeat of Christian Natural Law Ethics: Jesus Christ

As the above examples indicate, natural law is everywhere. From obeying road signs to fidelity to one's spouse, the natural law finds a way to show itself. Moral order and moral goods exist as dispensations of divine grace that a benevolent Creator makes known to his creation, even those who refuse to acknowledge him. As I will argue throughout the rest of this book, natural law is one of the central traditions to Christian ethics, if not its most historic and significant, as far as its impact on culture, civil law, and government.

One aspect of how the natural law has not traditionally been conceived of is in relationship to Christology. The natural law exists to hold human beings accountable to God's moral law and, in that sense, to bring us to the gospel.[4] It should also point us to Jesus Christ, by whom and for whom—according to Scripture—all reality is ordered, upheld and created (John 1:2; Col 1:15–20). It is Christ who provides the ultimate foundation and ultimate finality of where all moral good is directed. Christ is our *telos*—completion—and it is in knowing our *telos* that we best know ourselves. The natural law speaks to the very pattern of creation that Christ continues to sustain. It explains the orderliness that every person desires to participate

---

[4] For more on the relationship between natural law and the gospel, see Andrew T. Walker, "The Gospel and Natural Law," *First Things*, December 8, 2020, https://www.firstthings.com/web-exclusives/2020/12/the-gospel-and-the-natural-law.

in by virtue of the image of God inscribed upon them. It explains our desire for safety, our longing for justice, our knowledge of good and evil, the ends or goals of our existence, and the directiveness of our actions.

We err, of course, but every rational person is acting for an end that they believe completes them. The law written on our heart longs for peace with the Lawgiver. Even though fallen, humans strive for the good and can obtain the good in temporal form, as a shadow of the ultimate and beatific good found in Jesus Christ. As the natural law tradition teaches, moral goods exist with their own integrity such that non-Christians can experience true good; but Christians have a deeper grasp of the story of God's cosmic ordering. We are to choose and obtain these goods as a shadow of the highest good, Jesus Christ.

The glory of Jesus Christ exists for our ultimate good. He is true humanity and the highest good. He is the end or *telos* of our being that lets us be happy and complete beings. The finite human cannot perfectly grasp the infinite God. But the infinite God implants infinite longing and infinite inclination within finite creatures. In Christ, the infinite took on finite form so that the finite might have a manifest comprehension of the infinite's promise to us.

Thus, every grasp of moral goodness is an opportunity for us to live for God's glory and to experience the fulfilling happiness he intends for us as a reflection of his own character. This is what *Faithful Reason* hopes to achieve—a natural law ethics primer written from an evangelical perspective. Christian ethics are teleological ethics: it is by living with the ultimate end in view that we come to know ourselves now. We are to live in ways that bring glory to God (1 Cor 10:31) and as the truth of God's glory reflects back on his creatures, we experience the blessings, benefits, and goods he has made for us to enjoy and to know them at the deepest levels from which they are to be known. By having regenerative insights into the deepest interior realities of the moral law's existence and purpose, Christians are "the people who walked in darkness" but who "have seen a great light" (Isa 9:2). As Col 3:10 tells us, in Christ, we are awakened to the knowledge of what being made in the image of the Creator fully means. In Christ, humanity comes alive.

Christian ethics, therefore, is not primarily a field concerned with solving arcane debates about ethical dilemmas (important as those are), but about being awakened to how the moral life of the Christian is ordered to the obtainment of goods that simultaneously glorify God and cause us to enjoy his creation. Germain Grisez captures well the goal of this book's approach to ethics:

> Aware that they are created, people should acknowledge that they owe their very being and everything they have to the Creator. So, they should be grateful to him. Harmony with this transcendent source of meaning and value is one of the basic human goods. As children grateful to their parents love them for their own sakes, people grateful to the Creator can and should will the Creator's overall good for his own sake. If they do, they will fulfill their moral obligations as their contribution to that overall good. In this way, they will seek not only the harmony of submission to the Creator but the harmony of what can only be thought of as friendship.[5]

## Outline of the Book

*Faithful Reason* has two main sections: (1) The first section explains the theory of natural law by appeals to philosophical, theological, and biblical groundings. (2) The second section seeks to apply a natural law framework to a number of contemporary issues under the umbrella categories of (1) Life; (2) Relations; and (3) Order. The schematic organization of the applied section is very intentional, as I intend to show how the natural law explains the most rudimentary elements essential for survival, not an

---

[5] Germain G. Grisez, "Natural Law and the Transcendent Source of Human Fulfillment," in *Reason, Morality, and Law: The Philosophy of John Finnis*, ed. John Keown and Robert P. George (Oxford: Oxford University Press, 2013), 450.

exhaustive showcase that solves every ethical problem. Natural law thinkers disagree among themselves on all that the natural law entails. The natural law aims to articulate the basic lineaments of creation order necessary for human happiness and cultural survival. This volume will attempt to explain the structure of morality according to Christian natural law theory and how this tradition awakens Christians to both the enjoyment of this world and the obligations it posits for the common good.

In contrast to typical evangelical ethics volumes that I consider to be too long and redundantly formulaic, this volume proposes a different strategy: by laying a more substantive and coherent framework up front, less attention is necessary for explaining particulars of an issue of applied ethics once properly evaluated against an established framework.

The goal of *Faithful Reason* is simple: to produce an ethics volume that generates greater confidence in the Christian's understanding of the moral life. It seeks to (1) *frame* the importance of natural law in how it is conceptualized and utilized; (2) *explain* natural law theory in both philosophical and theological dimensions; and (3) *apply* the natural law in areas of practical application. Natural law ethics may not convince the hardened skeptic, but its approach will enhance Christians' ethical worldview. To that end, the book attempts to offer an apologetic for the rational coherence and superiority of Christian ethics.

## Ethics on Offense

The world both borrows from and obscures the ethics necessary for cultural survival from the Christian worldview. From the idea of human dignity to human rights, secularism offers no coherent way forward for cultural survival that will not eventually justify tragedy under its own banner. One goal of Christian natural law ethics, then, is for Christians to understand the enduring coherence and finality of God's creation order and to expose the absurdity of unbelief disguised as counterfeit ideology. For ethics to be Christian, we need Christian theological concepts like sin, kingdom, mission, salvation, and repentance. However, we need to operationalize those concepts into workable paradigms like human flourishing and the common good, both of which are tangible outputs of natural law ethics worked out in the lives of ordinary Christians who have the confidence and knowledge of the role that Christian ethics has and should play in our culture. We cannot afford to be caught flat-footed in explaining our ethics. Too much of our neighbor's good is at stake.

Because we insist upon the unwavering certainty of this, we must confess that Christianity is a religion of truthful assertion. We should not be embarrassed by what our faith teaches, but boldly proclaim it. If Christianity is indeed true, it means that all of its competitors bear a unique weakness of being false and thus liable to exposure. We are to avoid captivity to "philosophy and empty deceit" and "destroy arguments and every lofty opinion raised against the knowledge of God, and take every thought captive to obey Christ" (Col 2:8; 2 Cor 10:5).

Too often Christianity plays defense under a pietistic martyr complex. We valorize our disempowerment, surrendering responsibility to creation order and our neighbor under the belief that piety entails retreat. Since Christians believe the value of their ethics is not determined by their popularity but by their truthfulness, leavening the culture with the fruit of the gospel will necessarily imply seeking to influence it. Commenting on how the church has always sought to interact with the culture it lives in, Philip J. Wogaman writes,

> Efforts to influence the course of history entail interactions with centers of power and, if successful, lead to the empowerment of particular views and those who hold them. Efforts to maintain moral purity by sectarian withdrawal from the fallen world contribute to self-righteousness and illusions about the church's own moral perfections.[6]

---

[6] Philip J. Wogaman, *Christian Ethics: A Historical Introduction*, 2nd ed. (Louisville: WJK, 2011), 47–48.

Christians are not promised cultural victory. Indeed, cultural rejection for the sake of witnessing to the truth may be our lot. But to be salt and light in our world implies risk.

We are often inoffensive to a fault, choosing to placate cultured despisers through strategic silence or apologetic nuance, instead of giving "reason for the hope that is in you" (1 Pet 3:15). This volume seeks to play offense by giving reasons for the coherence of our convictions, but accomplished, as the apostle Peter instructs one verse later, "with gentleness and respect" (v. 16 HCSB). For better understanding our own ethics and in explaining our ethics to those who disagree with us, the natural law supplies us with reasons that we insist are reasonable in the explanation and defense of Christian ethics. Too much is at stake to stay cloistered in the hallowed halls of quietism. The path before us is a stark binary of options: paganism or Jesus Christ; chaos or order. Absurdity and barbarism can only work for so long as a strategy for cultural dissolution until nature strikes back. While we can never be sure how steep the descent may be, the West looks to be in the throes of a convulsive death rattle. In response, we must insist that apart from Christian renewal, there is to be no renovation to Western order or a confident assertion of Christianity's place in it, apart from a rehabilitation of Christian natural law ethics. But before we seek to persuade others, we need to be persuaded ourselves.

It is the tempest of cultural conflict that has required the Christian church to articulate its convictions in each age. It is the same today. In his best-selling volume *The Rise and Triumph of the Modern Self*, my dear friend and colleague, Carl Trueman, closed his book with an exhortation for how Christians can be faithful witnesses of Jesus in a darkening culture. His admonition was for greater Protestant exploration into natural law. Notice, too, that Trueman does not see the value of natural law only for its apologetical uses, but for internally shoring up our understanding of Christian moral principles. As Trueman writes,

> Protestants need to recover both natural law and a high view of the
> physical body. Some will immediately object that natural law will

not persuade the wider world to change its opinions about any-thing. I would concede that. My concern here is not primarily for the outside world but for the church herself. She needs to be able to teach her people coherently about moral principles. It is unlikely that an individual pastor is going to be able to shape a Supreme Court ruling on abortion (though he should certainly try as he is able), but he is very likely to be confronted with congregants asking questions about matters from surrogacy to transgenderism. And in such circumstances, a good grasp of the biblical position on natural law and the order of the created world will prove invaluable.[7]

Challenge accepted. As we will explore in this volume, there's no principle of Christian morality, whether decreed in Scripture or attested to in nature, that is not simultaneously ordered to the doxological and anthropological good. Christian natural law provides the most consistent, coherent account of morality necessary for the task of personal and social ethics. It offers God as the source of our ethics, reason as the basis of moral knowledge, and an all-encompassing goal behind it: our good, but chiefly, God's glory.

---

[7] Carl Trueman, *The Rise and Triumph of the Modern Self: Cultural Amnesia, Expressive Individualism, and the Road to Sexual Revolution* (Wheaton, IL: Crossway, 2020), 405.

# PART 1

# 1.

# Confidence in Creation

## Natural Law as Christian Catechesis and Cultural Renewal

In 2021, celebrity Oprah Winfrey sat down to interview the actress and celebrity "Elliot" Page. Page, born female and originally named "Ellen," had recently announced a transition to living as a transgender male. The announcement made headlines, including on the cover of *TIME Magazine*.

The look of Page during the interview evokes compassion and sorrow. Once beautiful, Page had undergone "top surgery" to remove her breasts. Her hair was now cropped short. With her small frame, she had the appearance of a young, gaunt teenage boy whose prepubescent voice was beginning to drop to a lower octave. The peace and self-acceptance that "transition" was supposed to offer gender-confused individuals like Page still appeared elusive on Page's troubled demeanor throughout the interview.

Obviously beset with continued identity issues and looking anguished, the frail and sunken appearance of Page is the result of a civilization like our own creating a worldview whose understanding of fulfillment and moral action are defined solely by the horizons of internal psychology and the subjective self's preferences and desires. It is achieved by a neglect or even disavowal of the body as an essential element of the "self." The self is merely a ghost inhabiting a machine. We are not our bodies and our bodies are not "us" in any corporeal sense. As the interview unfolds, observers see that Page understands her life's meaning by what her mind and self-chosen identity can impose onto physical reality. And it is, tragically, lauded by our elites as the essence of human flourishing. The question is whether physical reality allows for the body to be acted upon as a blank canvas without an equal and opposite reaction of human nature snapping back.

But in setting up the interview, Oprah opened the show by stating the following:

> . . . my hope is that this conversation can serve as an invitation for all of us to understand, for all of us to appreciate, and for all of us to know that inside ourselves that every human born to the planet wants the same thing and that is to be accepted, to be loved, and to live in health and safety as our authentic selves. And I really want to honor and celebrate your courage, Elliot, for sharing your truth on social media, then, on the cover of *Time Magazine*, and now in this conversation with me, so I honor that.[1]

It is important to not gloss over Winfrey's words. Three things are worth noticing. First, Winfrey pays homage to something central to this book's argument: a universal longing for goodness and wholeness that she considers built into the fabric of human nature. For Winfrey, there is a *universal, intelligible,* and *objective* longing for the human person to experience health, acceptance, and wholeness.[2] She believes the longings and aspirations that Page possesses are the same throughout humanity—that such longings exist to bring meaning that corresponds to how the person in question encounters

---

[1] "Elliot Page interview with Oprah Winfrey," *The Oprah Conversation*, Apple TV+, April 30, 2021.

[2] Throughout this volume, the categories of universal, objective, and intelligible will be invoked. I owe this helpful heuristic to the late Joseph Koterski, SJ.

their world. Importantly, Winfrey does not have to prove such an axiomatic truth to her audience; she simply assumes it.

Second, Winfrey proceeds to define those experiences and longings for personal wholeness by Page's own collapsed sense of autonomy and self-will. Such is the paradoxical irony of our age where universal longing is defined by the individual. Such is a feature of what scholars refer to as "expressive individualism," the framework that understands human happiness to be associated with unfettered fulfillment of one's deepest longings. Political philosopher Yuval Levin defines expressive individualism as:

> a desire to pursue one's own path but also a yearning for fulfillment through the definition and articulation of one's own identity. It is a drive both to be more like whatever you already are and also to live in society by fully asserting who you are. The capacity of individuals to define the terms of their own existence by defining their personal identities is increasingly equated with liberty and with the meaning of some of our basic rights, and it is given pride of place in our self-understanding.[3]

It is impossible to overstate just how permeated modern society is with expressive individualism. The highest self is the liberated self from the constraints of oppression and self-doubt. The moral horizon of expressive individualism is unbounded self-determination and self-definition. The worldview is regarded by many as perfectly encapsulated in the now-infamous phrase of Justice Anthony Kennedy where he defined "the heart of liberty" as "the right to define one's own concept of existence, of meaning, of the universe, and of the mystery of human life."[4] High-minded verbal pottage of this type is as vacuous as it is unsustainable to govern a civilization when "everyone did what was right in his own eyes" becomes the common

---

[3] Yuval Levin, *The Fractured Republic: Renewing America's Social Contract in the Age of Individualism* (New York: Basic, 2016), 148.

[4] *Planned Parenthood v. Casey*, 505 U.S. 833, 851 (1992), https://supreme.justia.com/cases/federal/us/505/833/.

moral currency (Judg 21:25). The collapsing of meaning, morality, and liberty toward subjective self-reference bears the hallmarks of what natural law historian Heinrich Rommen calls "metaphysicophobia"—the fear of moral norms being grounded outside the immanent self.[5]

Winfrey and Page, in turn, are prophets of expressive individualism. On screen, Page is cast as the arbiter of what health, acceptance, and wholeness entail. For Page, it means razing her body to the ground and attempting to re-organize it. Repressing her nature, augmenting her body, and subjecting it to the will are the conditions for her understanding of self-fulfillment. In this paradigm, there is no need to look externally outside one's own self. The expressive individual's own sense of self-worth and self-perception is the chief arbiter and chief ingredient to satisfaction.

Third, Winfrey—always quick to be the sagacious practitioner of tolerance—is quick to bow and even genuflect before Page's sense of self. If one asserts "their truth," then their interlocutor has nothing else to do but to affirm. This is the moral and social contract of our age: asserting one's identity silences dissent and requires the interlocutor to affirm or else run the risk of violating a secular blasphemy law. Those are the terms of our moral worldview in twenty-first-century America, and the West more broadly. At least on the issue of a woman willing her existence to be a man, Winfrey cannot invoke any sort of judgment. She wants to "honor" and "celebrate" Page and for Page to feel comfortable "sharing your truth" (one of the most banal phrases used today that captures the solipsistic essence of expressive individualism and moral relativism).

This episode is but a small microcosm of the challenge and opportunities facing Christian ethics at the dawn of the twenty-first century: human nature is eviscerated by emptying it of any normative account to give it grammar and poise, which in turn, invites an unending array of actions through which to tinker with a material substance that has no objective moral value

---

[5] Heinrich A. Rommen, *The Natural Law: A Study in Legal and Social History and Philosophy* (Indianapolis: Liberty Fund, 1998), 142.

apart from its own emotional satisfaction. Late modernism's loss of absolute value has created a cultural vacuum of valuelessness and despair.

## Striving against the Created Order

But a moral worldview of this type is an active striving against the world that God has made. As creatures made in God's image with a nature that reflects the natural longings he has implanted upon our inclinations, humans are no less morally animated than what they have been in previous generations, for it is inescapable that we search, divine, or construct systems of meaning. The quandary facing our civilization today is that moral longings have been radically *internalized*, *subjectivized*, and in turn, *relativized*. Objective accounts for morality and moral goodness have been deconstructed. What comprises self-hood in our cultural moment is self-constructing one's own sense of identity and never daring to suggest that one's own self-determination can be, in any authoritative sense, determinative for someone else. Psychological humanity seeks his or her fulfillment at the expense of body and soul's unity.

Meaning and morality have been emptied of teleology and collapsed into the horizon of the sovereign self.[6] Absent that larger purpose from which to define what human excellence is, we grapple and stumble about after any identity our post-rational society permits, even if the confluence of "identities" that gain mainstream acceptance are incoherent or contradicting of others' identities.

At best, however, we are only partly relativistic because as the individual purports to be the sole manufacturer of their sense of self, we still live in a world where grave evils like the Holocaust or ethnic supremacy remain recognizably evil and thus condemned. We are inconsistent creatures driven by utilitarian accounts of social justice. Progressive canons of social justice give

---

[6] For more on the relationship between the disenchantment of secular modernity making possible the construction of personal identity, see Charles Taylor, *Sources of the Self: The Making of the Modern Identity* (Cambridge, MA: Harvard University Press, 1992).

vivid expression to the reality that ours is a deeply anxious, but also a deeply moralistic age. The oddity of inhabiting a world that collapses morality into the subjective experience of individuals while at the same time righteously trumpeting the cause of social enlightenment with universal ideals like justice at every corner yields an inconsistent worldview.

The moral schizophrenia defining our civilizational moment is unrelenting. We are radically autonomous and non-judgmental while ferociously tribal and judgmental—even pharisaical—elsewhere. In this schematic, the only taboo act to commit is intolerance itself. Indeed, we are now living a real-life tale of C. S. Lewis's *Abolition of Man*. In that prescient little volume written in the 1940s, Lewis warned of a looming civilizational crisis where morality is evacuated of objective standards and reduced to emotive self-expression.

> When all that says "it is good" has been debunked, what says "I want" remains. . . . My point is that those who stand outside all judgements of value cannot have any ground for preferring one of their own impulses to another except the emotional strength of that impulse. We may legitimately hope that among the impulses which arise in minds thus emptied of all "rational" or "spiritual" motives, some will be benevolent. I am very doubtful myself whether the benevolent impulses, stripped of that preference and encouragement which the Tao teaches us to give them and left to their merely natural strength and frequency as psychological events, will have much influence. I am very doubtful whether history shows us one example of a man who, having stepped outside traditional morality and attained power, has used that power benevolently.[7]

Lewis's point is that moral judgment of certain stripes is inevitable because God has made us moral beings. We are creatures of judgment and reaction. How we ground and define those judgments, on the other hand, is the difference between a civilization that can form a consistent ethic and

---

[7] C. S. Lewis, *The Abolition of Man* (1947; repr. San Francisco: HarperOne, 2015), 66–67.

one that cannot. It is the difference of morality based on sound reason and morality based on emotional register. What concerns Lewis is the horizon from which moral judgment is issued. For Lewis, if the objective basis for morality (what he calls "the Tao") is jettisoned, humanity cannot summon a morality outside of its own internal, subjectivized expressions of emotive displeasure. As Lewis avers, filling the void of an objective morality will be a morality that is surreptitiously unstable and, eventually, malevolent.

## Pursuing Moral Intelligibility

This explains Oprah and Elliot Page: the admixture of universal longing defined, ironically, by the subjective self's own sense of happiness. It explains the dilemma of Western culture that everyone, from whatever ideological or religious persuasion, sees as conflict-prone, irreconcilable, and unsustainable. Western peoples lack a shared moral vision and no longer reason together. As a result, cultural fratricide defined by an intractable *kulturkampf* persists unabated. The culture war that plays out around us is little more than rival accounts of metaphysical order, what the non-Christian Philosopher Thomas Sowell refers to as a clash between a "constrained" vision of the world that accepts the imposition of order and human nature and an "unconstrained" vision that allows for unending re-invention of morality and calls into question whether "nature" exists at all.[8]

Winfrey and Page's moral schizophrenia, however, offers an opportunity for Christianity to begin an important and constructive dialogue with its secular neighbors. Christians also desire that all persons experience blessing, health, and self-acceptance. We are to genuinely love our neighbor and seek their unqualified good (Mark 12:31; Luke 10:25–37). We desire for justice to govern our society. Owing to our common nature, the universal longings for wholeness and fulfillment are the same between the Christian and the non-Christian while the starting point and ending points

---

[8] Thomas Sowell, *A Conflict of Visions: Ideological Origins of Political Struggles*, Revised edition (New York: Basic Books, 2007).

are viewed from different prisms. Our doctrine of sin reveals that though humans share the same cognitive faculties, we are now terminally prone to misuse them. Indeed, Christians have a long tradition of moral reasoning that insists upon some common moral agreement and partial epistemological agreement despite there being no foundational neutrality between competing philosophical or religious systems. Even though Christians believe morality ultimately sources back to a divine Being, we do not believe that moral knowledge is exclusive to Christians alone, even despite the descent of humanity into sin. A non-Christian may not be able to account for the grounds of their moral knowledge. But the lack of knowledge about an explicit foundation, however, does not dispel the reality that as creatures made in God's image, every creature retains some minimal awareness of moral principles that direct them to a true grasp of moral goods, even if error is possible or likely in how they grasp and execute their longings for the good.

## Acting for the Good

The fact that Page and Winfrey insist upon some understanding of an ideal state of affairs, even if wrongly understood and executed, shows that longing is itself evidence of a remnant morality trying to surface. We call this mode of moral reasoning natural law. I will offer several definitions of natural law throughout this book. I offer the following formal definition of natural law and natural law theory to begin our discussion:

> *Natural law is the God-ordained, God-upheld system of moral order engraved upon an image-bearer's conscience that enable them to rationally perceive moral goods and moral wrongs by interacting with their world through sapiential investigation. The natural law directs rational creatures to know what actions to do and what goods to fulfill consistent with their natural and supernatural ends, and correspondingly, what actions to avoid and vices to shun. The principles of natural law morality are principles that have no prior proof of their intelligibility*

*apart from obedience to these norms and the experiences of these goods*
*as goods and ends pursued for their own sake.*

This definition does not hold that persons know or execute the natural law perfectly, consistently, or exhaustively. Humans sinfully rebel against the moral law they do know and also err in their application of the natural law. Rather, the natural law demonstrates how human beings have implanted upon their nature the capacity for discerning moral truth from moral error. This discovery is made through an evaluation of our inclinations and the data of human experience that provides meaningful reason for action and for discovering what it means to flourish. The natural law is nothing else than moral obligation for rational creatures. Its terminology assumes the existence of an objective moral order that rational persons can grasp, and which supplies them with the data to attain their proper mode of being (i.e., their "flourishing").

To speak of the natural law is to speak of a mode of Christian moral reasoning based upon teleology and natural ends. *Telos* derives from "teleology" and the Greek language denoting "end," "goal," or "purpose." In a teleological moral system, actions are evaluated by their ability or inability to serve the purpose or goal of a given object's nature. That an object would have a particular purpose that fulfills what it means for that thing to complete itself (and its nature) stands as one of the greatest sources of cultural tumult. Indeed, the idea that "nature" resides immutably within a person and that there are actions and goods consistent with this nature is the very idea that expressive individualism (similar to Page and Winfrey) rejects. An identity based not on "nature" but what one *wants*, *wills*, or *chooses* without regard to their nature is appetitive and conflicts with the moral vision of Christianity, where God ascribes who we are as his image-bearers and what actions and goods find concord with the nature given to humanity.

I begin with this episode of Page and Winfrey because it frames the overall goal of this book: understanding the task of Christian ethics as ordered, simultaneously, to *God's glory*, but also *our good*. As an objective account of ethics, Christian natural law ethics from start to finish is an act of grace. Even the character of goodness—the quality of absolute excellence of X

arriving at what X is meant for—is itself of grace. That God creates human
beings and lets even fallen human beings experience moral goodness reflects
God's common grace and his creational bounty to his creatures. The goodness that humans can experience is a goodness that reflects God's own being.
Such an approach to Christian ethics is understood within a natural law
teleology: In His divine wisdom, God has seen fit to design a universe and a
field of moral action consistent with his own nature. God orders creaturely
activity to be consistent with the universe he has designed. To the extent we
obey God and fulfill what he demands of us within this moral order, we pursue God's glory by recognizing his authority and majestic creatorship. But
we also, simultaneously, pursue our own good as we align ourselves with the
Creator's intentions for our flourishing. All qualities of the "good," then, are
reflections of God's own nature since God could not impart anything less
than a measure of himself in ordering the moral world.

Glory and moral excellence are thus twin pillars of mutual reinforce-
ment. Such a configuration means that it is impossible for good moral
action not to reflect God's glory since both are a product of God's own
goodness. In acting for the good, we act for God's glory since all goodness
is but a mirror of his own being. Pursuing God's glory thus acts to fulfill
our good as well. No action or command in Scripture, then, is cordoned
off from implications of God's glory. Christian ethics is best understood
within two simultaneous horizons: the temporal (penultimate) and eternal
(ultimate). All creaturely activity, to the extent that it is good, fulfills what it
means to be human and accords with God's own being.

Without God disclosing himself both in nature and in his Word, humanity's knowledge of its ultimate good and its penultimate goods would be incomplete, speculative, and provisional. The natural, though possessing an integrity
of its own consistent with natural excellence as we understand it from general
revelation, requires the supernatural for the natural to understand itself in the
complete sense. With God and his revelation, humanity comes to understand
who it is made *by* and *for*. By "good," I mean obtaining a moral vision defined
by the existence of concrete moral goods that cause human beings to flourish.
It is by looking to God (our ultimate good) and God's special and natural

revelation (that discloses the good each in their own respective ways) that our penultimate and ultimate good, comes into focus. Only in the revelation of Jesus Christ do we come into a true, final, and complete knowledge of who we are and what completes us as rational and embodied beings.

## Fixed and Necessary Pathways

In Christ the richness of our nature is unlocked. Augustine famously said, "Our hearts are restless until they find their rest in thee."[9] By obeying the Creator, the Lord receives the glory and authority due to him. In exchange, we are confronted with the pathway necessary for true flourishing. Therefore, Christian ethics must simultaneously be organized around a concern for ultimate horizons (God's glory) while reflecting back on penultimate horizons (our good). It is a formula at the heart of Christian ethics. We will never be fully happy unless we are holy. Ethics is thus a measure of our joyful conformity to God's moral law, a law that is good and teaches us to live in accordance with his holiness. To practice holiness is to reflect the nature of God (1 Pet 1:14–15).

This is the chief theological motif of the book that will comprise our journey. I do this to anchor my vision for Christian ethics within a larger theological horizon that avoids the all-too-typical approach that sees Christian ethics as mere proof-texting. Texts matter, of course, to ground our reflection on the task of Christian ethics. But if texts are strung together in order to arrive at a proper conclusion of "what the Bible says about issue X," we can do so in an isolated and stunted way that divorces the reader from a richer theological tapestry that puts morality and moral action within focus of the grand sweep of Scripture's storyline.

At the heart of Christian ethics is the abiding reality of a morally ordered and morally intelligible universe. Christian ethics assumes that morality *exists* and is *knowable*. As Christians, we are moral realists, not

---

[9] Saint Augustine, *Confessions*, trans. Henry Chadwick (Oxford: Oxford University Press, 1991), 3.

moral agnostics, which means we believe our moral claims are accurate reflections of the way things truly are and ought to be. When we declare there to be a moral injustice, we are saying that an injustice exists, not merely that we feel that an injustice has occurred. This brings us back to our opening scene with Oprah Winfrey and Elliot Page. Winfrey is correct to highlight the universal longing for self-acceptance but is exactly wrong to collapse that longing into a person's own choices, preferences, or psychological frame of mind. We must look beyond ourselves to ground morality. From a Christian vantage point, creatures best know themselves by looking to their Creator. Oprah's exchange with Elliot Page gets this exactly backward. Hers, and the secular morality behind it, is an unsustainable morality that even she does not fully believe in if taken to its logical conclusion.

When erring humans are left to determine the grounds of their flourishing and happiness with indeterminate foundation, it ends, invariably, in some dystopic state of affairs. Human nature is not meant to bear the weight of searching endlessly after its nature, its fullness, and its finality. We should receive these as a givenness bestowed by our Creator. Even still, as fallen as we are, everyone draws limits, at least somewhere. Winfrey would not, for example, endorse rape, genocide, or torturing babies. She would not tell a serial murderer to be true to themselves. Her mistake is not a total lack of knowledge of the moral law per se, but the inconsistency, incompleteness, and her own volitional stubbornness to obey it.

What might Christianity have to say to this sense of moral inconsistency or moral incompleteness? Christianity declares that God's divine nature, being wholly and reliably good, encodes the world and his creatures with moral directives that reflect God's fundamental goodness while bringing the creature into blessed fulfillment. A morality ordered toward God's glory leads the creature in the pattern and form of human flourishing.

When God's glory is removed from our horizon, we ascribe glory to human ethical concoctions under the pretense that whatever it is—whether ideology, identity, or creature comforts—will complete us. Under a Christian rubric, false worship results in ethical rebellion and cultural decay (Rom 1:18–32). The obverse is also true: it is only in knowing God that humans are spared a descent into moral disrepair and cultural suicide. True worship, on the other hand, fuels human flourishing. The insidiousness of Winfrey's moral script is that non-judgmentalism can wreak havoc on impressionable persons swayed to and fro when morality becomes fluid. Postmodern morality offers individuals no fixed morality while biblical ethics does the exact opposite (Matt 7:24–27). One of the most understated aspects of Christian ethics in our day is that it dares to offer a fixed standard from which to ground one's center of moral gravity. In Christ, our souls are anchored to the only truth that can set us free to fulfill our callings as God's beloved and that allows us to reap a harvest of joy (John 14:6; 8:32; 10:10).

Indeed, in the absence of a mutually agreed-upon moral destiny defined by the Bible's own storyline, the inevitable end of irresolvable moral fragmentation is a world marked by cultural strife, human misery, and civilizational decline. The enterprise of Christian ethics is a lot of things, but it is never less than an enterprise whose goal is aligning ourselves and the places we inhabit with the order of creation and the pattern of morality that God has laid down in His creation. Recognizing the limits and operations of God's creation is to understand the beauty of His glory over creation. From there, it is an exercise in persuading our neighbor that their own good is bound up with recognizing Christ as their Creator, Lord, Savior, and Sustainer. Christian ethics, then, is ordered to the love of God, the love of one's neighbor and community, and the rightly ordered love of one's own self.

As culture continues to grow more secular, it will be increasingly important for Christians to gain greater facility with the foundations and intricacies of the Bible's moral witness. Morality, today, and even more acutely on matters of anthropology, are the primary theaters of cultural conflict. No Christian I'm aware of in the West is facing the loss of their job because they believe in the Trinity. They are, however, facing a bleak employment outlook in many professional careers if they refuse to affirm the full panoply of sexual and gender identities. This is so because in rejecting any natural ends to the human creature, we are prone to reject the Creator who inscribes such ends. This represents an opportunity, but also a challenge to how Christians have conceived of Christian ethics. Ethics, then, is as much apologetical in nature as it is anything else. Indeed, the book you are holding in your hands is a work of moral apologetics. But the apologetical nature of Christian ethics must be rightly understood. In any apologetical situation, one must ask: Who am I trying to persuade and why? For if the integrity of our moral apologetics is measured only against its ability to have our interlocutor agree with us, then the enterprise of moral apologetics will, more often than not, fail. We do not witness to the truth only on the grounds that we are successful. We are to witness to the truth for the sake of the truth itself. If, however, we understand moral apologetics to be not only outward-facing in its confrontations with skeptics, but also inward-facing as a method of ethical catechesis, the urgency of moral apologetics as a way of reinforcing the church's witness gains greater focus. A story I will never forget helps explain why I think this book and its methodology are needed.

## Reality Is Christian Reality

A few years ago, I gave a set of talks to a large, suburban Christian school in Florida. Having recently published a book on the rise of transgenderism, my talks endeavored to explain how we got to this moment in Western civilization, to understand the issue itself, to explain what it is that Christians believe when we confess that God created us male and female in his image, and to defend that confession's intelligibility. I was there to encourage a Christian audience to gain a better understanding of the issue in hopes that it would bolster their confidence to address the issue with others. Now, I believe my arguments provided rational grounds to reject transgenderism. But my goal that evening was not primarily to persuade a non-believer. My primary audience was young Christians who are daily bombarded by a culture peddling a deceitful and harmful ideology under the guise of tolerance and compassion.

Resigned to the possibility that I may not actually persuade the non-Christian of the unreasonableness of gender ideology because of their own wayward captivity to culture or peer pressure, I am repeatedly forced to ask myself a more fundamental question about the purpose of Christian ethics: What if I am chiefly concerned with Christians understanding the rationale and reasonableness of their ethical convictions before I'm concerned with persuading the gender-fluid ideologue of their foolish error? As 1 Pet 3:15 insists we do, we are to provide reasons and not merely brute assertions about the identity, purpose, and intelligibility of Christian ethics. This inflection point matters. Before Christians are to engage the world around them, it assumes a thoroughgoing understanding of their own moral beliefs. Apologetics assumes we have a sound grasp on the inherent reasonableness of our own convictions. We need moral catechesis if we are to be apologists for the moral superiority and eminent humaneness of Christian ethics. Too often, however, Christians are caught flatfooted in offering defenses for their convictions on the grounds of assertions, not reasons. That is not sufficient. Though the Bible is sufficient in what it teaches regarding creation order and male and female, we must also utilize the tools of inquiry that help us rationally explain why the Bible's understanding of this issue corresponds to what the best of philosophy and biology teach as well. Very little attention, it seems, is given to the rationale of Christian ethical imperatives. Ethics via fiat or by divine decree alone, we may believe, rescues us from having to defend the justification of Christian ethical commands, but it ends up producing a voluntarist ethic absent of there being intelligible reasons for action.

Though I had not used the phrase "natural law" in my talks the night before, that mode of argument was what my audience had been receiving. I wanted my audience to know that Christians were not eccentric cultists or crazed fideists for believing in the static categories of maleness and femaleness. Indeed, I wanted them to know that it was their secular progressive neighbors that were trafficking in absurd, delusional conclusions when they rejected the truths of nature and human embodiment. I wanted them to understand that special revelation's teaching on the male-female binary overlays with what we know is true about the male-female binary from the perspective of philosophy and biology.

Before the second night of my talks, a middle-aged teacher who taught at the school caught me in the hallway before the night's programming and said, "Thank you for your talk last night. I had no idea that we as Christians have good reasons to believe what we believe." This statement jarred me as it did sadden me. Here was a mature Christian who had just now been told that her ethical convictions were defensible on the grounds of rational coherence—that Christian convictions were not simply "beliefs" to tuck away piously and privately in the inner recesses of her heart, but truth that resounds throughout creation. Too often, Christians fall back on their "beliefs" without the due diligence to explain how those "beliefs" about controversial moral questions are grounded in truths knowable from reason and attested to in nature. This moment has stayed with me for years now because this teacher's admission of her ignorance of the objective soundness of Christian ethics captured the confused priorities for how Christians think about morality in general, and the use of the natural law in particular: Is the natural law utilized for the sake of the believer's own understanding of their ethical system, or for the sake of persuading the skeptic? While I do believe it can persuade and should be considered for that end, the burden of my argument in this book is to demonstrate the need for Christians to better grasp the natural law as a corollary to their discipleship. Christians need more rigorous instruction on the integrity of Christian ethics if there is to be any possibility of a future public witness.

My exchange with this teacher also demonstrated a fundamental gap in our thinking about the structure of Christian ethics—that they bear no intrinsic or teleological relationship to our doctrine of creation. It is as though God spins the world off as we do a top and simply lets time and inertia wind it down. In our time, a recovery of a natural law teleology grounded in a firm account of human goods and God's glory is what I believe is most urgently needed to offset the harming excesses of expressive individualism and cultural relativism.

The goal of building up the church's confidence with internal resolve concerning the coherence of its ethics is bound up with the Great Commission Christ has called us to advance. There will be no Great

Commission apart from a Christian moral confrontation with our world's hell-bent desire for self-abolition. These goals are not mutually exclusive. We need not choose between the shoring up of Christian doctrine and the building up of the church with a holy confidence in the triune God of order or believing that mere intellective arguments alone will salvage Christianity from its cultured despisers. In my talks at that church, and what I strive for as a professor, I was trying to accomplish one main goal: to bolster the confidence of the Christian that what we believe is not merely sectarian or fideistic, but correlated to reality as such, and that when objective categories of maleness and femaleness—or whatever topic regarding reasonableness is at hand—are jettisoned by secular progressivism, secular progressivism is not just abandoning Christian thought, but reality itself. In other words, Christianity possesses a body of ethical convictions that are true, regardless of whether a non-Christian accepts them as true. This has massive ramifications for our calling as disciples of Jesus Christ, but also our engagement with an unhealthy culture that we are called to speak the truth to in love (Eph 4:15).

## Ratifying Christian Ethics

Cultural disintegration ratifies the dire relevancy of Christian ethics. The war on reality waged by secular progressivism cannot continue apart from what Henry Kissinger called the "dissolution of all social bonds" where the outcome is "extremism, despair, and brutality"—what Kissinger spoke of the civilizational catastrophe wrought by totalitarianism.[10] Our culture is subject to another form of totalitarianism, the expressive self, an indomitable authority wrought by what the late Pope Benedict XVI referred to as the "Dictatorship of Relativism."[11] To see the stakes of contemporary

---

[10] Barry Gewen, *The Inevitability of Tragedy: Henry Kissinger and His World* (New York: W.W. Norton, 2020), 49.

[11] *Pro Eligendo Romano Pontifice*, Homily of His Eminence Card. Joseph Ratzinger, Vatican website, April 18, 2005, https://www.vatican.va/gpII/documents/homily-pro-eligendo-pontifice_20050418_en.html.

culture's decline as anything else than a reversion to totalitarian impulse is to overlook just how egregious our sins are as a culture. Abortion murders children. Rampant sexual promiscuity harms women and debases men. Pornography traffics women. Resurgent ethnonationalism imperils our ability to see all human beings as made in God's image. Euthanasia creates incentive structures for government-supported suicide. The failure to form marriages leads to isolation and demographic decline. Telling males and females to ingest hormones or amputate body parts is barbarism. Increased social isolation is leading to a suicide and an opioid epidemic. All because we have rejected God and, in turn, the creation he is Lord over.

When the culture rejects God's authority over nature like it has, the church must reassert its confidence in God's creation ordinances. Theology not only grounds ethics but explains why ethics can possess the rational explanation that they do as a creation ethic; and that's because Christian ethics promote human goods that are conducive to human flourishing. Human beings cannot flourish apart from obeying God's order of creation that we learn through the natural law. Thus, retrieving confidence in creation order constitutes an act of revolt against the anti-culture of secular progressivism. For the Christian to love their neighbor means for them to love their culture. There is no better way to love your neighbor and their culture than to proclaim the kingship of Jesus Christ and the moral foundations necessary for God's common grace to bless both neighbor and culture (Matt 5:13–16).

Such terms force us back to the "why" of the natural law. Consider Romans 1–2, the *locus classicus* of the Bible's teaching on the natural law. When Paul writes his statements on creation order and the law "written on their heart," Paul is writing this letter to Roman *Christians*. He's writing to explain the unfolding mystery of God's plan; that the universality of man's sinfulness corresponds to an indiscriminate, impartial need for justification. For Paul's audience to understand the perilous state of the world, they need vivid understanding of the world's revolt against God's moral law (Rom 1:18–32). His audience needed a confidence in creation order and a definitive interpretation of it to understand the world's rebellion against it. Against the backdrop of their revolt against God's authority do Paul's listeners understand their need for a Savior. Such is the same for our day. To understand cultural revolt, we must understand nature and the moral order God has imposed on the world. The world must be told of its revolt against reason and creation.

Part of the solution in recovering the natural law is rejecting the maxim that natural law's utility is measured only or even supremely by its ability to convince; or that we only deploy the natural law when we are seeking to translate Christian public ethics into publicly accessible terms. The use of natural law is never less than directed at these goals; but its legitimacy as a mode of ethical discourse for Christians ought not hinge upon its reception or its outside intelligibility by unbelieving individuals. Such an erroneous presupposition lies at the heart of Protestantism's rejection of natural law: Because we believe that man's reason is tainted by sin, we advert to a narrow biblicism to account for our public ethics. We end up in an epistemological ghetto proof-texting our way out of the cultural mess the contemporary West is in. That is not an effective strategy for a culture that rejects the theistic presuppositions of Scripture's authority. I want no fewer biblical citations, but for biblical citations to be informed by a confidence in the rational soundness and explanatory power of our ethics.

And therein is an irony: By immediately adverting to a narrowly defined biblicism for our ethics, we are admitting that creation in itself has no observable order; that the transgender activist has just as much reasonableness in cultural debates as does the Christian; that the Bible is the only (instead of the ultimate) way to appeal to what is true. The Bible, however, is not as restrictive about the epistemic abilities of fallen persons. The whole arc of the Bible assumes the capability of moral knowledge by the earth's inhabitants, even despite our sin. Surrounding nations are able to recognize the righteousness of Israel (Deut 4:5–8). Paul quotes pagans in the pages of the New Testament (Acts 17:28; 1 Cor 15:33). All of this merely suggests that in Scripture, there is no incongruency between what is true for a

Christian and a non-Christian if, in fact, the proposition coheres logically and corresponds to reality. As Christians, we should never want to cultivate an intellectual attitude and epistemological constraint that the Bible does not apply to itself.

But to my original point, it is the transgender activist who is the one thwarting creation. It is the Christian who is the one upholding creation's integrity. None of this is meant to diminish the authoritative significance of the Bible for Christian ethics, but to understand how the Bible speaks of creation. The Bible portrays creation as communicating truths about its design and its Creator that each living person is, in principle, capable of grasping. The Bible interprets nature as a self-attesting witness to God's orderly design. A homosexual activist may dispute the concept of "nature," or a pro-choice individual may question whether an unborn child is a "person," but disputes over what the Bible considers true about sexuality and human dignity are no more up for dispute than 2+2=4. That someone believes 2+2=5 does not make arithmetic any less true. The principle is what matters, not whether or not a given fact appears contestable to the unregenerate mind. Someone is right and someone is wrong. The Bible's authority is so supreme that it draws us outward to an engagement with the creation that God is Lord over. The Bible is the supreme authority over a Christian's life, but the Bible's declaration of creation's intelligibility likewise attests to the Bible's very own truthfulness about the universality of Christian ethics. Natural law discourse is thus out of bounds if and only if the Bible rejects natural law formulae within its pages. But it does no such thing.

## The Inevitability of the Natural Law

As one who stands proudly within the Reformed tradition, I believe reason is affected by sin, but what if redeemed reason restores our understanding of nature? What if Christians illumined by the Holy Spirit are to herald the divine standards for social righteousness (Isa 28:17; Jer

6:16)? What if our mission as God's agents in the world is to proclaim to the world what is true about the world, regardless of whether the world receives it? This forces us to re-evaluate the place of the natural law in the Christian life: What if the purpose of natural law is not first to convince the non-believer, but to explain the structure and practical outworking of morality and the moral goods that define human flourishing? In other words, what if natural law is less about apologetics, and *more* about discipleship? What if a system of natural law explains the grasp of goods (such as family life, the pursuit of beauty, and natural justice) that billions of non-Christians intuitively act upon countless times throughout their day? What if the natural law was the device that Christians use to explain the natural goodness that humans long for—that ideas like "equality" and "human rights" are unintelligible apart from its foundation. In this way, our ethics become a signpost to the wonder and majesty of a God-designed cosmos. Just imagine if Christians were catechized to have greater understanding of the world that God placed them in. We would move out from our theological ghettos to active confrontation with a secular world that cannot explain or resolve its haunting aches of despair and meaninglessness.

In Protestant circles, one of the primary objections raised to natural law is that it persuades a few who are not already committed to the Christian worldview. First, that's an overstatement, as even non-Christian intellectuals like Douglas Murray, Tom Holland, and Niall Ferguson seem to recognize that Christian morality best anchors and reflects universal moral dimensions benefitting civilization. How do we get to the position that life is valuable—valuable in an objective sense—if you start from the assumption that humanity's existence and its own self-consciousness are both accidents and an evolutionary contingency? Satisfying explanations have yet to be offered that do not borrow from objective foundations laid by theism.

Moreover, when non-Christians follow traffic signals and take care of their children, they are, in ways they may not even be aware of, reflecting on and participating in, the natural law. As I will argue later, much of the discussion related to the merits and strength of natural law are its definitions and assumptions about its uses.

The primary reason Christians should care about natural law is that it gives us rational, coherent ways of understanding the structure of God's creation order. Take marriage, for example. If the conjugal definition of marriage is dispensed with, it is not only the Bible's definition of marriage that is rejected, but also the soundness of marriage as a distinct institution apart from all other relationships. The *Obergefell* decision in 2015 was not just a revolt against the Bible, but against sound reason and logic. The reception of Christian ethics in a pagan world says nothing as to the truthfulness and binding reality of the natural law. Truth-claims are true or false, regardless of whether they are grounded in religious or secular truth claims. What natural law helps us to understand is that the truths of creation and natural order are, ultimately, truths anchored in a divine decree. Natural law theory helps give color to sound thinking about the structure and purpose of Christian ethics.

The result of rejecting the natural law tradition has been the deracination of Christian ethics, which leaves Christians with a two-fold dilemma: an inability to explain the coherence of Christian ethics to either the Christian or the non-Christian. As one of my mentors has said to me, "There is no truth without order, and without order there is no truth." Christians believe in truth. Our affirmation of a natural law is an affirmation about the structure of reality God has brought into being. We must now better understand that corresponding order, for in discovering the depth and intricacy of order we better glorify the truth that is there to set us free (John 8:32).

There is no shortage of confidence in the Bible among evangelicals. What is conspicuously missing is a confidence that the ethics we espouse from the Bible can be rationally articulated in ways that better benefit human flourishing and the common good than what its secular competitors offer. This is what we are called to do, as the apostle Peter instructs in 1 Pet 3:15. Christian ethics is too often playing defense within its own sectarian and epistemological ghetto. A better formulation of the task of Christian ethics is one that concerns not only our responsibilities to God as revealed in his Word, but also understands and explores how those responsibilities are bound up in explaining the way God has ordered creation. To jettison Christian ethics, then, is not merely to reject Scripture, but to reject the integrity of nature and reason that Scripture depicts God as the author of.

# 2.

# Grace in the Garden

## Worldview and Christian Natural Law Ethics

Before I explain more of natural law theory in later chapters, in the previous chapter and in this chapter, I am seeking to frame how we think about the natural law. One of the biggest obstacles keeping Protestants from utilizing natural law theory is misunderstanding its use. Rather than natural law being a primarily outward-facing apologetic used in defense of Christianity when talking with skeptics, my goal is to re-orient Protestants toward embracing the natural law as an approach to ethics that helps them understand the intelligibility and cogency of their own ethics for the sake of ethical catechesis.

The goal of this chapter, however, is to explore the moral and worldview milieus and paradigms that natural law must compete with for philosophical dominance. Natural law is an affront to competing moral philosophies that collapse moral rectitude down to emotion and pure consequentialist utility. It is against competing worldviews that natural law triumphs. Chapter 2 will touch upon the routine longings for universal morality and the dangers posed to society when universalized morality is jettisoned. This chapter will also define the precise components of the worldview behind natural law theory. This chapter serves as an appetizer, of sorts, for the next chapters' detailed explanations of natural law.

## Natural Law and Culture War

Jason Stanley is a philosophy professor at Yale University, one of America's most premier and elite institutions. An active Twitter user and expert on fascism, Stanley caused an uproar on social media in 2021 by calling natural law "White Christian Nationalism." The epithet came in response to American Enterprise Institute scholar Tim Carney calling for natural law to be taught in public school.[1] For Stanley, natural law represented a sort of fascistic and totalizing category that would dare to posit objective truths about the world that beckons people, law, and society to conform to its standards. "Metaphysicophobic" would be apropos to describe individuals who take this approach to ethics. In this instance, an elite philosopher conceived of objective truth as an exponent of invidious authoritarianism. Carney, it should be noted, is no fringe figure. He's a respected commentator in American politics, and his suggestion that American public schools teach natural law is completely in line with America's governing documents, especially the Declaration of Independence, which famously states that, "We hold these truths to be self-evident, that all men are created equal, that they are endowed by their Creator with certain unalienable Rights, that among these are Life, Liberty and the pursuit of Happiness."

Stanley's tweet was derided as appallingly ignorant and summarily deleted. Nevertheless, the episode was a revealing insight into both the chasm and hostility that natural law conjures in modern culture when

---

[1] John Daniel Davidson, "Calling Natural Law 'White Nationalism' Is Racist, Period," *The Federalist*, July 14, 2021, https://thefederalist.com/2021/07/14/calling -the-natural-law-white-nationalism-is-racist-period/.

brought up. For advocates, it is the backbone of Western order; for secular detractors, a smokescreen for religious-based oppression that desires to see all brought under its dogmatic sway. While I am unaware of Stanley's religious beliefs, he is a very vocal political progressive who has engaged in past verbal harassment of Christians.[2] What Stanley meant in his derisive labeling of natural law was to discredit the underlying philosophy of the worldview of the American Founders. And to be clear, that worldview is not beyond criticism. Whatever debates persist on whether the goal of the American founding was to gradually abolish slavery, the American founding embedded slavery into its foundation.

But for Stanley to suggest that the American founding and its underlying philosophies are as morally odious as he depicts them, doing so unwittingly relies on the categories of natural law for its moral assessment. To know that slavery is wrong, one must possess a standard of measurement to weigh the infraction against. Indeed, one helpful approach in deciphering the natural law is by way of *via negativa*; that is, gaining insight into what the natural law demands when its tenets are "disrespected and contravened."[3] Taking an approach such as this removes natural law from the domain of abstraction and into the domain of practical experience. The revulsion and repugnance of events like the Holocaust tell us, in other words, that wanton, indiscriminate killing of innocent persons is unjust. Therefore, one principle of the natural law is to respect life.

There is a logically antecedent axiomatic truth at play in this exchange that gets easily overlooked: Any moral judgment whatsoever assumes an underived moral premise from which the judgment itself is derived. That unassumed premise posits an obligatory "ought." Moral incumbency lurks everywhere, even among those who deny universal truths. The problem

---

[2] Jingyi Cui and Natalie Wright, "Philosophy Professor under Fire for Online Post," *Yale Daily News*, October 5, 2016, https://yaledailynews.com/blog/2016/10/05/philosophy-professor-under-fire-for-online-post/.

[3] Tom Angier, *Natural Law Theory*, Cambridge Elements: Ethics (Cambridge: Cambridge University Press, 2021), 18.

for those who deny the natural law is that they cannot escape it. To deny it, they must affirm it. An ineluctable reality, to deny the natural law is to affirm at least one law—that no moral law exists. But to deny the abiding presence of a moral order is sheer foolishness that no person or society can reasonably live by. Condemnation, in other words, implies a minimal knowledge of moral certainty about that which should be condemned. Honest intellectual inquiry would ask from whence that measurement or standard comes.

The natural law is instrumental for knowing why slavery and race-based supremacy are grave injustices. Justice Clarence Thomas, for example, once observed, "Those who deny the natural law cannot get me out of slavery."[4] Thomas's statement conveys an essential component to natural law: It is a system of moral judgment that imposes order on our interactions with the world. It gives finite directives on moral rights and moral wrongs that supersede even human courts or human custom. Thomas was appealing to the highest court of the universe to derive his principle of equality. If morality is merely an anthropological construct, it is hard to create a moral system that can principally forbid slavery *tout court*. This is the true brilliance of what natural law avails. It offers self-attesting evidence for its existence. Do you want to oppose racism? The natural law is necessary to establish the principle for *why* racial subjugation is wrong. Do you want to oppose sex-trafficking? The natural law is necessary to establish the principle for why subjugating female bodies is wrong. Do you want to oppose pornography? The natural law is necessary for establishing why misdirected use of sexual desire is wrong. We may not have explicit confirmation or even agreement about the full range of moral obligations that the natural law entails, but the quandary of searching is evidence itself of the natural law's abiding relevance to moral judgment. As Alasdair MacIntyre remarks, "Our everyday judgments about the good and the bad,

---

[4] Robert P. George, "The 1993 St. Ives Lecture—Natural Law and Civil Rights: From Jefferson's 'Letter to Henry Lee' to Martin Luther King's 'Letter from Birmingham Jail,'" *Catholic University Law Review* 43, no. 1 (1993): 145.

the better and the worse, at least when our evaluative language is in good order, presuppose some perhaps inchoate view of what it is that human flourishing consists in, even though it may be one that we ourselves have never spelled out."[5]

That an esteemed philosopher like Stanley at an elite institution would register the type of protest seen in his comments reveals the underlying explosiveness beneath the question of natural law in our age: Its reliance upon a particular worldview and underlying presuppositions that understands that morality is to be received, rather than constructed; that human flourishing is objectively ordered and achievable only according to rightly-ordered conduct. Natural law is thus an assault on human-made moral systems that gives a person the license to fulfill whatever it is that appears pleasing to his or her appetite or sense of aggrandizement. Natural law, in contrast, assumes the existence of a fixed moral order that determines the natural ends, goods, or goals of our existence, which, in turn, measures an action's worth based on the action's ability or inability to bring about the goal. Take slavery as an example.

Why, exactly, is slavery an invidious act of grave injustice? It is wrong, fundamentally, because it denies persons the essential properties of their personhood—equality, self-constitution, and freedom. To appraise equality and freedom as intrinsically valuable qualities connected to human flourishing assumes that human persons are beings whose nature requires these modalities for their flourishing. But all of these are grand assumptions about the moral excellencies of equality and freedom and the nobility of human beings. It assumes the existence of both norms and qualities of being that are rightly considered to be flourishing.

A Christian account of natural law offers a worldview where the moral values society esteems as necessary for its continuation finds foundation. Indeed, given the theory's connections to cosmology, ontology, epistemology, and teleology, it is not an overstatement to conclude that natural law

---

[5] Alasdair MacIntyre, *Ethics in the Conflicts of Modernity* (Cambridge: Cambridge University Press, 2020), 25.

posits a worldview, but is itself a worldview. One of history's most infamous atheists saw this for himself. Writing in *The Antichrist*, Friedrich Nietzsche criticized Christianity for propounding a worldview that he saw as an impediment to human advancement (which, for Nietzsche, meant the raw exercise of power). For Nietzsche, universal moral laws—like "equality" applied to all persons—impeded power struggles for dominating what materialist perspectives saw as weaker beings.

> Why be public-spirited? Why take any pride in descent and forefathers? Why labour together, trust one another, or concern one's self about the common welfare, and try to serve it? . . . Merely so many "temptations," so many strayings from the "straight path."—"One thing only is necessary". . . . That every man, because he has an "immortal soul," is as good as every other man; that in an infinite universe of things the "salvation" of every individual may lay claim to eternal importance; that insignificant bigots and the three-fourths insane may assume that the laws of nature are constantly suspended in their behalf—it is impossible to lavish too much contempt upon such a magnification of every sort of selfishness to infinity, to insolence. And yet Christianity has to thank precisely this miserable flattery of personal vanity for its triumph—it was thus that it lured all the botched, the dissatisfied, the fallen upon evil days, the whole refuse and off-scouring of humanity to its side. The "salvation of the soul"—in plain English: "the world revolves around me." . . . The poisonous doctrine, "equal rights for all," has been propagated as a Christian principle: out of the secret nooks and crannies of bad instinct Christianity has waged a deadly war upon all feelings of reverence and distance between man and man, which is to say, upon the first prerequisite to every step upward, to every development of civilization—out of the ressentiment of the masses it has forged its chief weapons against us, against everything noble, joyous and high-spirited on earth, against our happiness on earth. . . . To allow "immortality" to every Peter and Paul

was the greatest, the most vicious outrage upon noble humanity ever perpetrated.[6]

It is not hard to draw the conclusion for why Christian natural law is so scandalous to someone like Nietzsche. Because all persons bear ontological equality, justice entails like treatment. Power and domination of the weaker violate basic justice in this account. All other explanations for slavery's wrongfulness stem from that reality. Slavery denies that a slave's personhood is on the same level of their owner. As President Abraham Lincoln wrote to the same effect, drawing on a natural law principle that one sees in the Golden Rule, "As I would not be a slave, so I cannot be a master."[7] Slavery forces an individual to act against their will, robbing them of their agency and self-constitution, inducing inner fragmentation as the desire for liberty is left unquenched. Enslaved people cannot cooperate with their own capacities to reach their self-fulfilling ends. Fundamentally, the denial of their personhood results in the denial of their agency that is owed to them by virtue of their mere existence. This signals an injustice.

If one were to get to the foundation of natural law, it is a mode of moral reasoning that believes moral agency is perfected or fulfilled by the agent acting how he or she *ought* in accordance with a moral order that establishes and governs that agent's nature. Natural law refers to (1) the existence of a moral order (2) and norms that comprise that order's fulfillment of being. Natural law is thus a cosmically-rooted moral system in that we believe God gives it order and ordains oughtness as determinative of ends that satisfy both the cosmos and human nature. "Ought" is a loaded moral signifier in moral theology. "Ought" connotes directiveness, prescription, objectivity,

---

[6] Friedrich Wilhelm Nietzsche, *The Antichrist*, trans. H. L. Mencken (1895; repr., Waiheke Island: The Floating Press, 2010), 98–100.

[7] Quote by Abraham Lincoln in personal notes from 1858. For more on this note, see Christian McWhirter, "Lincoln Draws the Line on Slavery," Abraham Lincoln Presidential Library and Museum, February 23, 2021, https://presidentlincoln.illinois.gov/Blog/Posts/108/Abraham-Lincoln/2021/2/Lincoln-Draws-the-Line-on-Slavery/blog-post/.

intelligibility. In other words, natural law morality is a system of known moral norms and goods. It is a system of *moral realism*, a branch of cognitivist moral thought that insists upon the adequacy and coherency of language to describe moral actions and events *as such* and not simply as descriptions of emotional responses.

## Culture Wars as Metaphysical Wars

A framework such as atheism could not create a document like the Declaration of Independence. Consider: In an atheistic framework, from where do "inalienable" rights originate? What gives poise to the idea of inalienability? Why are the goods that rights exist to protect verifiably good? If left to the whims of convention, how are those rights protected from violation once human opinion shifts about the values protecting said rights? Why would the "pursuit of happiness" be at all intelligible, desirable, and worth protecting? On what grounds are these rights to be secured against? We are left with very few options when it concerns protecting human rights and securing justice. Justice and rights will be the result of objective beliefs about persons and certain states of affairs or else each are mere sundries left to the vicissitudes of humanity. In questions like these and so many more, there is an unstated but assumed standard from which to measure rectitude. Where atheism has been experimented with as a regime ideology, it has left carnage, death, and despair in its wake. Either this is purely coincidental, or circumstantial, or else atheism is materially responsible for entailing an ideology that fosters these outcomes. Ideas, it seems, do have consequences. This does not leave theism guiltless for the injustices sewn in its name, but it does leave open the question of whether injustices that follow from atheism are essential or accidental properties. The question is whether human rights and justice are left better protected by a consistent theism or a consistent atheism.

Understood against this backdrop, we come to understand that the so-called "culture wars" that besiege our culture are not as much ephemeral debates between liberals and conservatives but between rival visions for which metaphysical account of the world will predominate in society: Will it be one based on a wholly materialist account of the world, where the existence of the human soul is scoffed at, and its corresponding dignity denied? Or one anchored in a foundation of the transcendent-yet-imminent triune God who has revealed himself in nature and in his Word? At the risk of oversimplification, the option before us concerning Christian ethics and Christian worldview in today's world is a stark binary: we will acknowledge the centrality of God as the organizing principle of the universe or else toil in the vain pursuit of an illusory meaning that has no inherent safeguard keeping it from metastasizing into cultural barbarism.

Sociologists and historians have labored to explain the forces generating cultural strife. It is my own view that the culture wars, at root, are protracted conflicts about whether a natural law exists and to what extent its decrees must be obeyed. How we answer those two questions will be determinative of most of today's most contentious conflicts. Traced back to its irreducible origins, we might define culture war, at least theologically, as the ultimately futile resistance of cultural unbelief to the supremacy of Jesus Christ the Logos over his dominion of creation (Prov 8; John 1:3; 1 Cor 8:6; Col 1:17–17). Unbelief insists that reality belongs to it and is therefore bendable to human will. Christianity proposes a counter-vision, one that confesses that reality belongs to Christ and is fixed, and that no tranquility or flourishing is sustainable apart from recognizing God's authority. One recalls the famous words of Russian dissident Alexandr Solzhenitsyn on the cause of Russia's brutal history: "But if I were asked today to formulate as concisely as possible the main cause of the ruinous revolution that swallowed up some 60 million of our people, I could not put it more accurately than to repeat: 'Men have forgotten God; that's why all this has happened.'"[8] When humanity no longer conceives of itself as accountable to God's moral law,

---

[8] Aleksandr Solzhenitsyn, "Templeton Prize Acceptance Address by Mr. Aleksandr Solzhenitsyn" (London, May 10, 1983), https://www.templetonprize .org/laureate-sub/solzhenitsyn-acceptance-speech/.

barbarism is no further than one generation's experiment with atheism and moral relativism.

The denial of a shared, rightly ordered teleology signals not only intractable moral debate and cultural strife, but inevitable civilizational decline. The only way to recover a more human way to live is to return to the worldview of the Bible as the sure foundation for an objective account of morality. I am not the first to speak in this binary. Alasdair MacIntyre, one of this generation's most premier moral philosophers, has spoken similarly to the rival conflict of visions and the resulting irreconcilable contrasts they result in. According to MacIntyre,

> Modern moral utterance and practice can only be understood as a series of fragmented survivals from an older past and that the insoluble problems which they have generated for modern moral theorists will remain insoluble until this is well understood. If the deontological character of moral judgments is the ghost of conceptions of divine law which are quite alien to the metaphysics of modernity and if the teleological character is similarly the ghost of conceptions of human nature and activity which are equally not at home in the modern world, we should expect the problems of understanding and of assigning an intelligible status to moral judgments both continually to arise and as continually to prove inhospitable to philosophical solutions.[9]

MacIntyre's thinking is not to be quickly glossed over. According to MacIntyre, the ghosts of divine teleology haunt secular man's quest for ethical certainty. The problem of our culture, he avers, is, at root, a problem of ethics. The idea of a divinely transcendent moral order that determines the shape of human nature and the conduct befitting that nature, is, according to MacIntyre, extinct. We assume some norms, but secular culture has jettisoned the moral tradition that was seen as a cultural vehicle of those norms.

---

[9] Alasdair MacIntyre, *After Virtue: A Study in Moral Theory*, 3rd ed. (Notre Dame, IN: University of Notre Dame Press, 2007), 110.

Where our culture was once held together by a common moral grammar informed by Christianity, such a consensus gave rise not only to a shared destiny but a shared moral ecology informing our conceptions of moral norms, goods, and prohibitions. The Enlightenment, scientific and philosophical naturalism, as well global military conflicts and the attendant secularism they birthed created conditions for a disenchanted world emptied of moral purpose and a shared moral horizon.

As an abstraction, what's left is cultural fragmentation, moral disarray, and a vitiation of the common good. As a practical matter, the proliferation of cultural pathologies—among them abortion, ethnic strife, declining marriage rates, sexual promiscuity, and rampant sexual perversion and confusion in the forms of glamorized homosexuality and transgenderism—render it impossible for civilization to speak in moral harmony. That's because the melody itself is gone. Such a realization of cultural decay is contrasted with the vision of a divinely transcendent moral order where persons exhibit a moral worth to be realized, and where this realization is facilitated by a shared moral vision. Commenting on C. S. Lewis's understanding of the relationship between morality and the human person, Michael L. Peterson writes, "Moral law, then, has a normative force and morality is essential to human flourishing because personhood is intrinsically valuable. In a universe described by Christian theism, a perfectly good God creates finite personal beings with the capacity to reflect God's moral nature."[10] All of this is bounded by a morality defined by discrete goods with a corresponding nature. But where humanity lacks moral vision, he is robbed of the grounds that procure his flourishing.

Expressive individualism is the closest thing our culture exhibits as a totalizing worldview. It seeks to evade God by collapsing God into a mirror of the interior self. Today, culture is held together by the thinnest of margins borrowed from whatever remaining capital is left from Christianity's influence on the West. Not only is our situation dire in that Christianity's

---

[10] Michael L. Peterson, *C. S. Lewis and the Christian Worldview* (Oxford: Oxford University Press, 2020), 72.

ethics are no longer dominant, but now openly despised throughout many segments of the culture. A moral revolution has been undertaken that now interprets the moral foundations of the West as being a source of constraining bigotry. In turn, we are jettisoning even the most minimalist grounds of the natural law one must obtain for there to be civilization. MacIntyre's outlook is bleak, as it should be.

In the absence of even a modest moral consensus, MacIntyre asserts that reason takes a backseat to other forms of discourse, namely, emotional protest:

> It is easy also to understand why *protest* becomes a distinctive moral feature of the modern age and why *indignation* is a predominant modern emotion. . . . The self-assertive shrillness of protest arises because the facts of incommensurability ensure that protestors can never win an *argument*; the indignant self-righteousness of protest arises because the facts of incommensurability ensure equally that the protestors can never lose an argument either. Hence the *utterance* of protest is characteristically addressed to those who already *share* the protestors' premises. The effects of incommensurability ensure that protestors rarely have anyone else to talk to but themselves. This is not to say that protest cannot be effective; it is to say that it cannot be *rationally* effective and that its dominant modes of expression give evidence of a certain perhaps unconscious awareness of this.[11]

Because there is no shared teleology, that is, no sense of an ultimate goal to our civilization's existence that would inform our understanding of how to interact within society, rival cultural visions posit their own moral constitutions, cementing and entrenching an ever-widening degree of moral difference that these irreconcilable visions erect. The result, as MacIntyre famously quipped, is a context where "modern politics cannot be a matter of

---

[11] MacIntyre, *After Virtue*, 71.

genuine moral consensus. And it is not. Modern politics is civil war carried on by other means."[12] Protest, resentment, and indignation are the closest things Westerners have to a shared language and cultural grammar. Is it any surprise, then, that talk of an actual civil war among Americans is on the rise by commentators and statisticians?[13] It is under the weight of relativism and nihilism that society disintegrates. J. Daryl Charles notes the implications of moral fracture on the idea of a common good for society: "political judgments and the political process become impossible where there is no shared repository of values and priorities."[14] The pursuit of justice—the *sine qua non* of political communities—is rendered impossible without even a modest moral consensus.[15]

A teleology evacuated of transcendently grounded truth claims and exchanged for the expressive individualism of the autonomous and emotive self bears all the marks of what C. S. Lewis scholar Michael Ward calls a "post-truth" civilization in decline:

> The pervasive, almost ubiquitous acceptance of various kinds of emotivism and subjectivism in modern Western culture means there can be no persuasion—that is to say, rational argument leading to a freely adopted change of mind. Rather, as belief in objective value evaporates and the public square is evacuated of practical reason, what passes for moral discourse increasingly resembles a war zone in which political propagandists, commercial interests, private whims, and animal instincts fight tooth-and-nail in a permanent

---

[12] MacIntyre, 253.

[13] See, for example, Martin Pengelly, "More than 40% of Americans Think Civil War Likely within a Decade," *The Guardian*, August 30, 2022, https://www.theguardian.com/us-news/2022/aug/29/us-civil-war-fears-poll; David French, *Divided We Fall: America's Secession Threat and How to Restore Our Nation* (New York: St. Martin, 2020).

[14] J. Daryl Charles, *Retrieving the Natural Law: A Return to Moral First Things* (Grand Rapids: Eerdmans, 2008), 59.

[15] For more on the political repercussions of splintered concepts of political justice, see Charles, *Retrieving the Natural Law*, 60–62.

free-for-all. The leaders and the led, the rich and the poor, white-collar and the blue-collar, the religious and the secular: these parties look at one another with a rivalry bordering on hatred or simply with blank incomprehension. In this rational desert, the only way people can affect social or political or legislative change is to mobilise sufficiently large contingent of like-minded protestors and out-protest their opponents. The question of truth, as such, is relegated to a second- or third-order issue: the real question is one of power. And thus we arrive at our post-truth world.[16]

Notice the features of this culture: unmitigated strife battered by "blank incomprehension"—the notion that rival citizen groups are no longer simply in a disagreement on political matters but occupying divergent moral universes. The ability to empathize with another's outlook on the world grows more and more foreign, resulting in a nation with irreconcilable moral chasms. Where does that bring us? A moral vision set by raw power and raw majoritarianism. Where a denial of truth proliferates and natural moral goods are treated as exporters of discrimination, all that is left to manufacture morality is consent and majoritarianism.

These are the high stakes of what we are gambling with when it comes to the abandonment of any sort of Christian natural law-based civilizational vision: despair.

Ethics and morality originate from the wellspring of worldview. When looking at the conflicts that drive so much of our cultural tumult, we must look beyond the immediate horizon of politics and to the depths of theology. Buried deep within the annals of political dispute are theological questions. At root, political controversy is spiritual conflict related to self-ordering within community. Understood correctly, fraught battles over abortion, sexuality, and gender are really disputes about whether there is

---

[16] Michael Ward, *After Humanity: A Guide to C. S. Lewis's The Abolition of Man* (Park Ridge, IL: Word on Fire Academic, 2021), 42.

an objective basis on which to account for foundational truths that society must subscribe to for it to prosper. Our society cannot answer the questions of: What is a person? What is a male or female? What constitutes a family? The thinnest of natural law margins are being eclipsed by a literal abolition of humanity.

One of the insidious consequences, then, of secularism is its constant fluidity, fashionable fictions, and destabilizing fallacies. Jesus Christ is the opposite. In Christ, there is a place to stand. There is fixity and finality. It is easy to be dour about the prospects facing the viability of Christian influence in the West. But before looking to our own self-interest, let us be clear on what the decline of Christianity means: harm to individuals and society.

## Creation and Natural Law

These crises bring us to the dilemma of Christian ethics in late modernity. An issue plaguing Christian public engagement is the implied notion that Christian concerns about the world—mainly what is just and moral— are sectarian interests alone. By that, that our concerns about the world are "Christian concerns" rather than concerns about creation order more broadly. Of course, a concern about creation order is a "Christian concern." But there is a way of talking about what social pathologies concern Christians that unintentionally communicates that Christians are the only stakeholders in needing to see the issue resolved. For example, there is no shortage of Christian enthusiasm to marshal our resources to combat sex-trafficking. But the same quest for justice that animates our excitement in one arena demands equal attention in others if we are to be consistent in developing a robust natural law ethic, especially in the arenas that are far more controversial, such as insisting that marriage's redefinition is its own injustice. Christian engagement cannot stand, or fall, based on what is popular. What we need is a confidence that Christian reflection on addressing social ills is not determined by whether society accepts our claims as

Christians, but instead, whether society is living with or against the grain of a Christian universe. This is our Father's world, after all, whether the world realizes it or not.

That raises the question of impetus: Is there a moral backdrop that might give Christianity more confidence and consistency in our public proclamations? To make such proclamations means there are not two moralities, one for Christians and another for non-Christians. Instead, the way God has ordered the world means there's one moral order with two responses: obedience or disobedience. When we speak of Christian morality, therefore, we are speaking of reality itself with no bifurcated division between what the Christian believes is true and what the non-regenerate is required to obey.

We all know this to be true at some level. The command prohibiting murder is not a command that only Christians are obligated to obey. We believe in a common morality because we believe that God's creation has order, intelligibility, and reason behind it. To accept this is to accept a radical reorientation to engagement—instead of trying to make the world agree with Christians, we seek to persuade the world that the moral order of God's creation is real and good and true and can only be evaded to its own deprivation (Ps 24:1). The world must align itself with God's creation order for it to flourish.

Such commands as protecting life and forbidding murder are the products of a divinely mandated creation order. Whether we call it "General Revelation," "Creation Ordinances," or "Natural Law," the idea behind these terms is that a loving Creator orders our world and directs our actions and choices toward particular goods that fulfill the purpose of our design as humans. It assumes human nature exists and, as an essence, is not malleable by way of desire or will. There are truths realized through practical reason that all are bound by. We seek out beauty as something intrinsically beneficial for its own sake. Learning is a worthwhile pursuit because knowledge, as such, is intrinsically valuable. We follow traffic laws because preserving life is good; we reject racial animus because skin color is an irrelevant factor to take into consideration for constituting "dignity." The existence of moral goods and the moral laws that attend to them does not mean that all goods and laws are perfectly obeyed. Human existence testifies to the truth of our capacity for evil and error. But natural law, if it is indeed what God says it is, provides a forum and theater for the blessings of this life to be experienced even apart from a firm knowledge of where those norms and goods originate. Natural law truths are everywhere in Scripture. "The Golden Rule" laid down by Jesus in Luke 6:31 is a natural law principle: when we treat our neighbors with respect and kindness, we are seeking the integrity of their being in hopes that our integrity as persons is fulfilled as well. Magnified in the aggregate, something as simple as the reciprocal obligations we owe to one another is the building block of society.

But are morality and justice merely the innovations of human-made laws or of divine grace? Christianity asserts that all of creation, which includes the moral law, is itself a product of divine grace. While grace restores or "perfects" nature, grace presupposes the intelligibility and original goodness of nature. But nature, in a Christian rendering, is a product of grace as well. The reason we live, move, and have our being is the result of a benevolent Creator who wills such operations from eternity past. Understanding this dynamic is important for understanding the abiding relevance and authority of Christian ethics. The natural law is God's moral law disclosed through general revelation, within creation even now, and understood through practical reason. Grace was present even in the garden. As Eden was created by God, so is nature the product of grace. All aspects of creation order that reflect the givenness of reality are theaters of God's grace. As Bernd Wannenwetsch writes, "The Christian doctrine of creation is precisely such a way of explaining why there are aspects of reality that are invested with normative moral significance."[17] Precisely because the Christian believes

----

[17] Bernd Wannenwetsch, "Creation and Ethics: On the Legitimacy and Limitation of Appeals to 'Nature' in Christian Moral Reasoning," in *Within the Love of God: Essays on the Doctrine of God in Honour of Paul S. Fiddes*, ed. Anthony Clarke and Andrew Moore (Oxford: Oxford University Press, 2014), 209.

that reality belongs to a God who orders creation in the ways that he does, we hold that moral truths correspond to reality and existence as we know it.

We believe that righteousness and justice are the products of divine grace made intelligible within creation. A person need not be a Christian to be moral and justice-minded, but all accounts of morality and justice will, in the long run, be understood as means of grace given by God. There is no autonomous realm where God is not holding everything together through his logos, Jesus Christ. In Scripture, everything was made through him (John 1:3). In Colossians, he holds everything together, giving indication that the structure of creation and moral order has a scope and audience that is universal by nature (Col 1:15–17). As Oliver O'Donovan famously wrote in *Resurrection and Moral Order,*

> The order of things that God has made is there. It is objective, and mankind has a place within it. Christian ethics, therefore, has an objective reference because it is concerned with man's life in accordance with this order. The summons to live in it is addressed to all mankind, because the good news that we may live in it is addressed to all mankind. Thus Christian moral judgments in principle address every man. They are founded on reality as God has given it.[18]

It is our shared commonality as humans, not only as Christians, that gives us a license to enter the public square and make moral proclamations. That's not because being a Christian is unimportant to addressing social ills (surely, it is), but rather, our concern for addressing social ills is because we are all members of a creation ordered by God. Without a doctrine of creation at the forefront of our ethics, we lose the means to speak to an unbelieving world. For Christians, the question is not only what the Bible says, but what the Bible's description of an intelligible, stable order demands of those inhabiting it. Viewing the world's moral rebellion as a form of

---

[18] Oliver O'Donovan, *Resurrection and Moral Order: An Outline for Evangelical Ethics* (Grand Rapids: Eerdmans, 1994), 17.

estrangement from creation as it is, instead of seeing Christian moral claims as a foreign imposition on an otherwise malleable and fungible creation order, alters how we see the task of natural law ethics.

The full gamut of Christian engagement with the world requires the ability to enter the public arena and to debate with those who do not believe the Bible is God's Word. Confidence in God's creation is essential to our engagement with the world, whether that is in fighting poverty, addressing racial hostility, and promoting the dignity of unborn life. This does not mean that Christian thought offers every granular solution to poverty or the prudence of a minimum wage; it does mean that combating poverty is set against the backdrop of a creational mandate to exercise responsible dominion. Public witness and social ethics must begin with the belief that Christian truths are not sectarian truths. They are truths embedded in the very the structure of creation.

## The Necessity of Natural Law for Christian Social Ethics

A common line of argument in the relationship of Christian ethics to public engagement is asking why it is the government's responsibility to enforce Christian morals. As the argument is framed, if Christian ethics is primarily conversionist in nature, meaning that our ethics are only intelligible upon conversion, why expect non-Christians to uphold an ethical system they not only disagree with but cannot adequately act upon because of their unbelief? Moreover, what interest does the government have in promoting Christian ethics? Isn't it the job of the church to keep to itself and judge only those inside its midst? (1 Pet 4:17). Many who express these sentiments do so with well-meaning attempts to (rightly) keep Christians from panicking over misplaced trust in temporal earthly powers. Additionally, they want to remind themselves and fellow believers that to be a Christ-follower will always be, as Jesus promised, countercultural. I've even seen Christians invoke Paul's statement, "For what have I to do with judging outsiders? Is it not those inside the church whom you are to judge?" (1 Cor 5:12), as a way to excuse society's moral decadence—as though ecclesial accountability suspends moral obligation for others.

This line of approach misunderstands the very nature of Christian ethics and ignores how God ordered creation, morality, and the purpose he has given civil law for. Assumptions like those above can lead to disastrous consequences for how we understand moral obligation, creating stark binaries of "Christian morality" being a solely regenerate enterprise only.

In one sense, the Bible does describe the condition of humans, without Christ, as lost and depraved, incapable of pleasing God (Rom 3:9–20). Apart from Christ, we are in a state of rebellion, and until regenerated by the Holy Spirit, cannot understand the ways of God (1 Cor 2:14). It should not surprise us, then, when sinners act sinfully. Sin has been the human default ever since Eden.

However, by keeping the spotlight only on sinful humanity's inability to live lives of obedience to God, we overlook how failure to obey God shows that God's commands for human obedience are grounded in his good and holy nature, and therefore obligatory on all persons at all times. Morality reflects God's holiness (Lev 21:8). Thus, one function of the moral order is to expose our rebellion against God's moral law and God himself. We know the moral order is good because our guilty consciences indict us for failing to uphold it. This is the most basic of ethical principles. To say non-Christians can't be expected to live like Christians and obey God ignores the fact that God and the moral order he implanted in creation are to be obeyed universally. Making that claim leads to a consequence similar to what happens when we quit a book halfway in: we'll fail to see the full story and resolution.

At creation, God made humans as his image-bearers. Christian theology has long debated the definition and scope of what it means to image God. But on a functional level, to image God means at least that we possess the capacity to make sense of moral cues or moral demands. God endowed the mind to know right from wrong. Paul picks up on this theme of creation and moral order in Romans 1 and 2, where he describes particular sinful practices as unnatural. Not only that, but he also says that these practices are known to be immoral because they violate "the law . . . written on their hearts" (Rom 2:15). The "conscience also bears witness" to God's moral law. The fact that humanity is mired in sin does not excuse anyone from knowing or doing what their God-given conscience knows to be good or bad.

Every human, even in a fallen world, has some capacity to do good. Being made in God's image is what gives us the inclination to the moral life patterned after God's true and final image, Jesus Christ. The creaturely goods God enables us to fulfill are ordered by, and fulfilled in, Jesus Christ. As Matthew Levering writes, "All created reality, including human bodiliness, has inscribed within it this ecstatic ordering to its own fulfillment. Human reason shares receptively in God's knowing of his ecstatic ordering in creation, and this sharing, as imprinted in our minds, is natural law."[19] In one sense, then, Christology unlocks the fullness of human nature. Human nature is not a generic category for Christian ethics but is rooted in our belief that true human fulfillment is found in Christ. This is often referred to as common grace or general providence—that is, God's restraining us from exhaustive evil, and his enabling us to do good, though not unto salvation. But even common grace insofar as it upholds the pattern of creation—in order for creatures to come to know their Creator and his Son in whose image they embody—has a redemptive inflection to it. Christians do well, then, when they advocate Christian ethics in the public square, both as a word to the conscience of non-Christians, hoping they will repent before their Creator, and as a way to promote what is best for human flourishing.

But imagine we took the same laissez-faire approach toward enforcing Christian morality on others with a different issue—say, crime—that some do with sexuality and abortion. What if our approach toward murder or theft was to simply reply, "Well, you cannot expect non-Christians to live like Christians, so of course non-Christians will steal and kill." Of course,

---

[19] Matthew Levering, *Biblical Natural Law: A Theocentric and Teleological Approach* (Oxford: Oxford University Press, 2008), 180.

no one argues that theft and murder should go unpunished in society. Why? Why should we expect our neighbors not to murder? Why should we think non-Christians will act like believers and ought to obey the sixth and eighth commandments? Because theft and murder violate a fundamental principle of justice that all of our consciences know to be true: it is unjust to steal and murder. Stealing is a violation not only of God's revealed law, but also of the basic concept of justice that is written on the heart of every person. If our unbelieving neighbor steals from us, we don't excuse their behavior because they don't follow a Christian code of ethics. We simply expect them not to steal.

All Christians, if they are honest, hope non-Christians think and act like Christians—whether in maintaining a just and well-ordered society or when approaching issues like human trafficking, abortion, racial justice, child poverty, and other pressing issues. We fight for laws that reflect what we believe to be true about human dignity and human flourishing. Why? Because principles of morality are not limited to or binding on Christians only.

We must not shrink back from fighting for what we believe is God's design for human flourishing simply because it is controversial. That morality is contested and controversial simply displays how fractured societies are and how obstinate sinful humans are to God's design. We advocate for creational truths in the wider culture, not because we want to create a theocracy or because we need government sanction for our beliefs, but because we believe that the way God ordered human life offers the exclusive opportunity for human flourishing. Ending human trafficking or supporting the best marriage policy has real-world implications for the common good.

The second axiom of this laissez-faire approach to ethics is an appeal to the inability of civil law to shape human hearts. To this principle, I would simply add my whole-hearted agreement. Only a work of God's Spirit can regenerate the heart. There is no legal utopia that can convert and immediately sanctify.

However, this does not mean Christians should refrain from working for just laws and a well-ordered society. In fact, knowledge of human depravity should motivate Christians in a representative republic to fight for a government that promotes God's law. And we should do this for several reasons.

First, the Bible tells us that government is God's delegated authority to do good (Rom 13:4; 1 Pet 2:13–17). Christian ethics assumes the presence of sin and evil in society and therefore affirms the need for just leaders and just laws to punish evil and promote good. Human leaders, whether they realize it or not, are leading and serving in the place of God (Rom 13:1–7).

Second, it is fictitious to assume that laws are amoral. Every law reflects some moral principle. Laws that prohibit theft, for instance, reflect the belief that private property allows individuals to build their livelihoods without fear of arbitrary confiscation. Even something as anodyne as sugar subsidies exist in order to keep prices low so that humans can afford to eat and sustain themselves. Laws that govern food safety reflect the belief that corporations that sell food to the public should care about the health of the consumer. Laws that prohibit human slavery reflect the belief that humans possess inherent dignity. Each of these principles terminates at a particular goal: affirming that which is good, and shunning that which is evil.

All of our activism—our work to change laws and legislation in this country when necessary—flows from our moral beliefs. Sometimes activists acknowledge this more vocally, while others are more subtle. Imagine if Martin Luther King Jr. had not appealed to the Christian storyline in his march for civil rights. It is no surprise that King was a strong advocate for the enforcement of morality. He famously quipped that laws may be ineffectual to make a white supremacist like him, but laws can deter the white supremacist from physically harming him.[20] If Christians refuse to apply a Christian ethic while stewarding their influence on public policy, others will fill that void with their own moral ethic. A secular ethic is not a value-free ethic simply because it says so. Secular ethics are packed with their own

---

[20] "An Address by the Reverend Dr. Martin Luther King, Jr." (Speech, Cornell College, Mount Vernon, IA, October 15, 1962), https://news.cornellcollege.edu/dr-martin-luther-kings-visit-to-cornell-college/.

conceptions of what is true, good, beautiful, and worthwhile to pursue. The task of the Christian, therefore, is to contend for justice and truth in the public realm.

Third, it is impossible to work for justice without believing that laws *are* moral statements, because every belief in morality stems from the understanding that morality makes demands that we ought to follow. If as a Christian you work for justice at any level, you are bringing Christian ethics to bear on public policy, whether you realize it or not. Why? Because without a system where laws reflect some aspect of Christian ethics—principles of justice, dignity, and the common good more broadly—societies descend into anarchy, and the weak are preyed upon by the strong. Justice for the trafficked, eradication of poverty, compassion for the fatherless—these depend on a system where right and wrong are distinguished.

Some construe biblical texts to mean that Christians cannot morally evaluate what happens outside the church. "Judge not, that you be not judged," Jesus said in Matt 7:1. Some read this as a prohibition on making moral judgments about culture, for fear that Christians will appear morally scrupulous, petty, and judgmental. But what Jesus really says is this: the standard by which you judge will be the standard by which you are judged. The question, ultimately, is, Whose standard of judgment is true? As Christians, we believe unreservedly that God's moral judgments are holy, true, and for our good. Moral judgment is rooted in God's kindness and mercy to show a path toward righteousness and flourishing.

To be sure, Christians are to hold fellow Christians accountable within the life of the church. But neither Jesus nor the New Testament writers excuse misbehavior or unbelief carte blanche. It is not as though stepping outside the walls of a church grants one a license to be morally reckless. Much of the New Testament's moral witness is about Christian morality inside the life of the church. But that focus about Christian moral integrity doesn't welcome moral chaos *outside* the church.

If we insist that Christian ethics should have no bearing on public policy, we do a disservice to our theology and cripple the mission of the church. It is a retreat inward and a tacit approval of injustice in society. A public Christianity is not about imposing Christian ethics on an unwilling citizenry. Instead, public Christianity is about marshaling God's truth in service of our fellow image-bearers, using the conscience and persuasion as our means.

## Conclusion

In Augustine's *City of God*, he writes: "[I]t is not the honors or power of this life we should covet, since all things under the sun are vanity, but we should aim at using our position and influence, if these have been honorably attained, for the welfare of those who are under us . . ."[21]

In the quote above, Augustine sets forth a positive vision for why Christians should seek to exert influence within a society. This vision can guide us to an understanding of evangelical enactment. As Augustine says, we should not seek power or influence for power or influence's own sake. But because Christians have knowledge about the world and its attendant goods, one way we can tell the truth is to see the positive good that can come from Christians' using the levers of influence for the benefit of all. A Christian natural law ethic would not seek its own hegemonic dominance or privilege, but would seek to expose and point to the ultimate good using penultimate means. A justly ordered political society more aligned with God's intention for creation order is more apt to receive the message of redemption.

Sadly, any pronouncement about the need to recognize objective goods will be viewed as a form of moral imposition by adherents of expressive individualism. If this is the case, it should lead us to be forthright about where our marching orders come from—to be more explicit that the basis of moral goods is not located in the domain of "nature" alone, but ultimately, in Christ. This is where an evangelical point of origin for our deliberations

---

[21] Augustine, *City of God*, 19.19.

about the natural law can be established. Natural law is a signpost that lets us use penultimate goods in relationship to their ultimate reference point in Christology.

A vision for natural law rooted in the supremacy of Jesus Christ is what this book hopes to advance. To understand a theory of morality, however, means we must engage in actual theory, to which we must now turn.

# 3.

# Toward a Christotelic Natural Law

## Defining the Natural Law and Natural Law Theory

This chapter begins by offering introductory definitions of natural law and ends with exploring the relationship between natural law and Christology. What I will argue for is a Christotelic interpretation of the natural law, which I will explain at length.

Before going into the particulars of the definition below, it is worth noting at the outset of this definition that natural law is a theory. To speak of theory as such is to speak of the use of an analytical tool devised to give explanation to a particular mode of philosophical inquiry. A belief in the natural law speaks to the objective reality of moral law itself. A theory purports to offer a framework by which to understand the contours of how natural law functions. In that sense, natural law theory is an analytical tool that best explains the structure of morality imposed on the cosmos by God.[1]

Natural law *theory* seeks to explain the phenomenon of the concept of natural law. Natural law as a theory allows us to understand and intelligibly pursue alignment with the order that God has stamped upon creation. As a theory, it supplies us with the categories of ontology (existence), epistemology (knowledge), and teleology (purpose). Natural law's lineaments are what allows us to pursue a range of meaningful activities and disciplines such as science, art, and technology. It's what sets the stage for justice and jurisprudence. A neglected concept in modern day, natural law was the *sine qua non* of how previous centuries went about establishing political regimes and striving for just social orders. Natural law helps us understand the cosmos' laws set forth by the divine Legislator. Theory purports to explain how natural law operates as a comprehensive moral theory.

The idea of theory is a lacuna in much of Protestant ethics. Protestant Christian ethics, at least in the twentieth century, has often lacked theoretical foundations for the discipline's intelligibility outside explicit appeals to Scripture alone. This gives the appearance that the authority of Christian ethics rests upon theological voluntarism and mere fideism *alone*—the notion that ethics are simply an exertion of will, instead of reason. But the natural law tradition argues that any ethical claim of Scripture can be presented with a reasoned defense to go alongside it, regardless of whether the person one is dialoguing with believes in biblical inspiration.

Natural law, in a complementary way, enables us to take the moral rules of Scripture and explain their reasonableness, choiceworthiness, and purpose since Christian ethics rests upon the intelligible goodness of the moral claims themselves as a reflection of God's own nature, where the will is understood to reflect God's goodness. As C. S. Lewis writes, "God's will is determined by His wisdom which always perceives, and His goodness

---

[1] Beyond that even, there are various schools of natural law theory. Readers may find it of interest to know that the natural law theory I subscribe to is a slightly modified form of what is called "New Natural Law" theory.

which always embraces, the intrinsically good."[2] To be clear, ethics done via proof-text is not wrong. Citing Scripture's authority as the foundation of Christian ethics is an eminent entailment of *sola Scriptura*. Indeed, without confirmation from the data of Scripture, adverting to reason alone will leave us in speculation. We most certainly should look to Scripture as our inspired, highest authority to ground our ethical convictions. But as previously discussed, without attesting to the reasonableness of Scripture's moral demands, citing Scripture without answering "why" the Bible is commanding what it is commanding can make Christian ethics appear denuded. The question we must ask and what the natural law tradition assists in answering is: Do we have valid *reasons* for holding the moral position that we do? For example, when the Bible prohibits murder as it does in Exod 20:13, that is our cue to go searching after the rationale and principles behind the prohibition for why the unlawful taking of life is wrong (it unjustly robs someone of a life they are due to live). That is where natural law becomes complementary to the task of biblical ethics.

## Biblical Sufficiency and the Natural Law

Conservative Protestants pledge fealty to the Bible as the supreme authority for ethics, but one reason that Protestant ethics can disagree amongst its proponents is that adverting to texts divorced from any sort of overarching theory or ethical method can posit conflicting conclusions. A theory like the one being proposed here is not intended to impose a theory on the Bible; rather, what I argue is that the Bible's own structuring of its moral content is best understood within a natural law framework.

There are right ways and wrong ways to cite Scripture in ethics. For one, merely looking for a verse to cite to positively affirm or prohibit an issue can, depending on how one goes about it, leave readers in a potential cul-de-sac because it may assume that the teaching of Scripture is authoritative

---

[2] C. S. Lewis, *The Problem of Pain* (1940; repr., New York: HarperOne, 2001), 100.

only insofar as its authority is accepted. Natural law theory, on the other hand, broadens our understanding of Scripture's authority by expanding and extending our understanding of its intelligibility and therefore, its authority. The truthfulness of a moral claim in the Bible is not binding if and only if the Bible's authority is accepted by an interlocutor. Rather, the morality that the Bible posits is, by virtue of having been ordered by God, authoritative regardless of whether one accepts the truthfulness of Scripture or not. That's because we are saying something about morality itself when Christians make moral claims, not just *biblical* morality. A sound natural law theory will help us understand that the Bible's truthfulness and philosophical truthfulness are never independent realities.

Secondly, a narrow reading of the Bible that understands ethics as merely the recitation of Bible verses can unintentionally undermine biblical sufficiency. Scripture is entirely sufficient to address the moral conflicts that the world throws at Christianity. But it often requires formulating theological methods that inform us of how the moral grammar of the Bible functions. The knowledge that murder is wrong, to cite one easy example, is straightforward scripturally speaking, but what about in vitro fertilization (IVF)? Or cloning? No verse explicitly prohibits either. Does that mean both are allowed? If we are left looking only for a solitary Bible verse to end the debate one way or another, we will not find it on the topic of IVF or cloning.

Without some way of reading Scripture ethically, the Bible can appear, however unintentionally, truncated and insufficient to the task of moral reflection. Moreover, when the Bible speaks morally, we need to explain the underlying rationale of the Bible's moral claim. We need to, for example, explain why murder is wrong not only because Exodus prohibits it, but because murder vitiates moral goods that Scripture implies are in the background. With the assistance of natural law theory, the Bible's apparent silence on an issue comes alive. Though I'll write about this later, the Bible's teaching that begetting children is an embodied and sexually exclusive act should cause us to register concern with technologies like IVF, which produce embryos outside an embodied union and through third-party interventions.

Natural law helps explain the underlying rationale of the Bible's moral teachings so that its ethics is not mere casuistry alone. Providing a full-body account of morality, natural law ethics concerns our reasoned reflection on what human goods fulfill our being and what norms or principles of moral action lead us *to* or *away* from our fulfillment as God's image-bearers. As Mark Murphy notes, "the natural law constitutes the principles of practical rationality, those principles by which human action is to be judged reasonable or unreasonable."[3] Natural law seeks to adumbrate, for example, why the prohibition on murder is not only a legitimate rule we are to follow from Scripture, but the reasonableness and choiceworthiness of the good the rule seeks to protect. Behind every ethical command is a *reason* for the action it is commanding. Natural law seeks to explain the reasons behind the command so as to give intelligible explanation for morality's reasonableness and corresponding obligation. Natural law ethics is thus fundamentally about articulating the underlying and theoretical reasonableness of biblical ethics. No prescription or decree of biblical morality will ever reject sound reason because morality issues from God's own eternal Wisdom.

My formal philosophical definition of natural law and natural law theory is the following:

*The moral theory that a divinely ordered and self-evident universal moral order exists that human reason can, in principle, grasp as intellectually knowable, which serves to direct our behavior toward morally choiceworthy goods and away from moral evils. This comprehension of the moral order and its basic, non-instrumental goods defines and identifies which actions are reasonable and worth pursuing—even apart from an immediate appeal to divine revelation—by achieving the purposes or goals necessary to human nature's fulfillment and*

---

[3] Mark Murphy, "The Natural Law Tradition in Ethics," *The Stanford Encyclopedia of Philosophy*, ed. Edward N. Zalta, Summer 2019, https://plato.stanford.edu/archives/sum2019/entries/natural-law-ethics.

*society's proper coordination. Natural law is thus action-guiding and action-explaining. It explains what we ought to do and why we ought to do it by providing reasons for action and reasons for restraint.*

While the rest of this chapter will be devoted to unpacking this definition in greater detail, a few initial observations are worth making. First, natural law theory applies to two simultaneous domains of moral consideration. It concerns the *external* or *extrinsic* moral order established by God. By this, I merely mean to suggest that God as the divine architect has promulgated an actual moral law that is universal, intelligible, and objective. Second, there is an *intrinsic* referent: natural law refers to the practical reasonableness and justification for any worthwhile choice or action directed toward the fulfillment of an intelligible human good grasped by reason. "Practical reason" is what it sounds like: the mind "working as a principle of action, not simply as a recipient of objective reality. It is the mind charting what is to be, not merely recording what already is."[4] Behind natural law is a commitment to basic goods—purposes, ends, or goods that are intelligible to order one's life around for their achievement. From start to finish, an ultimately coherent natural law must emanate from a divine source. As Paul Helm writes, "the natural law, being given for mankind's good, is part of the practical reason, and so it is teleological in its operation."[5] Among the range of possible goods debated by natural law theorists are life, family, health, integrity, knowledge of the truth, justice, friendship, play, vocation, integrity, skillfulness, aesthetic experience, authenticity, practical reasonableness, and religion. When the goods are pursued in harmony, a will toward integral human fulfillment is achieved, thus integrating all goods under the canopy of an ultimate good.[6] While there is a debate about defining the number of

---

[4] Germain G. Grisez, "The First Principle of Practical Reason: A Commentary on the Summa Theologiae, 1-2, Question 94, Article 2," *Natural Law Forum* 10 (1965): 175.

[5] Paul Helm, *Human Nature from Calvin to Edwards* (Grand Rapids: Reformation Heritage Books, 2018), 79.

[6] For more on the basic goods of the natural law, see Robert P. George, *Making Men Moral: Civil Liberties and Public Morality* (Oxford: Oxford University Press,

possible goods, what's less important is a strict adumbration of all possible goods than the underlying principle that any action pursued for its own sake would qualify as a good in itself.

Robert P. George offers a similar definition of natural law:

> Theories of natural law are reflective critical accounts of the constitutive aspects of the well-being and fulfillment of human persons and the communities they form. The propositions that pick out fundamental aspects of human flourishing are directive (that is, prescriptive) in our thinking about what to do and refrain from doing (our practical reason)—they are, or provide, more than merely instrumental reasons for action and self-restraint. When these foundational principles of practical reflection are taken together (that is, integrally), they entail norms that may exclude certain options and require other options in situations of morally significant choosing. Natural law theories, then, propose to identify principles of right action moral principles—specifying the first and most general principle of morality, namely, that one should choose and act in ways that are compatible with a will towards integral human fulfillment. Among these principles is a respect for rights people possess simply by virtue of their humanity—rights which, as a matter of justice, others are bound to respect and governments are bound not only to respect but, to the extent possible, also to protect.[7]

Though George's definition may sound overly technical, we should not miss the real simplicity of the point he's trying to make. What he focuses

---

1993); John Finnis, *Natural Law and Natural Rights*, 2nd ed. (Oxford: Oxford University Press, 2011); Alfonso Gómez-Lobo, *Morality and the Human Goods* (Washington, DC: Georgetown University Press, 2002); Germain G. Grisez, *The Way of the Lord Jesus: Christian Moral Principles*, vol. 1, 3 vols. (Quincy, IL: Franciscan Press, 1997); Mark C. Murphy, *Natural Law and Practical Rationality* (Cambridge, UK: Cambridge University Press, 2001).

[7] Robert P. George, "Natural Law," *Harvard Journal of Law & Public Policy* 31, no. 1 (Winter 2008): 172.

on is how the natural law facilitates, fundamentally, an order of justice and human flourishing. As we understand through the practical intellect the moral norms that lead or direct us to the goods that come to define our "nature" so to speak, we are able to establish what is necessarily "owed" to all persons. Because, for example, upholding one's life is a good pursued for its own sake, persons are owed protection against actions or persons who would seek to do bodily harm to them. Justice within a political community thus entails that law enforcement punish individuals who threaten a person's well-being. Narrower determinations, such as whether someone is owed healthcare by the state, is a debate that the natural law does not fully address. That is not a shortcoming of the natural law. Natural law concerns only those most foundational moral realities from which prudential applications by appropriate authorities and decision-makers are further elaborated.

Niels Hemmingsen, a sixteenth-century protégé of Philip Melanchthon, offers a definition of the natural law that parallels with the previous definitions:

> The law of nature is a certain knowledge, imprinted on the minds of men by God, of the principles of knowing and acting, and of the conclusions proved from these principles that are in agreement with the proper end of man. Reason constructs these conclusions from the principles by necessary consequence for the government of human life, so that man may recognize, want, choose, and do the things that are right, and avoid their opposites; and God has bestowed on men the conscience as the witness and judge of all these things.[8]

Natural law concerns the ability of practical reason to discern the moral goods that complete us. Moral goods just are those non-instrumental reasons for action. For example, we do not harm ourselves because self-harm is, well, bad in itself or, alternately, we pursue marriage for the sake of procreative

---

[8] Niels Hemmingsen, *On the Law of Nature: A Demonstrative Method* (Grand Rapids: CLP Academic, 2018), 30.

and relational fulfillment for their own sake. Goods are those completing activities that require no additional reason for their choiceworthiness.

As one studies the definitions above, one will see that the natural law is simultaneously theoretical and practical in nature. It concerns the existence and identification of our nature and assumes there are goods, purposes, or ends that constitute us in real fulfillment. As Hemmingsen notes, the "law of nature is a certain knowledge of the first principles of contemplation and of acting."[9] It concerns the existence of a moral order, our grasp of it, and our action in accordance with it. Thus, the natural law is a divinely inscribed and universally known moral order discovered through a body of intelligible reasons for action and restraint that provide norms and principles for directing persons to act in the fulfillment of goals and goods of human fulfillment.

Reformed theologian and ethicist David VanDrunen defines the natural law as "the idea that God makes known the basic substance of his moral law through the created order itself. Human beings therefore know this law simply by virtue of being human, even apart from access to Scripture or other forms of special revelation."[10] As a later chapter will explore, VanDrunen correctly observes in his definition how creation itself is a form of natural law or natural revelation. Similar to the definition above, VanDrunen defines the natural law as the "moral order that directs people to proper human goals corresponding to the purposes for which God made them."[11] A teleological undercurrent is what animates natural law theory under the axiom that a moral law exists that humans should strive—in their persons and in their societies—to honor and achieve so as to prosper.

At its most basic, then, the natural law is God's moral law implanted in human beings that allow them to understand basic principles of right and wrong action that correlate with their flourishing or, conversely, act

---

[9] Hemmingsen, 62.

[10] David VanDrunen, *Politics after Christendom: Political Theology in a Fractured World* (Grand Rapids: Zondervan, 2020), 126.

[11] VanDrunen, 138.

parasitically to it. French Catholic philosopher Jacques Maritain echoes the idea that the natural law is not simply about knowing that a moral order exists above us and within us, but "the natural law of all beings existing in nature is the proper way in which, by reason of their specific nature and specific ends, they *should* achieve fulness of being in their behaviour."[12] Natural law is nothing else than creatures learning to inhabit their existence to a maximal degree of personal happiness.

Though the topic of "law" as an isolated concept will receive deeper treatment below, I want to conclude this section with Thomas Aquinas's famous definition of law as it will serve as a helpful reference point throughout the rest of the chapter as we delve more deeply into the natural law. Law, according to Aquinas, is "an ordinance of reason for the common good, made by him who has care of the community, and promulgated."[13]

Having defined the natural law, it is important to establish four components of the natural law in greater detail that will receive treatment later in the book: The *origin* of the natural law, the *knowability* of the natural law, the actual *content* of the natural law, and the *utility* of the natural law. Before getting to that task, it is necessary to establish the forgotten or neglected relationship between natural law and Jesus Christ.

## Natural Law and Jesus Christ

Every aspect of Christian ethics begins and ends with the revelation Jesus Christ. To pit Christ against the creation that Scripture declares that he orders and holds together is to miss the coherence and scope of the Christian ethical program's relationship to the world. To do ethics as a Christian means we do ethics in light of the revelation of Jesus Christ. Anything less and ethics ceases to be Christian. Oliver O'Donovan writes, "A belief in

---

[12] Jacques Maritain, *Natural Law: Reflections on Theory and Practice* (South Bend, IN: St. Augustine, 1952), 29.

[13] *ST* I-II, q. 90, a. 4, s. c.

Christian ethics is a belief that certain ethical and moral judgments belong to the gospel itself; a belief, in other words, that the church can be committed to ethics without moderating the tone of its voice as a bearer of glad tidings."[14] O'Donovan's statement must inform our reflections on the natural law and natural law theory. The concern that natural law is insufficiently Christological has justifiably contributed to the suspicion of natural law as an insufficiently faithful expression of Christian ethics. After all, if natural law refers to a system of morality that non-Christians could in principle grasp, how is it Christian? A dilemma facing evangelical ethics is how to argue for the inherent naturalness of Christian morality, as the natural law teaches is the case, while not sacrificing the ontological and epistemological priority of Christology.

An evangelical approach to natural law necessarily entails that we begin and end our reflections of it with Jesus Christ, in whom "all things hold together" (Col 1:17). Contrary to other systems of moral reasoning, Christians do not hypothesize as to the foundation of its ethical system. That is, indeed, the true scandal of Christian ethics: A revealed system of normative ethics that claims binding judgment through its norms and principles not only on its adherents, but also on those who inhabit the creation ordered by the God who is revealed. In turn, we do not do our moral reasoning abstracted from the person of Jesus Christ. Ethics forever changed with the dawning of Jesus Christ. The realms of creation and redemption were conjoined in Christ. Moral infractions, then, are not violations against an impersonal force or a mere "principal," but against the Son of God. This includes our conceptualizations regarding the natural law.

To speak of the centrality of Jesus Christ for Christian ethics is to speak of the unfolding mystery of God's plan now made known in Christ. The apostle Paul speaks of the dawning of Christ as God "making known to us the mystery of his will, according to his purpose, which he set forth in Christ as a plan for the fullness of time, to unite all things in him,

---

[14] O'Donovan, *Resurrection and Moral Order*, 12 (see chap. 2, n. 18).

things in heaven and things on earth" (Eph 1:9–10). To speak of natural law without reference to Christ is to advert to the errors of generic moral inquiry, what Christian theologian Carl F. H. Henry called "speculative ethics."[15] On its own terms, moral reasoning is of course necessary for there to be clear moral boundaries established and categorized. Coherent concepts like "morality," "goodness," "action," "obligation," need to be carefully delineated. All, however, must be interpreted by Christ. We must take every thought captive to obey Christ, in whom the fullness of knowledge resides (2 Cor 10:5; Col 2:3).

One of the challenges, then, is to speak of the natural law in Christological forms. This is a reality often missing or muted in natural law literature. Natural law as a function of "Divine Law" is replete throughout the field's literature (more on this in the next chapter), but its connection to Christology is conspicuously absent.

This challenge represents both an opportunity and a task; an opportunity, that is, to bring the full weight of Christ's supremacy to Christianity's historic mode of moral reasoning, and a task in formulating biblical-theological expression that gives rightful expression to both. In the absence of natural law being spoken of in explicitly Christocentric language, I am advocating a Christotelic understanding of natural law. Doing so more fulsomely locates natural law to its true foundation in Jesus Christ and drives away suspicions that have kept Protestants from warmly embracing it. The explanation below coincides with the concern raised by Oliver O'Donovan that evangelical ethics is perpetually hamstrung by its failure to relate the domain of creation. While O'Donovan's focus was on the resurrection to bridge those domains, my goal is to establish a complementary perspective for how moral goods retain their creational integrity in view of Christ as the very Logos of creation order yet also how those creational goods become heightened as one understands them in light of the gospel.

---

[15] For example, see Section 1 of Carl F. H. Henry, *Christian Personal Ethics*, 2nd ed. (Grand Rapids: Eerdmans, 1977).

"Telic" derives from *telos*, from which we derive our understanding of a particular thing's nature by the goal, end, or purpose of the thing's features. The proper teleological end, for example, of a team with nine players who wear gloves and hit baseballs with bats is to coordinate their activity for competition, hopefully winning as a result. This crude comparison is mentioned only to highlight the significance of Christ for moral reflection. If all things are summed up in Jesus Christ (Eph 1:10), so too is the moral law and our moral reflection of it. The late theologian John Webster remarked that "theological apprehension of Christ and his dominion is at once metaphysical and moral—only moral because metaphysical, and because metaphysical necessarily moral."[16] This is a profound theological proposition that communicates the magnitude of Christian ethics. It is what gives Christian ethics the binding nature of its theological axioms. Because Christians confess that there is order to the universe, there must be corresponding truth that follows from order. If we espouse a binding, objective truth to the character of our ethics, that presupposes a prerequisite order to promulgate it in the first place.

Christian ethics cannot be, though it attempts to be in all human constructs, a self-contained *ex nihilo* enterprise. Christian ethics is *extra nos*, a reality outside of us and imposed on us by God. The scandal of Christian ethics is that we believe there to be, objectively, a real moral law. As all things are summed up in Jesus Christ, so, too, must be the moral order. Thus, behind the natural law are metaphysical assumptions about the cosmos, among them the notion of an uncaused cause we call God. God orders the universe and promulgates intelligible law throughout it. Despite sin's impact on human reason, this law is known to human creatures through our capacity of reason. Humans may know moral law most acutely when their conscience condemns them for breaking it, but even the glimmer of moral truth that breaks through the darkness of the heart's inner recesses testifies to the reifying persistence of God's moral law.

---

[16] John Webster, *God Without Measure: Working Papers in Christian Theology*, vol. 2 (London: T&T Clark, 2015), 6.

# Christology: Ontology, Agency, and End

The "uncaused cause," however, is not left unknown. The unveiling of Christian ethics is similar to Paul's announcement at Mars Hill (Acts 17:22–34). In the same way that Paul's pagan audience possessed a general knowledge of the "unknown God," Christians espouse both a general and specific character to our morality. The innate moral law written on the heart is a Christological emanation. All longings for moral goodness and the satisfaction of justice are dim reflections for ultimate goodness and satisfaction that emanate from their source, Jesus Christ. What pagans speculate concerning the source and culmination of morality, Christians ratify with specifying clarity.

In considering how to connect Christology to natural law, we must turn to Scripture. In John's prologue, he describes Jesus Christ as the divine ordering principle of the cosmos.

> In the beginning was the Word, and the Word was with God, and the Word was God. He was in the beginning with God. All things were made through him, and without him was not any thing made that was made. In him was life, and the life was the light of men. The light shines in the darkness, and the darkness has not overcome it. There was a man sent from God, whose name was John. He came as a witness, to bear witness about the light, that all might believe through him. He was not the light, but came to bear witness about the light. The true light, which gives light to everyone, was coming into the world. (John 1:1–9)

We see three essential pillars of natural law thought reflected in John's introduction: ontology, agency, and *telos*. Christology is cosmology, according to John. Ontology refers to the nature of existence; agency to the mode of operation that achieves an ontic end; and *telos* to the notion of a final end existing that ontology orders and action strives for. According to John, everything was made through the divine person of Jesus. Ontology is the product of Christ's self-ordering wisdom. Christ is the divine agency through which this self-ordering occurs, and all things reach their ultimate end in relationship to knowing Jesus Christ. Order and natural law are thus the Christological outworking of creation composed through the divine reason of Jesus. Christology, as it were, is the very grain of the universe. As Scripture attests to, Jesus is being (ontology), means (agency), and ultimate end (teleology). According to Herman Bavinck, "General revelation is due to the Word, who in the beginning was with God, who made all things, and whose lights shines in the darkness, and coming into the world gives light to every man."[17]

We read that in Christ, there is "life," and he is the "light of men." He is both the substance and perfective end of the complete good. He is the "true light, which gives light to everyone." Jesus is the font of our and the cosmos's existence. We are to understand all of reality—why anything exists at all—through Jesus. He is the beginning and end of all things. As the "true light," he is the illuminating principle behind humankind's intelligible interactions within the world, regardless of whether he is expressly known to all as Savior. The practical implications of this are, literally, without end. When non-Christians gather for a party and enjoy one another's company (experiencing friendship) and the delight of bodily nourishment through delicious foods (fostering the conditions of life), Christians attest that it is because the physical, relational, intellective, and moral properties of the universe have been ordered by Christ. We do not believe in a self-created or self-sustaining universe. There is no part of the universe's existence, or our own, from which Christ is not responsible for the active creating, upholding, and fulfilling of all things. Jesus Christ is the reason for reason and the rationale for rationale.

Similarly, in Col 1:15–18, Paul likewise offers another high Christology that positions Christ as the basis and rationale for creation's existence, order, and intelligibility.

---

[17] Herman Bavinck, *Guidebook for Instruction in the Christian Religions* (Peabody, MA: Hendrickson, 2022), 22.

He is the image of the invisible God, the firstborn of all creation. For by him all things were created, in heaven and on earth, visible and invisible, whether thrones or dominions or rulers or authorities— all things were created through him and for him. And he is before all things, and in him all things hold together. And he is the head of the body, the church. He is the beginning, the firstborn from the dead, that in everything he might be preeminent.

Once again, we see the pillars of ontology, agency, and *telos* in the background. If we take these Johannine and Pauline Christologies at face value, we deduce profound entailments for natural law theory as Christotelic in nature. The moral order of the universe is intelligible only in reference to Jesus Christ. The operations of the conscience to grasp moral duties and moral wrongs are patterned after the intelligible logos, Jesus Christ. Matthew Levering argues that our participation in the eternal law is the grounds of our participation in Christ himself. Says Levering,

In so far as human beings participate by reason in God's eternal law, such participation belongs to the (primarily receptive, secondarily active) dynamism of the imitation of God, instantiated in the practice of *imitatio Christi*, whereby human beings become more and more fully the image of God that, as created, we are. As participation in the eternal law, the natural law is the imprint of the pattern of divine *ecstasis*, divine wisdom and love as revealed in Christ.[18]

All things, including all moral operations, are held together because of Jesus Christ. The reason we understand morally intelligible propositions such as "it is evil to torture babies," is because Jesus Christ has structured the universe and our awareness of this moral reality to be what it is. The reason our language can convey meaningful moral propositions is because Jesus has ordered our language to correspond to a reality that his supremacy

---

[18] Levering, *Biblical Natural Law: A Theocentric and Teleological Approach*, 182 (see chap. 2, n. 19).

has conditioned as a product of divine reason. If we understand natural law as a divinely imposed moral order made known through a body of intelligible reasons that direct persons to act for particular ends, we must understand that Jesus Christ is the origin of that order and the fulfillment of its directiveness. Moral order is imposed on existence by the prescriptivity of the Son.

Prior to what political philosophers call the Rule of Law, there must be law itself. Law is undergirded by reason that makes the law intelligible and binding. In the same way that law undergirds the Rule of Law, so Jesus Christ is the *ratio legis* of the moral law. Herman Bavinck, in *Reformed Ethics*, calls Christ "the moral ideal, the living law."[19] He is the source and culmination of moral reality and moral norms. Natural law theory for Christians amounts to a supernatural order revealed within the natural; one that even non-Christians have a share in participating in due to the sheer fact of their existence. Thomas Aquinas might not have spoken in such categories, but when he defined the natural law as the "rational creature's participation in the eternal law," we should see this in view of a Christological gloss.[20] Christ is the divine law through which all order derives. Human participation in this law does not mean that they are Christian in any universalist sense, but that their capacity as an image-bearer of God is ordered to respond to a universe patterned and upheld by Christ.

## Christology and Final Ends

We will go into further detail in the next chapter, but central to natural law theory is the proposition that every agent (i.e., person) acts for an end. Creatures, in other words, move themselves in the direction of some perceived good that they seek after and which they believe will complete them. At one level, this forms one of the most fundamental aspects of natural

---

[19] Herman Bavinck, *Reformed Ethics: Created, Fallen, and Converted Humanity*, ed. John Bolt, vol. 1 (Grand Rapids: Baker Academic, 2019), 341.

[20] *ST* I-II, q. 91, a. 2., co.

law. Whether the end is our personal happiness, sexual unity with a spouse, the mere act of eating food to sustain ourselves, or the delight one receives in watching a skillful athletic performance, every action with free choice assumes there is desirability built into and behind the agent's motivation for action.

As we consider a Christological reading of the natural law, it is necessary to distinguish between penultimate ends and ultimate ends or penultimate desires versus ultimate desires. This is essential to the book's overarching thesis of rooting our theory of moral action in God's glory and our good. A Christian theory of natural law must always factor the supremacy of God into its formula while also demonstrating how the pursuit of heavenly ends mirrors back to the fulfillment of true creaturely and earthly ends.

Human creatures desire happiness; they seek after an end they believe—whether rightly or wrongly—will complete them. They desire temporal happiness and whether humans admit it, we desire and even yearn after an ultimate form of happiness that informs what penultimate forms of happiness are. This is the place of God. God is the author of our inclinations and desires and for whom our knowledge of illuminates all other subordinate forms of happiness. On the one hand, a rational creature is deemed "happy" insofar as their personal selves are thriving and basic needs met. But a Christological reading of the natural law would suggest that unless the person is aware of the ultimate horizon giving reason for desirability's existence in the first place, they are left unfulfilled and robbed of the creature's ultimate horizon and ultimate satisfaction. Human nature retains its own integrity as the ends that it seeks are truly good for human nature's fulfillment. From the vantage point of eternal law and Christology, however, the natural good requires the supernatural good to complete it in its fullness. Natural law, then, must be understood against ultimate finality—Jesus Christ. Our happiness is fulfilled in God who in turn fulfills and gives explanation to all other forms of subordinate happiness.

A Christological reading of the natural law expands our awareness of the theory of moral action that God has providentially constituted. Consider a verse as seemingly innocuous as 1 Cor 10:31: "So, whether you eat or drink, or whatever you do, do all to the glory of God."

Paul's concern is that his audience govern their actions by a particular *telos* or end—namely, the expansion of God's glory. Bodies need food and drink to sustain themselves, so at the forefront of Paul's exhortation is an assumption that sustaining one's body offers a rational reason to direct one's actions. That's the penultimate horizon: life. Paul heightens the meaning of moral action by measuring its value not only by its ability to further biological life, but by the ability of the action to obtain an even greater *telos*, the glory of God.

Christian natural law ethics, then, poses an objective for Christians on at least two levels. It offers us a framework for determining whether and how the action being considered fulfills or violates a moral good. Secondly, it enlarges the theater of moral action to considerations of God's glory. Thusly stated, all moral action gives God glory and satisfies our longings as moral agents. The converse is also true: all immoral action robs God of his glory and degrades us of the type of fulfillment that is meant to bring us lasting fulfillment. As God's own excellency is his proper and due end, so humanity's end is in knowing God. In the law of reason that God has implanted within us, enabling us to know Him and the goods he has ordered for our proper and fitting end, it is man's grasp of this ultimate, eternal end that orders his grasp of all lesser, penultimate, and creaturely ends. To know God is to know the good. To seek the good is, from the vantage point of he who orders the good, to seek God. As Proverbs 16:4 states that the "Lord has made everything for its purpose," to know our purpose in Christ means to know the "riches" and "treasures" that God has for his creation (Phil 4:19; Col 2:3).

The attainment of God's glory done by ordering our actions in accordance with his will and sound reason reflects back on the creature in the form of blessing and flourishing. For the non-Christian who engages in rightfully-ordered conduct, they are participating in the Creator's *general* moral governance. For the Christian who engages in rightfully-ordered conduct, they are participating in the Lord's *saving* moral governance that awakens them to true creaturely satisfaction. As Herman Bavinck writes, quoting Johann Christoph Blumhardt, "Man must be twice converted, first from the natural to the spiritual life, and then from the spiritual to the natural."[21] Christian ethics exists on two domains: (1) moral action considered as such from the vantage point of creaturely good; (2) moral action considered as such from the vantage point of the beatific good. The latter is the grounds of the former, but the scriptural formula sees their enactment as each possessing their own integrity yet both mutually reinforcing from the perspective of the Christian.

It is hard to overstate the significance of this formula for gaining clarity on Christian ethics: all moral commands handed down to us in Scripture must necessarily entail both creaturely benefit and God's glory. Ethical action is thus rational action aligning with penultimate human good and ultimate divine glory. Flourishing and moral excellence occur when beings act according to their proper end in both penultimate and ultimate perspective.

Whatever is good comports with God's order of creation and produces temporal, even if imperfect, joy, while that which comports with God's order of redemption produces eternal, perfect, and beatific joy. The natural law is a temporal signpost to the eternal realm. As Baptist theologian Albert Mohler argued similarly, "The natural law means that in creation, God has actually given us adequate instructions to know much of what we have to know for life in this world, and implying also, in the age to come."[22]

John Piper's famous dictum that "God is most glorified in us when we are most satisfied in him" takes on a significant ethical gloss considering the preceding discussion. Spiritually happy individuals will revel and delight in the goodness of God's moral commands because they know the attainment of these goods will mean not only that God receives glory, but that they

---

[21] Herman Bavinck, *The Philosophy of Revelation: The Stone Lectures for 1908-1909, Princeton Theological Seminary* (Grand Rapids: Eerdmans, 1953), 242.

[22] R. Albert Mohler Jr., "Friday, August 12, 2022," *The Briefing*, accessed December 14, 2022, https://albertmohler.com/2022/08/12/briefing-8-12-22.

themselves will know fulfillment and completeness by acting in accord with what God's decrees are good for their nature.

Understanding our nature in the fullest sense is unlocked by the gospel of Jesus Christ. According to Paul,

> In their case the god of this world has blinded the minds of the unbelievers, to keep them from seeing the light of the gospel of the glory of Christ, who is the image of God. For what we proclaim is not ourselves, but Jesus Christ as Lord, with ourselves as your servants for Jesus' sake. For God, who said, "Let light shine out of darkness," has shone in our hearts to give the light of the knowledge of the glory of God in the face of Jesus Christ. (2 Cor 4:4–6)

Paul's argument is that knowing Jesus Christ gives persons the fullest epistemological clarity as to ultimate reality. This, however, in no way explodes, undermines, or negates the integrity and intelligibility of penultimate reality. Natural morality retains the constitutive properties to fulfill rational beings. I thus agree with Herman Bavinck when he writes, "Temporal life has great value in itself for humanity and also in the goal of life that lies beyond us."[23] The gospel heightens natural morality to the plane of supernatural fulfillment. Morally, Christians come to see the world in color, whereas non-Christians see in black and white. Christotelic reality helps us understand that generic appeals to "universal morality" or even the "natural law" are shadows of realities established, patterned, and upheld by Jesus Christ.

Relating this back to moral action, in Christ, Christians are made aware of just how high the stakes are for ethics. It is not only the difference in sorting good conduct from bad conduct, but from knowing ultimate causation from indeterminate causation. It is by fallen moral action that we rob ourselves of fullest human felicity. The reverse is true as well. As creatures encounter the saving grace of Jesus Christ, they learn the substance

---

[23] Bavinck, *Reformed Ethics: Created, Fallen, and Converted Humanity*, 1:231.

and destiny of their earthly nature. There should be no more of a satisfied creature who delights in the earthly good than the Christian, even if their delight is set supremely on the eternal good. It is the eternal good that gives maximal poise and subordinate placement to the earthly good. According to John Owen,

> Those who engage this nature in the service of sensual lusts and pleasures—who think that its felicity and utmost capacities consist in their satisfaction, with the accomplishment of other earthly, temporal desires—are satisfied with it in its state of apostasy from God; but those who have received the light of faith and grace, so as rightly to understand the being and end of that nature whereof they are partakers, cannot but rejoice in its deliverance from the utmost debasement, into that glorious exaltation which it has received in the person of Christ.[24]

The horizons that Christians gain access to because of their knowledge of morality's ultimate convergence is what satisfies their being in both their natural and supernatural dimensions.

Natural law is thus eschatologically inflected. The need in the present age to explain why real moral longings exist in the first place should drive such concerns to the future of eschatological dawning. Lutheran theologian Carl Braaten is correct to note that for natural law to be *Christian*, it must affix itself to the domain of eschatology:

> The final truth of all things is revealed by the arrival of the eschatological future in the person of Jesus Christ. The eschatological future of the kingdom is the power that draws all people, whether they know it or not. This power has been revealed in Jesus Christ as the highest good which all people implicitly seek in their quest for fulfillment. Therefore, when people strive for justice under the

---

[24] John Owen, *The Glory of Christ: His Office and Grace* (Fearn, Scotland: Christian Heritage, 2008), 23–24.

conditions of its absence—and this goes on in all societies—they are in quest of something true and transcendent that for them is still future and yet to be fulfilled. From the Christian point of view, this highest good is the kingdom of God which Jesus proclaimed and embodied in his very person. The universal human quest for justice can be seen to be the anticipatory prescence of the kingdom of God at work throughout the created order, even under the conditions of sin and estrangement.[25]

Here, natural law and mission become inter-related. The natural law that individuals wish to see fulfilled is also the natural law that each of them break in their revolt against God. "Humanity is hurt and needy, yet not because it is lost in a sea of infinite chaos but because it is out of alignment with the moral order by which God governs the world," writes David VanDrunen. He goes on: "If a contemporary world tempted to nihilism is to hear the gospel—really to hear it—it needs to understand that the world actually has a purpose and that the evil and suffering surrounding us are not the way things are supposed to be. There is nothing more important for the church than proclaiming the good news of salvation for the world in Jesus Christ. Far from undermining the message, natural law provides the scaffold."[26] The natural law provides the scaffolding of the gospel by announcing the terms of the gospel's indictment. Our moral failings and our moral longings must, then, be understood against the reality of a Holy God who orders those desires and whose standard of perfection we rebel against. Whether admitted or not due to acts of self-deception that occurs within persons, humanity knows it is rebellion against a Creator. Christian theology provides the clarifying revelation of the identity of that Creator and the pathway toward reconciliation. We must see the importance of natural law to the gospel and

---

[25] Carl E. Braaten, "Protestants and Natural Law," *First Things*, no. 19 (January 1, 1992): 25.

[26] David VanDrunen, "Natural Law for Reformed Theology: A Proposal for Contemporary Reappropriation," *Journal of Reformed Theology* 9, no. 2 (2015): 129, https://doi.org/10.1163/15697312-00902018.

Christology but also in our ongoing mission to uphold the structures of the creation for the awaited dawning of Jesus's kingdom. Braaten goes on to similarly link the cause of natural law's advocacy as "believers cooperating with God in preserving the world so that the world may be given time to learn of its true destiny in the kingdom of God."[27]

Natural law may not persuade. There is no promise that any mode of moral reason will persuade a person hellbent in their rejection of God from accepting the intermediate grace of the natural law. Yet, as David VanDrunen notes, natural law provides the "theological explanation for the reality of the universal revelation and perception of God's law and for the possibility of genuine and substantive moral communication among people of differing religious convictions."[28] The natural law thus provides the connective tissue to bring all human beings to an awareness of their status before God. We owe such truths to our neighbors. John Barton remarks to this end that "morality is first and foremost a matter of human beings recognizing their finite created status and seeking a way of life which embodies their sense of belonging in the hierarchical universe whose head and origin is God."[29] As considerations of the natural law move forward, we may suggest that to know the human good in the fullest sense, we must know "no one is good except God alone" (Mark 10:18).

## Is Natural Law Religious?

A frustrating element to considerations of the natural law is the degree to which its theological presuppositions are sometimes cloaked under the guise of ideological or philosophical neutrality. At least one element of its neutrality is true: natural law does offer a platform for common moral grammar. The truth of moral commonality, however, does not imply moral or epistemological neutrality as to its foundation. Natural law is, at its foundation

---

[27] Braaten, "Protestants and Natural Law," 26.
[28] VanDrunen, "Natural Law for Reformed Theology," 126.
[29] John Barton, *Ethics and the Old Testament* (London: SCM, 1998), 67.

and terminus, a religious doctrine. It is a metaphysical system, even if its proponents are demure in saying so in full.[30] Admitting its ultimately religious foundation, in fact, allows us to state out in the open what is true of all other belief systems as well—they stem from deep-seated faith commitments of some sort. A hardened secular evolutionist must arrive at a position of human rights out of faith since reason on their own terms can do no such thing. Every single human being is placing their faith in something—whether ideology, sense perception, or biological instinct. To admit the religious orientation of the natural law does not blunt the forcefulness of the natural law. Rather, it is my conviction that grounding the natural law, ultimately, in divine causation, grounds it more durably in an authority outside of itself—an authority that gives it existence, structure, and direction. To deny it as grounded in metaphysical claims about the nature of the universe is duplicitous. Christians should not, and indeed cannot, cloak their moral suppositions in a veneer of pure neutrality. We do not believe in a view of the world where neutral observers approach their convictions without presuppositional commitments to basic worldview elements. There is no such thing as disinterested metaphysics.

Neither does the natural law's religious foundation negate its effectiveness as an explanatory or apologetical device. While Christians believe that claims of the natural law can be, and indeed are, compelling on their own terms since the natural law merely corresponds to that which is true, those terms are *never* independent of divine order. The natural law is nothing else but divine order recognizable—even if imperfectly because of sin's impact on the reason and will—through natural means. Natural law, and the moral goods comprising it, are the product of divine authorization. What natural law advances is a theory of morality that, while divine in origin, nonetheless corresponds to states of affairs that rightly ordered minds recognize as true,

---

[30] For example, one of the criticisms, particularly of New Natural Law methodology, is its reluctance to foreground its metaphysical presuppositions. For more on this line of critique, see Phillip E. Johnson, "Metaphysics Matters," *First Things*, no. 97 (November 1999): 70–74.

regardless of whether one recognizes the divine origins of the claim. The natural law being natural (though religious in origin), makes a claim that its persuasiveness and coherence can be understood as intelligible without *immediate* reference to revealed religion. To deny this as self-evidently true is to say that no non-Christian has ever known true moral facts. That belies reality. Non-Christians may not have a satisfying answer as to the moral foundation of the claim they understand correctly, but the lack of foundation does not vitiate the otherwise truthfulness of their position, if it is in fact true.

Within a natural law paradigm, though an unbeliever cannot account for the *foundations* of what amounts to true moral knowledge, this does not mean that the knowledge they do possess is any less true. A non-believer can have true moral knowledge that he or she cannot account for. Not being able to give an account for moral sensibility does not mean that moral knowledge is less valid, only that the unbeliever lacks adequate foundation. To word it differently: God's existence is a necessary prerequisite for the laws of morality in the same way that God's existence is necessary for the laws of logic and a reliable trust in sense perception. Whether a person himself or herself believes in God individually (as desirable as that is) says virtually nothing about whether the person can possess true moral knowledge. It should be noted, however, that a person who recognizes the moral law and seeks to align themselves with it, but not with the moral Lawgiver, possesses an internally inconsistent worldview. A non-Christian relying upon a worldview that he or she will not admit explains the coherency of their own ethical convictions is an example of what the presuppositionalist camp of apologetics calls the "borrowed capital" of Christian theism.

What we should insist upon is that truthfulness with regard to the natural law demands that we have the integrity to state these presuppositions clearly and unapologetically. Natural law is a religious belief in the same way that atheism is religious disbelief. But atheist disbelief is hardly irreligious or ideologically disinterested. Its claims, like the ones made by natural law, are comprehensive claims and ultimate commitments about the type of universe we inhabit. No one, whether the Christian natural lawyer or the atheist, is arguing from a vantage point of pure neutrality or pure, disinterested rationality.

Every propositional axiom about morality is made on the basis of faith in *something*. Christian ethics is no more controversial than Christ himself was. Christ taught that he was "the way, the truth, and the life," not just "a" way or "a" truth or "a" life. Christian ethics is but a reflection of the way and order of Jesus in a world that persists in unbelief. Creation order and the goods that comprise it are monarchical facts inscribed within the grain of the universe by a heavenly King, Jesus Christ. At minimum, natural law is an expression of common grace; maximally, it demonstrates what revealed theology says to be true about the world.[31]

To be sure, the natural law tradition is broader than just the Christian tradition, but it is my conviction that it is Christianity that is most responsible for codifying the natural law as a coherent theory. In other words, Christianity is the carrier vehicle in which the pillars and tenets of the natural law are best distilled and disclosed. Instead of seeing this as a problem to natural law's intelligibility, we should see how it is that the natural law tradition comes to its fulfillment within the Christian narrative. In Christ, tensions that plague the natural law in other traditions are resolved. According to Christianity, the universal is made specific and the specific is universal. Christianity, more than any other tradition, clarifies the natural law by solving the universal problem of relating finite comprehensibility with universality. The Christian natural law tradition solves the problem of indeterminacy. Even if one adopts the position of Jean Porter, as I do, that "natural law must draw on specifically theological elements in order to function prescriptively," this fact does not elide what it is that natural law seeks to posit: "resources for defending and evaluating substantive moral

---

[31] I am indebted to R. Albert Mohler, Jr., for offering this insight to me in conversation.

claims on the basis of rational considerations that we might reasonably hope to be persuasive, even across boundaries of distinct traditions of rational inquiry."[32] Whether one finds those claims persuasive or not, a rejection of the claims of the Christian natural law tradition does not invalidate their truthfulness. It only reaffirms the obstinance of human nature.

But even still, we are left stating a fundamental axiom of natural law and natural law theory: the value and utility of the natural law is not primarily found in its apologetical prowess for unbelief or even its value as a common moral grammar for politics (however valuable both are), but its explanatory power for Christian ethical catechesis.

---

[32] Jean Porter, "Does the Natural Law Provide a Universally Valid Morality?," in *Intractable Disputes about the Natural Law*, ed. Lawrence S. Cunningham (South Bend, IN: Notre Dame University Press, 2009), 90–91.

# 4.

# Faith, Reason, and Moral Epistemology

Every claim of Christian morality is ratified by the canons of reason and every rational moral claim will always cohere with Scripture. In this chapter, we will unpack that statement and how the Bible as a medium of special revelation communicates truths that are true by virtue of what general revelation says is true of creation.

Before looking at how the natural law is known in itself, an important prerequisite to that reality are the preconditions for knowledge itself within a natural law rubric. Beliefs about the natural law assume beliefs about the nature of knowledge itself. Natural law holds that reality is truly knowable and that our sense perceptions are reliable and correspond to things as they are and ought to be. Knowledge is not socially constructed or constructed simply by what our minds impose on it. Natural law, in other words, does not countenance existential ways of knowing where existence precedes essence. In a cognitive framework such as natural law, essence determines existence within a moral realist framework.

A later chapter will look at God's eternal law as the ultimate source of natural law and our capacity for reason to know the natural. This chapter looks to examine the relationship between (1) natural theology and natural law, (2) how faith and reason reinforce one another, (3) and how special revelation and general revelation harmonize to speak in a morally complementary relationship. All three of these tasks will result in an epistemological foundation for knowledge of the natural law. Without clarifying and relating such concepts, the task of Christian ethics can implicitly sever religious moral claims from rational moral claims into hermetically distinct domains.

## The Necessary Nexus of Natural Theology and Natural Law

"Natural theology" understood apart from Scripture provokes no small amount of confusion and derision in Protestant thought. A basic definition for natural theology is the philosophical study of God's Being and action in creation. For some critics of natural law theory, natural theology is a handmaiden to natural law and is associated with overtures to Deism, where God is a mere "watchmaker" who creates but cannot be known in any relational sense. In this vein, natural theology is opposed to special revelation in that it sees the created order as the only possible medium for revelation at all. Natural theology can tend toward the dismissal of the miraculous since what can be known by God is only a product of philosophy and nature. Natural theology is thus the theology of the philosophers. If science accepts categories of divinity at all, it is in the vein of a natural theology that services agnosticism or theistic evolution.

Natural theology for others is a catalyst to variations of Pelagian theology that relies upon the inner strength of humanity to "work" their way to God apart from intervening and supernatural grace. This could also be referred to as "natural religion." Natural theology divorced from Scripture downplays or rejects the effects of sin on humanity's nature. That approach to natural theology is not within view in this volume. Natural theology is an immanentized form of theology that locates the "divine" within the experience of the subjective self. It forms the theological superstructure that can metastasize into theological liberalism where the spiritual becomes coequal with human longing for the sublime. If natural theology is used in either of these ways, disavowal is necessary. But going about defining natural theology is similar to the saga of defining natural law: terminology and specificity matter. Much Protestant antipathy toward natural theology and natural law are the result of imprecise definition and caricature.

But there are right and wrong uses of natural theology. Dispensing with a biblical approach to natural theology because of possible abuse is unwarranted. What matters is discovering whether Scripture speaks in its own categories of natural theology.

Natural theology as referenced in this book excludes any possibility of natural theology being salvific in any way. Natural theology as this book argues for is deduced from the scriptural teaching that the order of creation reveals truths about God the Creator apart from special revelation—among them that God exists and is responsible for organizing the splendor of an orderly universe. Special revelation, as I will argue, posits a form of natural theology that provides the seedbed for natural law. Scripture teaches of a natural theology revealed by means of natural revelation. Here, the focus is not on the salvific capability of natural theology but the intelligibility of nature as bearing witness to God's handiwork. As David Haines rightly notes, conflating natural theology as an all-sufficient natural religion with the belief in reason's exhaustive knowledge of God leads to an unnecessary rejection of creation as its own type of authority under God's general revelation.[1] In other words, we should not throw the baby out with the bathwater.

Frequently referenced verses such as Genesis 1; Psalm 19; Acts 14:15–17; 17:26–27; Rom 1:19–21, 28–32; and Rom 2:14–15 come to mind as examples where Scripture speaks of how creation and the experience of human nature itself testifies to God's existence and moral order (these verses will be explored further below). David appeals to creation as

---

[1] David Haines, *Natural Theology: A Biblical and Historical Introduction and Defense* (Landrum, SC: Davenant, 2021), 15.

giving witness to God's existence and glory. For Paul, appeals to both creation order and human cognitive ability witness to God's design, but also to humanity's condemnation for having rejected this design. Jesus points to God's care for the animals and flowers of creation to reflect the benevolent providence of God the Father (Matt 6:26–34). The Reformed theologian Peter Martyr Vermigli argues similarly about Christ's relationship to creation order: "Christ sends us to the birds of the air, to the lilies and grass of the field, that we might acknowledge the singular providence of God in preserving those things that he created."[2] Also tacit in Jesus's words is a natural law principle of acknowledging creaturely distinction between the Creator and the created. Haines offers a helpful metaphor to understand natural theology: "Knowledge of God through nature can, therefore, be compared to the light given off by a candle, the Scriptures to a spotlight (casting direct light on certain very important things that we know about God), and the beatific vision like looking directly into the sun (or being absorbed by it)."[3]

Even taking into consideration fallen human nature, natural theology is Scripture's own way of making the design argument for God's existence and the ongoing persistence of those moral obligations based on that design's redounding persistence. Though sin mars our grasp of God, Scripture boldly asserts that even fallen humanity knows of God's existence through the created order. In turn, natural theology surfaces in a myriad of ways today. When tragedy strikes, quickly adverting to "thoughts and prayers" to bring solace reminds us that humanity seeks consolation outside of its own control. Traveling to well-known geographic landmarks to partake of their beauty and splendor summons us to a grandeur and awe-inspiring holiness. The fact that professed atheism is still, despite its vocal proponents, quite marginal is a statistical reminder that belief in the divine seems to be the average default of persons. The inexplicable loveliness that comes

---

[2] Peter Martyr Vermigli, quoted in Stephen J. Grabill, *Rediscovering the Natural Law in Reformed Theological Ethics* (Grand Rapids: Eerdmans, 2006), 110.

[3] Haines, *Natural Theology*, 93.

from experiencing life's blessings makes people want to cry out in worship or gratitude. The reminder that science, despite its ability to explain the universe's physical laws, cannot offer a comprehensive moral theory that accounts for the awfulness of such events as the Holocaust tells us that people go looking for moral grounding in systems outside of philosophical materialism alone.

The importance of natural law to natural theology is that natural law is a necessary entailment and species of natural theology. Natural law theorists simply articulate the axioms and moral entailments that extend from natural theology. Because Scripture posits a natural theology, natural law exists as its by-product. Natural law is nothing other than the rational cognizance of natural theology. Natural theology engraves a moral order we call the natural law in all persons enabling them to know right and wrong. As I will explore further below, the existence of natural law brought about by natural theology does not mean that awareness of natural law is unaffected by sin. Hardly. The question left after the fall is in what manner the natural law functions once accommodated to the reality of sin.

Understanding that God has knit eternity into human nature (Eccl 3:11), natural theology and general revelation give a non-salvific awareness of:

- God's existence
- God's benevolence in upholding the structure of creation
- God's grandeur and awesomeness as Creator
- Creaturely longing for eternal satisfaction
- Humanity's proclivity to ascribe ultimate worship
- The orderly design of creation necessary to produce life
- The orderly design of creation necessary to sustain life
- God's providential guiding and watchfulness over human affairs
- Humanity's "cosmic guilt" in having violated God's law
- Moral culpability (guilt)
- Retributive justice for moral law-breaking
- Moral obligation
- Natural law (rational capacity for knowing right and wrong)

We should be interested in natural theology insofar as Scripture is. Yet, as J. V. Fesko writes summarizing Aquinas's view on natural theology, so too is the lesson relevant for us: "Reason can discover God because the Bible says so."[4]

Inescapably, then, as discussion of the natural law arises, questions related to the relationship of faith and reason necessarily surface. For a law that is religious in origin to be available to natural humanity, the natural person must possess the category for apprehending religious claims, even if those claims do not appear, at first, to be religious. We indeed possess such a capacity, namely, reason. Thus, moral claims that appear only rational in origin, from the perspective argued for in this volume, find their deepest reality in the domain of religion. Reason helps us to discern the natural truths that faith posits.

To foreground the rest of the chapter, it's important to clarify *how* the two categories of faith and reason relate to one another and how this relationship will serve as a backdrop to arguments made in later chapters. In our discussion about the epistemic foundations of natural law, and before we even discuss what the natural law *is*, that natural law flows out of natural theology still requires us to stipulate how we can know such claims in the first place.

### Faith and Reason

There are truths of faith that cannot be grasped by pure reason alone (e.g., the Trinity). Reason's limitation, however, does not imply that the truths of faith are therefore unreasonable. Though distinct ways of knowing, faith and reason are complementary and integrated. Because Christianity teaches that an orderly cosmos exists that is discernible by reason, sound reason will always comport with the order of faith as such. Faith, in other words, should never require the suspension of sound thinking. Why this

---

[4] J. V. Fesko, *Reforming Apologetics: Retrieving the Classic Reformed Approach to Defending the Faith* (Grand Rapids: Baker Academic, 2019), 90.

relationship matters for Christian ethics is that driving a wedge between Christian ethics as a theological system and the soundness of natural law as a philosophical system risks forging a false dichotomy. Faith and reason relate not only to the natural law, but to the very integrity of Christian ethics. Christian morality, whether decreed in Scripture or attested to by reason, stands or falls according to its own reasonableness and self-attesting coherence. While Christian morality is chiefly revelatory owing to our belief that the triune God has revealed himself, Christian morality also believes itself to be eminently reasonable: All Christian morality is an ordinance of reason—if reasonable, it is sound; if sound, it is binding as a measure of continuing validity; if binding, it has God as its ultimate author; if God-ordered, it must be reasonable since God is the very essence of reason himself. To go against the grain of the universe that we discern through reason is to go against God's Word because both affirm, each in their own way, the same reality of givenness ordered by a holy and good God.

To accept a Christian account of the natural law is to be a metaphysical and moral realist. To claim a theory that accepts reality for what it is—and to insist upon obeying its limitations—is to put one at odds with the vast sweep of contemporary moral philosophy. Reality and morality are not mere linguistic exercises as positivism and emotivism claim them to be. Natural law accounts for access to true reality, not an existential and phenomenal realm of imagined speculating. We insist upon saying propositionally true things about existence itself; namely, that reality has ontological structure and meaning given to it by God. This, of course, is one of the most obvious statements that can be made about a Christian interpretation of reality, one that lies at the heart of what secularism disputes.

As reality is not a mere construct, neither is morality. The world is not only physically constituted by physical laws explainable by philosophical inquiry, but also constituted by actual moral laws that contain a moral grammar explainable by reason as well. The natural law seeks to explicate these realities as *being* true, not merely *appearing* true. Faith and reason (philosophy) must necessarily then work together as neither can posit contradictory truths. Faith and reason harmonize into a singular melody. There are truths to theology that reason may not fully grasp. But the inability of reason to attain the highest planes of knowledge, however, signifies no fallibility of reason, but only a limitation of its reach. Even still, reason grasps what theology grounds and theology confirms what reason posits. As Robert P. George writes, "Just as faith illuminates the truths that reason can identify, reason can help us understand the meaning of what is revealed."[5] No principle of biblically revealed morality or natural law morality will ever be at odds since both faith and reason reflect what is true in different modes of knowing. Reason will never posit a truth that is truly false according to revelation and revelation will never require the abandonment of sound reason. Philosopher John Searle makes a critical observation for how reason should function in this light:

> If we have justifications for our beliefs, and if the justifications meet rational criteria, then the fact that there are all sorts of elements in our social situation that incline us to believe one thing rather than another may be of historical or psychological interest, but it is really quite beside the point of the justifications and of the truth or falsity of the original claim.[6]

Searle's point is salient in that he's saying a principle is true or false depending on its own soundness and irrespective of its cultural embeddedness. If what we say is true of natural law concerning reason's foundation for it, it will necessary be true of theology as well. Why this is of such importance in relating reason and revelation is that reason and revelation emanate from the same point of origin for its justification—God. Thus, both bear witness to the same ontological reality though in different modalities and cannot come to contradictory conclusions.

---

[5] *Social Conservatism for the Common Good: A Protestant Engagement with Robert P. George*, ed. Andrew T. Walker (Wheaton, IL: Crossway, 2023), 284.

[6] John R. Searle, "The Word Turned Upside Down," *New York Review of Books*, October 27, 1983, https://www.nybooks.com/articles/1983/10/27/the-word-turned-upside-down/.

The beauty of Christian ethics is that properly ordered reason always harmonizes with what Scripture teaches is true. Reason is indeed subordinate to Scripture, but never at odds with it. There is no tension and can never be in God's ordering of reason and revelation since both emanate from God himself. Natural law is neither superior to, nor a substitute for, special revelation.

## Moral Epistemology and Biblical Hermeneutics: Relating Special and General Revelation[7]

While the last section sought to define natural law in relationship to natural theology, it is necessary to explore how natural law and natural theology harmonize within the context of special and general revelation. General revelation, writes Christian philosopher Owen Anderson, "provides the foundation of natural law thinking."[8] General revelation is the doctrine that God communicates true things about himself through creation. These truths are discernible apart from special revelation even if special revelation provides the definitive interpretation of what general revelation posits. The existence of the moral law and our knowledge of the moral law are enabled by a God who orders its existence and our capacity for understanding its obligations in the world. Knowledge of actual truth, according to Scripture, is intelligible apart from special revelation. We glean truths known apart from Scripture through general revelation—a mode of God communicating

---

[7] I would like to briefly clarify my use of "Natural" and "General" when speaking of revelation. Both are generally regarded as synonyms, which I largely agree with. "Natural" in my view tends best to speak of the realm of the "natural order" pertaining to creation itself whereas "General" denotes its wide epistemic availability. Natural revelation can also speak to one's *interpersonal* grasp of God's existence through nature while general revelation could speak of the Bible's own depiction of creation giving truths about God's nature through creation. I'm cautious to draw too many distinctions in otherwise closely related terms.

[8] Owen Anderson, "Natural Law and Philosophical Presuppositions," in *Christianity and Natural Law: An Introduction*, ed. Norman Doe (Cambridge: Cambridge University Press, 2017), 205.

his being and attributes through the lineaments of creation order and human rationality. Scripture testifies to a two-fold reality along these lines: (1) Special revelation has an integrity of its own as God's self-disclosed way of communication; (2) Special revelation attests to the reality that creation order is intelligible and suffused with moral directives.

As a metaphor to explain this relationship, think of the Christmas carol "Joy to the World." The lyrics "And heaven and nature sing" captures the complementary relationship between special and general revelation. Heaven and nature each sing, but in their own way. There is heavenly singing that we learn about in Scripture (Rev 5:11–13) and also creational singing (Ps 19:1). Creation itself manifests God's glory. If it did not and nature had no moral intelligibility inherent in it, we would be without grounds to argue for nature positing moral truths. Now, we gain greater clarity about nature through special revelation by what Scripture says about nature, but Scripture concludes that creation is an intelligible medium. If nature only has integrity because Scripture informs us that it does and this integrity is not apparent on its own apart from Scripture, it means that nature has no self-attesting integrity within itself. Such a conclusion is disastrous for ethics. It means, for example, that claims defending abortion, same-sex marriage, and transgenderism have just as much authority as do Christian interpretations of the same canvas. We are not left in this position, however.

The beauty of the relationship posed in Scripture is that special and general revelation each have their own integrity. Heavenly beatitude (known by special revelation) makes nature's divine resplendency explicit (known by general revelation). But creation, as Scripture describes it, corresponds to, and communicates divine order in the sense that nature is a form of revelation. The divine is suffused within the natural while the natural communicates a divinity of its own mode.

Scripture's aperture of creation is wide. It describes reality and creation as an orderly, self-contained system. This is another way of saying that moral truths known by reason are not moral truths incompatible with faith, or that moral truths that comport with faith bear no relation to moral truths known by reason. If Scripture's portrayal of creation is true, there can be no inherent disjunction between faith and reason. In a natural law paradigm, if Scripture does not lie, neither can creation. If creation tells truth, they are the same truths of Scripture. This is so because Scripture speaks to God's design as an integrated whole, meaning that dichotomies between faith and reason can never be justified because reality is not constituted by either faith or reason, but both, when properly related. Scripture, in other words, attests to the possibility of human reason, even fallen human reason, understanding the world, its operations, and humanity's place within it—albeit imperfectly. If creation had no integrity of its own or was operational only if the persons involved were regenerate, disciplines such as ethics, medicine, engineering, and physics would be moot.

A tendency, however, exists in Protestant ethics that dichotomizes truths known from Scripture from truths also known from reason. For example: Why is murder wrong? Is it wrong only because the Bible says so? If we did not have special revelation, would the prohibition on murder have no integrity of its own? Or does human reason recognize truths that comport with Scripture's depiction of human life's value? We should reject any dichotomy that pits reason and revelation against one another. While it is true that ethics is ultimately revelatory owing to our belief about what Scripture is, Scripture is speaking truthfully about reality *as such*. It would thus be a mistake to view ethics as issuing from special revelation *alone*. Ethics are ultimately existent by appeal to divine warrant because of what we believe Scripture says about God, but not exclusively intelligible by divine warrant alone. Ethics as a meaningful discipline has order to it because God has promulgated a moral order into existence, but true knowledge of that moral order can exist apart from individuals having a perfect grasp of where that moral order originates. We can say this in confidence because natural law truths known from reason are always compatible with moral truths known from Scripture because of the type of moral universe God has brought into being. We know that an objective moral order exists because of Scripture. Knowledge of that moral order, however, is intelligible apart from Scripture because Scripture deems creation order and human reason as integrated and mutually-reinforcing channels of moral communication.

Were we to assume that ethics is intelligible by appeal to Scripture alone, it would call into question the intelligibility of our ethics, as though ethics are intelligible solely on the basis of revelation. We may have ethics definitively because revelation provides an authoritative account of creation and moral order, but the account of ethics revelation provides must accord with sound reason gleaned from the data of general revelation.

From our belief that Scripture speaks to the whole of created reality, when the Christian engages in natural law ethics, he or she does so under the assumption that Scripture's portrayal of creation is not sectarian and fideistic but comprehensive and intelligible. Scripture's rendering of creation is not one with Christian reality "over here" and a materialist rendering "over there." Scripture is more sufficient than many who claim its highest attributes even recognize. As the Westminster Confession of Faith says, "The whole counsel of God, concerning all things necessary for His own glory, man's salvation, faith, and life, is either expressly set down in Scripture, or by good and necessary consequence may be deduced from Scripture."[9] These deducements are what entailments from living within God's creation order allow for. It means, for example, that there are cultural issues that arise that Scripture can speak to, even if the topic is not expressly mentioned in the text. Take, for example, human sex-trafficking. There is no Bible verse addressing this evil modern practice directly, but human sex-trafficking does not become permissible because the Bible lacks a verse prohibiting it. Rather, the moral order God has posited teaches us that sex-trafficking is wrong because of the value humans intrinsically possess. We cannot respect the human person in their fullness and then enslave them to sexual abuse. This we view as a paralleling of Scripture speaking about the created value of human beings and the sanctity of marital intercourse. If creation is the intelligible order that we believe it is, it must necessarily align with how Scripture describes that order.

---

9 "The Westminster Confession of Faith," *Ligonier Ministries*, May 12, 2021, https://www.ligonier.org/learn/articles/westminster-confession-faith, 1.6.

Understanding the moral epistemology of Scripture, then, requires understanding how Scripture speaks about reality. Let me use a metaphor and then a famous passage of Scripture to explain in greater depth the moral epistemology of Scripture in relation to general and special revelation.[10] No metaphor is perfect, but some help illustrate complex ideas.

In *The Wizard of Oz*, viewers see two dimensions or layers for how reality is interpreted: black-and-white and eventually in color. We should compare non-Christians to those who see the world in black-and-white. They still see the world *as* the world. Toto is still known as a dog in the world of black-and-white because the principles of classification for identifying animals from human life are intelligible. Persons can still make meaningful sense of the world. Inhabiting creation provides participants with real moral insights from the data of human experience. Protecting one's life from a tornado is intelligible because of the human desire for self-preservation. A teenager running away from home is viewed as a fretful situation because of the disruption it poses to family.

Christians, on the other hand, see the world in color. Their moral knowledge is illuminative of morality's deeper significance and eternal foundation. They both *see* and *know* at a deeper level than those who see in black-and-white. Dogs like Toto are still dogs, but dogs, like all animals, are understood as creatures brought into existence by God, not blind chance. We understand that we protect our lives because God deems life inherently valuable. A child running away from home is a deviation from God's plan in Genesis for families to remain intact. To offer another example, murder violates not only a basic moral good, such as life, but murder is an affront against a principle of human dignity given to humanity by the triune God. Murder violates a basic good (black-and-white) while Christians know murder defaces the image of God (color) ordered by God (the metaphorical "Wizard" so to speak, behind the curtain). Or take marriage to use as another example. Non-Christians might understand that marriage provides

---

[10] I'm indebted to Robert P. George who first used this illustration with me in personal conversation.

society with a basic good of social stability and child protection. But it is Christians who understand that marriage's ultimate horizon bears relationship to the Christ-church union, not just social stability. At no point in the metaphor do the moral principles become any more or less true. Their *realness* as a matter of origin and ultimate meaning is, however, heightened.

Special revelation clarifies general revelation, but general revelation is a platform for, and prerequisite to, special revelation—meaning that general revelation is intelligible on its own grounds. If we did not have the cognitive capacity given to us by a God-given nature, the supernatural truths of grace would be of no benefit. Grace restores nature but grace also presupposes nature. General revelation must be intelligible for us to believe that creation has truth built into its foundations and for us to interpret Scripture properly. It is sufficient for what natural revelation is designed to do—to posit a natural theology of creation and morality, which, given man's state, functions to both illuminate and condemn. General revelation and special revelation are distinct forms or modes of revelation, but both are of divine origin. As J. Daryl Charles writes, "The existence of natural law, it must be emphasized, is independent of salvific faith, even when it is an intricate part of divine revelation."[11] Charles is emphasizing the point I made earlier—that natural law is a form of revelation, but of a generic sort.

Special revelation builds off the foundation that truths of general revelation make possible. To know the moral properties that Scripture speaks of requires an antecedent knowledge of what those properties are. Consider, for example, that to understand "Jesus loves me," I must have the cognitive capacity at hand to know beforehand what love *is* for me to know of the value and uniqueness of my Redeemer's love. According to Joe Rigney, "The existence of created reality *and* experiential knowledge of created reality are both necessary in order for Scripture to be intelligible."[12] A certain mutuality thus exists between special and general revelation: Special

---

[11] Charles, *Retrieving the Natural Law*, 43 (see chap. 2, n. 14).

[12] Joe Rigney, "With One Voice: Scripture and Nature for Ethics and Discipleship," *Eikon: A Journal for Biblical Anthropology* 1, no. 1 (Spring 2019): 29.

revelation is disclosed within the realm of general revelation even while special revelation clarifies the contours of general revelation's intelligibility. Francis Turretin argues to the same effect, writing that "The special knowledge of true faith (by which believers please God and have access to him, of which Paul speaks) does not exclude, but supposes the general knowledge from nature."[13] J. V. Fesko summarizes Thomas Aquinas as teaching the same principle: "Aquinas argues that human beings cannot conceive of faith apart from natural knowledge because supernatural knowledge (special revelation) always comes to us within the context of general revelation."[14]

Rigney goes on to argue similarly: "Both general revelation and special revelation are necessary for us. They are authoritative, clear, and sufficient for different purposes. One is sufficient to condemn. The other is sufficient to save. But they both work together to give us true knowledge of our Creator and Redeemer."[15] "Scripture and nature are mutually interpreting for each other," Rigney writes. "They are mutually meaningless without each other and mutually fruitful with each other. You can't understand the Bible rightly without some general revelation. You can't understand nature rightly without the illumination of the Bible."[16] Special revelation and general revelation are therefore complementary to one another. To deny one is to render the other meaningless. For natural law to gain definitive clarity in its demands and to account for the errors of human nature due to the wounds of sin, it needs special revelation as an authoritative and God-given capstone. But for Scripture to have interpretive intelligibility, the cognitive capacities given to us by nature are required as well. Special revelation (grace) and general or natural revelation (nature) require one another for their mutual support and intelligibility. Though spoken in the context of science's need for God, what John Frame says below speaks to morality as well:

---

[13] Francis Turretin, *Institutes of Elenctic Theology*, trans. George Musgrave Giger (Phillipsburg, NJ: P&R, 1992), 1:3.10, 8.

[14] Fesko, *Reforming Apologetics*, 78.

[15] Rigney, 32.

[16] Rigney, 32.

Science itself presupposes the absolute personal God of the Bible to validate the relative uniformity of nature and the possibility of intelligible thought about the world. If the universe is fundamentally impersonal, there is no reason why we should feel obligated to seek truth rather than error, or any reason why we should think our intellectual faculties capable of finding truth.[17]

Frame's point is highly relevant for considerations of the natural law. The structure of creation itself requires the existence of properties and modalities that are assumed for meaningful communication, among them the laws of logic, the uniformity of nature, and reliable trust in sense perception.[18] The existence of a moral universe requires that linguistic constructions communicate true propositions that accord with reality, that creation functions with predictability, and that when we engage in perception of right and wrong, that our senses are corresponding to moral facts as they truly are. In other words, consciousness provides a reliable grasp on true reality. This line of argument is why a figure like C. S. Lewis would argue that one of the shortcomings of naturalism is that the worldview denies what it presupposes: an accurate perception of the world as it is. Perception has no inherent stability to it given the accidental properties that brought it about.[19] Atoms that gain the appearance of consciousness have no built-in assurances that consciousness is intelligible or trustworthy.

To know what the Bible declares as God's love for sinners, cognitive abilities exercised through sapiential wisdom, implies my correct understanding of what divinity and love conceptually refer to. But to deny that special revelation bears any authority to moral issues means that morality is irretrievably lost to empty speculation. Scripture provides definitive authority over a creation order that sinful humanity is prone to misinterpret.

---

[17] John M. Frame, *The Doctrine of the Word of God* (Phillipsburg, NJ: P & R, 2010), 199.

[18] Jason Lisle, *Ultimate Proof of Creation* (Green Forest, AR: Master Books, 2009), 45–73, 92–95.

[19] C. S. Lewis, *God in the Dock* (Grand Rapids: Eerdmans, 1970), 52–53.

## *Psalm 19 and the Intelligibility of Creation Order*[20]

To understand the epistemological paradigm of this chapter, a brief study of Psalm 19 will help demonstrate the synchronicity between Scripture as special revelation itself and Scripture depicting the natural order as a mode of general revelation enclosed within special revelation.

One of the most cited Scriptures for general revelation through the natural order is Psalm 19. Even if we take this to be special revelation, the backdrop of Psalm 19 (and the rest of Wisdom literature) shows how "the doctrine of creation appears as undergirding God's work even in Israel, and thus God's commandments themselves already possess a framework in the created order."[21] As Jonathan Burnside helpfully observes, Psalm 19 can be broken down in a three-fold division focusing on the heavens (1–6), the law (7–11) and the human heart (12–14). Psalm 19 demonstrates how revelation moves from the general to the specific—from creation → covenant → individual. A naturally-formulated heuristic like this captures the trifold foci of God's law. Both the expansiveness of the law in its universal and individual capacities are brought into focus. Psalm 19 shows how moral law transmitted through creational law and covenantal law results in personal transformation. Psalm 19 thus functions as special revelation describing the divine intelligibility of natural revelation. We learn from this passage that creation teaches intelligible truths about its own order that special revelation then codifies for the sake of clarifying the rudimentary truths of creation. It is worth stressing how this sequence parallels the general thrust of natural law being a basic moral system whose entailments become more precise as special revelation comes into focus.

**The Heavens (1–6).** In these initial verses, creation itself tells of God's existence. In Hebrew, God is revealed as the Hebrew "El," meaning

---

[20] For this section, I am relying heavily on the work of Jonathan Burnside, "Natural Law and Biblical Law," in *Research Handbook on Natural Law Theory*, ed. Jonathan Crowe and Constance Youngwon Lee, Research Handbooks in Legal Theory (Cheltenham, UK: Edward Elgar, 2019), 181–203.

[21] Levering, *Biblical Natural Law: A Theocentric and Teleological Approach*, 45.

the God of creation order. Creation does not speak in a verbal sense, of course. Instead, creation manifests order and design and both are speech acts testifying to the availability of knowledge of God the Creator through creation. The response to this knowledge is worship, which suggests there is even a general moral obligation to respond to God for his sovereignty in creation. Psalm 19 suggests there is a covenant of creation at work that establishes a natural desire for worship. Humanity is thus *homo religiosus* in its response to creation teeming with grandeur.[22] Citing Psalm 14, which has thematic similarity to Psalm 19, the English Puritan Stephen Charnock wrote that humanity's deception to worship false deity or even creation itself is established by a "notion of a real one." Though humanity errs in the object of its worship, "the difference is in the manner and immediate object of worship, not in the formal ground of worship. The worship sprang from a true principle, though it was not applied to a right object."[23] Burnside argues that the ancient Near East language of "sun" in verse 4 denotes associations with kingship, justice, and order; that the psalmist describes the Creator God as ruling in justice.[24] Burnside summarizes verses 1–7 as demonstrating a "(1) universal knowledge that can potentially be accessed by all human beings; (2) knowledge that is normative for all human beings; (3) an idea of normativity that is rooted in objective reality, independent of human knowledge of that reality; and (4) an idea of normativity based on a conception of what is required for true human flourishing."[25]

**The Law (7–11).** The Hebrew shifts to the covenantal God, YHWH, thus signifying that the God of creation does not remain hidden but is the covenant God of Israel. Here the psalmist moves from *creational* law

---

[22] See Timothy Samuel Shah and Jack Friedman, eds., *Homo Religiosus? Exploring the Roots of Religion and Religious Freedom in Human Experience* (Cambridge: Cambridge University Press, 2018).

[23] Stephen Charnock, *The Existence and Attributes of God*, vol. 1 (Wheaton: Crossway, 2022), 51.

[24] Burnside, "Natural Law and Biblical Law," 184–85.

[25] Burnside, 185.

to *covenantal* law, demonstrating the interplay of the two. The two are not at odds, but mutually reinforce one another. The focus moves from creation as a *law* itself to Torah as the *Law*, God's special revelation to Israel. As God's covenant message to Israel, Torah is the written law that is intended to distill the creational ordinances of natural revelation into special revelation. Special revelation in no way cancels the authority of creation; it merely gives an authoritative interpretation of it. God's covenantal law with Israel particularizes his creation law. Torah is rooted in an objective creation order. As Burnside summarizes, "the words of *Torah* and the message of the heavens imply there are substantive connections between them. There is continuity between a heavenly message that is universal and a body of law (*Torah*) that is authoritative for a particular people."[26]

**The Heart (12–14).** As Burnside notes, Torah functions as a "bridge between the words of the heavens and the words of the psalmist."[27] The psalmist understands that it is only obedience to God's law, Torah, that can take the elements of creation order and fashion it from chaos into order.[28] After the fall of humanity into sin, we need God's Word as the final authority over our misinterpreting God's creation. So it is today. Though God's creational law remains in effect and binding, humanity's descent into sin renders us unable to understand it in full or perfectly obey it. This is no way suggests that creation itself is less intelligible; only that we are apt to misinterpret it and suppress our obedience to it. We need God's Word to bring authoritative clarity. Alignment with God's creation order as crystallized in God's law is the pathway to true human flourishing.

Psalm 19 amplifies what was originally given in the Torah. As Deut 4:5–8 shows us, God's law was never intended as a sectarian project beholden to Israel's scope only. God's written *law* was meant to refract the abiding authority of the moral *law* and bring it into focus.

---

[26] Burnside, 188.
[27] Burnside, 188.
[28] Burnside, 189.

"See, I have taught you statutes and rules, as the LORD my God commanded me, that you should do them in the land that you are entering to take possession of it. Keep them and do them, for that will be your wisdom and your understanding in the sight of the peoples, who, when they hear all these statutes, will say, 'Surely this great nation is a wise and understanding people.' For what great nation is there that has a god so near to it as the LORD our God is to us, whenever we call upon him? And what great nation is there, that has statutes and rules so righteous as all this law that I set before you today?"

It is Israel's obedience to YHWH's law that makes the Gentiles aware of their futile strivings against God's moral order. Echoes of this theme abound in 1 Pet 2:12 where Peter tells his audience to "Keep your conduct among the Gentiles honorable, so that when they speak against you as evildoers, they may see your good deeds and glorify God on the day of visitation." The reality of such a standard comports elsewhere in Scripture where non-Christian peoples have true moral knowledge and surrounding nations are held accountable to God's moral standards for righteousness (Amos 1–2; Deut 4:5–7).

In summation, creation and God's Word are complementary, though distinct, mediums of revelation. God's existence can be genuinely known in the ordering of creation and its attendant teleological structuring. If true knowledge of God the Creator were not available, humanity could not be held liable for punishment because they would *not* be "without excuse" (Rom 1:20). As VanDrunen writes, "If God holds all people accountable before his judgment, then all people must also know what his justice demands."[29] God the Redeemer is disclosed only in a covenantal framework where the disguised theism of natural revelation becomes intimately known as YWHW. The God who speaks through creation is the same God who speaks in inscripturated form. Psalm 19 demonstrates how God's word

---

[29] VanDrunen, "Natural Law for Reformed Theology," 123.

gives its own account of natural revelation in the form of special revelation. Psalm 19 is the Bible's account of natural law. We see creation order through the looking glass of Scripture, so to speak. God's covenantal law is rooted in creation order and is the final arbiter in human disputes over morality. God's law codifies the natural law into written form, thus giving an authoritative account for morality and order.

## Reason, Faith, and Moral Knowledge: An Application to Ethics

Following from this, we understand that general revelation and special revelation are two modes of God's revelation that reason is able to grasp. Truths deduced from natural law are the result of general revelation's sufficiency in positing a universal moral order. The tendency to pit natural law *against* Scripture, therefore, is thus unwarranted and to be rejected. Mutually reinforcing one another, reason and revelation speak in harmony according to the Bible's own account of created reality.

Understanding *how* Scripture speaks about creation's intelligibility is the difference between furnishing an ethic that narrowly focuses on ethics-as-proof-texting or concordance-based ethics versus an ethics that encompasses creation order. A narrow sufficiency that does ethics only by proof-text alone will, unintentionally, leave Christians without answers to a whole host of questions. A broader sufficiency, one that encompasses how Scripture speaks over all created reality, broadens our understanding of the Bible's relevancy to ethics.

Though perhaps controversial at first blush, the task of ethics will, at times, require us to think beyond the immediate horizon of individual verses and instead see Scripture's wider aperture as a canonical witness to creation order. Scripture is not an exhaustive repository addressing every dilemma we face as modern Christians. For fear that that may sound like I'm advocating for a "trajectory hermeneutic," no such thing is in view. No, the concern expressed here, as I stated in a previous chapter, is that sufficiency understood in the narrowest of ways can lead to ethical malpractice;

creating ethical systems where if Scripture does not prohibit it, it is therefore permissible.

We never speak against Scripture nor Scripture's teaching on creation order. God is the source of all moral knowledge, but a God-implanted moral knowledge is broader than what is contained in Scripture alone. A non-Christian heart surgeon, for example, may better understand the operations of the heart and how it ought to function better than a Christian heart surgeon. This is where the Westminster Confession's teaching is helpful and worth re-stating: "The whole counsel of God, concerning all things necessary for His own glory, man's salvation, faith, and life, is either expressly set down in Scripture, or by good and necessary consequence may be deduced from Scripture." We can and must "deduce" moral truths *from* Scripture that are not directly stated from Scripture on a host of contemporary ethical issues that surpass specific mention within the text of Scripture itself (e.g., IVF, surrogacy, same-sex marriage).

True moral knowledge resides in all persons regardless of their perfectly acknowledging God. He gives humanity the powers of reason and cognition to know whether something is true or false on its own grounds (Rom 2:14–15). We may suppress the truth or err in our application of the moral law (Rom 1:18–21), but Scripture attests to the reality of the moral law. Nowhere does Scripture argue that non-Christians are incapable of knowing any truth. Scripture argues that non-Christians suppress the truth, which suggests that the truth is known but rebelled against.

The world the Lord creates is known to us by a divinely endowed capacity for reason. To say that image-bearers can know by reasoning is to insist that the Lord does not make the splendor of this world unintelligible. Sin mars our reason, but it does not render us blind to the knowledge of a creation that "proclaims his handiwork" or deaf to a world that "pours out speech" (Ps 19:1–3).

What does this have to do with natural law ethics? Natural law calls for reasoned debate about deeply moral questions. All moral law certainly emanates from God, but that does not mean one who does not believe in

God does not have actual moral knowledge. The unbeliever may have no solid ground upon which to base their morality, but unstable foundations do not invalidate the true knowledge they do possess. That may sound like I am investing too much weight or optimism in reason itself. That's not my intention. Instead, I want us to understand that a secular progressive's refusal to agree with Scripture also signals their refusal to agree with what are ultimately the sound principles of morality as such. Principles of morality will be sound, or they will not be, regardless of the non-believer's understanding of their foundation. A non-believer may want to argue that an apple is an orange, or a man can be a woman, but if they insist upon an irrational conclusion, a part of the task of sound moral reasoning is not only offering sound foundations but also sound principles for determining the nature of reality and truth as such. We can and should debate ethical origins, but we should be preeminently concerned with truthfulness. If God's world is one of order, in principle then, truth must be able to be understood by all even if the interlocutor suppresses this knowledge or self-deceives themselves in denying such knowledge.

God speaks with one voice in two ways: in Scripture and in creation. Suppose we pit these two against each other, as though faith and reason are antipodes. In that case, we do violence to Scripture and send the wrong signal to unbelievers that they are justified to sever reason from faith, as though there are degrees of knowledge incompatible with faith. Such a description is a false dichotomy. Special revelation builds off the platform provided by general revelation even while it brings focus and clarity to it. As Francis Turretin so aptly states,

> [N]o lie against the truth can be sheltered under the protection of true reason, nor can one truth be destroyed by another (although one may transcend and surpass the other) because whatever the one may be—whether below, according to or above reason, and apprehended by the senses, the intellect or faith—it has come from no other source than God, the parent of truth. So grace does not

destroy nature, but makes it perfect. Nor does supernatural revelation abrogate the natural, but makes it sure.[30]

Some aspects of reason may be incomplete, but they are never incompatible with faith. For example, a non-Christian might not know God as triune. Still, the same triune God—Father, Son, and Holy Spirit—is also the God who rationally ordered a universe where all can know injustice exists and should be rectified. An unbeliever may not be able to give account for the identity of the triune God, but they could, in principle, understand that abortion is wrong. And that's because the world God created is intelligible. It explains why non-Christians can make wonderful discoveries or become experts in medicine: The world has order to it.

Scripture speaks in a panoramic way when it comes to morality. The whole edifice of Christian morality should cause us to point our interlocutor to God because, without God, there can be no stable foundation of morality to begin with. We should not let our secular neighbors off the hook because they reject Scripture. We should also ask them: From whence does your understanding of sound ethics derive? Morality reduces to two options: either (1) a transcendently given morality that is universally true and objectively accords with reason and reality as such, or (2) a convention, consensus, or majority-contingent, and ever-evolving neural mechanism promoting dopamine-like sensations based upon group, preference, and power.

If all moral knowledge is known *exclusively* from Scripture rather than *ultimately* by Scripture's testimony of God's sovereignty, we might unintentionally forfeit the ground on which we're called to witness to God's glory and creative majesty. But neither should we ever grant the premise that the morality Scripture speaks of is anything ever less than truly reasonable. Thus, to jettison Scripture, in other words, is to jettison reason itself because the Lord is a God of reason, not sheer will. God does not create Christian

---

[30] Turretin, *Institutes of Elenctic Theology*, 1:44.

morality "over here" and non-Christian secular morality "over there." The triune God is not only the God over salvation but also creation, which means when God rationally orders the universe, the morality that goes with it is not bifurcated between "Christian" and "non-Christian."

We see this in Genesis 1.

Genesis describes a creational order that bears witness to creation as such, not simply a Christian view of creation as though the world we inhabit as Christians is different for non-Christians. No, there is one God, one cosmos, one world, and one morality. The beauty of Christian ethics is that properly ordered reason will always harmonize with what Scripture teaches is true. Reason is subordinate to Scripture but never at odds with it. There is no tension and can never truly be. God is not a God of chaos, irrationality, or contradiction.

Our ethics are never less than biblically rooted, but biblically rooted ethics necessarily posit rational truths. Our knowledge is not valid insofar as it only agrees with Scripture, but reason as well. But if it's reasonable, it will never be at odds with Scripture. If there are reasoned justifications for the ethics we espouse that satisfy the criteria for rational soundness, then where that truth is located—whether in special revelation or general revelation—is irrelevant to the integrity of the issue at hand. If true of reason, it will necessarily be true of Scripture. To say otherwise is to traffic in ethical dualism.

What matters is whether the argument in question is true or false. No tenet of Christian ethics will ever be at odds with what reason can know as true. Therefore, when we speak of "Christian Ethics," we speak of an inherently public discipline because Christian ethics are grounded in creation, divinely attested to in Scripture, and confirmed by sound reason. The truthfulness of our ethics is not a private, self-disclosed reality.

But I'd like to suggest that grounding our ethics and the call to ethics in Scripture *alone* is to bypass the full range of arguments that God gives us. We should never appeal any less to Scripture. We are, after all, Protestants who believe in sola Scriptura. But *sola* Scriptura is not *solo* Scriptura. It has never been the position of Christian ethics that authority is found only within Scripture, but that Scripture is our ultimate authority. What questions this raises is whether there are other valid sources of authority that Christians should consider when making public arguments. Sound reason that comports with God's creation is one of them.

All matters of public policy and cultural flashpoints subject to intense debate in the public arena, if they are essential to organizing our shared life around, ought to and can be debated on the basis of reason, which is never disconnected from theology, but merely its entailment.[31] Further, any principle of public policy that a Christian would want to see codified as a sound reflection of biblical morality would necessarily be grounded in the natural law. Any cultural debate that requires Christians to offer a definitive response must never be at odds with reason; if it were, it would not be grounded in God's eternal law from the start.

In a natural law framework, faith is indeed a precondition to rationality because we believe God orders rationality itself. The beginning point of any notion of truth requires placing trust in something. Reason itself requires a source. Christians call this source "God." In every moral debate, everyone borrows on some form of an assumed "ought." Christianity provides the foundational "is" that foregrounds the very possibility of oughtness and to the very idea of practical reason and reasonableness to start with. John Finnis provides an outstanding summary on the connection between the principles of practical reason and their grounding in God's nature.

> The principles of practical reasonableness are now understandable as having the force and depth of a kind of sharing in God's creative purpose and providence. The good of practical reasonableness (*bonum rationis*) is now understandable as good not only intrinsically and for its own sake but also as a constituent in the good of *assimilatio* (making oneself like) and *adhesio* (uniting oneself) to the omnipotent creator's practical wisdom and choice. The truth of the practical principles is now understandable not only as the

---

[31] I owe this thought to the work of Richard John Neuhaus.

anticipation of the human fulfillment to which they direct us, but also as their conformity to the most real of all realities, the divine creative mind, the mind which is nothing other than the very reality of that pure and simple act, God.[32]

The purpose of this chapter has been to demonstrate the epistemic foundations of natural law: Knowledge of the natural law springs from the capacity of our mind to respond to God's activity of furnishing a natural order knowable through general revelation and special revelation. Natural law is a species of natural theology in the way that general revelation is a species of revelation proper. From the canopies of natural theology and general revelation to the specificity provided by special revelation, we deduce the synchronicity and complementarity between faith and reason that allows the Christian to obtain genuine moral knowledge and to maintain the superiority of Christianity in providing a coherent moral account for life in this world. Though general revelation and special revelation differ in form, and faith and reason's horizons differ as to end, the author of each is the same—God.

---

[32] John Finnis, *Aquinas: Moral, Legal, and Political Theory* (Oxford: Oxford University Press, 1998), 308–9.

# 5.

# Philosophical Foundations for the Natural Law, Part 1

## Origins and Knowability

We now begin our formal inquiry into the philosophical underpinnings of the natural law and natural law theory. It should be noted that entire volumes have been composed just on what this chapter hopes to explore. While not everything that ought to be said can be said here, it will provide the reader with the necessary philosophical orientation to understand the basic outline of natural law and natural law theory from the domain of philosophy. While overtures to theology will be made along the way, the purpose of this chapter is to set forth natural law as a coherent philosophical category.

In this chapter, we are concerned with exploring the philosophical foundations of natural law theory and how the natural law is known. These categories concern the topics of ontology and epistemology. The existence of the natural law beckons us to learn of its essence and for us to formulate how it can be known. As in any debate, we are driven back to the fundamental questions that the natural law helps us answer: What is the good, and from where does it come? These questions force us to answer questions about the philosophical origins of the natural law and how we come to know it.

Though the topic of "law" as an isolated concept will receive deeper treatment below, I want to briefly mention Thomas Aquinas's famous definition of law as it will serve as a helpful reference point throughout the rest of the chapter as we delve more deeply into the natural law. Law, according to Aquinas, is "an ordinance of reason for the common good, made by him who has care of the community, and promulgated."[1] This is one of the most important phrases in all of the natural law tradition.

## Natural Law as Metaethics

As Aristotle famously set forth centuries ago, "Every art and every inquiry, and similarly every action and pursuit, is thought to aim at some good."[2] Thus began in finite form the natural law and teleological trajectories of ethics. While Aristotle's notion of the good does not draw us immediately to theism, the idea that an arrival at an end that satisfies a thing's nature is a repudiation *tout court* of all ethical relativism. The notion of created things reaching their created potential has left dents in the history of ethical inquiry that cannot be removed.

"The good" that all aim for is a contentious topic that this volume has already previously established. Some dispute the objectivity of goodness existing at all, while others so radically relativize it to where goodness becomes just another form of "what I want." At least from the Christian vantage point, what someone "wants" cannot be assumed to be naturally good because of fallen inclinations which disorder both our passions and our reasoning. Definitionally, "Goodness" is the quality of a thing reaching the end that perfects its nature. In Aristotelian terms, such a state is

---

[1] *ST* I-II, q. 90, a. 4, s. c.

[2] Aristotle, Nicomachean Ethics, ed. and trans. Roger Crisp (Cambridge: Cambridge University Press, 2000), 1094a.

"eudemonic." Eudemonia refers to a contented felicity that accords with human happiness being obtained. "Nature," of course, assumes the created essence of things-in-themselves that exist for an ultimate purpose, which is also disputed in secular moral philosophy. "Goodness" also requires a referent outside of itself to order its being and to bring it into conformity with the quality of excellence that subsists within the unconditional grounds of goodness. Goodness also requires the application of itself to things with natures. That referent, in both ordering and applying the good, we call God. Without God, the best that could be said about goodness is that it is a brute concept inexplicable apart from the emotional or volitional satisfaction we assign to its object. Goodness, then, assumes objective excellence and the objective existence of things with natures that can attain this excellence.

While the paragraph above is admittedly complex, the metaethical realities it mentions are what lurk beneath the surface of cultural conflict and explain the contentious cultural strife of our age and its rival conceptions of the good that people aim for. A commitment to some understanding of the good is impossible to resist. It motivates every action so that every agent is striving toward some end that they see as choiceworthy and beneficial. Regardless of whether the end each strives for is actually good is irrespective of the teleological truth that human beings all aim for actions they believe enhance their being. So let us begin our analysis by insisting on the maxim that all persons begin from an original position of pursuing some perception of the good.

How "the good" is assessed in our culture reveals an unequal type of evaluation. If one submits their version of "the good" without reference to God, it enjoys a special privilege in the most elite sectors of culture that are largely secular. Secularism believes it operates from a point of Archimedean neutrality untainted by ideology and religion, a state of pure belief in facts and objectivity. This is the most extravagant lie our civilization tells itself. It is not only patently false; it is unspeakably biased in its own favor and rife with the potential for evil. When morality is left without a transcendent and objective reference point, the notion of good collapses into whatever a society considers good *to them*. A society that defines the good only by its own horizon is a society that can easily fall into the abyss of totalitarianism.

Secularism enjoys a presumption of neutrality that should be called into question. A story explaining the inherent biases of secularism and how it operates with regard to claims about moral goods will help us as we begin our philosophical investigation into the natural law.

I was once interviewed by a journalist for a book project I was organizing. The journalist was fair-minded, inquisitive, and from what I could tell, deeply committed to the idea that if one is going to make certain moral claims in society and on society, arguing on the basis of religion is out of bounds because, as secularism tells us, someone may not share the same presuppositions. And not sharing the same presuppositions about the world when engaging in public debate is a violation of public decorum. To argue in society, everyone must supposedly empty themselves of any ultimate claims about the world and debate on terms sanitized of religion. But notice that this is a claim itself on the world: That religious claims are disfavored and disallowed—that religious claims somehow pose a threat to civic order, that the "good" just naturally exists without deeper metaphysical grounding.

Civic order and its boundaries, then, are operating according to certain assumptions about the moral good of social order: social order is harmed when religiously motivated claims are inflicted because not everyone shares the same religion. Notice, however, that excluding religion tends to assume the exclusion of moral goods that stem from religion. Such a declaration of religion's disavowal assumes that moral claims issuing from a religion are only intelligible if those religious presuppositions are shared. But that elides an important question: If we do not share the same religion, do we share the same capacity to reason about what is good, irrespective of our claims about the good's origin? Notice, fundamentally, how secularism tilts the scales in its favor by barring religious argument. Secularism rigs public debate by imposing asymmetrical judgments on the types of claims that are allowed.

I was asked a question about the imposition of religious claims on secular society. In fact, the conversation went like this, "Individuals who do not want to arrange flowers or bake a cake for a same-sex wedding are imposing their religious convictions on others. Isn't that wrong?"

I answered the journalist, saying, "Well, actually, this is not exclusively a debate about a religious claim. It's a moral debate about the definition of marriage. Some secular individuals have one definition of marriage. Evangelical Christians have a different definition of marriage. The question for legal matters is not, ultimately, about whether someone is imposing one's religion on another or whether Christians or secularists are correct. For I could just as easily reply that secular individuals are imposing their convictions about marriage on evangelicals. No, the question at the heart of this dispute is a moral and philosophical debate over whose definition of marriage is most reasonable, compelling, and conducive to the common good."

To my shock, the journalist replied, "Well, that's really helpful. I hadn't thought about it like that. So, you're saying this is really a debate about moral goods, not ultimately about religion?" "Yes," I replied, "while I'm willing to debate what my religion teaches about marriage, my faith also teaches me that its moral principles are moral principles that correspond to reality as it truly is. So that means we ought to be able to debate whose understanding of marriage is most coherent or persuasive without relying, exclusively, on religion."

I can't say that I walked away from this conversation having changed the journalist's mind about my convictions on this matter, but what did happen is that a journalist uncovered the fact that what passes for "religious debates" in our society—while ultimately religious in one sense—are not *exclusively* religious. That's because the natural law, if it is what this book argues it is, avails itself of truth claims that should be falsifiable on the grounds of their own internal coherence and reasonableness, not just whether one accepts a presupposition about divine revelation. Religious arguments are fine in society and people should be free to make them. The test of a religion's claim is whether its entailments that derive from religion pose a moral claim about moral goods that bear relevance to others who may not share the same faith. The famous public theologian Richard John Neuhaus argued to similar effect when in a debate with secular philosophers, he noted, "There's nothing necessary in the public realm to answering the question 'how ought we to order our life together?' That cannot be debated and considered reasonably on the basis of arguments that are accessible to everybody."[3] I offer this anecdote to explain that as Christians reason about moral conflict in society, we are not just reasoning about religious claims in an ultimate sense, we are reasoning about the coherence of morality in a penultimate sense, as well. Behind all moral quests are questions about the source of moral goodness itself that makes all other moral discourse possible.

## The Origin of the Natural Law

Behind the natural law stands a basic metaphysical truth: there is a cosmic order to the world.[4] As David Oderberg writes, "It is impossible to know how the world ought to go, more specifically how one ought to act (or what makes a state of affairs or action good, or worthwhile, praiseworthy, etc.) without prior knowledge of how the world is."[5] The effects of the natural law spring from an eternal first cause, God. According to Richard Hooker, the eternal law speaks of how "all things work, in their own way, to a law. Nearly everything works according to a law subject to some superior, who has authored it; only the works and operations of God have him as both their worker and their law. The very being of God is a sort of law to his working, for the perfection that God is, gives perfection to what God does."[6] God thus orders all things to their predetermined ends according to his internal operations. To say that a goal or end exists for natural law, then,

---

[3] This quote comes from Richard John Neuhaus in a Firing Line Debate: "Resolved: That the Wall of Separation of Church and State Should be Lowered," September 8, 1994.

[4] David S. Oderberg, "The Metaphysical Foundations of Natural Law," in *Natural Moral Law in Contemporary Society*, ed. Holger Zaborowski (Washington, DC: Catholic University of America Press, 2010), 48.

[5] Oderberg, 45.

[6] Richard Hooker, *The Laws of Ecclesiastical Polity*, ed. W. Bradford Littlejohn, Bradley Belschner, and Brian Marr, vol. 1: Preface-Book IV, Library of Early English Protestantism (Landrum, SC: The Davenant Institute, 2019), 50.

presupposes the existence of God who orders all things to subscribe to the goal or end he has in mind.

At its deepest backstop, natural law is a religious doctrine since we believe that it exists because of an eternal being ordering it into existence. How this order came about, how we know it, and where it is ultimately headed are questions that theology is designed to answer. But theology and philosophy are never at odds with one another. They represent two ways God has ordered our minds to know him and his moral law. Thus, to speak of natural law is to speak of a moral theory that virtually all understand to be divine in origin. Cosmic order, as this book understands it, is the result of divine ordination. Apart from God, the tenability and enforcement of natural law becomes exponentially more difficult. For there to be a "law" to speak of, there must be a Law-Giver. As Germain Grisez writes,

> When we consider other things and ourselves as creatures of an intelligent and free Creator, we naturally attribute to him the order we find in the world around us and in ourselves. Included in that order is the directiveness of the principles of practical reason. Just as the truth that a universe of contingent things exists is obvious but points to the Creator, so the truth that our human goods are to be realized is evident but points to the directive intelligence of the Creator, who is in and of himself completely real and so not like us, who must act to realize (*real*-ize) ourselves.[7]

To say there is a natural end of humanity assumes a designer fitting humans with such natural ends from the start. John Calvin helpfully articulates the same idea, observing that God "directs everything by his incomprehensible wisdom and disposes it to his own end."[8] Striking a teleological chord to God's ordering of nature, Calvin writes that God is what directs things

---

[7] Grisez, "Natural Law and the Transcendent Source of Human Fulfillment," 448 (see introduction, n. 5).

[8] John Calvin, *Institutes of the Christian Religion*, ed. John T. McNeill, trans. Ford Lewis Battles (Philadelphia: WJK, 1960), 1.16.4.

to their own end consistent with the nature implanted upon them: "It is, indeed, true that the several kinds of things are moved by a secret impulse of nature, as if they obeyed God's eternal command, and what God has once determined flows on by itself."[9] The uncaused cause of the natural law must necessarily be a non-contingent Being who enacts the natural law and gives to it the structure of its existence and the binding force of law, prescriptivity, and obligation. A finite mind cannot be the source of an eternal law. A transcendently given law requires a transcendent Being. This Being cannot be given any authority outside of itself or else it would lack the authority to order things to an ultimate end. It would be impossible to insist upon the universality of morality without God's moral law issuing from God's divine aseity. A Being like this must be perfectly good and must possess the authority to prescribe us to obey his moral law. That Being is what we call God and is the principal and efficient cause of all moral order. Brian McCall, author of the magisterial volume, *The Architecture of Law*, grounds the natural law in the eternal law of God, which he defines as:

> The idea of the universe in all its particulars flowing from the mind of God. It contains the due end to which all things are directed. It also contains the exemplar or the pattern for the universe, the style each creature is to use in pursuing that end. Finally, it contains the skill or art needed to achieve the particular idea.[10]

Consider an artist. Before the artist goes about painting her portrait, she envisions in her own mind what form the artwork will take. A design exists within her mind that will impose structure on the canvas from which she draws. She thus imagines within her own mind what design both the form of the artwork's appearance will be and the means by which it will be brought about.

Understandably, these are deep waters to swim in, because to speak of the origin of the natural law is to speak of the inner workings of God's

---

[9] Calvin, *Institutes*, 1.16.4.

[10] Brian M. McCall, *The Architecture of Law: Rebuilding Law in the Classical Tradition* (Notre Dame, IN: University of Notre Dame Press, 2018), 53.

own mind. We should tremble to speak more than we ought on these matters. But to say there is a natural law is to merely extend out the principle that God decrees that such a law exist. The eternal law of God attempts to explain the inscrutable foundations of God's own being. It is my own position that natural law loses the *fullest* force of its persuasiveness absent God's being and revelation.[11] God is the directing agent of the natural law who assigns the pattern of inclinations that directs individuals toward the grasping and obtaining of their due ends as agents. As Steven A. Long writes to the same effect, "We are subjects of the commonwealth of being, and the law of our being is promulgated at creation by the author and supreme governor of our being."[12] From a philosophical standpoint, natural law assumes the goodness of God as a benevolent Creator. Natural law is the eternal law directed toward the rational creature's participation in it. If God is benevolent, the ends for which God orders our capacities for fulfillment must be good—and never capricious or arbitrary—as well.

God is the *a priori* basis of natural law. According to Aquinas, "If they [laws] be just, they have the power of binding in conscience, from the eternal law whence they are derived."[13] The necessity for God's existence is no more simply explained than when McCall states, "Classical natural law jurisprudence is intellectually unsustainable without teleology, and teleology requires a being that is above teleological reality."[14] The ordering agent of the natural law, traced back to ultimate origins, must be God. Yet, God's existence as the foundational superstructure of the natural law does not, on its own, offer the grounds of its persuasiveness, only its origin. The

---

[11] I should state that I think natural law stands or falls on its own claims of rational soundness and persuasiveness, regardless of whether one accepts God's existence. Denying God's existence does, however, blunt the authorizing force for why there is any law to speak of, thus forfeiting ultimate causation.

[12] Steven A. Long, "God, Teleology, and the Natural Law," in *Natural Law: The Present State of the Perennial Philosophy*, ed. Christopher Wolfe and Steven Brust (Lanham, MD: Lexington Books, 2018), 9.

[13] *ST* I-II, q. 96, a. 4. co.

[14] McCall, *The Architecture of Law: Rebuilding Law in the Classical Tradition*, 422.

blunt assertion, "God exists," is not a self-attesting witness to the knowledge of natural law or its persuasiveness. Hypothetically, God could exist and there not be a natural law. So God must promulgate a moral law that his creatures are capable of grasping.

On its own terms, then, natural law must have practical reasons for its ability to command obedience apart simply from, "God exists." There must be reasons for its choiceworthiness. God's existence tells us only about natural law's origins, not whether or how it is knowable. Now, the natural law, being a law, attests to its promulgation so that it is indeed knowable through reason. But the natural law is either compelling on its own terms as a body of natural, choiceworthy truths or it is not, regardless of whether one believes the natural law is divinely ordained. But, since Christians believe God exists, and that the contours of natural law are a product of God's eternal law, it is always the case that natural law is God-ordained and, under ideal conditions, persuasive. Patrick Lee writes, "since God is the author of both our nature and our intelligence, these moral principles are indeed directives from God, a part of God's wise plan for his creation."[15] But whether one acknowledges the source of these principles accurately says nothing about whether the principles can be rationally understood. While the natural law tradition holds that people, in principle, can grasp the natural law with reason alone (and, of course, err in their grasp of it), the fact of God's Being provides an oughtness to the natural law that removes it from accusations of arbitrariness. At the end of the day, the natural law is obligatory because it issues from God; and to the extent that we know God, we can amplify our understanding of the moral law and why it is worth obeying.

At the same time, on the practical side of the natural law, we do not say to people that they are correct in their convictions if and only if they have the source of that knowledge correct as well. We may wish them to acknowledge the correct source while appreciating their grasp of truth as best as they grasp it. As Patrick Lee writes further,

---

[15] Patrick Lee, "God and New Natural Law Theory," *The National Catholic Bioethics Quarterly* 19, no. 2 (Summer 2019): 280.

One need only distinguish between knowing certain moral truths and knowing their source, that is, between knowing moral precepts that in fact are part of the natural law and knowing that they are part of a law—which of course by definition includes the notion of a legislator. NNLT [New Natural Law Tradition] holds that the former occurs—people who do not know that God exists still know some moral truths. But it also holds that, of course, to know that these moral truths are part of the natural law requires knowing or believing in God the legislator.[16]

This is not to say that God's existence is irrelevant to considerations of the natural law (far be it, in fact). Rather, either the natural law is compelling on its own terms as such, or it is not. The nature of obligation that undergirds ethical normativity requires that individuals have reasons to fulfill what is knowable about the natural law. As Germain Grisez writes, "[M]oral normativity arises from the prescriptivity of the principles of practical reason."[17] The question of practical reason's existence and its prescriptivity, however, requires a cause outside of practical reason to give order to it. The cause that orders prescriptivity that the mind grasps must require divine authorization for it to have absolute, unconditional authority for it to command such existence. This divine authorization is what gives a moral command the character of universal obligation—by virtue of the kind of obligation it is, in that since it stems from a divine source, it just *is* obligatory because it is universal; and because it is universal, therefore, it is obligatory. As Oliver O'Donovan writes, "No command or principle, biblical or Platonic, could be justified ethically except by reference to a universal; an ethic without universals would be no ethic, a series of disconnected, arbitrary imperatives."[18] If a moral claim were not binding, it would not have

---

[16] Lee, 287.

[17] Grisez, "Natural Law and the Transcendent Source of Human Fulfillment," 449.

[18] Oliver M. T. O'Donovan, "The Possibility of a Biblical Ethic," *Theological Students Fellowship Bulletin* 67 (1973): 18.

the character of a moral claim. Moral claims, by nature, are universal claims about what obligations exist.

God is the authorizing agent of a moral order that is compelling as a natural explanation to knowing good from evil. But people may know moral truths apart from recognizing their source.[19] If natural law is what it says it is, people ought to be able, in principle, to agree to fundamental moral truths regardless of whether they assent to belief in God. In this sense, it is not that the individual has disconnected themselves from a God-ordained order, but that individuals are considered as unwitting participants within a created order that they claim not to know or deceive themselves into denying. As Aquinas states, "The human being has a share of the Eternal Reason, whereby it has a natural inclination to its proper act and end: and this participation of the eternal law in the rational creature is called the natural law."[20] Simply by virtue of the capacities that God has ordered us with, we are able to identify aspects of the natural law, whether incompletely or completely, by our nature as reasoning beings since reason is how the natural law is grasped.

## The Knowability of the Natural Law

How do we come to know the natural law? For example, on what basis do we know that murder is wrong? While the next chapter's focus will be on what Scripture refers to as those who "by nature do what the law requires" because of "the law" that is "written on their hearts" (Rom 2:14–15), approaching this question philosophically requires us to think about the acquisition of moral knowledge at its most basic level.

### Per Se Nota Truths

Per se nota truths are truths that we consider indemonstrable or self-evident. They are brute facts comprising human knowledge. They are the propositional

---

[19] Lee, 287.
[20] ST I-II, q. 91, a. 2., co.

truths whose conclusion is assumed in the premise. C. S. Lewis wrote, "I believe that the primary moral principles on which all others depend are rationally perceived. . . . Their intrinsic reasonableness shines by its own light. It is because all morality is based on such self-evident principles that we can say to a man, when we recall him to right conduct, 'Be reasonable.'"[21] By "its own light," Lewis means that some moral principles are self-attesting. For example: Why is it wrong to steal my neighbor's wallet? Because that robs him of his possessions. But why is it wrong to rob him of his possessions? Because it violates the basic principles of justice. Why is it wrong to violate the basic principles of justice? Because it disrupts affairs from how they ought to be. Why is it bad to disrupt affairs from how they ought to be? *Because it just is.* Disorder and privation are bad ends in themselves and to be avoided. Moral realism attests to our desire for moral equilibrium. Think of the converse: It is dastardly to accept states of affairs that allow irrationality and evil to go unchecked. Humans desire satisfaction of a sort that we believe is natural and good as attested to in our nature. It is impossible, in other words, for me to be indifferent about abuse toward one of my daughters (were one of them to be abused) because God *just has* ordered human nature to be of the type that *just is* inherently responsive to moral affairs.     → Nat'l Law!

I cannot prove to you why it is bad for affairs to not be how they ought to be apart from just knowing that certain things ought not to be. If I have to prove this, it means there is no moral foundation from which to base all other moral judgments. For there to be a moral position to aspire to requires an absolute backstop from which to derive a moral conclusion. As one author notes, this is an essential operation to all moral reasoning: "We would be lost in our train of reasoning if we had no fixed points that guided our reasoning . . . [I]t would be impossible to reason at all without fixed principles."[22] Humans reason from stated or unstated moral premises by virtue of the kinds

---

[21] C. S. Lewis, *Miracles: A Preliminary Study* (New York: Macmillan, 1960), 34–35.

[22] Pauline C. Westerman, *The Disintegration of Natural Law Theory: Aquinas to Finnis* (Leiden: Brill, 1997), 52.

of beings we are. This is an inexplicable feature of our nature that exists as a brute fact. Elsewhere, Lewis observes to similar effect, "If nothing is self-evident, nothing can be proved. Similarly, if nothing is obligatory for its own sake, nothing is obligatory at all."[23] Lewis is emphasizing that, at root, there must be some foundational, unprovable, and immutable principle of morality that makes sense of all rational considerations and moral obligations.

The importance of this concept cannot be overlooked—if not only for its necessity, then also for its simplicity. Self-evident truths simply mean that there are fundamental moral realities we cannot justify apart from the experience of their own intrinsic reasonableness and choiceworthiness. It may appear as though this is a form of circular reasoning. To some degree, it is, and that is because all moral knowledge relies upon some stated or unstated foundation. If the natural law is indeed true, it would imply that there are necessary truths at no lower level of explanation than their own existence. Jacques Maritain rightly notes that, far from this being a disqualifying quality, it speaks to the "greater validity" and "essential naturality" of the natural law.[24] If the natural law is truly natural law, the obviousness of some underlying moral principle ought to be implied. This shows the practical genius of the natural law: its simplicity. Though natural lawyers debate the application of the natural law to specific situations, the natural law holds that foundational moral principles (e.g., "pursue good, avoid evil") are not hard to grasp. We can pursue knowledge, generally, and grasp the natural law, more particularly, because God saw fit to order our cognitive capacity to function as he designed it.

## First Principle of Practical Reason

The First Principle of Practical Reason (FPPR) is another foundational element to natural law theory that builds on the idea of the necessity of some underived, self-evident moral truth that presupposes all other intelligible

---

[23] Lewis, *The Abolition of Man*, 40, (see chap. 1, n. 7).

[24] Jacques Maritain, *Natural Law: Reflections on Theory and Practice* (South Bend, IN: St. Augustine's Press, 1952), 21.

moral action. It is akin to the law of non-contradiction, but for ethics.[25] As Patrick Lee writes, the FPPR is "self-evident in that the predicate [*is to be done and pursued*] is immediately apprehended in the intelligibility of the subject, *Good*."[26] According to the FPPR, there cannot be a moral universe without the FPPR. There is no proving it; it just is. Philosopher Paul DeHart is correct to observe that natural lawyers do no further work to derive an ought before the primary ought is given from the FPPR; rather, they assume it from the start as that which explains why there is any morally obligating action whatsoever.[27]

Developed from Thomas Aquinas, the FPPR is the sort of principle and guideline that explains all other precepts of rational morality. It goes like this: "Good is to be done and pursued, and evil is to be avoided." Thomas goes on to write how "all other precepts of the natural law are based upon this: so that whatever the practical reason naturally apprehends as man's good (or evil), belongs to the precepts of the natural law as something to be done or avoided."[28] Developed in the thought of Aquinas, the FPPR assumes that all agents act for an end, which is to say, their good. Rational persons pursue practical activity that the person perceives will further their flourishing. If a rational creature pursued what harms them as an equally choiceworthy end, there would be no moral action to speak of since pursuing evil would be just as beneficial as pursuing the good. For example, if it was "good" to put one's hand on a hot stove and harm one's self, it means that arriving at goodness is incoherent. It cannot be good to do the bad. If it were, there could be no directive end to a moral norm because no moral good exists. If moral goods do not exist, the point of having moral norms is moot. Aquinas continues: "The good or evil of an action, as of other things,

---

[25] Patrick Lee, "The New Natural Law Theory," in *The Cambridge Companion to Natural Law Ethics*, ed. Tom Angier (Cambridge: Cambridge University Press, 2019), 75.

[26] Lee, 75.

[27] Paul R. Dehart, "On the First Principle of Practical Reason," *Public Discourse*, July 6, 2020, https://www.thepublicdiscourse.com/2020/07/64302/.

[28] *ST* I-II, q. 94, a. 2, co.

depends on its fullness of being or its lack of that fullness."[29] For Aquinas, an action is good and reasonable if it leads to the rational creature's completing itself. In other words, no rational agent seeks its detriment. If it did, meaningful action would be unintelligible since action taken that is contrary to one's good would be considered "good." That is nonsensical. Since "good is that which all things seek after," there is no antecedent premise for explaining the basis for all other actions apart from the FPPR.[30] Denying the FPPR means denying that ends or goods exist that complete us or obligate us to obtain them. Without the FPPR, we would be unable to say whether something like suicide, abortion, or lying are morally good or bad. We would be inhabiting a world with no moral meaningfulness whatsoever. If evil is just as desirable as good, chaos would ensue.

FPPR helps us understand that a person who eats food does so not merely for taste, but to preserve their life. Why do they want to preserve their life? Just because a person in their right mind understands that life is better than death. In contrast, an individual who willingly chooses to place their hand on a stove's burner would be conducting action considered "unreasonable" because it would be intentionally undermining the agent's good. Whatever the mind grasps as practically beneficial—whether as an apparent good or an actual good depending on the accuracy of the mind's grasp—to their existence, that thing ought to be done.

Lest one think that these categories borrow exclusively from Catholic categories, the Protestant Reformers Franciscus Junius and John Calvin arrive at the same principle in terms starkly reminiscent of Thomas Aquinas. Junius observes: "Moreover, the end of that practical reason, which has been placed in both the just and the unjust, is one's own good, and for this reason it is the first and highest precept of the natural law. The good, as the end of nature, must be pursued and done; evil must be avoided."[31] As Calvin him-

---

[29] *ST* I-II, q. 18, a. 2, co.
[30] *ST* I-II, q. 94 a. 2.
[31] Franciscus Junius, *The Mosaic Polity*, trans. Todd M. Rester (Grand Rapids: Christian's Library Press, 2015), 45.

self states, "God provided man's soul with a mind, by which to distinguish good from evil, right from wrong; and, with the light of reason as guide, to distinguish what should be followed from what should be avoided."[32]

Neils Hemmingsen also captures this same principle at greater length:

> For if what is concluded is honorable or useful or pleasant, a man thereupon is carried along by a natural impulse to obtain it; but if the reason discovers that what is concluded is shameful, use-less, or unpleasant, then just as the mind judges that that thing ought not to be embraced, so the will turns away from it in dis-gust. Consequently, one ought to be amazed at the workmanship of God, who created man in such a way that in him are both cogni-tive and appetitive faculties, that is, the faculties by which things are perceived and desired. It is fitting to gaze upon and wonder at these, so that we may be grateful to our creator, who has adorned this miniature world—that is, man—with gifts so wondrous.[33]

The argument from Junius, Calvin, and Hemmingsen tells us that God has implanted a most elementary principle for moral action in humanity. It is a feature of our natures being made in God's image and possessing the capacity for reason. Importantly, the focus here is on the operation of how we grasp moral knowledge. Fundamentally, it is through practical reason's reflections on behavior that either completes or perfects us (or which fails to complete us) that we come to understand the contents of human nature. God assigns a nature to us that we learn how to complete and fulfill through reasoned reflection on the goods that reasoned creatures see as completing them. The simplicity of the FPPR reflects a certain inevitability as to our awareness of the natural law. If the natural law is "natural," its most basic tenets should not be hard to discover. It means that goods that complete us

---

[32] John Calvin, *Calvin: Institutes of the Christian Religion*, ed. John T. McNeill, trans. Ford Lewis Battles, (Philadelphia: WJK, 1960), 1.5.18.

[33] Niels Hemmingsen, *On the Law of Nature: A Demonstrative Method* (Grand Rapids: CLP Academic, 2018), 49.

and which comprise our nature should be self-evident and "basic," even if an agent misunderstands the good or errs in the entailments of what truly completes or fulfills them.

## Practical Reason or Speculative Reason?

A significant debate engulfs natural law theory as to the basis of how we perceive the content of the natural law. Do we perceive it through theoretical reflections about human nature or through practical considerations of human nature? For example: Does the physiological structure of male and female and their capacity for bodily union tell us that any heterosexual act is moral? Or does reasoned consideration of what context their union takes shape in and their corresponding potencies define what licit sexual practices are? In other words, is any sexual act moral if its heterosexual? Is that the only threshold? Or is a sexual act moral only to the extent that it sees man and woman join together within the estate of marriage that bonds them to any children that are present? The answer is the latter. A heterosexual sex act, contrary to a sodomitical one, could produce children without caring for them as the children are owed. We should be able to discern how not to use the body (and sodomitical acts indeed harm the body) but the naturally occurring facts of opposite sex design do not, on their own, tell us that marriage is the moral good we ought to pursue. We come to know that marriage is the basic moral good constituting our sexual design by understanding marriage's unique aptitude for social stability. So, the moral good of a sex act is not just through heterosexual expression but expression in the proper outlet—marriage and family life. The fact of our heterosexual design needing to be channeled in the direction of marriage is something we learn through practical reasoning about what states of affairs best complete us.

Or consider lying. Do we understand lying to be wrong by looking at human nature? But what is nature? Is nature merely a description of propositional phrases describing existence? Or do we learn what our nature is by experience, sapiential wisdom, and investigation into the acts that promote flourishing? These considerations redound to practical axioms that lead us to ask questions about what activities or actions complete or thwart our fulfillment as persons. My own view is that while nature is ontologically necessary to us being created in God's image, our knowledge of that divinely stamped human nature is based on capacities and potentialities that realize, perfect, or complete us as rational beings. Knowledge of human nature—though authored and ordered by God, of course—is derived first from practical reason; not speculative reason. It is through activities and performances and the pursuit of particular ends or goods that we come to constitute human nature.[34]

Ethicist Alfonso Gómez-Lobo argues similarly:

A grasp of human nature that demands sophisticated intellectual training to be understood would not provide proof that friendship is a basic good; it would assume it. That man is endowed with a natural capacity for friendship (or has a natural inclination to sociability) would have to be derived from our realization that it is good to have friends, not the other way around. Indeed, it is not because we have an inclination to X that we may infer that X is good for us. It is our prior grasp of X as good that justifies the claim that our inclination to X is a natural inclination. The appeal to natural inclinations is part of the theoretical enterprise to understand our nature, but it does not have a foundational role in the practical enterprise.[35]

It is my own conviction that despite human nature existing as an ontological reality owing to the natural law, it is through our epistemological knowledge and practical awareness of those goods that comprise human nature

---

[34] I am indebted to Robert P. George for this insight. Robert P. George, "Natural Law Ethics," in *Companion to Philosophy of Religion*, ed. Philip L. Quinn and Charles Taliaferro (Malden, MA: Wiley-Blackwell, 1999), 463.

[35] Alfonso Gómez-Lobo, *Morality and the Human Goods* (Washington, DC: Georgetown University Press, 2002), 127.

that human nature comes to be known. Knowledge of what *is* is gained by practical knowledge. To put this in the plainest and simplest terms that resonate with categories for organizing human knowledge, knowledge of what comprises human nature is derived inductively, rather than deductively. The assertion that humanity has a nature to it requires practical insights into what activities complete or fulfill that nature. In other words, ontological nature is derived first, practically, and, secondly, speculatively. While as a Christian I can argue from the assumption that nature exists because God has ordered human nature to be what it is by way of deductive reasoning, knowledge of that nature arrives, cognitively speaking, from our experience and interaction within the world by way of inductive reasoning.

To put this in practical terms, that there are other male humans whose presence I enjoy being with tells me nothing necessarily *moral* or directive about my behavior. It tells me only a fact. Now, that fact may exist because God has made me with a nature to that end. But for me to gain an awareness of that fact being morally directive, it requires my reflection about whether it is good or not. Morality, if it is to satisfy the criteria for moral approval, is fundamentally *directive*. It is my reflection through my use of reason that tells me that friendship is a good for which I ought to pursue friendships because it helps realize my nature as a social being.

Admittedly, this is complex, and it would be an error to reduce debate about the natural law down to this question of epistemology alone or to pit practical and theoretical reasoning against one another. Alasdair MacIntyre rightfully reminds us that both practical reasoning and speculative reason share an interdependent relationship: "there is then no form of philosophical enquiry . . . which is not practical in its implication, just as there is no practical enquiry which is not philosophical [i.e., speculative] in its presuppositions."[36] Brian McCall similarly argues, "Speculative reason is necessary to understand the basic truths on which the existence and

---

[36] Alasdair MacIntyre, *Three Rival Versions of Moral Enquiry: Encyclopedia, Genealogy, and Tradition* (Notre Dame, IN: University of Notre Dame Press, 1990), 128.

obligatory nature of natural law rest: the end and nature of man. Practical reason is necessary to reach conclusions oriented toward actions based on these truths."[37]

## On the Meaning of "Flourish" and "Nature"

To speak of *nature* is to say that there exists an ideal form and function of what something ought to be. "Purpose," "goal," "design," and "finality" are terms that come to mind when defining nature. The nature of a family, for example, is to care for and raise offspring. To say that something has a *nature* is to insist upon the existence of perfections to that thing's being, which supplies our understanding of what the thing in question truly is and how we ought to treat it.

Nature can speak to both moral and physical properties. Actions that allow us as rational beings to complete ourselves are moral actions that help constitute our nature. When we say something/someone is living in accordance with one's nature, there is moral excellence occurring that allows the physical aspects of the thing to flourish as it was designed by God. "Nature" means something in a philosophical way that is fore-grounded in theology: "God intended for this thing's purpose to be X." A football has a certain design. The nature of a football is different than the nature of a basketball or baseball. Consequently, the shape and look and *telos* of a football is different. Now, you can try to play baseball or basketball with a football. It's not impossible to play something like baseball with a football or to play something like basketball with a football, but it's not really the same sport with a different ball. In time, trying to play the same sport with a ball of a different nature will lead to frustration and failure. And the degree to which it "works" with a ball of a different nature will only be because the game itself has been changed.[38] If there is a design and purpose to how we have been created, we are obligated to act

---

[37] McCall, *The Architecture of Law*, 178.

[38] I'm indebted to my friend Kevin DeYoung for this illustration.

within our nature's limits—that's what 'nature' means." We should not frustrate, impede, or harm a thing's ability to attain flourishing consistent to its nature. Barring men and women from marriage, for example, would be contrary to nature because the nature of marriage and its orientation to the common good requires the free choice of men and women to enter it.

The term "nature" is inherently constricting because it tells us that God's creation has purpose built into the structure of it. Learning our nature means learning what our purpose is and to know who we are, what is possible, what to do, and what not to do. There is no happiness apart from obeying and fulfilling what our nature is. As Kody W. Cooper and Justin Buckley Dyer rightfully state, "to act in accordance with our nature means to act consistently with the way we are designed to function. It is proper to human nature to act according to reason, that is, for reason to order our passions and appetites to appropriate ends."[39] This has profound implications for moral debates that we will explore in later chapters.

*Flourish* is a term that describes the fullness of a thing's being. A thing is flourishing to the degree that conformity to its nature is obtained. For example, a person flourishes if there are not active attempts to end their life since it is in their nature to want to exist as a rational being who is able to attain the life of virtue. A flourishing family is a family with no disruptions or privations undermining its operations, such as divorce. A "same-sex marriage," in contrast, can never be marital because it lacks the essential quality or nature of marriage: conjugality between the sexes (more on this later in chapter 11). A thing experiences its fullness of being or *excellence* when it lives according to what it is and what it is designed to do. Whatever enables us to flourish consistent with our nature obtains the force of a "law."

---

[39] Kody W. Cooper and Justin Buckley Dyer, *The Classical and Christian Origins of American Politics: Political Theology, Natural Law, and the American Founding* (Cambridge: Cambridge University Press, 2022), 9.

Niels Hemmingsen offers a helpful summation: "Because, therefore, it commands and forbids, it is called 'law,' and because it is implanted in nature, it is called 'natural.'"[40] "Nature" and "natural" are subject to immense debate. For our purposes, "natural" speaks to the reality that the principles are knowable by all—by nature, that is.[41] We need no special insights not available to others to know how to live and thrive. It is important to clarify that "natural" does not mean what naturally occurs. That someone experiences intense lust as a simple fact of their existence does not justify their acting out their sexual desire. Second, "nature" speaks to the concrete existence of things acting toward their proper end. To say that human beings have a nature means they have actions that complete their structure, which allows them to realize their end.

Determining nature can be complex, but a four-fold way of evaluating nature has long been espoused by the natural law tradition:

1. Material Cause—What is X made of?
2. Efficient Cause—Who made X?
3. Formal Cause—What is X?
4. Final Cause—What is X for?

It is by asking these questions that we can understand an object's nature—what its true and ultimate purpose is that informs what actions help complete its nature. Alistair MacIntyre captures the idea of nature well: "Every craft is informed by some conception of a finally perfected work which serves as the shared *telos* of that craft. And what are actually produced as the best judgments or actions or objects so far are judged so because they stand in some determinate relationship to that *telos*, which furnishes them with their final cause."[42] MacIntyre is speaking of something painfully obvious, but important: the display of a thing's excellence.

---

[40] Hemmingsen, *On the Law of Nature*, 29 (see chap. 3, n. 8).

[41] Samuel Gregg, *The Essential Natural Law* (Vancouver: Frasier Institute, 2021), 7.

[42] MacIntyre, *Three Rival Versions of Moral Enquiry*, 64.

To know the thing is living excellently requires that there is a standard from which to measure the excellence. Take marriage. To say that marriage has a "nature" means its existence is completed by those activities or features that comprise it.

Importantly, here we must differentiate between ultimate ends and subordinate ends in determining nature. For example, John Corvino, an LGBT activist from Wayne State University, has a popular video on YouTube where he seeks to dismiss the argument that homosexual sodomy is against nature.[43] Corvino argues that because the mouth can be used for eating, talking, and kissing, it reveals that there are multiple legitimate uses for certain parts of the body, including the rectum. Corvino, however, fails to distinguish between ultimate ends and subordinate ends and actions that run contrary to both. Jonathan Edwards powerfully explains the difference:

> A chief end is opposite to an inferior end; an ultimate end is opposite to a subordinate end. A subordinate end is something that an agent seeks and aims at in what he does; but yet don't seek it, or regard it at all upon its own account, but wholly on the account of a further end, or in order to some other thing which it is considered as a means of. Thus when a man that goes on a journey to obtain a medicine to cure him of some disease, and restore his health, the obtaining that medicine is his subordinate end; because 'tis not an end that he seeks for itself, or values at all upon its own account; but wholly as a means of a further end, viz. his health: separate the medicine from that further end, and it is esteemed good for nothing; nor is it at all desired. An ultimate end is that which the agent seeks in what he does for its own sake; that he has respect to, as what he loves, values and takes pleasure in on its own account, and not merely as a means of a further end: as when a man loves

---

[43] John Corvino "Is Homosexuality Unnatural?" September 18, 2012, YouTube video, 4:13, https://www.youtube.com/watch?v=UlQvf7IVxao.

the taste of some particular sort of fruit, and is at pains and cost to obtain it, for the sake of the pleasure of that taste, which he values upon its own account, as he loves his own pleasure; and not merely for the sake of any other good, which he supposes his enjoying that pleasure will be the means of.[44]

Applying Edwards's argument, the fact that one can forcibly insert one body part into a man's (or woman's) rectum does not mean the use of the body for that end is licit. Placing one's member into a body cavity does not constitute that the purpose of either body parts has been achieved. Yes, the mouth is used to eat and talk but those actions require no thwarting harm done to them in the process. A subordinate end (pleasure) cannot be used to thwart an ultimate end (expelling waste). Corvino's argument makes as much sense as saying that sticking one's index finger in the ear of their partner means the ear can be used for things apart from hearing. It can, but that does not mean the thing is being used according to its ultimate end. Penultimate ends like using the mouth to eat may be legitimate if not used in opposition to its ultimate end (communication). Like an index finger is a foreign object obstructing hearing, so are sodomitical acts against the use of the body as well, which means, to use the apostle Paul's language, such acts are "contrary to nature"—against the created essence for which the thing was created (Rom 1:26).

## Law

Though it certainly underscores our concept of human statutory law, it is important to develop a broader, macro-level understanding of "law." A "law" is any function of reason that directs our behavior toward good ends. It is a standard of measurement by which to evaluate our actions and judgments. Laws exist as ordinances of reason to measure our action against. To

---

[44] Jonathan Edwards, *Works of Jonathan Edwards, Volume 8, Ethical Writings*, ed. Paul Ramsey (New Haven: Yale University Press, 1989), 405.

the extent we follow the moral law and conform ourselves to its dictates, we are flourishing.

To restate Aquinas's famous definition: law is "an ordinance of reason for the common good, made by him who has care of the community, and promulgated."[45] The most important part to dwell on is "ordinance of reason." Reason is what sets humans apart from the rest of creation. Our capacity for deliberation and free choice means humans act on the basis of valid reasons to bring about good ends. We would say that a compelled action is not free action because the person did not choose to do X when they would have preferred Y. Moreover, to hark back to the First Principle of Practical Reason that tells us that humans intuitively pursue what is good and avoid what is evil, a "law" is any authoritative reason for acting that satisfies human fulfillment of the good.

What does this mean, practically speaking? There is no human statute that says I cannot gossip about my friend. But gossip is a form of slander that belittles my friend's character. Gossip is fundamentally unjust because it damages the person's character inflicted by it. So, there is a "law" at play here: As I discern that gossip harms my friend, I recognize that it is wrong and refrain from doing it because it harms my friend's integrity and damages my own as well. It fails to love my neighbor as myself, and is therefore a violation of the order of justice. Refraining from action upon learning of its unsound conclusion is fundamentally directive of one's behavior. *So a law is a measure or standard of right action grasped through right reason to which humanity must conform itself.*[46] Our capacity for reason informs us of whether our actions satisfy the demands of justice.

One would not, for example, be bound to starve themselves by the force of any "law" because starvation is akin to pursuing evil. Starvation is opposed to the good of bodily life so there would be no moral obligation to

---

[45] *ST* I-II, q. 90, a. 4, s. c.

[46] I wish to acknowledge my appreciation for Mark Murphy's essay, "The Natural Law Tradition in Ethics," in *The Stanford Encyclopedia of Philosophy*, 2019, https://plato.stanford.edu/entries/natural-law-ethics/.

starve one's self. Further, a law must aim for the common good rather than private interest, meaning any command that benefits some, and not all, cannot have the force of law by its own definition. If a law truly is an ordinance of reason, it beckons all persons to follow its decrees.

Let's go back to the question of human statutory law. When a speed limit says one must go no further than 70 mph on a highway, the law is commanding your obedience to its precepts. We are right to question: What precept is the law advancing? A speed limit is there to set a standard of speeds to regulate travel for everyone's safety. The law is there for every individual to follow, no exceptions. *self evident*

To vividly capture the binding nature of law, recall Martin Luther King Jr.'s *Letter from a Birmingham Jail*. If you will recall, one of the reasons he gives for breaking the law and going to jail is his belief that laws of racial supremacy enacted in Alabama were fundamentally unjust. They violated the sense of natural justice that comes from the natural law. If a human law violates the natural law, that means it is out of sync with the eternal law. If this is the case, according to King, the law in question does not actually retain the force of true law because its precepts are irrational in that it pursues evil rather than good.

While we will focus next chapter on God's place in natural law, a quote from Philip Melanchthon offers a helpful explanation for what sense "law" is a decreed promulgation issuing from the eternal law:

> The law of God, which is called the moral law, is the eternal and immovable wisdom in God, and the norm of righteousness in the will of God that distinguishes between good and evil. It was revealed to rational creatures in creation, and afterwards was often repeated and ratified by God's voice in the church. It shows what God is, and of what sort, and that he is judge. It binds all rational creatures to be conformed to the norm of God, and condemns all and declares horrible destruction on all who do not adhere to the norm of God, unless reconciliation should be made on account of a mediator, according to what Moses has said [Deut 27:26]:

"Cursed is he who does not abide by all that has been written in the Law."[47]

Melanchthon's definition has much to commend to it. Fundamentally, law is an ordinance of God imparted by the Creator to rational creatures that enable them to discern good and evil according to the Creator's standard of righteousness. Law is coercive to the extent it evaluates our actions and commands our obedience to it according to norms of justice and human nature.

## Conclusion

I began this chapter by quoting Aquinas's definition of law as "an ordinance of reason for the common good, made by him who has care of the community, and promulgated." This definition aligns with what I have tried to accomplish in this chapter; that is, to begin our discussion by highlighting that the natural law is promulgated or ordered by a universal sovereign (God) because God has rightful care of the universe he has created. In God's sovereign ordering of the natural law, he made us agents capable of grasping the natural law through our capacity of reason. These two pillars of the natural law thus satisfy how we think about the natural law's origins and its knowability. In the next chapter, we turn to the content and utility of the natural law.

---

47 E. J. Hutchinson, "What Is the Law of God?" *Ad Fontes*, November 8, 2021, https://adfontesjournal.com/ej-hutchinson/what-is-the-law-of-god/.

# 6.

# Philosophical Foundations for the Natural Law, Part 2

## Content and Utility

Eliud Kipchoge is the best runner in history. As of this writing, he's still competing. In 2019, he set an unofficial world record in the marathon by running it in 1:59:40. As a runner myself, I can only say that such a feat seems other-worldly. The event he ran that time in was designed and optimized for him to break the two-hour barrier on the marathon. Running with perfect conditions and a team of pacers in front of him, watching him run is like watching a machine glide through an action with perfect ease. From his cadence to his posture, Kipchoge's form, combined with native physiological gifting, makes him unlike anything else the world has ever seen.

In the 2019 competition, with just under four hundred meters to go and well under the pace necessary to break the record, Kipchoge motioned for his pacers to step aside so he could finish the race on his own. You can find the video on YouTube today. Watching Kipchoge finish the last part

of the race with a roaring crowd cheering him on and his joyful countenance aware that he was about to break the record is nothing short of awe-
inspiring. I distinctly recall staying up super late so I would watch the race
live from Austria. In those last few meters, tears began to stream down my
face at what I was witnessing. Why on earth was I crying?

Consider another story.

In 2015, *Vanity Fair* ran a long-form essay on the rise of Tinder's use
among New York's City's upwardly mobile denizens.[1] The essay spun off no
small amount of public commentary on how the rise of such apps as Tinder
were making the availability of sex easier than ever to obtain. The reason
for the public commentary about the article itself, though, wasn't the fact
that people were celebrating even greater access to sex. Quite the opposite,
in fact. The public was shocked by what users of the app were disclosing
about the state of their lives to a journalist: utter misery. Here were twenty-
somethings in one of the world's most glamorous cities with access to the
very thing that our culture tells young people they ought to have: unencumbered sexual autonomy.

The problem is that sexual autonomy did not bring about the liberation
and ecstasy it promised. The women felt used, objectified, and dejected.
The men, ever prone to find as many partners as are willing, are portrayed
as ravenous conquerors with sexual appetites unable to be controlled. They
are unwilling to commit to a single partner, instead looking for their next
sexual escapade as soon as the previous one could be walked away from. The
article was a walking advertisement for the virtues of chastity and marriage.

One last episode is worth considering. A trend across the global West is
the expanding regime of euthanasia, physician-assisted suicide, or what is also
called "Medical Assistance in Dying" (MAiD). A common trend among all
the countries that have begun to implement euthanasia is the ever-expanding eligibility criteria permitting its use. What began as a "treatment" for

---

[1] Nancy Jo Sales, "Tinder and the Dawn of the Dating Apocalypse," *Vanity
Fair*, August 6, 2015, https://www.vanityfair.com/culture/2015/08/tinder-hook-up
-culture-end-of-dating.

terminal conditions has metastasized into justifying suicide for alcoholism, sexual trauma, and depression. Younger populations are now accessing it. In 2022, a physician in Canada testified before Canadian law-makers that severely disabled infants should be able to access physician-assisted suicide.[2]

Why do I recount the episodes above involving athleticism, sexual disarray, and euthanasia? Because each, in their own way, reflect the presence, abuse, or negation of a moral good that the natural law exists to help us understand and live faithfully in response to as befits our nature.

When one considers the athletic display put on by Kipchoge, one sees the beauty of both skillful excellence and aesthetic wonderment at the joy of seeing human fitness at its highest potential. The fact that something as seemingly routine as watching someone run can evoke tears speaks to the inherent goodness of watching human excellence in peak condition display itself with glory and wonderment.

Looking at the episode of young New Yorkers engorging themselves with sexual freedom and experiencing sadness and cheapened self-debasement is a reminder that even heterosexuality, to say nothing of homosexuality, is rife with abuse all on its own. What we observe in this tragedy are the intoxicating seductions that come with believing that the use of one's body in a sex act has no moral content it, that sex can be stripped from marriage with the belief of few to no attendant consequences. We are seeing in very real time just how morally freighted sexual acts really are. When society sends the signal that sexuality is divorced from marriage and family life, all we're left with is the pottage and destruction that come from creating situations where children get abandoned and aborted and where women are treated as though their bodies exist for someone else's gratification.

Lastly, euthanasia is the result of a worldview that places human dignity on a sliding scale of worth. The preciousness of life is compromised and the absolute principle of "Do No Harm" is jeopardized once we license

---

[2] Michael Cook, "Quebec Doctors Back Euthanasia for Newborns," *BioEdge* (blog), October 12, 2022, https://bioedge.org/end-of-life-issues/euthanasia/quebec-doctors-back-euthanasia-for-newborns/.

into public policy the permissibility of killing for some end other than self-defense. Whether abortion or euthanasia, both spring from devaluing the intrinsic worthiness of life and treat it as discardable and subject to human passion.

Beauty, marriage and family, and life. Each of these tenets of the natural law are their own good to be enjoyed, respected, and protected in their own right and in their own proper context. They are not an exhaustive list of moral goods, of course, but examples for us to reflect on about the nature of basic moral goods. In this chapter, we will (1) examine the content of the natural law, focusing on the rules and norms for moral action and identity; (2) reflect on the existence of moral goods; and (3) reflect on the purposes for why the natural law is to be utilized.

## The Content of the Natural Law: Rules, Norms, and Principles for Moral Action

While natural law is a theory of moral origins rooted in God's nature, it is also a theory of moral action. Regarding the natural law as a theory of moral action, Baptist theologian Albert Mohler states that, as a theory, it teaches, "Everyone knows enough to know a very great deal about how human beings are to act, who human beings are by nature, what God's purpose is for human beings. There are certain [moral] 'oughts' that are just so universally known that every civilization in its own way has found its way to that ought without the necessity of anything beyond nature."[3] One of the unsung elements of the natural law that often gets overlooked is its attention to practical matters, not just theoretical abstraction. The tenets of the natural law are meant to be known, obeyed, and experienced.

Thus far in our discussion, we have been focusing our attention on the conceptual foundation of the natural law as a theory. As we have established, natural law is, at root, little else than reason's deliberations on identifying

---

[3] Mohler, Jr., *The Briefing* (see chap. 3, n. 22).

the range of activities and goods that fulfill us as persons. That is how natural law is determined—by reflecting on moral obligations for rational agents. The capacity to reason enables individuals to understand and act to promote and protect their own and others' well-being. We've discussed where the natural law comes from (God) and how we know it (reason). We are left to specify what it is concerning its contours and prescriptions; that is, its content. Often, when discussions of the natural law arise, rarely are the actual contents of the natural law explicated. This is partly because natural law refers to a self-evident order more than it does a highly distilled set of actual laws and rules. Nonetheless, we come to know the natural law by two main operations that stem from our practical deliberation: (1) Self-evident primary principles known in themselves; and (2) secondary principles derived from primary principles. For example: (1) Life is a good to pursue and protect; and (2) Do not murder. What the natural law directs us to understand, in a general way that becomes more specific in each area of application, is how a morally good act is one that brings about good and a morally evil act is one that which robs deprives, abuses, thwarts or negates good.[4] One should never knowingly act against the obtaining of the good.

Germain Grisez, one of the most significant theorists of the natural law in the twentieth century postulated what he called the "First Principle of Morality," which states the following: "In voluntarily acting for human goods and avoiding what is opposed to them, one ought to choose and otherwise will those and only those possibilities whose willing is compatible with a will toward integral human fulfillment."[5]

What Grisez means is that any action that intentionally wills harm or intentionally thwarts or disrupts well-being is not only immoral action but irrational because it works against our obtaining the goods constitutive of

---

[4] Patrick Lee, "God and New Natural Law Theory," *The National Catholic Bioethics Quarterly* 19, no. 2 (Summer 2019): 279.

[5] John M. Finnis, Germain G. Grisez, and Joseph Boyle, "Practical Principles, Moral Truth, and Ultimate Ends," *The American Journal of Jurisprudence* 32, no. 1 (1987): 128.

our flourishing. A moral action is an action that wills the good. For example, one should not will—or bring about—the murder of another human being because murder robs someone of their life, which is a good in and of itself. To say there are morally bad acts implies that acts occur which are contrary to a nature that truly exists. As Aquinas notes, "There must be definite kinds of operations which are appropriate to a definite nature, whenever things have such a definite nature. In fact, the operation appropriate to a given being is a consequent of that nature. Now, it is obvious that there is a determinate kind of nature for man. Therefore, there must be some operations that are in themselves appropriate for man."[6] What Aquinas means to communicate is that human action should act commensurately with whatever aligns with or fulfills its nature. As murder is the negation of life and life is a good worthy for its own sake, we discover that we should not murder.

Well-being in natural law theory is discussed in terms of obtaining basic goods that we grasp by reflecting on the data of everyday experience. According to Robert P. George, the natural law tends toward the view that "practical knowledge (i.e., knowledge of human goods and moral norms and the reasons they provide) is a *source* of our knowledge of human nature."[7] As reason reflects on experience, it should, ideally, direct toward the goods "appropriate" to our inclinations.[8] Moral goods are the sources of that practical knowledge we come to reflect upon. Proper moral action is willed action to achieve human flourishing. Human flourishing is thus directive and prescriptive in that it is action-guiding and action-explaining. As we understand what our nature is, we come to understand how we ought to act and why the action in question completes us. According to George,

---

[6] Thomas Aquinas, *Summa Contra Gentiles*, trans. Vernon J. Bourke (Notre Dame, IN: University of Notre Dame Press, 1975), 3.129.

[7] Robert P. George, "Natural Law Ethics," in *Companion to Philosophy of Religion*, ed. Philip L. Quinn and Charles Taliaferro (Malden, MA: Wiley-Blackwell, 1999), 462.

[8] Grisez, "The First Principle of Practical Reason: A Commentary on the Summa Theologiae, 1-2, Question 94, Article 2," 180.

An entity's nature is understood by understanding its potentialities or capacities; these are in turn understood by understanding its activities and performances; and these finally are understood by understanding the *objects* of its acts or performances. Human nature, then, is known by understanding the objects of human acts; and these are the basic human goods which, by providing non-instrumental reasons, give human acts their intelligible point.[9]

We act only in regard to the conditions that enable flourishing. To flourish, in other words, we must know what it means to flourish and what actions make obtaining it possible. Human flourishing both explains what we do and why we do it. Practical reason is the means by which we grasp these conditions. This is where our concept of "human nature" is grasped. As John Finnis writes, "Epistemologically, (knowledge of) human nature is not 'the basis of ethics'; rather, ethics is an indispensable preliminary to a full and soundly based knowledge of human nature."[10] Of course, we should insist from the vantage point of a Christian view of reality that all of these realities are the consequence of divine ordering. Even if we believe the natural law functions as an intelligible ethical system, we should always understand that the natural law, ultimately, springs from our understanding of Christian reality.[11] Robert P. George writes elsewhere on why practical reason factors so centrally in our understanding of moral goods that comprise human nature:

> In the ontological mode of inquiry, an account of human goods will refer back to human nature: "Why are these the ends fulfilling of human beings?" "Because human nature is constituted as it is." But this answer in no way entails that our knowledge of the ends

---

[9] George, 463.

[10] John Finnis, *Fundamentals of Ethics* (Washington, DC: Georgetown University Press, 1983), 21.

[11] Rufus Black, "Is the New Natural Law Theory Christian?," in *The Revival of Natural Law: Philosophical, Theological and Ethical Responses to the Finnis-Grisez School*, ed. Rufus Black and Nigel Biggar (Burlington, VT: Ashgate, 2001), 158.

as human fulfillments is derived from prior speculative knowledge of human nature.[12]

When humans act in ways that benefit themselves and their political community, moral norms of justice are established. That's really what natural law principles are—principles of justice that allow human beings to mature into the types of beings that they are. The natural law tradition refers to proper action as "modes of responsibility," which include the Golden Rule (Matt 7:12) and the Pauline Principle of rejecting the idea that evil can be done in service to good (Rom 3:8).[13] Another mode of responsibility, "Human Integral Fulfillment," means acting to pursue all goods in harmony. All rightly ordered action is intelligible and justified by its directiveness to individual goods and common goods. A law that prevents murder, for example, is protecting the good of life while also creating a norm that all of society must abide by if the political community is to flourish.

What are these goods that are said to cause our flourishing or fulfill or complete us? First, it is to establish what a "good" is in the first place. According to David Haines and Andrew Fulford, "The general notion of good, then, is that the good is that which each thing desires for itself (and not for something else), and that end toward which each thing directs itself

---

[12] Robert P. George, "Natural Law and Human Nature," in *Natural Law Theory: Contemporary Essays*, ed. Robert P. George (Oxford: Oxford University Press, 1992), 34. For a contrary approach that relies on speculative reason and teleology, see Steven J. Jensen, *Knowing the Natural Law: From Precepts and Inclinations to Deriving Oughts* (Washington, DC: Catholic University of America Press, 2015). The careful reader will observe that I think the so-called divide between "New" Natural Law and "Classical" Natural Law poses false dichotomies because their approaches begin from different starting points even though their end points are the same.

[13] For more on the modes of responsibility, see Germain Grisez, "A Contemporary Natural Law Ethics," in *Moral Philosophy: Historical and Contemporary Essays*, ed. William C. Starr and Richard C. Taylor (Milwaukee: Marquette University Press, 1989), 131–36.

according to its nature. The end of each being is, therefore, its good, and each being is good in the measure that it obtains its good—that is, its end."[14] Similarly, Edward Feser comments that:

> Practical reason is directed by nature towards the pursuit of what the intellect perceives as good; what is in fact good is the realization or fulfillment of the various ends inherent in human nature; and thus a rational person will perceive this and, accordingly, direct his or her actions towards the realization or fulfillment of those ends. In this sense, good action is just that which is "in accord with reason" (ST I-II.21.1; cf. ST I-II.90.1), and the moral skeptic's question "Why should I do what is good?" has an obvious answer: because to be rational just is (in part) to do what is good, to fulfill the ends set for us by nature.[15]

A good is any intelligible end that a person directs himself or herself to in pursuit of their flourishing as rational beings. But moral goods are ends pursued *for their own sake*, meaning one does not pursue them as a means to some higher or greater good. They are "basic" in that they are self-evident and "nothing more fundamental" than the good itself is at stake.[16] These are the grounds for our reasons for action. A good means we can derive no greater fulfillment out of the good than the experience of the good itself. Called "non-instrumental," a moral good is a good unto itself. We will elaborate on the content of these goods in later chapters, but here is a list to begin our consideration:

- Life—One acts to preserve their life and well-being. Something as simple as taking vitamins or getting regular sleep serves the end of health, which inexorably contributes to the totality of health. In

---

[14] David Haines and Andrew A. Fulford, *Natural Law: A Brief Introduction and Biblical Defense* (Lincoln, NE: Davenant, 2017), 35.

[15] Edward Feser, *Aquinas: A Beginner's Guide* (London: Oneworld, 2009), 184–85.

[16] George, "Natural Law and Human Nature," 34.

general, the moral good of life means we respect life's existence and take no unlawful or unethical action to harm it.

- Family life—Cultivating family life founded on and centered around the conjugal union of husband and wife. It is from their union that family life takes shape. Here, we understand that mere heterosexuality is not its own good (though that constitutes rightly ordered sexual desire), but heterosexuality in service to the proper *telos* of its end, which is marriage.

- Friendship (sociability)—As social beings, human beings enjoy companionship with like-minded persons for the sole purpose of community, sharing one's life, and enjoying each other's company.

- Knowledge—Learning and engaging in intellectually-stimulating activities are worthwhile endeavors done for their own sake. When a person reads, for example, they are gaining knowledge or appreciation for something their mind understands as beneficial.

- Aesthetic appreciation (beauty)—Beauty inspires persons to engage in a range of activities that drive them to pursue it (e.g., painting, listening to music, visiting the Grand Canyon).

- Practical reasonableness—A person should use their intellectual faculties in the right way to make possible the realization of other basic goods. Someone being "in their right mind" is a moral good.

- Integrity—A person should pursue internal and external harmony in one's motives and actions in contrast to hypocrisy, inner fragmentation, and illicit motive.

- Religion—Knowing and contemplating God and aligning oneself with God's plan is always good and architectonic in shaping the values and ethics of persons.

- Play—Rest, leisure, and skillful activity are to be pursued for their own sake (e.g., running a marathon, watching a skillful athlete perform).

Scholars within the natural law tradition differ on the full-range of what defines a good. For example, scholars like Mark C. Murphy develop a similar list: life, knowledge, aesthetic experience, excellence in play and

work, excellence in agency, inner peace, friendship and community, religion, and happiness.[17] A scholar like the deceased Alfonso Gómez-Lobo
include in their list of basic goods: life, family, friendship, work and play,
the experience of beauty, knowledge, theoretical knowledge, integrity,
religion.[18] What's less important in this discussion is identifying a number of moral goods that provide sufficient reason for action than it is to
understand that whatever is pursued for its own sake qualifies as a potential good.

Again, these goods are said to be "non-instrumental." Non-instrumental
goods are pursued for their own sake and for no other reason than the choiceworthiness of meriting or striving for their own obtainment. Understanding
a moral good is deeply significant for explaining the range of activities that
we do. In choosing to attend a concert, we learn that the underlying motive
for spending a high figure on a concert ticket and battling boisterous crowds
is that we believe we will receive a benefit from which no greater benefit is
derived or explained. We attend a concert, for example, just because concert
attendance conduces to an aesthetic good pursued for its sake. Moral goods
are thus explanatory for the reasons we pursue all rightly ordered and rationally motivated activity.

Contrast this with what are known as "instrumental goods." Money
and pleasure, for example, are only instrumental goods. They are pursued because they facilitate some greater end than just themselves. Money
is meant to provide for one's livelihood. Pleasure is meant to facilitate
the spousal love of husband and wife within the context of marriage.
But money sought for its own sake produces greed. The accumulation of
wealth has no intrinsic good in itself. The use of wealth is always determined by the ends for how one's wealth is used. Pleasure sought for its
own sake is the cause for no small amount of society's descent into sexual
anarchy. When instrumental goods function as non-instrumental goods as

---

[17] Murphy, *Natural Law and Practical Rationality*, 96–138 (see chap. 3, n. 6).
[18] Alfonso Gómez-Lobo, *Morality and the Human Goods* (Washington, DC:
Georgetown University Press, 2002), 6–25.

the primary reason for action, the occasion for disordering abuse or misuse of a thing follows. Failing to acknowledge a true and final end of a thing or activity or ascribing a final end to that which is not owed it, ensures the misuse of a thing toward an end it cannot sufficiently serve. One recalls, for example, that it is the inordinate love of money that Scripture warns against, not money itself (1 Tim 6:10). This principle speaks to how the use of instrumental goods as non-instrumental goods in themselves cause a moral misfire.

It is from this list of goods that we derive our sense of the moral goods we ought always to pursue and never act to violate or thwart. Natural law theorists debate the full range of goods. What's less important is enumerating an exhaustive list of goods than identifying what goods we pursue whose intelligibility as a grounds for action depends on no further reason for its choiceworthiness.[19] It is the knowledge and realization of these goods that provide the basic reasons for all rationally motivated action. "Only those ends or purposes that are intrinsically worthwhile," writes Robert P. George, "provide basic reasons for action."[20]

## *The Norming Activity of the Natural Law*

The list of "goods" above provides reasons for action that assume the availability and recognition of norms enabling their fulfillment. Norms are nothing else but laws for action undertaken to safeguard and procure moral goods. "Norms" are prescriptive and authoritative claims of moral obligation, not simply preference or suggestion.

The question arises as to whether the norms can be distilled into axiomatic laws. I believe they can and, for the sake of clarity, must. Though my list of norms defining the directiveness of natural law toward fulfilling the good

---

[19] I am indebted to Robert P. George for this insight given to me in personal correspondence.

[20] Robert P. George, *Making Men Moral: Civil Liberties and Public Morality* (Oxford: Oxford University Press, 1993), 11.

is by no means intended to be exhaustive, below is a codified list of natural law norms. The first four are borrowed from J. Budziszewski.[21]

- Law of Consequence: Violations of the moral law result in negative consequences that ought to reform our behavior. Moral violations teach us what conduct is needed to not repeat our error.

- Law of Conscience: The law of conscience refers to the inner pangs of the mind knowing it has violated the moral law, known as *synderesis. Synderesis* speaks to the existence of the moral law itself and the conscience alerts the individual of their violating synderesis.

- Law of Human Design: From the procreative complementarity of male and female bodies to the need for social cooperation, humans tend toward the propagation and furtherance of their species.

- Law of Creational Design: That the world exhibits physical design as well as moral design tells us that the design is the product of a masterful Designer, God. God is the uncaused cause of all design as such.

- Law of Natural Duties: Humans tend to extend higher levels of devotion and duty the closer one is related to another.

- Law of Beneficence: Acting benevolently for the sake of others is universally lauded as virtuous since promoting the good of others promotes the good of all.

- Law of Justice: A principle of reciprocity, we are to give others what they are due.

- Law of Non-Contradiction: All intelligible propositions cannot be self-refuting.

- Law of Self-Preservation: Moral agents act to preserve their lives.

- Law of Honor: Showing honor to whom honor is due is recognizable universally.

---

[21] For extended analysis on these first four categories, see chapters 4 and 5 of J. Budziszewski, *What We Can't Not Know: A Guide* (Dallas: Spence, 2004).

- Law of Worship: Individuals self-direct and organize themselves (and even their communities) around some concept of ultimate reality.

That different scholars would find similar patterns to organize human conduct by speaks to the existence and universality of the natural law. The natural law is meant to be totalizing in that it provides an account for why humans act the way we do (descriptive), the way we ought (normative), and why moral inclinations exist in the first place (ontological). Budziszewski offers a helpful summary in understanding the comprehensiveness of natural law theory: "the authority of the natural law has been found in the Creator, its content in the design He imparted to us, and the power by which we recognize it in the faculty of reason."[22]

## Natural Law and the Naturalistic Fallacy

One of the most frequent criticisms against the natural law is that it is impossible to derive an "ought" from an "is." Or, alternately categorized as the "fact-value" dichotomy. So, the criticism might go: There is no way to say that intercourse between a husband and wife is any more morally superior than sexual conduct between two men. According to this line of criticism against the natural law, the fact of same-sex attraction does not tell us any moral wrong or moral right issuing from it. Facts of nature, in other words, do not contain moral instruction or moral impetus. Surmising a value from the fact of a thing or natural occurrence of a thing is thus rendered impossible.

Does the natural law fall apart at this criticism? By no means. It should be acknowledged, though, that if one is a committed philosophical naturalist, there is no objective moral content to anything, so natural law (alongside giving any care to the is-ought fallacy) is simply a discardable theory, as all others are as well. Morality would be little else than a tragic comedy where one encounters the world with the gusto of nihilism. But according

---

[22] Budziszewski, 107.

to J. Budziszewski, where the natural law is understood as God-ordered, the criticism retains less punch: "An 'is' which merely 'happens to be' has no moral significance because it is arbitrary; that is why it cannot imply an 'ought.' But an 'is' which expresses the purpose of the Creator is fraught with an 'ought' already. Such are the inbuilt features of our design, including the design of deep conscience."[23] Budziszewski's argument is that, because of the eternal law's organization of the natural law, "is" statements or "is" realities are infused with divine causation and divine coordination directing the person or inclination to a proper end. If it does, it means that facts of nature have self-directing ends built into them by a Creator, which means we cannot, as Christians, separate *ought* from *is* because *is* has *oughtness* built into it by a wise Creator. Natural law denies that nature or actions are valueless and arbitrary. As I wrote above, the natural law tradition does not argue from an "ought," but rather assumes it. It assumes it because without it, there can be no foundation to morality otherwise. Divorced from teleology, morality reduces to a species of either speculation, nihilism, or emotivism. Either morality is divinely charged or else, at best, morality is a brute fact with no *real* obligation intrinsic to it.

Furthermore, the very terms of "natural" and "law" satisfy, or at least address, the objection of the "is-ought" and "fact-values" dilemma in their own usage. "Natural" connotes just what *is* by virtue of there being a presupposed "is" to the structure of the universe. "Law" connotes goal-directedness in its own term. "Natural" thus corresponds to "is" or "fact" and "law" corresponds to "ought" and "value" by virtue of goal-directness inhering within the natural order itself. The description of nature-as-it-is joined to the prescription of what-is-to-be only makes sense in a worldview where intelligent design is presupposed.[24] Of course, this may not satisfy the moral skeptic. But it should not go unnoticed that the moral skeptic has no grounds upon which to make compelling counterclaims, since, according to

---

[23] Budziszewski, 108.

[24] I am indebted to my Ethics and Public Policy Colleague Brad Littlejohn for making this very helpful observation.

their own philosophically naturalist worldview, all forms of obligation are either arbitrary, brute, or illusory.

Natural law, as I argue, does not deny the ontological existence of "nature" as secular approaches do, but instead argues that *knowledge* of nature is derived preeminently through practical reason's grasp of basic moral goods, not primarily speculative reason's grasp of "nature" as an abstraction. Nature is grasped as a secondary reality stemming from the antecedent use of reason. There is no prior concept of human nature apart from determining what goods—and the norms to achieve those goods—comprise human nature. Though God orders all that exists, our chain of reasoning means that our knowledge of right and wrong through practical reason comes prior to our speculative knowledge about the universe and its origins. We may rightly assume God as the authorizing intelligence behind reason, but that reality is expressed through reason's operation. Of course, it should be acknowledged that even one's grasp of practical principles about what constitutes human nature assumes reflection about what practical reason is in itself—namely, it is an intelligible operation whose function we can rely upon. As Rufus Black rightly notes, "the nature of practical reason will still be dependent upon a person's theoretical conception of human nature and the conditions for human life."[25] Thus, "nature" comes pre-programmed by a God who orders nature, but nature is grasped through sapiential investigation in one's interactions with the world.

### Natural Law Misfiring?

One of the primary objections to the natural law is that sin's impact on human cognition makes knowledge of the natural law more difficult. While I will address this question in greater details in a later chapter dealing with theological objections to natural law, the question needs addressed philosophically.

---

[25] Black, "Is the New Natural Law Theory Christian?," 158.

Immorality occurs all around us. If we *know* the natural law as the natural law purports, why is our world so rife with sin and injustice? Why are supposedly self-evident truths not self-evident to some? Why is there abortion and sex trafficking? How can gratuitous evil occur if we know we should only act to pursue good? Why do some people seem to appear evil then? Putting it at its most basic, we might ask: If the natural law is true, how could unspeakable evil like the Holocaust ever have occurred? Would not Nazis know that what they were doing was wrong?

There are several explanations. No proponent of the natural law has ever argued that the existence of the natural law entails either exhaustive knowledge of its full entailments or its perfect obedience. That people err in mathematical calculation does not vitiate mathematics as an intelligible discipline. But the beauty of the natural law is that even by violating it, we are held accountable to it. There are certain truths we cannot deny, though; for example, that every agent is to pursue what they perceive as an apparent good and avoid what they perceive as an evil, even if they are mistaken in their grasp of both. Thomas Aquinas argued that there is a multitude of reasons for why someone would disobey the natural law: "[T]he natural law can be blotted out from the human heart, either by evil persuasions, just as in speculative matters errors occur in respect of necessary conclusions; or by vicious customs and corrupt habits, as among some men, theft, and even unnatural vices . . ."[26] Here, Aquinas hints at the possibility of corrupting behavior, true evil, and error in the application of the natural law as explanations for why evil and sin exist.

There are several responses and qualifications needed to understand why the natural law is disobeyed. Budziszewski has introduced the helpful category of guilty feelings versus guilty knowledge.[27] This bears resemblance to what Scripture teaches as possessing a seared conscience (1 Tim 4:2). The idea behind this distinction is that one could possess knowledge of their actions violating the natural law, but lacking remorse in doing so. And the

---

[26] *ST* I-II, q. 94, a. 6, co.
[27] Budziszewski, *What We Can't Not Know*, 87 (see chap. 6, n. 21).

fact that one could know it is wrong to lack remorse for committing an evil act is a witness of the abiding function of conscience. Individuals can also engage in acts of self-deception where they deny what they do know in order to justify whatever it is they want to do. Others can also be so irrationally committed to a cause or conviction that no amount of reason will work to dissuade them from something they are presuppositionally endeared to.

Individuals can also be self-deceived into justifying or rationalizing what they know is wrong for the sake of some supposed good. A thief might steal a wallet under the guise that having more money—even if gained by theft— is beneficial for them, thus serving some "good" in their mind. Though a person who steals to gain money to feed their family is violating justice and truthfulness, that person believes their action of stealing is still bringing about a good, namely, feeding their family. Even in the act of theft, there is an understandable and good aim at the end—avoiding starvation and caring for one's family.

Others can misapply the natural law. Take "same-sex marriage." Even proponents of same-sex marriage extol the good of marriage as do traditional proponents. Revisionists do not dispute that marriage exists. Advocates for same-sex marriage wish merely to expand the pool of individuals eligible to enter marriage, namely, same-sex couples. Now, as I will argue later, this teaching is erroneous in that it is irrational and in violation of Scripture. But the debate around marriage's definition centers on its definition, not its existence. Or take abortion. The debate over abortion in America is *not*, primarily, that murder is a positive good. Rare and extreme are voices who are arguing for the positive moral good of killing unborn children. Christians rightly believe that abortion *is* murder, but proponents of abortion do not believe that it is. Rather, the debate over abortion in America is whether the  unborn child is a *person* deserving of equal legal protection as that of the mother's bodily autonomy.

I also affirm the possibility that humanity's wickedness and depravity would lead them to desire evil for evil's sake. So a moral agent could either be confused in their sin or willfully choose to do what they know is sin because of the volitional impact of sin on the will and reason. An evil person could pursue evil for the sake of evil, but this we would understand to be the extreme minority of cases as might be indicative of sociopaths. Still, even a sociopath may want to be treated kindly if being waited on at a restaurant. All this shows is that blotting out all remnants of morality is impossible.

The apostle Paul does talk of individuals "suppressing" the conscience, which leads to the unreliability and searing of it. Even a seared conscience, however, would still be acting for an end, even if wrongly perceived. A crazed serial killer, despite their homicidal madness, would still desire to be treated with respect, I assume. So the Golden Rule would still be in effect. Or, the serial killer would understand that theft is wrong too. Absent from the historical record is anyone so evil and vicious that he or she did not possess even an iota of moral knowledge. Despite sin, and despite the fact that humanity is evil, that does not elide the reality that humans still have a moral law, of some degree, written on the heart that is not fully extinguished because of their sinful estate. To emphasize this point, the most gruesome and morbid serial killer in American history, Jeffrey Dahmer (after a purported conversion to Christianity in prison) exhibited knowledge of the moral law: "If a person doesn't think that there is a God to be accountable to, then what's the point of trying to modify your behavior to keep it within acceptable ranges?" Dahmer went on in the same interview to explain his murderous rampages as indebted to an evolutionary account of the universe.[28]

But let's take one of the worst instances of evil we can think of—the Holocaust. How could German military officers oversee the execution of millions of men, women, and children? There are several answers to this question: first, cowardice. Individuals could have been following orders that they knew were wrong, but simply refused to resist for fear of

---

[28] Jeffrey Dahmer interview with Stone Phillips, *Dateline NBC*, February 1994.

endangering themselves. Many German officials insisted they were obeying lawfully passed legislation that must be followed as ordered. This relates to another condition called groupthink where individuals simply go along with herd morality. Secondly, it is no doubt the case that certain members of the Nazi regime actually believed they were carrying out a positive good by ridding the world of Jews. That brings us back to the idea that all agents act for ends irrespective of whether the end in question is actually good or not. Nazis wishing to rid the world of Jews believed they were doing the world an actual favor. Of course, this is unspeakably heinous, but it does explain how some could justify or rationalize their behavior, especially if they were convinced that Jews were guilty of such behavior that merited extinction. What is also relevant to this discussion is the inconsistent application of the natural law. Herman Göring, one of Hitler's top lieutenants known for his cruelty, in biographical accounts, was also known as a doting father to his daughter. That raises the question: What could bring a man who knew to love his *own* daughter with fatherly affection to also oversee barbaric evil? Doubtlessly, individuals do pursue evil for evil's sake. But they also act irrationally by their willingness to extend principles of fair, equitable treatment to some that they turn around and deny to others. According to Aquinas, "a rational creature chooses evil because it perversely judges it to fall under the category of the good." That's what true perversion means: a misapprehension of what the true good is such that one desires the moribund.[29]

The natural law tradition has never argued that individuals all share a comprehensive knowledge of the moral law. There are some moral principles that cannot be blotted out entirely (among them the First Principle

___

[29] *De Malo*, q. 3, a. 9, ad. 4. Quoted in Peterson, *C.S. Lewis and the Christian Worldview*, 24 (see chap. 2, n. 10). The above quote from Aquinas is a translation from Michael Peterson. The Clarendon Press edition states, "But sin is not in the will insofar as the will's object is a true good. Therefore, every sin is in the will insofar as the will's object is an apparent and not a real good." Thomas Aquinas, *On Evil*, ed. Brian Davies, trans. Richard Regan, 1st edition (Oxford: Oxford University Press, 2003), 168.

of Practical Reason) even if applied erringly, inconsistently, or evilly. Every agent is *necessarily* acting for an end. The question is whether the end in sight is a true good or furthers a true good.

## The Utility of the Natural Law

Thus far, I have left unexplained the catalogue of reasons I think Protestants should retrieve the natural law. As I explained in a previous chapter, one of the major reasons Protestants have rejected the natural law is its inability to persuade non-Christians about the tenets of our ethical convictions. As I have been at pains to make clear, I wish to dispose once and for all the idea that natural law is primarily of value for its apologetical power. To give outsized focus on apologetics and persuasion would mean overlooking how most of Christian history has understood natural law and natural law theory. At its foundation, Christianity has valued natural law for the simple fact of it giving explanation to the world's affairs and our place as rational creatures within it. Below are reasons why I think natural law deserves a larger role in Protestant ethics.

### *Common Moral Grammar*

Christians are rational creatures just like their unbelieving neighbors, meaning that we share common experiences, common longings, common reactions, and common emotions (albeit with different explanations and understandings around each). We may not share a commonality as to the foundation of that knowledge, but the knowledge is nonetheless real. To love our neighbor, Christians must be able to empathize with their unbelieving neighbors and friends. When tragedy or injustice strikes, the natural law provides a common moral grammar for relating to one another. When seeking to influence society for the good, Christians must be able to couch their arguments in ways that non-Christians can understand. Natural law offers this. It is a moral signpost that allows us to take the natural intuitions and inclinations common to humankind and redirects them to questions of eternal origin and eternal destiny.

## Rational Articulation of Moral Norms

Connected to the category above, Christians must be able to explain why our ethical convictions not only align with Scripture, but why they are rationally valid to begin with. If abortion is indeed a grave moral wrong, we should be able to explain why abortion is wrong without immediately adverting to Scripture. This once again harks us back to an earlier chapter about how we understand the relationship between faith and reason: they can never be in conflict. Rather, the knowledge of one helps us better understand the other. Reason can deepen faith while faith can give explanation to reason's deepest inquiries. Natural law is thus catechetical in helping Christians understand the integrity of their ethics.

## Exposing Error

One of the values of natural law is its usefulness to explain the shortcomings or irrationalities of secular beliefs. As just one example, take abortion: On what rational basis does it make sense to assign personhood and legal protection on the basis of whether the child has passed through the birthing canal? Reason can be a powerful tool to expose erroneous thinking. In the same vein, natural law is a useful device to expose the shallow foundations for secular morality in general. Honest atheists will admit that their view of the universe has no inherent meaning. While intellectual honesty may be commendable, atheists have a bad track record of living consistently with atheism's tenets.

## Ubiquity

One of the reasons Christians should have greater facility with the natural law is that, understood properly, natural law is all around us. From obeying traffic signals to caring for our children, we do all of these activities on the basis of their helping us to live a well-ordered life. One evening my family went to have dinner at a restaurant. The restaurant was a pro-military BBQ restaurant that often showcases famous quotes from soldiers. One quote from General Norman Schwarzkopf read: "The truth of the matter is that you always know the right thing to do. The hard part is doing it." Whether this famous military figure was aware of it, his statement captured the underived nature of self-evident truth claims.

## Designedness for Joy

If natural law really is true, it is the pathway that offers individuals and cultures the availability of common grace. From family life, to leisure, to beauty, to the notion of public justice, the natural law offers a rationale for the fulfilling ways that God has ordered our existence for our good. At a bare minimum, the natural law allows us to assert that apart from obeying its precepts, human beings will never reach their optimal flourishing.

## Concern for the Common Good and Human Flourishing

The natural law necessarily draws us as believers into contending for the patterns of living that cause individuals and societies to flourish. To fight against an injustice, we need to know why, at its ultimate depths, the action or event in question is truly wrong. Sex trafficking, for example, is wrong on at least two major horizons. One, it dishonors God as the sovereign Creator of persons who bear his image and reflect his design for sexuality. Secondly, to force an individual into labor against their will and abusing them sexually is a fundamental denial of justice, robbing persons of their agency and, in turn, their dignity. The call of the natural law is the call to loving one's neighbor with a commitment to public justice. Unless government acknowledges at least some foundational truths of the natural law, society will devolve into moral anarchy.

## *Persuasion*

At the end of the list is persuasion. Placing it here was very intentional. I've done so to demonstrate that natural law is relevant for a whole host of reasons apart from persuasion. We do not utilize the natural law only because we are trying to seek to persuade others (though we certainly do not avoid appealing to it, either), but because as the prior categories explained, we cannot help but be familiar with it if we hope to interact with the world around us. As one of my mentors rightly observed, if someone did not reach their position by way of reason (but because of power or groupthink), reason will not likely argue them out of their position either.[30] One of the effects of sin is to allow individuals to rest contently in their irrational claims.

There are other valuable reasons for why natural law as a theory is worth Protestant attention: Natural law allows us to better understand reality as we are confronted with it and the intricacies of moral knowledge; in other words, natural law helps us understand the order and operation of God's world. Natural law seen in this light is within the realm of learning wisdom, the idea that our encounters with the world provide the raw data for our investigation of what conduces and does not conduce to human flourishing. Through the natural law, we come to know not only what a moral act is, but why, in fact, it is good. It provides explanations for the rational and sub-rational faculties of human conduct.

What this chapter and the previous one has attempted to do is offer a theory of natural law on philosophical grounds. The next chapter will argue that the theoretical underpinnings of natural law parallel with Scripture's account of moral knowledge and moral action as well.

# Conclusion

One morning, as one of my daughters was getting ready to go to a birthday party, I said to her with a wry smile, "Catherine, I hope you have a very bad

---

[30] I'm indebted to Ryan T. Anderson for this insight.

day where no fun is had by anyone." Flummoxed, she looked at me (age 7), and said, "Why would you say that? The whole point of today is to have fun." I quipped back to her, "You know I'm joking. I hope you have a wonderful day full of fun memories." She replied, "Aww, Dad, I knew you were joking, because no one tells people to have a miserable day."

This singular exchange, in summary fashion, encapsulates all the components of the natural law. She could not articulate it this way, but in this moment, my daughter was in possession of facts about birthday parties that knew to direct her to certain choiceworthy outcomes, namely, having fun. She would not want to go to a birthday party if it was going to work against what she understood as some good worthwhile for its own sake. She did not have elaborate justification for why she wanted to have fun at a birthday party; she just knew that the whole point of a birthday celebration was to engage in the sort of activity that would accomplish the goal of play and celebration of a friend's life.

Of course, questions about natural law grow far more complex than this situation as situations become more complex. But at its core, natural law—God's eternal law, known through reason—identifies whether actions are reasonable or unreasonable consistent with the ends of our design that cause us to flourish. To the extent that we grasp and live in accordance with these goods, we are truly free in fullest sense of what it means to be human. As we partake and understand the order God brought about, we participate in God's common, creaturely grace to us as humans. "The light of natural reason, whereby we discern what is good and what is evil, which is the function of the natural law," according to Aquinas, "is nothing else than an imprint on us of the divine light."[31]

The natural law teaches us is that the universe runs according to goodness—not fully realized, of course, because of sin—but a goodness that awaits us all. And for those who know God as he is revealed in Jesus Christ, he is the highest good that makes all lesser goods resplendent with joy and

---

[31] *ST* I-II, q. 91, a. 2, co.

grandeur. To that end, C. S. Lewis ends our chapter well with the importance of "goodness" as a moral property reflecting God's loving providence
over us:

> If the universe is not governed by an absolute goodness, then all our
> efforts are in the long run hopeless. But if it is, then we are making
> ourselves enemies to that goodness every day, and are not in the
> least likely to do any better to-morrow, and so our case is hopeless
> again. We cannot do without it, and we cannot do with it. God is
> the only comfort, He is also the supreme terror: the thing we most
> need and the thing we most want to hide from. He is our only
> possible ally, and we have made ourselves His enemies. Some peo-
> ple talk as if meeting the gaze of absolute goodness would be fun.
> They need to think again. They are still only playing with religion.
> Goodness is either the great safety or the great danger—according
> to the way you react to it.[32]

---

[32] C. S. Lewis, *Mere Christianity*, rev. ed. (San Francisco: HarperOne, 2015),
29.

# 7.

# The Biblical Case
# for Natural Law

In previous chapters, I have sought to explain how it is that natural law speaks about the whole of created reality. While I have made overtures to Scripture, my goal in those chapters was focused less on expounding at length on biblical texts than furnishing a paradigm for how Scripture portrays its own account of creation as orderly and intelligible and what truths are necessary entailments from that reality.

I have focused on two main aspects: (1) Scripture speaks panoramically in positing a harmony between special and general revelation. Scripture portrays its account of creation and reality as both accurate descriptions of reality that contain normative truths about its operations. In other words, special revelation attests to how nature is a different, though complementary, mode of revelation. Revelation thus provides no grounds for a bifurcation between "Christian reality" and "reality." Christian ethics presupposes the intelligibility of reality *as such* for a horizon to do ethics within. (2) I have also sought to demonstrate how truths of revelation cannot be severed from the truths and evidences of reason. These are prolegomena backdrops to understand *how* Scripture speaks regarding the idea of a universal, objective, and intelligible moral law.

For natural law to be biblically grounded, however, the case for natural law should rely on explicit references to the *concept* of universal moral order as a descriptive and normative reality, as well as the *existence* of moral goods that Christians and non-Christians can both, in principle, grasp. Following from this, moral norms should be self-evident that allow persons to grasp goods consistent with the reality of the natural law. Scripture indeed posits the idea of a natural law, the existence of moral goods, and the ability to grasp them.

If none of these conditions are met, natural law would be little else than an artificial construct imposed on Scripture. But as this chapter will argue, no imposition is necessary. Far too often in considerations of the natural law, the creational blueprint of Scripture is diminished. The Bible, however, makes no sense apart from our grasp of its words and moral horizons having actual conceptual meaning. Apart from the faculties that make it possible to truly know the moral realities that God's Word speaks of, Scripture would be unintelligible itself. Hence, the operations of natural law stand at the forefront not only of what enables us to understand Scripture but to make sense of the overall moral arc of Scripture.

At the same time, it is not necessary for the Bible to posit an elaborate natural law theory (nor should we expect it to speak of a "theory"). It must only speak in ways that intimate that a natural law exists and is cognizable. Natural law is an idea suffused throughout Scripture's self-attesting intelligibility. There are biblical references to its concepts, but to explicate a biblical concept of natural law, we must understand it alongside the crystallizing and illuminating authority of God's Word, too. I therefore agree with J. Budziszewski who argues for a complementary relationship between the natural law and the doctrine of Scripture:

> There is a natural law, and it can be known and philosophically analyzed. But that which is beside the Scripture can be vindicated

only with the help of Scripture; that which is revealed before the gospel can be secured against evasion only in light of the gospel. The doctrine of Natural Law is best grounded not in the study of nature independent of God's Word but in the Word of God itself.[1]

When considering the biblical lineaments of natural law, we should return to an earlier reference for how moral theory is considered in the first place. A natural law theory (or any moral theory, really) should contain: (1) an explanation for the origin of the moral system in question (existence); (2) what norming authority there is to give the moral system its structure (prescriptivity); and (3) a *telos* of its reason for action (e.g., "goal")—we need to be clear the moral system and its norms are putting us on a trajectory whose destination is known. A moral theory needs to explain where it came from, why it is obligatory, and the purposiveness of its directives.

Natural law is thus "biblical," scripturally speaking, in two ways. In the first sense, Scripture portrays nature as an intelligible stage where moral actors understand their world and how to act within it, even if in a state of suppression, rebellion, and error. Scripture never portrays humanity as having its moral compass comprehensively extinguished. In a second sense, as I'll demonstrate in this chapter, Scripture also speaks of the natural law itself and the basic lineaments of a theory of natural law. Natural law theory is not an imposition on the text but a gleaning one naturally receives from the text's own depiction of the moral order and moral agents. Scripture thus speaks both implicitly and explicitly in natural law categories; it offers an account of the natural law itself and an account of how agents grasp the natural law. To that end, as Carl Braaten echoes, "the choice between biblical revelation and natural law is a false one."[2] If Scripture speaks in these categories, even indirectly, it will be shown to have an inchoate natural law

*→ Total depravity = comprehensive depravity*

---

[1] J. Budziszewski, *Written on the Heart: The Case for Natural Law* (Downers Grove, IL: InterVarsity, 1997), 183–84.

[2] Braaten, "Protestants and Natural Law," 24 (see chap. 3, n. 25).

theory. As I will demonstrate below, the origin for the natural law is God, its norming authority and knowability is the product of divine reason's communication to human reason. Its content is the knowledge of right and wrong achieved by norms that fulfill human goods that comprise human nature and human flourishing. From a biblical perspective, the natural law offers moral instruction as well as moral caution and prepares persons for encountering the gospel.

Rather than offer an encyclopedic list of Old Testament and New Testament verses pertaining to the natural law, the present chapter categorizes how the select verses in question relate to, and posit, a natural law doctrine. Let it be noted that some of the Scriptures referenced could understandably be placed in overlapping categories.

Natural law is not only a philosophical theory; it is also a doctrinal output that follows from reading Scripture in its textual, epochal (covenantal), and canonical context. Natural law is a metaphysical school issuing from the mind of God who acts in creation. Natural law helps put together the manifold ways that morality is presented to us throughout Scripture and reminds us that if there are not absolute moral prohibitions and obligations binding Christians to act that correspond to reality as such, it follows that there must not be absolute doctrinal prohibitions and obligations binding Christians to believe. In this schematic, ethics is doctrinal because it relates to the very essence of Christian theological truth claims. Orthodoxy (doctrine) and orthopraxy (ethics) are mutually reinforcing. The natural law can help illuminate the reasons why.

Christian ethics is premised on its morality not only objectively existing, but positing the goods necessary to fulfill human longing: "The reality is that Christians who define Christianity in terms of historic Christian doctrine and moral teachings do not believe merely that these teachings are true," writes theologian Albert Mohler, "but that they point to the only truth that will produce real and lasting human happiness."[3]

---

[3] R. Albert Mohler Jr., *The Gathering Storm: Secularism, Culture, and the Church* (Nashville: Nelson Books, 2020), 117.

The value of the Bible for principles of natural law is that the Bible gives epistemic clarity and authoritative declaration where the frailties of human reason are prone to err. As J. Budziszewski writes, "Biblical law illuminates the natural law by making many remote implications of the natural law clearer than they would have been through human reasoning alone; it also explains the means of salvation, which reason could never have figured out for itself."[4] Though marred and wounded after the fall, nature and reason retain an integrity proper to their own end. But it is grace that enables us to understand why reason errs and what nature's ultimate fulfillment truly is. As we ponder the natural law from the biblical perspective, we should do so from the perspective that natural law stands behind, through, and beneath the text of Scripture while Scripture brings clarifying authority to areas where the natural law does not provide exacting detail.

## The Existence of an Objective Creation Order

The whole drama of Scripture assumes a teleological order from whence humans are directed to obtain what is objectively good for them. The stage that Genesis shows unfolding is one of moral purpose. A scriptural worldview is incomprehensible apart from its depiction of created reality as orderly and moral. From communion with God in his kingdom, to persons aligning themselves with the grain of the universe made known through wisdom and natural inclinations, Scripture directs humanity toward a particular direction: God's glory. God's glory and humanity's good are dual, mutually reinforcing realities. God inscribes a moral order that reflects his own character. Alignment with said order is conducive to human flourishing. Such an order assumes meaningful moral agency is intelligible—it is orderly, observable, and agents can act to protect and further their good.

---

[4] J. Budziszewski, *Natural Law for Lawyers* (Phoenix: Alliance Defending Freedom, 2019), 18.

The setting of Genesis portrays creation as purposeful and opposed to chaos and anarchy. Were humans unable to draw moral conclusions from the world that God has placed them in, Scripture's storyline would be unintelligible. God inscribes creation order with an ethic consistent with it fulfilling its moral purpose. God establishes a fixed moral order by creating the world and by placing moral agents within it who are endowed with moral agency and tacked with moral purpose. Everything in Genesis's depiction of creation suggests that God has imposed right and wrong ways for his creation to operate for everything to act according to the purpose he has ordered it. It is a moral universe whose antithesis is chaos, accidents, and directionlessness. That creation is described as "good" is a repudiation of worldviews that see no inherent moral meaning within creation itself.

Natural law is thus more than a set of concrete rules or goods (though it is never less than that); it is a whole "moral order directing people to ways of life that promote and attain purposes for which God designed them."[5] We can recall how in Acts, the earliest Christians were subscribing what was referred to as "the Way" (Acts 9:1–2). "The Way" denotes a mode of existence within a realm of understanding. Natural law is its own "way" in that it communicates the necessity of aligning oneself with the order of wisdom. It is "sapiential" in that the creation order of Genesis 1 is an ontological stage of moral realism learned by way of wisdom and interaction with the world.[6]

Whether we agree on the exhaustive knowledge of these moral goods within the moral order, Scripture speaks of an inclination to our design that knows objective goods exist. According to Jonathan Burnside, "The Bible's understanding of human nature is radically teleological because it presumes the existence of created human natural inclinations towards the goods of human flourishing (e.g., Genesis 1–2 and Genesis 1:28)."[7] Or as

---

[5] VanDrunen, *Politics after Christendom: Political Theology in a Fractured World*, 135 (see chap. 3, n. 10).

[6] VanDrunen, 145.

[7] Burnside, "Natural Law and Biblical Law," 200 (see chap. 4, n. 20).

Matthew Levering similarly observes, "God creates human beings so that they are naturally ordered to preserve the good of their human existence. Without the inclination to preserve this good, God's warning about the tree of the knowledge of good and evil would not be intelligible."[8] That Scripture portrays creation as a platform for God's ordering of meaningful human interaction and divine redemption captures the teleological nature of life within God's creation. Nothing about the existence of an objective order changes from the Old Testament to the New Testament. As Markus Bockmuehl writes concerning New Testament authors, there is a "theologically based presupposition of a universal ontology."[9]

Other passages of Scripture express a continuity between divine providence and an intelligible creation order include:

- *Psalm 19*—As mentioned earlier, Psalm 19 is a rich presentation of an orderly creation witnessing to God's creation exhibiting design and uniformity.

- *Jer 31:35–36; 33:25*—God explicitly cites his own covenant with creation order in these two sections, noting "If I have not established my covenant with day and night and the fixed order of heaven and earth . . ." (33:25) In both sections, YHWH expresses the permanency of his covenantal bond with Israel as he does the fixity of his covenant with creation.

- *Acts 14:15–18*—Rejecting that he and Barnabas should be worshipped, Paul redirects the impulse to worship to the true God. Paul insists the pagans have an unregenerate knowledge of God through an understanding of God's providential ordering of creation. In verse 17, the upholding of their lives through basic goods is proof that "God does not leave himself without witness" and that creational continuity is a witness for their preservation and for their

---

[8] Levering, *Biblical Natural Law*, 59 (see chap. 2, n. 19).

[9] Markus Bockmuehl, *Jewish Law in Gentile Churches: Halakhah and the Beginning of Christian Public Ethics* (Grand Rapids: Baker Academic, 2003), 116.

"gladness." Creation itself and creational goods are semblances of an objective order ordained by God.

- *Acts 17*—One of the best-known natural theology passages, in Acts 17, Paul moves from a creational argument to a redemptive argument. He acknowledges the impulse to worship an "unknown god" (v. 23). Paul states as a matter of observation that pagans understand God's ordering of creation and providence, but then redirects that impulse to its ultimate *telos*: Jesus Christ (vv. 30–31). Paul cites pagan poets (Epimenides of Crete and Aratus's *Phainomena*) as saying true things about God, giving textual evidence that even pagan thinkers can say true things about God.[10] The argument in verses 22–34 demonstrates the proper way to utilize natural law in relationship to special revelation by moving from general creational truths to specificity regarding the exclusivity of Christ.

- *Isa 24:5–6*—These verses teach a correspondence between obeying creation order, disobedient human behavior, and negative human consequence. According to the logic of Isaiah, failing to obey the "everlasting covenant" and its laws and statutes (which is, presumably, the Noahic covenant) results in a world marked by curse, suffering, and decay.

- *Rom 1:18–32*—Though these verses could apply to other natural law categories as well, Romans 1 is a natural theology lodestar which teaches that a failure to obey creation order leads to moral anarchy, social decay, and futility of mind. It does so by teaching that God has made certain truths "plain" (v. 19) to Jew and Gentile alike. God has "shown" himself through creation order (v. 19), meaning that humanity retains knowledge of God despite its sin. Paul is not speaking conditionally, but factually to the existence and necessary observance of an order imposed on creation by God that

---

[10] Haines, *Natural Theology*, 87 (see chap. 4, n. 1).

determines the fixed patterns and *teloi* of creation. Hence, there are homosexual actions that are "contrary to nature" (v. 26) and heterosexual actions that evidence "natural relations" (v. 27). The juxtaposition is striking in the vividness of offense against nature by the misuse of the body and revealing of the ways in which Paul's understanding of a fixed creation order forms the backdrop of homosexuality's illicitness.[11]

Humans do have knowledge of God and God's law (Rom 2:14–16). Creation reveals the attributes of God in his eternality, majesty, and moral order. The fact that Paul demonstrates this rejection of creaturely limitation by referencing homosexuality speaks to the teleology behind Paul's overall argument. His argument is that rejecting the bodily design of the creature is to reject the heavenly design of the Creator.[12] Commenting on 1 Cor 6:18, but which applies here as well, Haines and Fulford aptly state how "to sin sexually is to offend against the right order inscribed by God into the body he created for human beings."[13] According to Paul, a refusal to honor God as Creator results in abandoning creational limits and living "contrary to nature." Thus, to reject creation order is to reject God. Like Isaiah 24, the natural law is often known most acutely when breaking it and experiencing the consequences that follow from breaking it. Moreover, according to Paul's logic, humanity's plight is not primarily epistemological in nature. There is additional weight to the natural law in

---

[11] Douglas J. Moo, *The Epistle to the Romans*, The New International Commentary on the New Testament (Grand Rapids: Eerdmans, 1996), 114. See also Angier, *Natural Law Theory*, 1 (see chap. 2, n. 3).

[12] For more of this argument, Richard Hays writes, "When human being engage in homosexual activity, they enact an outward and visible sign of an inward and spiritual reality: the rejection of the Creator's design. Thus, Paul's choice of homosexuality as an illustration of human depravity is not merely random: it serves his rhetorical purposes by providing a vivid image of humanity's primary rejection of the sovereignty of God the Creator." Hays, *The Moral Vision of the New Testament* (San Francisco: HarperOne, 1996), 386.

[13] Haines, *Natural Theology*, 103 (see chap. 4, n. 1).

this passage as it teaches that humanity's violation of the natural law is not due primarily because of ignorance. Our indictment is not our ignorance of the natural law but our stubbornness to submit to it. It is a volitionally based ethical rejection of God's divine decrees self-evident in creation.[14] C. S. Lewis argued similarly, stating that "the general tenor of scripture does not encourage us to believe that our knowledge of the Law has been depraved in the same degree as our power to fulfill it."[15] It is not that we lack knowledge of the moral law or of God the Creator. It is the opposite in fact. Paul says that aspects of God's moral attributes are self-evident. It is, rather, that human beings "suppress the truth" (Rom 1:18). To invoke the natural law, then, is not to impose an alien and external morality on an interlocutor but to draw out a morality that Scripture considers present from within a person's knowledge of the world. The natural law are those principles that a person with the proper use of their reason would gladly accept. The natural law is not something that a rational agent would actually choose to reject if they were using their mind properly. In the same way that Paul warns against men exchanging customs denoting manhood for womanhood, nature is creation's object lesson giving its participants a foothold for discerning the moral law and acting cooperatively in response to it (1 Corinthians 11).

David VanDrunen rightly captures how the existence of an "objectively meaningful natural order" contributes to our understanding of natural law:

> Natural law, in other words, is not first and foremost a means for making moral or apologetic arguments to which unbelievers will be compelled to give assent, but a means by which Christians express their conviction that God has made this universe in such a manner that there is a morally appropriate way for human beings to live within it, and that, furthermore, the moral law God has

---

[14] Fesko, *Reforming Apologetics*, 123 (see chap. 4, n. 4).

[15] C. S. Lewis, "The Poison of Subjectivism," *Christian Reflections* (Grand Rapids: Eerdmans, 2014), 97.

explicitly revealed in Scripture is not arbitrary but a reflection of this created reality.[16]

As a function of apologetics, Scripture teaches of an objective creation order that rebellious individuals are subject to regardless of their willingness to obey it or not. Our duty toward our neighbor who persists in rejecting the natural law is not simply to insist upon its existence but as a warning of the carnage to person and culture as both strive against it.

To summarize, the whole of creation is under the sway of a sovereign Creator who communicates himself through a natural order teeming with design. One of the most basic elements of the natural law is the law of negative consequences that follows from shirking this design and its natural limitations. As humans reject the Creator, it leads to rejecting their own creational guardrails. The order God creates and governs by his providential rule is objective, universal, and fixed. When natural law is depicted as creation order or a creation ethic, it is done so with these categories in mind.

## The Existence of Universal Moral Laws

- *Rom 1:32*—Whatever degeneracy there is from earlier in Romans 1, it apparently does not extinguish knowledge of "God's righteous decree," which everyone is presumed to know. Knowing God's decree and disobeying it is what indicts humanity for its descent into the vices listed in 1:28–31. Indeed, it is knowledge of God's law that fills out the larger sections of Romans 1–3 that tells of humanity's culpability and need of redemption. In knowing God's moral law, Paul says the world is "without excuse" (v. 20) for disobeying it. It is disobedience resulting from an obstinate will, not ignorance.

---

[16] VanDrunen, "Natural Law for Reformed Theology," 120 (see chap. 3, n. 26).

- *Rom 2:14–15*—Employing the metaphorical language he does, Paul's language of a law "written on their hearts" (referring to non-Christian Gentiles, in my view) must refer to a non-codified moral law since laws are not physically written on bodily organs. In the history of the Christian natural law tradition, it is these two verses that are most often appealed to as the *locus classicus* of the Bible's teaching on the natural law. According to Paul, God has inscribed a body of moral knowledge within non-Christian persons that their conscience bears witness to when obeying it and defying it.[17] As Paul writes in verse 14, non-Christian Gentiles "by nature do what the law requires," indicating that the law they have "to themselves" most likely refers to the natural law, not the Mosaic Law. I identify this moral law as the First Principle of Practical Reason, which is that "good is to be pursued and evil avoided." As was written in the previous chapter, this is the elementary first moral principle upon which all other moral principles are constituted. It self-evidently true and cannot be proven, and if attempted to be proven would signal the elimination of all sound foundations on which morality rests. The conscience in verse 15 is not the moral law. The conscience is the internal mechanism God has implanted within us to remind us of when we're about to breach the moral law or have indeed done so implicitly or explicitly. Douglas Moo defines conscience as a "reflective mechanism by which people can measure their conformity to a norm."[18] Another scholar refers to the conscience as the "intuitive attunement to creational normativity."[19] The pang

---

[17] I hold to the majority view of Rom 2:14–15 that Paul is speaking of non-Christian Gentiles. For more on this debate, see Douglas J. Moo, *The Epistle to the Romans*, The New International Commentary on the New Testament (Grand Rapids: Eerdmans, 1996), 148–53.

[18] Moo, 152.

[19] Albert M. Wolters, *Creation Regained: Biblical Basics for a Reformational Worldview*, 2nd ed. (Grand Rapids: Eerdmans, 2005), 29.

of a guilty conscience testifies to our having broken the moral law of God. John Calvin highlights these verses to conclude: "If the Gentiles have the righteousness of the law naturally engraven on their minds, we certainly cannot say that they are altogether blind as to the rule of life. Nothing indeed is more common than for man to be sufficiently instructed in a right course of conduct by natural law, of which the Apostle here speaks."[20]

- *Deut 4:5–6*—In these verses, Moses instructs Israel to follow God's law. But the horizon of impact of Israel's obedience is promised to extend beyond just Israel. Their obedience to God's universal law will be recognized by the Gentile nations, who see in Israel's obedience, their own hope for redemption. How can the nations recognize Israel's wisdom and understanding apart from a prerequisite moral knowledge that such behavior conforms to the moral law? Israel is to exhibit par excellence the way of existing that the world looks for in futile wandering.

- *Rom 13:1–7; 1 Pet 2:13–17*—These verses are essential to government's purpose to oversee political communities that are ordered around the pursuit and obtainment of justice. The fact that governments and magistrates are held accountable to this command suggests they possess the reasoning capacities to differentiate justice from injustice.

- *Isa 5:20; Amos 5:15*—Though the contexts of these verses are directed toward the nation Israel, they assume a knowledge of what principles constitutes "evil," "good," and "justice." Perversely exchanging "good" for "evil" is an occasion of judgment in Isaiah, while in Amos, aligning oneself with good and not with evil is a sign of blessing. Alignment with what Scripture assumes are objective goods testifies to their tacit creational existence, the knowledge of each, and the corresponding objectivity to states of affairs that

---

[20] Calvin, *Institutes*, 2.2.22.

are truly evil or truly good. Both sets of verses demonstrate that natural law's existence by the positive consequences that follow from obeying it and negative consequences that follow from violating it.

- *Exodus 1*—The Hebrew midwives in Exodus 1 were assigned by Pharoah to care for other Hebrew women during birth, killing any newborn males to prevent their population from growing. Knowing it would be wrong to kill innocent children, they subverted Pharoah's command to kill and disobeyed a kingly decree. This is an example of a moral law written on the heart, a law that was higher in authority than a law issued by Pharaoh.

- *Ps 119:52*—In these verses, "rules from of old" are taken to mean the creational moral law. We may take this to mean the psalmist rejoicing in the codified expression of the natural law. Calvin states, similarly, "Why does the [the psalmist] say that the law of God has been from everlasting? This may to some extent be accounted for from the righteousness here mentioned not being of recent growth, but truly everlasting, because the written law is just an attestation of the law of nature, through means of which God recalls to our memory that which he has previously engraved on our hearts."[21] Written law distills and clarifies the principles of moral law in authoritative form.

- *Amos 1–2*—In these two chapters, Amos communicates judgment upon the nations, indicating the nations' accountability to the moral law of God.

- *Book of Jonah*—Gentile Nineveh was condemned for practices that it should have known not to do. Of course, Nineveh was not a recipient of the law, so its moral knowledge must have been the result of an implanted moral knowledge.[22]

---

[21] John Calvin, *Commentary on the Book of Psalms,* vol. 4, trans. James Anderson (Grand Rapids: Eerdmans, 1949), 38.

[22] Jesse Covington, Bryan T. McGraw, and Micah Watson, "Hopeful Realism: Renewing Evangelical Political Morality," *Public Discourse,* July 21, 2022, https://

- *Prov 20:10*—Unjust social practices are critiqued as an abomination. This again attests to the knowledge of a form of general equity justice.[23]

- *1 Cor 5:1*—Paul is upset that the Corinthian church is allowing for sexual practices that even pagans would not practice or tolerate. That, of course, assumes some knowledge of universal moral laws governing proper sexual relations.

- *2 Cor 8:21*—Here, Paul says his ministry aims at what is "honorable" not only to the Lord, but also "in the sight of man." Again, that non-Christians can recognize what is honorable speaks to the existence and recognition of universal moral laws. Colossians 4:5, 1 Thess 4:12, and 1 Tim 3:7 command us to walk in appropriate ways as we interact with non-believers. In other words, we should not let unreasonableness or outlandishness serve as a stumbling block to the gospel.

- *Matt 12:12*—Though it may seem odd, there is a kernel of natural law insight in this passage where Jesus says, "Of how much more value is a man than a sheep!" Jesus's rhetoric communicates an apparently obvious and important truth that humans have an intuitive recognition of a person's worth over an animal's worth. Such an observation may seem tedious, but distinguishing types of creatures and their corresponding value assumes that the natural order finds ways to communicate human worth over and above animal worth. Jesus also assumes the durability of his audience's knowledge that can rightfully differentiate animal life from human life. Beastly distinction is part of God's creational law stipulating how God has created animal life according to its own kind (Gen 1:25).

---

www.thepublicdiscourse.com/2022/07/83450/.
[23] Covington, McGraw, and Watson, *Public Discourse*.

Even among the survey offered here, the conclusion can be drawn from Scripture that the natural law exists and is discernible as a moral order by even fallen human beings. A natural law knowledge of right from wrong, life's intrinsic value, honor from dishonor, an acknowledgment of sexual design, and the differentiation between human and animal species dictates their respective treatments are present in the biblical witness.

## The Existence of Cognizable Moral Goods

As I've discussed previously, the natural law is not simply an abstract "law" but an order known through ordinances of practical reason that the mind grasps, which helps direct us to moral goods. Moral goods, as a reminder, are those non-instrumental reasons for action whose intelligibility depends on no further or deeper ends than they are means to the good itself. Moral goods are what we pursue for their own sakes. Intrinsically valuable and choiceworthy in themselves, moral goods exist because God orders them as a reflection of his holy and just nature. Any experience of the good or emanation of justice we can experience as finite beings are reflections of the infinite good and just God.

Recall from a previous chapter that we benefit from a moral good in and of itself. Undoubtedly, God is the giver of such goods. Goods are those things which we desire proportionate to natural inclinations that direct us toward natural and fulfilling ends for their own sake. The "good," then, is simply what a rational person understands as truly completive of his or her being. To the extent that a moral agent grasps its true end and pursues it, it more fully experiences its nature.

 What is good? Whatever end fulfills our being. Why is it reasonable to pursue a good? Because rational persons just naturally seek whatever ends naturally complete them. Why is it reasonable? Because it fulfills what is natural for obtaining the human good. But why should someone seek their true end? Because God ordered our nature to be so. Moral goods, are, in fact, natural goods rooted in divinely authorized goods. General and special revelation testify to the same truth about moral goodness in their own unique and complementary way.

While the natural law posits goods that non-Christians can, in principle grasp, natural law in this scheme is ultimately a natural law of religious presuppositions. Indeed, when Scripture depicts humanity knowing certain moral facts and knowing that God is the author of these facts and goods, non-Christians are correct to view the entailments of the natural law as ultimately religious in nature. Thus, when non-Christians object to the natural law on the grounds that it is religious in nature, Christians should not disagree. We would merely wish to explain why the moral debate in question can be explained on the grounds of reason apart from religion, even if the point of origin is religious in nature. Every moral claim, even if religious in origin, must have a rational output for it to be obligatory on all persons, irrespective of whether the audience agrees with the religious presuppositions in question.

This is the case because Christians must assert that morality is not self-subsisting but requires God for its ultimate grounding. Natural law should make no attempt to disguise its religiously grounded metaphysic. There are always metaphysical commitments lurking behind everyone's moral proclamations. The question is whether the metaphysical commitments are intelligible. Scripture teaches that they are. They are considered true and can be understood as one learns about what best fulfills their nature. Christian natural lawyers who would deny or under-emphasize that the natural law is ultimately religious in nature, albeit with conclusions reachable from reason, are not being faithful to Scripture or the natural law tradition, properly understood. Life, for example, may be a moral good worthy for its own sake but, ultimately, because God is the author of the lives that we seek to safeguard.[24] As Germain Grisez rightly notes, all moral reality and moral obligation is given ordination, directiveness, and force by the Creator. Therefore, alignment with, and conformity to, the moral goods is not alignment or

---

[24] I am indebted to my friend Abigail Dodds for helping refine this insight.

conformity, ultimately, with moral goods for their sake alone, but with the Creator who orders them:

> When we understand that directiveness as guidance provided by our Creator, our sense of its dependability deepens, and with that the normative force of the moral *ought* which it generates increases, and general moral obligation emerges. This emergence can be explained. Children who follow their parents' guidance cooperate with their parents. Similarly, if one thinks that the Creator has provided the principles of practical reason to guide us to our fulfillment, one will suppose that one is cooperating with the Creator when one follows the direction of practical reason in promoting and protecting basic human goods. By the same token, following emotions against reasons will be failing to cooperate with the Creator and disobeying his guidance.[25]

We see here once again how alignment with God's order reflects our obedience to him, giving the glory due to a Being who orders moral goods to benefit his creatures.

Scripture does not speak of a discrete, highly enumerated set of moral goods as such—it assumes them. When Scripture prohibits murder in the Ten Commandments, such a prohibition is against a moral backdrop that assumes a moral good. The moral rule "Do not murder" provides norming guidelines around the moral good that preserving life is its own end. The prohibition "Do not murder" simply commands action of a type that allows for obtaining the moral good. When we are instructed to not bear false witness in the Ninth Commandment, we are implicitly directed to speak only that which is true. Now, God is the ground of all truth, but truthful communication that allows for us to meaningfully communicate and cooperate toward the common good testifies to the fact that truthfulness is a moral good all on its own.

---

[25] Grisez, "Natural Law and the Transcendent Source of Human Fulfillment," 449 (see introduction, n. 5).

Elsewhere, when Paul tells his audience to "think about these things" which are "true," "honorable," "just," "pure," "lovely," "commendable," and possess "excellence," such a moral command is done against a backdrop that assumes the capacity to grasp things of said qualities. Scripture thus speaks positively and apophatically concerning moral goods. One cannot understand the intelligibility of moral obligations and prohibitions of Scripture apart from their choiceworthy and directive prescriptivity to protect and facilitate the good. There are realities (e.g., justice), institutions (e.g., government), and relationships (e.g., marriage) that the Bible considers goods worthy of obtaining, protecting, and respecting by providing norms of restraint and obligation.

One additional note is necessary to explain why a discussion about the nature and reasonableness of moral goods is appropriate to pursue in these pages. As far as a survey of Christian ethics texts I have reviewed, I cannot locate a contemporary Protestant ethics volume that focuses on what moral goods are in themselves—as far as their intelligibility and oughtness. While standard ethics texts discuss illicit and permissible actions to arrive at what Scripture considers lawful or unlawful, no text I am aware of discusses the rational coherence of what constitutes a moral good and why the moral good is to be pursued for its own sake. This confirms my suspicion that most of Protestant ethics, while more than just divine-command-oriented in their explanation, are thought of as primarily divine-command-oriented.

Below is a survey of the range of moral goods that Scripture speaks of. I would begin our list by observing Ps 34:14, a verse which speaks in the same categories of the First Principle of Practical Reason, and which assumes that all rational moral action directs individuals toward pursuing moral goods: "Turn away from evil and do good; seek peace and pursue it." Included here is a chart that demonstrates the continuity between creational ordinances, their identification as a natural moral good, and their abiding obligation in light of the New Testament and the covenant of redemption. Once again, I must stress that the New Testament does not suspend or abrogate *all* Old

Testament law; it only suspends those laws which were unique in defining the covenantal boundary markers of Israel to YHWH. Since YHWH's creational laws are, by definition, applicable to all, laws or ordinances set forth in creation persist into the present day and it is on that basis we can insist on their continued obligation.

## The Enduring Goods of the Moral Law from Creation to Redemption

| Creational Ordinance | Non-instrumental Natural Moral Good | Redemptive Ratification of Creational Ordinance |
|---|---|---|
| Existence and self-constitution (Gen 1:26–27; Exod 20:13) | Life | Luke 18:20; Rom 13:9 |
| Embodiment (Gen 1:26–27; Gen 2:18-24; Exod 20:13) | Life | Matt 19:4–6 |
| Marriage (Gen 2:18–24; Gen 9:1; Exod 20:14) | Family | Matt 19:4–6; Eph 5:22–33; 1 Tim. 4:1-5 |
| Children (Gen 1:28; Gen 9:1; Ps 127:3–5) | Family | Matt 19:14; Eph 6:1–4; Col 3:20 |
| Political Authority (Gen 9:5–6; Exod 20:12) | Order | Rom 13:1–7; 1 Pet 2:13–17 |
| Beauty (Gen 2:23; Ps 19:1–6) | Aesthetic Appreciation | Phil 4:8 |
| Rest (Gen 2:1–3; Exod 20:8–11) | Leisure and Recreation | Mark 6:31; Matt 11:28–30 |

| Vocation/Labor (Gen 1:28; Gen 2:15; Exod 20:8; Prov 22:29) | Skillful Performance | 2 Thess 3:10; Eph 4:28; 1 Tim 5:8 |
|---|---|---|
| Political Justice (Gen 9:5–6) | Justice | Rom 13:1–7 |
| Friendship (Prov 18:24; Prov 27:17) | Sociability | Matt 5:21–23; John 15:12–15 |
| Wisdom, moral sensibility, moral obligation (Psalm 1 & 8; Prov 34:12) | Prudence and Practical Reasonableness | 1 Cor 10:31; Col 3:17 |
| Advancement of Knowledge and Industry (Gen 4:21–22) | Knowledge | Phil 4:8; 1 Cor 10:31; Col 1:10, 3:10 |
| Worship and Orientation to the Divine (Gen 1:26–27; Exod 20:2–7) | Alignment with Transcendent Reality | Acts 17:16–34 |
| Commutative Justice (Exod 20:15) | Justice | 1 Thess 4:6; Eph 4:28 |
| God's Providential Rule and Divine Illumination (Gen 1:1; Ps 36:9) | Alignment with Transcendent Reality | Acts 14:13-18 |
| Truthful Communication (Exod 20:16) | Truth | Eph 4:25; James 3 |
| Internal Motive and Integrity (Gen 2:16; Exod 20:17; Prov 2) | Integral Human Fulfillment | Matt 15:11; Phil 4:7 |

We should not quickly move on from the discussion of moral goods in Scripture. Moral goodness is what Herman Bavinck referred to as "natural morality." Bavinck saw no bifurcation between what moral realities non-Christians and Christians were called to obey. Moral goods do not subsist in different kind or degree of obligation. What is afforded the Christian is the ability to "discern better than others with the light of the Word what is in nature and thereby have learned to distinguish between nature and grace."[26] Bavinck more or less affirms the classical Greek traditions articulation of the virtues as an accurate reflection of moral goodness. Echoing the thought of Germain Grisez and John Finnis, Bavinck goes on to affirm such goods as bodily life, marriage, family, friendship, vocation and industry, the advancement of knowledge, aesthetics, liberty of conscience, and public justice upheld through a system of law.[27] These goods are goods in themselves according to Bavinck, and while they do not bring someone to salvation, they "bring us closer to the kingdom of heaven, but it can never bring us in."[28] The moral goods mentioned above, for Bavinck, are what allow for civic virtue, human survival, and modest tranquility to persist despite sin. Natural human longing for moral goodness is what Bavinck uses as confirmation for Christianity's supremacy against other systems of thought that cannot account for morality in a coherent way. Because Christianity accounts for what pagans aspire after in their common life, Christianity embodied ultimate moral fulfillment and can explain the enduring reality of why moral longing exists and what it is.[29] Regeneration does not suspend the abiding validity of the moral goods; rather, the heavenly good should "animate the moral life, control it, subject it, and make it its instrument" so that the task of ethics "is therefore to describe how regenerate people

---

[26] Bavinck, *Reformed Ethics: Created, Fallen, and Converted Humanity*, 1:228.

[27] Bavinck, 1:230–32.

[28] Bavinck, 1:232.

[29] Herman Bavinck, *Reformed Dogmatics: Prolegomena*, ed. John Bolt, trans. John Vriend, vol. 1 (Grand Rapids: Baker Academic, 2004), 319–20.

are to manifest their eternal heavenly life in the form of the temporal earthly life."[30]

Two other comments are worth making regarding the existence of these goods; the first concerns the taxonomy of moral goods and the second concerns how moral goods are enforced. First, regarding the identity of these moral goods, one will observe that many of the moral goods mentioned find resonance with the Ten Commandments. In the view offered here, the Ten Commandments represent the distillation and codification of the natural law. Though the audience of the Ten Commandments was covenantal Israel, the principles behind the Ten Commandments are natural law principles. As David Clyde Jones states,

> The Ten Commandments are universal moral norms because they represent the will of God for human nature as he has created it—to be fulfilled through his ordinances of worship, rest, authority, life, sex, property, and communication; they are grounded in his purposes and instructions for human beings always and everywhere.[31]

In similar fashion, John Murray describes the Ten Commandments as the "concrete and practical form of enunciating principles" that neither began with the Sinaitic covenant or concluded at the Sinaitic covenant's expiration.[32] The principles, as it were, are creational principles expressed in concrete ordinances graspable through even fallen reason. Secondly, as regards the enforcement of the natural law in order to secure and procure moral goods, as I have previously stated, the natural law does not, on its own, give self-evident guidance on the best way to enforce its principles. How the natural law's goods are enforced is a matter of prudence. Natural law principles and moral goods do not necessitate that the mandate of

---

[30] Bavinck, *Reformed Ethics: Created, Fallen, and Converted Humanity*, 1:235 (see chap. 3, n. 19).

[31] David Clyde Jones, *Biblical Christian Ethics*, First Edition (Grand Rapids: Baker Academic, 1994), 116.

[32] John Murray, *Principles of Conduct: Aspects of Biblical Ethics* (Grand Rapids: Eerdmans, 1957), 7.

their obligation be enforced in all the same ways. The natural law testifies more to the existence of said laws, not granular specificity as to how each is enforced. Commands 1–4, for example, are binding natural law principles; their existence and the people's accountability to them does not necessitate the state's enforcement. Even if one were to say, for example, that because the family is tasked with leading its members in the direction of religion, therefore the state must as well, nothing implies that state is authorized to enforce "true religion" in the same way that another natural institution, for example, the family, is. Of course, many creation order decrees fall within the state's interest due to their facilitation of the common good and, in turn, common harm. Considering that the New Covenant does not negate the natural law whatsoever, how the state determines whether to incentivize, be indifferent to, or punish that which is in its interest in view of the natural law is a matter of prudence.

Lastly, though Christians partake in an eschatological ethic that results in a "partial" release from the creational structures of the natural law, the moral goods of the natural law are not to be torn asunder or disrespected by Christians living in this age. Our "release" from such goods does not tarnish their intelligibility. Rather, Christians are to go beyond the mere lineaments of the natural law in obedience to a law born of the Spirit. Creation order persists even while Christians are called to embody an eschatological ethic that is promised to reign over all in the new creation. Moral goods do not themselves *change* from a state of unregeneracy to regeneration. Rather, our perspective from the vantage point of our *knowledge* about natural moral goods and their creaturely limitations changes. Hence, while Christians are called to participate in earthly political communities and economic activity and to propagate the species through the family, an eschatological ethic informs how a Christian: (1) differentiates legal justice from ecclesial mercy, (2) subordinates the good of earthly family relations to the reality of spiritual kinship in the gathered body, and (3) practices a radical generosity.[33]

---

[33] For additional perspective along the lines of what I am arguing in this paragraph, see David VanDrunen, *Divine Covenants and Moral Order: A Biblical*

We are called, in other words, to embody the coming Kingdom within the present natural order, thus respecting the natural order for its continued platform for the propagation of the gospel.

## The Existence of Justice

At the heart of the natural law is conformity to an order of justice. Natural law and justice may be considered synonymous in that conformity to one assumes conformity to the other. Alignment with how things *ought* to be is characteristic of both justice and natural law. Classically defined, justice is "giving each their due." It represents a state of affairs rightly ordered, bringing parity and equilibrium to the issue or situation at hand. Justice is fulfilled when any circumstance and action aligns with God's order for creation. A human law is considered just when it is in conformity with eternal law, divine law, and natural law. Justice rejects, and is thwarted by, irrational actions, unfair procedures, biased standards, and exploitative circumstances.

Critically, knowledge of the moral goods is a prerequisite to justice. To know what we ought to do assumes possession of a knowledge about what it is that is good to obtain. Justice, in other words, assumes the existence of states of affairs defined by the obtainment of moral goods. Natural law thus affords the order of justice to which we must confirm but also provides us with the critical faculties necessary to grasp the goods and duties of the natural law. Without trying to sound too sweeping in my generalization, justice is at the heart of the Bible's entire narrative concerning natural law. God's Word is a grand testament to God's mission of reclamation. The Bible speaks about justice with such abundance that to excise the priority of justice is to tear apart the entire drama of Scripture.

At the heart of Scripture is the idea of justice as *general equity*. Established as part of the reconstituted social order in the Noahic covenant

---

*Theology of Natural Law* (Grand Rapids: Eerdmans, 2014), 448–79.

in Gen 8:20–9:17, Gen 9:5–6 embodies the central framing of reciprocal and rectifying justice:

> And for your lifeblood I will require a reckoning: from every beast I will require it and from man. From his fellow man I will require a reckoning for the life of man.

> "Whoever sheds the blood of man,
>     by man shall his blood be shed,
> for God made man in his own image."

I point to these verses in particular because I think they provide the overarching canopy from which the rest of Scripture's pronouncements about justice are issued in this age. Noahic justice is, after all, the form of justice issuing from the covenant that God makes with all humans that remains abiding into the present. Noahic justice is the justice of the natural law.[34]

Several conclusions are worth drawing from the requirement of Noahic justice. First, God requires an order of justice to rectify wrongs as a matter of settling disputes between humans and humans only. Justice is aimed at repairing a breakdown to a properly ordered state of affairs. If God requires an order of justice, he must necessarily instill within the order of creation the ability to understand, pursue, and rectify it. Second, God does just that. Given the non-salvific nature of the Noahic covenant, the call to justice continues unabated and is obligatory on all participants within human society down to the present day. Natural law is, if nothing else, the universal form of justice made accessible to rational creatures

---

[34] I should acknowledge that my understanding of the Noahic covenant has been deeply influenced by the work of David VanDrunen's *Divine Covenants and Moral Order: A Biblical Theology of Natural Law* (Grand Rapids: Eerdmans, 2014), as well as Jonathan Leeman, *Political Church: The Local Assembly as Embassy of Christ's Rule* (Downers Grove, IL: InterVarsity, 2016). I consider both gentlemen to be friends and theological mentors.

who bear God's image. Third, the account of justice established by Noahic covenant establishes how the form of justice established by the natural law is necessarily minimalist in nature; meaning, natural law does not give detailed specifications on every last iota of moral conflict—only those areas of moral necessity that are essential for continued survival and civilizational order. Fourth, the picture of justice pictured in the Noahic covenant is not a soteriologically-inflected version of justice. The justice of the natural law does not save, but reflects a broadly theistic account of justice that, coherent on its own terms, should direct image-bearers toward questions of ultimate justice.

The Noahic covenant, which is still operative today and provides the theological justification for natural law's durability into the present, directs earth's inhabitants toward the "good" of justice that is primarily preservative, protectionist, and rectifying in nature. The Noahic covenant does not predicate a person's apprehension of justice on a perfect knowledge of God the Redeemer, only God the Creator. I grant, for the sake of the overall structure of justice having coherence, that it must have a theistic foundation. It is the durability of Noahic justice into the present day that accounts for how non-Christians (who may espouse relativism or subjectivism) still appeal for justice and desire its satisfaction, albeit with incoherence.

Echoes of natural justice can be seen in Gen 20:9 where Abimelech castigates Abraham for doing "things that ought not to be done." Abimelech was a pagan king with no revealed knowledge of right and wrong. Though God had spoken to Abimelech in a dream (v. 3), that dream imparted only the previously unknown reality that Sarah was in fact Abraham's wife, not that Abimelech had no knowledge that it would have been wrong to sleep with another man's wife.[35] Abimelech possessed an innate knowledge that sleeping with someone else's wife would be wrong.

---

[35] For more on this exchange, see David VanDrunen, *A Biblical Case for Natural Law* (Grand Rapids: Acton Institute, 2006), 42–45.

## Jesus Christ, Justice, and the Natural Law

Additional echoes of this justice principle can be located in Jesus's statements in Matt 7:12, "So whatever you wish that others would do to you,
do also to them. For this is the Law and the Prophets," and in Mark 12:31,
"You shall love your neighbor as yourself." Martin Luther pointed to how
Matthew 7 points to the natural law:

> Not an individual is there who does not realize, and who is not
> forced to confess, the justice and truth of the natural law outlined
> in the command, "All things therefore whatsoever ye would that
> men should do unto you, even so do ye also unto them." The light
> of this law shines in the inborn reason of all men. Did they but
> regard it, what need have they of books, teachers or laws? They
> carry with them in the depths of their hearts a living book, fitted to
> teach them fully what to do and what to omit, what to accept and
> what to reject, and what decision to make.[36]

It would seem, then, that the love of God and the love for neighbor are
ratifications of the first and second table of the Decalogue, which many in
the Reformed tradition consider a distilled and codified expression of the
natural law woven into the creation order.[37]

C. S. Lewis has shown how the Golden Rule has parallels around the
world in different cultures and religions, including some predating Jesus,
evidence of humanity's ability to grasp the principle of reciprocal justice
without special revelation or regeneration.[38] Markus Bockmuehl comments
similarly on how "the uncomplicated assumption of a kind of natural reciprocity and commonality of human needs suggests the acceptance of a moral

---

[36] Martin Luther, *Sermons for the Fourth Sunday after Epiphany: Romans 13:8-
10*, in *Luther's Epistle Sermons: Epiphany, Easter, and Pentecost*, ed. John Nicholas
(Minneapolis: Lutheran Press, 1909), 73.

[37] Grabill, *Rediscovering the Natural Law in Reformed Theological Ethics*, 146
(see chap. 4, n. 2).

[38] C. S. Lewis, *The Abolition of Man*, 83ff (see chap. 1, n. 7).

category that is general and self-evident, rather than positively revealed in the Torah."[39] Haines and Fulford also observe natural law reciprocity behind our Lord's words:

> Jesus teaches his disciples to take their own basic desires as ones that every human being has. Secondly, by telling them to satisfy those basic desires of others, he affirms those desiderata as good. The implication of these two premises is that Jesus teaches all people actually know what is good for them, on some level, since they have desires that ought to be met.[40]

What loving one's neighbor foregrounds is the most basic principle necessary to sustain life in society: a reciprocal assurance that decency and kindness will be faithfully returned if given. In that, moral trust undergirds the principle to love one's neighbor. An unstated truth of social cooperation is the abiding trust in trust itself that is required for there to be intelligible cooperation in society. If we have no assurance that our cooperation in society—not simply our niceties—will be returned, that would be the end of society itself. Reciprocity means cooperation toward moral goods prevails. Study any dystopic novel and one will quickly see that society breaks down when trust in moral interaction collapses. Trust in moral reciprocity, then, makes life in society not only manageable but potentially even promising as the mutual exchange of moral goods is realized between agents.

The love of neighbor assumes, of course, that people intuit the inherent good that one's own self should be treated fairly. Built into the principle is an indemonstrable or *per se nota* moral "ought" that persons just should act in this way if they are in their right minds. The teaching's principle is as simple as it is profound, which is why it is not uncommon for it to be among the first bits of moral instruction that parents teach their children (as was the

---

[39] Markus Bockmuehl, *Jewish Law in Gentile Churches: Halakhah and the Beginning of Christian Public Ethics* (Grand Rapids: Baker Academic, 2003), 118–19.

[40] Haines and Fulford, *Natural Law*, 82 (see chap. 6, n. 14).

case for our own children, for example). We teach this principle because it easily captures the most intuitive of principles: people innately understand what it means to prosper and feel respected as persons. Achieving a state of affairs where this is realized is hindered or even vitiated if we are unwilling to grant this state of affairs to others. The moral order requires the reciprocal execution of its norms in order for the individual and society's good to be realized. The possibility of obtaining our good is enhanced in proportion to our willing the good of our neighbor.

When we think of such ideas as the just society, we understand that the common good is loving one's neighbor in the aggregate. My safety on the road depends on another's safety on the road. As I want to be protected from wanton endangerment, so I should avoid wantonly endangering others. I do this not out of any pleasure-seeking utilitarian contract where pleasure is whatever society deems as desirable, but out of a belief in the concrete existence of goods that are valuable for their own sake.

When we, as Christians, love our neighbors, we do not do this only with generic commitment to the natural law (as valuable as that is), but out of a commitment to the ultimate finality of revelation given in Scripture. In Scripture is deposited the fullness of our neighbor's good, which is not merely temporal and penultimate, but eternal and ultimate. Loving our neighbor, then, requires us to operate on two horizons. The beatific good is not in conflict with the temporal good but all instances of the temporal good are opportunities for us to use them as signposts for the beatific good. Whatever is the neighborly good comports with God's order of creation and produces temporal joy while that which comports with God's order of redemption produces eternal and beatific good. Our neighbor's good is not only their neighborly safety, but their eternal destiny secured in Jesus Christ, who is goodness incarnated (Mark 10:18). The love of neighbor as Christians means we insist that people are made to know God. He is their ultimate good and happiness.

We are to genuinely seek after the fulfillment of our neighbor's good, which has both positive and negative dimensions. As a positive reality, I should treat my neighbor with the dignity and respect befitting their existence. As a negative reality, I should work to restrain—by either my own agency or the political agency of the community—privations from raining down on my neighbor. I should not personally hinder their good nor seek after policies that will their privation.

In Matt 12:25, Jesus appeals to the law of non-contradiction to communicate that "no city or house divided against itself will stand." Critics of the natural law are right to raise the concern that natural law, as far as how some of its proponents frame the topic, can appear to bypass the issue of Christology. Were natural law a method of ethics used to omit the name of Jesus Christ or to cordon ourselves off from the radical demands that Jesus places on his followers, I would join in that criticism. The issue, however, is that Jesus invokes creation order and natural law in his own ministry. That, coupled with the reality that the New Testament does not suspend the natural law, but rather clarifies it and heightens it, helps us understand that divorcing natural law considerations from issues of Christology is unwarranted.

# Conclusion

As we have seen in this chapter, the Bible's storyline is unintelligible apart from the natural law playing a vital role in it. As Protestants reflect upon their legacy of *sola Scriptura*, we would do well to re-center discussions of the natural law away from perceived negative associations that attend to it and focus more extensively on relating the ways in which natural law's teleological offerings demonstrate—and not merely assert—the substance of creation order and its signpost to the order or redemption. Such a task is theological in nature, which we turn to next.

# 8.

# The Theological Case for Natural Law

The famous legal philosopher and historian, Harold J. Berman, once observed that, "at the highest level, surely, the just and the holy are one, and our sense of each rests partly on our sense of the other. It is necessary to say this because conventional wisdom has separated them to the point of disaster."[1] An axiom of this formulation comes in response to the devastating shift in the twentieth century away from law's conception as anchored in divine reality and toward a positivist conception that reduced law merely to matters of judicial will and legislative decree. Berman's phrase is merely capturing what had previously been an uncontroversial thought: reason can grasp, and is even ordered to, a realm of justice that reflects the holy character of God.

---

[1] Harold J. Berman, *Faith and Order: The Reconciliation of Law and Religion* (Grand Rapids: Eerdmans, 1993), x.

The effect of this shift coincided with a twentieth century that saw a degree of barbarity and bloodshed that the world had not previously known. Of course, one must be cautious from hastily assuming a correlation-causation relationship between law's anthropocentric turn and corresponding bloodshed but let us begin with the proposition that once legal systems see themselves as accountable to no authority outside of their own decreeing, law can and will be used to the advantage of powerful interests.

If law is simply what any authority decrees, there is no end in sight at what is morally justifiable. It should come as no surprise that one of the defenses made by Nazi war criminals was their simply obeying Nazi law as it was duly enacted. If they were following a law, so the line of reasoning went, how could they be guilty of law breaking? This dilemma and many others like it, represent the perpetual conflict between law, religion, and morality. The law's deracination and emptying of divine impetus in the twentieth century shows what happens when legal regimes rule with unchecked moral accountability and with no view toward justice outside its own purview.

The linking of the just and the holy, as reconnected by Berman, reminds us that the natural law arises out of God's own being and nature. Law is just in accordance with its alignment with divine order and divine Being. The moral goods of the natural law are good in that their choiceworthiness as ends in themselves reflect the beatific good of God as the ultimate good and first cause and final end of all things. While the natural law's persuasiveness will stand or fall on its own claims as a testament to its own self-evidence, even those who refuse to give God his due as the architect of the natural law cannot fully evade the contours of the natural law. There is nowhere humanity can run and not be under the watchful gaze and constraints of God's moral order. We may try, and, indeed, we are trying. But such fleeing is futile. We cannot outrun or evade a God whose goodness—both internal to himself and external as communicated to us—are eternal. The natural law is thus an ineluctable reality that we will either learn from and reform or reject and regress into cultural devolution.

In this last explanatory chapter, we turn to the role of theology in formulating natural law theory. In particular, this chapter looks at a theological justification for knowledge of the natural law and provides summarizing axioms as to the relationship between theology and the natural law. It concludes by looking at the relationship between the creation order, the kingdom of God, and natural law.

## The Two-Fold Horizon of the Moral Order

The Bible presents a two-fold horizon for the moral order that natural law is cabined under. Heuristically, the first two chapters of Romans help illustrate those horizons. Let us, for the sake of argument, categorize Rom 1:18–32 as representing "Natural Law from Above" and Rom 2:14–15 representing "Natural Law from Below." The realms of each taken together as a whole will help us build a holistic theological account of natural law.

What I mean with these designations is that when Scripture speaks about its own moral order, it does so with reference to (1) the existence of the moral order itself and (2) our cognizance of the precepts within that moral order. We may liken this to the reality that with, say, baseball, there is the playing of the game itself as well as the rules that determine the proper operation of the game. So, too, does Scripture speak to this reality concerning the natural law. The two-fold horizon spoken of here references the existence of the natural law and, from it, our knowledge of the natural law as grasped by reason.

Romans 1 as referenced above testifies to the existence and orderliness of the natural law as a form of revelation within creation. God speaks through creation in the vastness and majesty of its design. Romans 2, on the other hand, speaks to human perception of the natural law as a function of reason and conscience. In a previous chapter, we discussed whether Scripture speaks with an explicit "theory" of natural law. We can say, in light of the last chapter, that Scripture speaks implicitly of a natural law theory since Scripture witnesses to both the existence of the natural law and our grasp of the natural law.

# Theological Justification for Knowledge of the Natural Law

Two of the most significant objections to the natural law is our knowledge of it and our capacity to obey it. There are two aspects to these objections: (1) What enables human beings to understand the substance of the natural law? (2) To what extent can the capacity to know the natural law be sustained in a world marred by sin?

At its most basic explanation, the natural law continues to persist because of God's common grace and general providence to uphold the lineament of creation order for the world's continued maintenance. Because human beings are made in God's image, they possess the requisite capacities as beings made in God's image (choice, deliberation, judgment) to understand moral knowledge and pursue moral goods. The powers of cognition, though marred, are not extinguished. Humanity cannot be so depraved so as to be unaware of its depravity. If we were so depraved as to not know any good, we would not know that goodness even exists and thus, morality and ethics would be a futile enterprise from the start. That we can name our sin and injustices evidences how glimmers of the natural law still break through the darkness of the human heart.

Our ability to grasp or discern the natural law comes to us through the capacities given to us as God's image-bearers. It is the image of God, writes David VanDrunen, that carries with it man's responsibility to bear that image: "Being created in the image of God carried with it a moral purpose, a commission."[2] God communicates the principles of righteousness and justice to us, his creatures, for us to reflect those qualities in our everyday life. The human person, by nature, just *is* a rational being capable of discerning moral truths. As humans live with an internal harmony that conduces to sound mind and sound action, they are pursuing what the natural law tradition considers "practical reasonabless" and what Scripture refers to as "wisdom."

---

[2] VanDrunen, *A Biblical Case for Natural Law*, 13 (see chap. 7, n. 35).

God's common grace reflects his commitment to the covenant of creation established in the Noahic covenant.[3] The natural law reflects God's covenantal relationship with creation. The continuation of creation order is God's commitment to uphold the most basic foundation of creation and elements of moral knowledge necessary for human survival. [A civilization is considered flourishing to the extent that it aligns itself with this order.] Indeed, there is no human flourishing apart from individuals and societies aligning themselves with creation order and natural law.

While humanity may err, suppress, and deceive themselves, the moral law remains engraved on their hearts, but impaired. Because of sin, individuals misapprehend the full entailments of morality and worse, willfully disobeying what they do know. But total eradication or extinguishment of the moral law would, however, be impossible as a practical matter for human civilization. Moreover, an argument that humanity retains no knowledge of the moral law would contravene a doctrine of God's common grace.

As fallen individuals, we continue to have access to the natural law because God upholds the structure of creation through common grace. Even the staunchest critics of the natural law cannot dismiss its abiding authority over non-Christians. If the Bible is to be taken seriously, humanity's relationship to the natural law is not its complete ignorance of it, but its refusal to obey what is known and cannot not be known. It is impossible for us not to know, for example, that the law of non-contradiction is what stands behind rational communication. Or it is impossible for humans to not have some underived knowledge of right or wrong, regardless of whether they admit to it or not. Yes, non-Christians may obscure, reject, obfuscate, and err in their grasp and application of the natural law, but such misfiring does not blot out the natural law and, indeed, cannot extinguish the natural law either.

---

[3] For an exhaustive survey on the relationship between natural law and the Noahic covenant, see David VanDrunen, *Divine Covenants and Moral Order: A Biblical Theology of Natural Law* (Grand Rapids: Eerdmans, 2014), 95–132; VanDrunen, *Politics after Christendom*, 124–49 (see chap. 3, n. 10).

Though it may sound controversial at first blush, we can insist upon the abiding validity of knowing the natural law because our intellects, wills, and passions—though fallen—are not fundamentally extinguished. Herman Bavinck rightly argues that with regard to our intellect, though it is "dulled, enfeebled and sometimes even suspended (in the mentally ill), it is not lost."[4] Regarding the will, though it can be "inflexible, stiff-necked, and willful or double-minded," as a native capacity inherent to our nature, it, too, "has not been lost."[5] Bavinck brilliantly summarizes the condition of the will, even in a state of sin: "We can freely and spontaneously, without compulsion, do what we do. We can even direct our will in accordance with our mind; that is, we can will only those things that the mind prescribes as good. This enables us to act rationally, reasonably, in accord with the voice of reason."[6] So, too, can our emotions or passions "express themselves too feebly or too strongly (when they become extreme, excessive, or unregulated), or are disharmonious and conflict with one another."[7] But even the emotions have not lost the capacity to know and rejoice what is appropriate to their due end and "directed in proper measure to the right goals."[8]

Despite fallen humanity's contentment to holding to a morality it cannot give an account for, no matter how hard we run in the opposite direction, humanity cannot evade the natural law in full. Running headlong against it only serves to reinforce the limits and contours of God's creation. As history reveals in such evil events as the Holocaust or wicked practices such as the North Atlantic slave trade, we come to re-learn the natural law either gladly or stubbornly. Either way, it cannot be rejected in perpetuity without it striking back in the fiercest of ways.  *Agree.*

John Calvin's thoughts on the epistemology of the natural law are particularly illuminating. In Calvin's view, there is a two-fold knowledge of

---

[4] Bavinck, *Reformed Ethics: Created, Fallen, and Converted Humanity*, 1:151 (see chap. 3, n. 19).

[5] Bavinck, 1:151.

[6] Bavinck, 1:151.

[7] Bavinck, 1:151–52.

[8] Bavinck, 1:152.

God—the "*duplex cognito Dei*."[9] There is knowledge of God as Creator and knowledge of God as Redeemer. Similar categorization can be found in the work of Anglican Divine Richard Hooker who divided knowledge of God salvifically as "Revelation" and regarding a general knowledge of God's moral law as common "Reason." Whether from Calvin or Hooker, salvific and non-salvific knowledge are both a divine dispensation.[10] There is thus a duality of epistemological scope without forging a dualistic knowledge of God. God the Redeemer is hidden from the unregenerate while God the Creator is universally present to his creation. For our purposes, we can envisage this God as the God of "In God We Trust" on American coinage. It is a conception of God as the Creator of all things. We maintain a general assent and awareness to this understanding of God through what Calvin refers to as the *sensus divinitatis*. By nature, persons possess a divine sense perception akin to the power of other senses. There persists within humanity as divine image-bearers a mechanism of nature that enables their knowledge of God in the most creational and generic of senses. According to this view, there subsists within humanity the natural ability to know God as Creator through general revelation and common operation in the world or what Calvin calls "things below."[11]

This represents a non-salvific understanding of God's existence. The knowledge of God in view with the *sensus divinitatis* is both an illuminating and condemning knowledge. According to Calvin, "To prevent anyone from taking refuge in the pretense of ignorance, God himself has implanted in all men a certain understanding of his divine majesty."[12] God holds all humanity

---

[9] For a detailed examination of this concept and John Calvin's broader natural law theory, see Grabill, *Rediscovering the Natural Law in Reformed Theological Ethics*, 70–97 (see chap. 4, n. 2).

[10] Richard Hooker, "The Laws of Ecclesiastical Polity" in *The Works of That Learned and Judicious Divine Mr. Richard Hooker with an Account of His Life and Death by Isaac Walton*, rev. R.W. Church and F. Paget, 7th ed. (Oxford: Clarendon, 1888), vol. 1, 150.

[11] Calvin, *Institutes*, 1:2.2.13.

[12] Calvin, 1:1.3.1.

culpable because all of humanity has some general awareness of God. In a well-known passage, Calvin writes: "First, as much in the fashioning of the universe as in the general teaching of Scripture the Lord shows himself to be simply the Creator. Then in the face of Christ he shows himself the Redeemer."[13] I hold that the incomplete knowledge of God as Creator is a true knowledge of God as such that humanity errs in how it is prone to "misperceive, suppress, distort, deny, and abuse in the true knowledge of God."[14] As Stephen Grabill writes, this general knowledge of God and his moral laws are a "constitutive aspect of the human mind and thus justly hold people accountable for their implicit moral sense and their awareness of God's existence."[15]

There is one very powerful reason for why some liminal knowledge of God's natural law is necessary for the storyline of Scripture: for humans to be guilty in their sin, it is required that they have a true knowledge of whom they are rejecting. The blindness we have is willed blindness. Our blindness is not imposed from outside of us but emanates from our fallen natures. It is this willed blindness that makes us sinners by choice and by nature and fully deserving of just condemnation.[16] According to Calvin, despite sin's effect on both the will and the mind, it has not erased all moral residue from human nature:

> When we so condemn human understanding for its perpetual blindness as to leave it no perception of any object whatever, we not only go against God's Word, but also run counter to the experience of common sense. For we see implanted in human nature some sort of desire to search out the truth to which man would not at all aspire if he had not already savored it. Human understanding then possesses some power of perception, since it is by nature captivated by love of truth.[17]

---

[13] Calvin, 1:1.2.1.

[14] Grabill, *Rediscovering the Natural Law in Reformed Theological Ethics*, 84.

[15] Grabill, 71.

[16] I'm indebted to my student Michael Carlino for this insight.

[17] Calvin, *Institutes*, 1:2.2.12.

For Calvin, even fallen humanity's desire for truth reflects a prerequisite knowledge of its existence and God's existence. Calvin writes,

> All the Gentiles alike instituted religious rites, they made laws to punish adultery, and theft, and murder, they commended good faith in bargains and contracts. They have thus indeed proved, that God ought to be worshipped, that adultery, and theft, and murder are evils, that honesty is commendable. It is not to our purpose to inquire what sort of God they imagined him to be, or how many gods they devised; it is enough to know, that they thought that there is a God, and that honor and worship are due to him. It matters not whether they permitted the coveting of another man's wife, or of his possessions, or of any thing which was his,—whether they connived at wrath and hatred; inasmuch as it was not right for them to covet what they knew to be evil when done.[18]

Calvin goes on to define the natural law as such: "natural law is that apprehension of the conscience that distinguishes sufficiently between just and unjust, and which deprives men of the excuse of ignorance, while it proves them guilty by their own testimony."[19] The *duplex cognito Dei* and the *sensus divinitatis*[20] by no means impart any salvific knowledge of God. In fact, it imparts only a sense of culpability in the guilty knowledge one possesses for having broken God's law, and the cosmic debt one senses is owed to a Supreme Being. Christians, in contrast, profess a revelational knowledge of God as redeemer. The Christian knowledge of God is based on special revelation. God is not merely the "Creator," but the redeemer God known as Father, Son, and Holy Spirit. If willed blindness was our estate while in

---

[18] John Calvin, *Commentaries on the Epistle of Paul the Apostle to the Romans*, trans. John Owen (Grand Rapids: Christian Classics Ethereal Library, n.d.), https://www.ccel.org/ccel/calvin/calcom38.vi.iv.html.

[19] Calvin, *Institutes*, 1:2.2.22.

[20] Calvin, 1:1.3.1.

a state of perdition, the gift of the Spirit awakens us to the spectacles of revealed religion that allows us to see creation in all resplendent glory.

We might structure this division as follows in the following table:

| Doctrinal Issue | Creation | Redemption |
|---|---|---|
| Realm | Nature | Grace |
| God's covenantal constituency: | Humanity | The Church |
| God's expression of Grace: | Common | Saving |
| God known as: | Creator | Redeemer |
| God's law revealed through: | Natural revelation and reason (creation) | Special revelation and redeemed reason |
| God's law grasped by: | Conscience | Conscience, Scripture and the Holy Spirit |
| Ethics: | General equity, justice, prudence, temperance, and fortitude | Faith, hope, and love |
| End of humanity: | Human flourishing and social cooperation | Beatific vision; membership in God's kingdom |
| Authority: | Civil rulers | Church and pastors |
| Authority's mode: | Coercion and civil law | The law of Christ (Gal 6:2) |
| Natural law's purpose: | Basic knowledge of right and wrong of moral goods; indicting for sin; restraining evil; instruction in wisdom | Knowledge of right and wrong; indicting for sin; instruction in wisdom; illuminates toward righteousness, ratifies creation order |
| Purpose of moral goods | Flourishing (earthly good); civil tranquility | Doxological Flourishing (complete good) |

| Institutional duration: | Temporal (e.g., government) | Eternal (e.g., church) |
|---|---|---|
| Authority's locus: | Unregenerate people | Regenerate people |

These realities enable the natural law to function within humanity while allowing the church to know the ultimate foundation and ultimate terminus of the natural law. Elsewhere Calvin speaks favorably of the natural law's engravement on human nature:

> Now, as it is evident that the law of God which we call moral, is nothing else than the testimony of natural law, and of that conscience which God has engraven on the minds of men, the whole of this equity of which we now speak is prescribed in it. Hence it alone ought to be the aim, the rule, and the end of all laws. Wherever laws are formed after this rule, directed to this aim, and restricted to this end, there is no reason why they should be disapproved by us, however much they may differ from the Jewish law, or from each other.[21]

Calvin is clear to suggest that the natural law retains its own sufficiency proportionate to its own end, which is to supply humanity with a basic understanding of "equity," or natural justice. Much in the same way as the previous quote, for Calvin, the natural law also serves as the creational backdrop making possible the continued durability and intelligibility of creation: "Since man is sociable by nature, he has a natural tendency to want to maintain and preserve society. Thus we see stamped on the minds of all men common ideas concerning decency and social order."[22]

Contrary to depictions of Calvin as denying the possibility of true moral knowledge because of human depravity, Calvin's doctrine demonstrates a

---

[21] Calvin, *Institutes*, 4.20.16.
[22] Calvin, *Institutes*, 2.2.13.

clear doctrine of natural law that helpfully explains the current status of unregenerate humanity in relation to the natural law.

## Theological Axioms of the Natural Law

Putting together the previous chapters and now this chapter as well, below are what I would consider axiomatic theological summaries of natural law ethics.

*The natural law teaches that morality is ultimately theistic, ordered, and objective. It is therefore ineluctable.* Natural law, by definition, assumes the concrete existence of real moral goods and moral norms. The existence of moral goods and moral "oughts" emanate from "the directive intelligence of the Creator."[23] Within metaphysical categories, existence implies objectivity. Objectivity denotes conformity to a standard of true being. "Objective" in this sense means "corresponds with what is true of reality," or as C. S. Lewis says, the "belief that certain attitudes are really true, and others really false, to the kind of thing that universe is and the kind of things we are."[24] Thus, natural law is a moral theory entirely opposed to relativism, emotivism, behaviorism, socio-biological constructivism, existentialism, and hedonism. As moral realists, Christians affirm that our actions have actual (not perceived) moral freight to them and are subject to moral evaluation. For example, fornication does not "appear" to be wrong because of mere consensus or emotional register. No, fornication is a morally wrong action because it subverts the objective good of marriage that God designed as the exclusive bounds of sexual intimacy. Moral goods are obtained by morally upright actions constituted within a moral universe. To say that a moral good has objective goodness to it means that its goodness cannot be undone. A moral good is not subject to change, decay, or enhancement. Furthermore, the natural law, since it is embedded into the structure of the universe, is

---

[23] Grisez, "Natural Law and the Transcendent Source of Human Fulfillment," 448 (see introduction, n. 5).

[24] C. S. Lewis, *The Abolition of Man* (see chap 1, n. 7).

unavoidable. We will always play by its rules, whether to our fortune or misfortune. The quotidian realities of the natural law are an ineluctable reality in that its order reflects the givenness of creation.

*The natural law relies on indemonstrable principles of God's existence for*  *its ultimate intelligibility.* While I am not a presuppositionalist by traditional categories, natural law is, from an ultimate vantage point, incoherent without presupposing its ultimately theistic foundation. According to Franciscus Junius,

> We call principles those that are known in themselves, are immovable, and are indemonstrable, that is . . . for example, the principle of knowledge that is innate to the mind is 'God exists,' and in life is 'preserving our existence, our species, and justice.' We call common conclusions, however, those things that natural reason, with the light of nature leading the way, constructs from the principles, such as, for example, that God must be worshiped, and that our life, our species, and the supports of justice must be cared for.[25]

These moral axioms *just are* and cannot be proven apart from assuming the intelligibility of the principles as sound premises in themselves. Only God can be the first cause of indemonstrable principles, or else the principles cannot be proven or otherwise obligatory.[26] Natural law *just is* by virtue of the universe God has ordered. This is not a fallback or simplistic explanation; it is, rather, the necessary premise to the conclusion that the natural law exists.

*The natural law demands the necessity of an ultimate Lawgiver.* While natural law theorists debate the possibility of a self-emanating moral law,

---

[25] Franciscus Junius, *The Mosaic Polity*, trans. Todd M. Rester (Grand Rapids: Christian's Library Press, 2015), 46.

[26] Once again, C. S. Lewis's remarks are helpful on this point. He wrote, "But you cannot go on 'explaining away' for ever: you will find that you have explained explanation itself away. You cannot go on 'seeing through' things for ever. The whole point of seeing through something is to see something through it." See Lewis, *The Abolition of Man*, 81.

the vision for natural law described in this book is one ordered by the triune God. For a moral system to be objective, its objectivity must be given to it by an ultimate source of objectivity. Appeals to non-instrumental goods may be valid, but their validity requires an ordination for the goods' existence in the first place. This source we call God. Otherwise, morality is merely a self-contained system invented from thin air. The Lawgiver promulgates moral law as a reflection of the Lawgiver's own nature and rationality. As stated in the previous chapter, eternal reason emanating outward is the basis for the natural law's existence. The standard for a moral law is thus the lawgiver's own being and character. Moral goodness, then, reflects God's own goodness (1 Pet 1:15–16). While basic moral goods are irreducibly and ineluctably absolute in that their intelligibility is true by the sheer force of their own reasonableness and choiceworthiness, the existence of the good and the determination of its goodness is a set of conditions that the good cannot achieve on its own. God gives moral goodness out of his own character. No moral "good" could ever be anything other than the good it possesses if the good reflects God. If God is immutable, so must be the moral goods consistent with his being. As what C. S. Lewis says about the impossibility of there being a new "ethics" relates to the impossibility of there being new moral goods coming into existence: "Let us very clearly understand that, in a certain sense, it is no more possible to invent a new ethics than to place a new sun in the sky. Some precept from traditional morality always has to be assumed."[27] While moral goods can be discovered (not invented) under the auspices of practical reason, all moral goods reflect the eternal goodness of God.

   *The natural law reminds fallen humanity of its culpability and the righteousness of judgment.* The most enduring reality of the natural law for sinners is its power to indict human sinfulness for our failure to live up to its ideals. Every vain, wicked, cruel, and perverse thought or action reveals humanity's condition. The existence of an objective moral law stands to

----

[27] Lewis, "On Ethics," *Christian Reflections*, 66 (see chap. 7, n. 15).

witness to our rebellion and attempted evasion not only of the law itself, but of the Lawgiver. Despite attempts at rationalization and self-justification, every human being's conscience knows they owe a debt they cannot pay—a failure to live up to a standard of goodness that every person wishes they followed but know they cannot. John Henry Cardinal Newman offers a powerful example of how the witness of conscience testifies to our breaking the law of the Lawgiver:

> If, as is the case, we feel responsibility, are ashamed, are frightened, at transgressing the voice of conscience, this implies that there is one to whom we are responsible, before whom we are ashamed, whose claims upon us we fear. If, on doing wrong, we feel the same tearful, broken-hearted sorrow which overwhelms us in hurting a mother; if, on doing right, we enjoy the same sunny serenity of mind, the same soothing satisfactory delight which follows on our receiving praise from a father, we certainly have within us the image of some person, to whom our love and veneration look, in whose smile we find our happiness, for whom we yearn, towards whom we direct our pleadings, in whose anger we are troubled and waste away. These feelings in us are such as require for their exciting cause an intelligent being; we are not affectionate towards a stone, nor do we feel shame before a horse or a dog; we have no remorse or compunction on breaking mere human law: yet, so it is, conscience excites all these painful emotions, confusion, foreboding, self-condemnation; and on the other hand it sheds upon us a deep peace, a sense of security, a resignation, and a hope, which there is no sensible, no earthly object to elicit. "The wicked flees when no one pursueth;" then why does he flee? Whence his terror? Who is it that he sees in solitude, in darkness, in the hidden chambers of his heart? If the cause of these emotions does not belong to this visible world, the object towards which his perception is directed must be supernatural and divine; and thus the phenomena of conscience, as a dictate, avail to impress the imagination with the picture of a

supreme governor, a judge, holy, just, powerful, all-seeing, retributive, and is the creative principle of religion, as the moral sense is
the principle of ethics.[28]

6) *The natural law illuminates our understanding of creation order, human
design, and life in society.* One of the most valuable aspects of natural law is
how it illuminates the order of God's world. Rather than walking blind, the
principles of the natural law guide us into alignment with creation order.
Natural law itself may well as be shorthand for creation order—the way
creation is structured and our obligation to live within its natural boundaries. All this flows downstream from the idea that natural law is objective
morality issued by a Lawgiver. As a teleological ethical system, natural law
ethics teaches that a thing's purpose exists and is actually knowable, that
its purpose is evident in its design, and that the purpose of a thing determines which sound principles of morality are necessary to the thing in question's proper use. From protecting human life to the knowledge of what
marriage is, natural law provides teleological categories that provide inviolable boundaries from which to both define and act to secure them. The
Christian's insistence that morality exists and is knowable is one of the biggest elements of common grace we can give a world awash in moral nihilism
and relativism. Where moral relativism offers the appearance of inclusion
and kindness, the true hideousness of moral skepticism is the harm it does
to individuals and societies told to live with virtually no moral restraints.
If the purpose of a thing is to know what it is to *do* in order for it to know
itself in a complete way, natural law theory explains both proper function
and ultimate destiny—modalities that our culture rejects.

7) *The natural law is a pedagogical and evangelistic tool to be appealed to for
directing an interlocutor's moral awareness to God's existence and the need for
salvation.* From natural longings for injustice to be rectified, to the general
call to love our neighbor and see them thrive under a regime of just laws that

---

[28] John Henry Newman, *An Essay in Aid of a Grammar of Assent* (Oxford:
Oxford University Press, 1985), 76.

enable them to flourish, the natural law is a device that provides a common moral grammar that should enable us to question our neighbor's desire for justice and natural obligation. As Paul aptly demonstrates at Mars Hill, the use of natural theology and natural law can serve the purposes of directing individuals from a vague awareness of morality and divinity to the specific realty of Jesus's divinity and resurrection.

*The natural law demonstrates that Christian ethics centers primarily on*  *the existence and obtainment of moral goods guided by sound moral principles; not following rules as ends-in-themselves or aggregative accounts of morality that are based on consequence, pleasure, or situationism.* Natural law thus aides against legalism and subjectivism. A perennial debate in ethics centers on whether ethics ought to be understood by a focus on goods, consequences, or means (e.g., action, conduct, or rules). Deontology focuses on means. Utilitarianism focuses on consequences (ends). Classical teleology focuses on goods. Classical teleology—which is where natural law is cabined under—has also gotten moral principles wrong. For example, Aristotle taught that the natural law sanctioned human hierarchy and slavery.[29] A Christian natural law theory, on the other hand, has the benefit of focusing on the concrete obtaining of goods regulated by rightful action as handed down definitively in Scripture.

Since consequentialism finds it difficult to arrive at limiting principles and rules-as-ends-in-themselves can become legalistic, Christian natural law ethics rejects extreme forms of consequentialism while also rejecting an inordinate focus on rules-as-ends-in-themselves as the locus of ethics. Regarding deontology, focusing on obedience to rules (means) apart from the existence of moral goods (ends) can lead to a rigid moral casuistry where the goal of ethics are the rules themselves. Where conformity to expected behavior is taken as the *summum bonum* of ethics, it leads to moralism. Christian natural law ethics offers not just a clear pathway for moral action but moral purpose guarded by real moral limits. Scripture speaking about the existence

---

[29] Aristotle, *Politics*, I.v.

of moral goods under the canopy of God's glory offers a two-fold rationale for ethics: (1) All action is pursued for the highest good, God's glory; and (2) All God-glorifying action is action commensurate with obtaining the goods necessary for human flourishing.

*The Christian life does not negate the natural law or natural moral goods but illuminates them and allows for even greater obedience to their precepts and greater joy upon their obtainment.* Nowhere in the New Testament are the principles of the natural law nullified, suspended, or abrogated. Because the principles of the natural law are part of a created whole by God, they can no more be suspended than God could suspend his own being. The New Testament offers a pathway for greater conformity to the natural law, which, by the power of the Holy Spirit, helps our nature learn the glory of the very first act of grace, which is creation itself (e.g., 1 Cor 6:12–20). While common grace preserves nature, saving grace ratifies nature's original intelligibility and illuminates nature's fulfillment in Jesus Christ. Saving grace restores nature to our ultimate end in knowing God as beings designed to be in relationship with him. Saving grace situates nature's economy within the realm of redemption such that, in Christ, the fullness of humanity is both repristinated and reaches its highest fulfillment even as we await a new creation. As Bernd Wannenwetsch writes, "Christ restores creation by helping those who after the Fall have to live 'natural lives' to reconnect with the divine purpose of all creation so as to become what they have been destined for in the beginning."[30] Or, as Jonathan Edwards said to the same effect, "But in the sanctifying work of the Holy Ghost, not only remaining principles are assisted to do their work to a greater degree, but those principles are restored that were utterly destroyed by the fall; [so that] the mind habitually exerts those acts that the dominion of sin had made the soul wholly destitute of."[31]

---

[30] Wannenwetsch, "Creation and Ethics: On the Legitimacy and Limitation of Appeals to 'Nature' in Christian Moral Reasoning," 210 (see chap. 2, n. 17).

[31] Jonathan Edwards, *The Works of Jonathan Edwards*, 13:513.

The gospel's effect on the Christian's life does not eradicate their human nature so as to propose a whole new ethics at odds with creaturely being, "but from a changed understanding of the human condition" that comes from the Holy Spirit, we are made aware of what constitutes true creaturely fulfillment and happiness.[32] The content of morality is not so much transformed as is the framework for how it is activated and achieved within and upon the Christian agent, namely, the Holy Spirit's regenerating effect on human understanding and human agency (Rom 12:1–2; 1 Cor 6:9–10; Col 3:10, 17). Even if we grant that our relationship to the natural law has changed as those who are regenerated are no longer condemned by failing to obey it, the fact remains that Christ obeyed the natural law in its fullness and, in doing so, demonstrates how "original human destiny is achieved for those who believe in him."[33] The moral law and the moral goods *themselves* do not undergo an ontological change from unregeneracy to regeneracy. Natural principles of morality must have their own integrity, or else general morality does not have what is required for it to be true morality—universality. Christianity takes natural principles and gives them directional and eschatological fullness in light of the gospel of Jesus Christ. Those within the realm of creation cannot attain the realm of redemption without the intervening grace of God, but neither does the Christian's participation in the realm of redemption negate their participation within the order of creation. A Christian has a heightened plane of awareness of what their participation in the order of creation means and are to leaven the order of creation with the truths of redemption's promised fulfillment.[34]

---

[32] Black, "Is the New Natural Law Theory Christian?" 157 (see chap. 6, n. 11).

[33] VanDrunen, *Divine Covenants and Moral Order*, 436 (see chap. 8, n. 3).

[34] Readers may note that the position I argue for aligns with Progressive Covenantalism. For a helpful chapter that explains how ethics functions explicitly and hermeneutically within Progressive Covenantalism, see Stephen J. Wellum, "Progressive Covenantalism and the Doing of Ethics," in *Progressive Covenantalism*, ed. Stephen J. Wellum and Brent E. Parker (Nashville: B&H Academic, 2016), 215–33.

Here is where I must agree and disagree with someone like David
VanDrunen, who argues from "an ultimate level" that Christians "have
been released from the natural law through their union with the crucified
and exalted Christ and yet, at a penultimate level, must continue to live
within the structures of this present world that exist under the authority
of the natural law through the Noahic Covenant."[35] The problem is that
VanDrunen's notion of "release" is too strong. While VanDrunen is correct that we live in an era of overlapping ages, we are not released from
the authority and necessity of the moral goods stemming from the natural
law. We merely attain a heightened understanding of their origin and *telos*.
In the same section of writing, he goes on to insist that Christians have
no need of "basic institutions" like the state and family because we have
been "released from the authority of the Noahic natural law."[36] That is too
strong. The covenant of redemption does not negate the validity of creation
order. VanDrunen seems to blur categories when he negates the timeless-
ness and authority of the natural law and moral goods with membership in
the New Covenant.

Interestingly enough, he writes that "determining how to witness to
the moral order of the new creation while also honoring the natural moral
order perhaps constitutes the principal challenge for Christian ethics."[37]
This volume has sought to take up that challenge by insisting on the ongoing authority of the natural law as refracted through the eschatological
lens of Christ as the *telos* of creation. In fairness to VanDrunen, his understanding of "release" stems from his argument that Christians are no longer
under the covenant of works that he associates with the natural law. In that
sense, he is correct that we as Christians are not "under the law" from the
perspective of works-righteousness. We are, though, still governed by an
objective moral order meant for us to experience temporal flourishing. Even
still, VanDrunen's rhetoric seems to throw the baby (abiding moral goods,

[35] VanDrunen, *Divine Covenants and Moral Order*, 416.
[36] VanDrunen, 416.
[37] VanDrunen, 417.

which should be kept) out with the bathwater (covenant of works, which we are no longer under). We may no longer live under the "oversight" of the natural law from an Old Testament covenantal perspective, but we do live under its auspices as a grant of eternal law and especially in light of the New Testament's confirmation of the abiding reality of that eternal law.[38] Christians are called to uphold, defend, honor, publicly support, and participate in the institutions of creation order and natural law even as they live in light of a new eschatological age borne witness through the institutional church that transforms and guides by an ethic of love.

The nature of moral goods does not change from a state of unregeneracy to regeneration; modes of motivation to obtain them change and knowledge of them deepens. The moral goods are what they are as expressions of God's eternal law; what changes is the understanding of the framework from which those goods are grasped and what their purpose is in relationship to ultimate matters. The Christian and the non-Christian can both grasp the good of family life. But it is only the Christian who can rightly order their understanding of family in relationship to the kingdom of God. My brother in Christ, Matt, does not cause me to forsake or detach the earthly brotherhood of my biological sibling, Chris. Christians and non-Christians can both grasp the good of political authority and political justice, even while the church preaches an ethic of radical mercy and forgiveness in view of redemption. Christians and non-Christians can both grasp the good of vocational labor and supporting one's family even while the church practices a radical command to hold all things in common (Acts 4:32–35).

The in-breaking of an eschatological ethic does not undermine or negate the durability of natural law's moral goods. Nor could they, since moral goods are a product of an eternal law. Every moral reality obtains a heightened gloss from the vantage point of redemption. As Germain Grisez writes, "For nothing one does—nothing hard one must do and no suffering one must undergo—is merely for the present age's future. Rather, all of it is

---

[38] VanDrunen, 441.

for the far more important future of the age to come. And in that age, the real meaning and value of everything one did, in the Spirit of the Lord and in accord with his command, to promote and protect human goods in the present age will be gloriously manifest."[39] In contrast, though the same in substance, moral goods serve a different purpose for non-Christians. Even though fallen humanity is hostile to God and its spiritual relationship to God is broken, humanity retains knowledge of the moral goods appropriate to their due end as creaturely goods in themselves. Non-salvific, they are nonetheless real moral goods worthy of non-Christians to pursue. According to Bavinck, "In spiritual, heavenly matters, knowledge, will, and ability have been entirely lost. In moral and civil matters, in temporal, earthly matters, knowledge, will, and ability have been weakened, but not entirely taken away. There is therefore a certain good, measured by an earthly, temporal standard—and by natural persons themselves—that acquires temporal rewards. In themselves those virtues are good. But evaluated by the measure of God's holiness, the best virtues are splendid vices."[40] Above all, we should insist that moral goods retain the character of goodness by virtue of their reflection and grounding in God's own being.

 *The natural law guards against the encroachment of arbitrary absolutes in determining moral content.* A perennial question in ethics is the Euthyphro dilemma, which is traditionally described as the dilemma of whether something is good only because God wills what is good or whether because something is good, therefore God wills it. Is goodness independent of God? If so, is God fully God if goodness exists independent of him? At the crux of this question is an important debate for applied ethics: Are truth, justice, and moral goodness arbitrary by sheer force of God's will? In other words: If God willed torturing babies, would it be good? A question of this nature also strikes at important downstream topics like political authority. Is political authority legitimate by sheer command alone or must the authorities

---

[39] Grisez, "Natural Law and the Transcendent Source of Human Fulfillment," 456.

[40] Bavinck, *Reformed Ethics: Created, Fallen, and Converted Humanity*, 1:161.

command what is truly good and just in order to be legitimate? If a political authority does not wield its power for what is truly good, how can its law be truly binding? A Christian natural law approach can help answer these questions. It does so by positing the synchronicity of goodness and authority as co-extensive with God's own nature. God, in other words, has legitimate authority because his authority springs from the goodness of His own being. Political authority, in turn, can be truly legitimate and commanding of our obedience under the assurances that its authority is being meted out for what is truly good and in the interest of the political community. As Cooper and Dyer write,

> a theology that roots moral obligation in the arbitrary will of God alone suggests that God's superior strength is the source of his authority, setting the pattern for human rule founded on force, the strong doing what they will and the weak suffering what they must. On the other hand, a theology that affirms a standard of goodness outside of God's will lacks any authoritative prescription. It can do no more than establish hypothetical, rather than categorical, imperatives. Power without goodness does not entail authority, and goodness without authority does not entail law. The unity of power and goodness is necessary for the establishment of the rule of law founded on the idea of an authority who may legitimately legislate for the common good.[41]

To summarize, a Christian can insist upon the unity of goodness and authority by virtue of which God has revealed himself to be in his Word.

*The natural law reflects the divine reason of the Logos, Jesus Christ* Supremely, Christians must have a concern for the natural law because we are called to love Jesus Christ. Jesus Christ is the origin and terminus of the natural law. He is truth (John 14:6) who sets humanity free to pursue communion with him (John 8:32). He testifies to the enduring authority and

---

[41] Cooper and Dyer, *The Classical and Christian Origins of American Politics: Political Theology, Natural Law, and the American Founding*, 18.

intelligibility of creation order (Matt 19:4–6). He is reason, the rationale for reason, and reason personified. In this, Christ is the *ratio, ratio legis*, and *ratione personae* of the natural law.[42] Christ as the *ratio* of the natural law means he is the basis of reason itself. To say Christ is the *ratio legis* of the natural law means he is "the logical element of the law, or the purpose that animated the legislator in the issuance of the law."[43] Christ's own glory is the reason any such law exists. As the *ratione personae*, in contrast to traditional expressions of natural law theory that depict law as an impersonal "ordinance of reason"—or *Tao,* to use C. S. Lewis's term in *The Abolition of Man*—a Protestant and evangelical account of natural law sees the logic and instantiation of the natural law as inextricably bound with God's plan to sum up all things, even the principles of sound moral reasoning, in the *person*, Jesus Christ (Eph 1:9–10). Reflecting this truth, later in his life, C. S. Lewis would go on to state, "Is not the Tao the Word Himself, considered from a particular point of view?"[44] Lewis elsewhere reflects on the relationship between Christ and the natural law:

> [W]hat lies beyond existence, what admits no contingency, what lends divinity to all else, what is the ground of all existence, is not simply a law but also a begetting love, a love begotten, and the love which, being between these two, is also imminent in all those who are caught up to share the unity of their self-caused life. God is not merely good, but goodness; goodness is not merely divine, but God.[45]

---

[42] Aaron X. Fellmeth and Maurice Horwitz, eds., "Ratio," in *Guide to Latin in International Law* (Oxford: Oxford University Press, 2009); Aaron X. Fellmeth and Maurice Horwitz, eds., "Ratio Legis," in *Guide to Latin in International Law* (Oxford: Oxford University Press, 2009); Aaron X. Fellmeth and Maurice Horwitz, eds., "Ratione Personae," in *Guide to Latin in International Law* (Oxford: Oxford University Press, 2009).

[43] "Ratio legis," Educalingo, accessed December 2, 2022, https://educalingo.com/en/dic-it/ratio-legis.

[44] Letter to Clyde S. Kilby, January 11, 1961 (CLIII1226-1227) quoted in Peterson, *C. S. Lewis and the Christian Worldview*, 74 (see chap. 2, n. 10).

[45] Lewis, "The Poison of Subjectivism," 99 (see chap. 7, n. 15).

In previous chapters, I spoke of the natural law in the categories of its origin, knowability, substance, and utility. The same can apply within the theological horizon. Natural law has God as its origin. It is known through an orderly creation made accessible by God's endowment of reason in human beings. Knowledge of right and wrong, as well as moral goods that complete human beings, comprises its substance. Understanding the structure of morality for human flourishing and the necessity of natural law to sound social order are the grounds of its utility. It also an apologetic tool to draw people to Christ by appealing to their innate sense of justice and morality.

## Kingdom, Creation, and the Eclipse of Natural Law

Despite decades-long concerns about the direction of American culture, even among more conservative sectors of Protestantism, there is a reluctance toward and absence of natural law thinking. In the opinion of this author, among other reasons for this situation discussed later, this lacuna is the result of an indeterminate relationship between the realms of redemption and creation, or a disproportionate fixation on "Grace" to the neglect of "Nature."

At the risk of being misunderstood, my criticism is not that prioritizing the doctrine of salvation and redemption as the primary mission of the church is somehow wrong or should be less of a priority than it is. Who could argue that the church's mission should be anything less than primarily salvation-centric? Rather, locating Christian mission primarily within the realm of redemption and omitting how creation functions within that drama helps explain part of the lacuna facing evangelical ethics. If salvation is about escape from the material creation, it can easily veer toward a rejection of creation's ongoing authority over our common creaturely lives. This incipient soteriological Gnosticism focusing disproportionately on redemption alone in evangelical theology has allowed for redemption to subsume considerations related to creation and nature. In the words of J. Daryl Charles:

At the heart of the rejection of natural law by Protestant social ethics is the erection of a false dichotomy between nature and grace,
leading to the mistaken assumption, particularly among evangelical
Protestants, that the natural law is distinct from "Christian social
ethics." This mistaken distinction fails to see the role our common
human nature plays in moral theory and moral discourse—and
thus it undermines any attempts to enter the public square, where
critical ethical issues are at stake.[46]

Charles's criticism is a valid one because he rightly captures not only
the significance of nature but the tendency for Protestant social ethics to pit
grace versus nature in a hostile relationship, as though our spiritual regeneration is disjointed from creational considerations.

Solving this gordian knot is thus vital to re-balancing the realms of
creation and redemption into a happier relationship that honors both sepa-
rately and in their relationship to one another. Grace assumes the original
ontological goodness of nature. Creation (or nature) is thus a prerequisite to
redemption, but redemption (grace) does not repudiate or vitiate creation
order; it ratifies its enduring intelligibility. Common grace preserves nature
while saving grace fulfills nature.[47] The preservation of nature, despite sin,
is an undeserved but non-salvific grace. Creation remains an "ontological
priority" as a "prerequisite for the reception of divine grace."[48] Rather than
dismissing creation, a fully orbed kingdom ethics understands that the fullness of creation is unlocked for the Christian, whose responsibility includes
telling the world about the creation order it is hellbent to reject.

When preoccupied almost exclusively on kingdom ethics, its proponents tend to forge a false bifurcation on the kingdom's ongoing relationship to creation. It results in an ethic that focuses on special revelation to
the neglect of natural revelation. It creates a theology of evacuation instead

---

[46] J. Daryl Charles, "Protestants and Natural Law," *First Things*, no. 168
(December 1, 2006): 37.

[47] I'm indebted to the categories of David VanDrunen in this rendering.

[48] Charles, *Retrieving the Natural Law*, 55 (see chap. 2, n. 14).

of a homesteading theology. It tends to offer an over-idealized version of the church as an alien community (hence "Resident Aliens" vis-à-vis Hauerwas)[49] whose mission is divorced from worldly affairs and whose radical rejection of creation ordinances (e.g., the state) or subjugation of creation ordinances (e.g., marriage) leaves Christians with no responsibility to the world as the world. The world, according to this view, has no inherent integrity worth trying to rehabilitate and recalibrate in light of the gospel.

The resurrection of Jesus Christ furnishes us with a better relationship between creation and redemption. As Oliver O'Donovan writes, the resurrection connects the severed relationship between creation and redemption, exhibiting "confirmation of the world-order which God has made. Man's life on earth is important to God; he has given it its order; it matters that it should conform to the order he has given it."[50] As O'Donovan rightly notes, it is the resurrection that enables us to grasp the threat of de-creation by a world inclined to reject it while at the same time pointing persons to their eschatological destiny without abrogating the authority of creation itself.[51]

The natural law, as argued for in this volume, bears an eschatological inflection. That is, from the perspective of the Christian, "nature" is not just a neutral substance or blank canvas for inhabitants to create, raze to the ground, and re-create at will. No, from the perspective of Christians, natural law reflects the order of creation that we see fulfilled in the resurrection of Jesus Christ. That creation retains ontological significance in light of Jesus Christ, "the summons to live in it is addressed to all mankind, because the good news that we may live in it is addressed to all mankind. Thus Christian moral judgments in principle address every man."[52]

A kingdom ethics that fails to understand the underlying ontology and abiding authority of creation fails to fully love the neighbor still anchored

---

[49] Stanley Hauerwas and William H. Willimon, *Resident Aliens: Life in the Christian Colony* (Nashville: Abingdon, 1989), 11.

[50] O'Donovan, *Resurrection and Moral Order*, 15–16 (see chap. 2, n. 18).

[51] O'Donovan, 15.

[52] O'Donovan, 17.

within creation. Kingdom ethics advocates thus ignore considerations of nature, general revelation, and natural law. Rather than "resident aliens," we should understand ourselves as "alien residents."[53] We are the redeemed who inherit creation, explaining its relevance to human flourishing in the present while pointing those within creation to the ultimate climax that awaits it. Christian ethics, then, extends to explaining nature to those who refuse to acknowledge the existence of ontological nature. We have a postlapsarian responsibility to tell sinful humanity what it refuses to believe about itself. We need those who exercise knowledge of redemption to tell creation's occupants what they refuse to believe about the divinely ordered nature they inhabit. A Great Commission focus that incorporates a stronger doctrine of creation understands that apart from aligning oneself with creation order, there can be no hope for human flourishing or relationship with the Savior-Creator.

## Conclusion

Natural law is the moral order we must reckon with whether we acknowledge it or want to play on its terms. It's there. To deny it is there is to deny the possibility of moral coherence and moral communication. The Bible's presentation of morality is that it is universal in scope, objective in its truthfulness, and intelligible as a reflection of its reasons for commanding our obligation to obey it. Biblical morality is, therefore, a matter of law. It exists and is for our good.

If this is true, we cannot act as though it isn't, nor can we refuse to bring its ethics to bear in every arena where ethics apply. If Christianity possesses a body of metaphysical truth claims oriented to the common good, it is the duty of the Christian to proclaim those truths and to counteract any claim to the truth based in evil or error. This is not pursued so as to defend a Christian hegemony over society, but to bring social order into

---

[53] I am indebted to my friend and colleague Paul Akin for this rendering.

alignment with what is true. We can be indifferent to ethics and the common good only if there are no fundamental ethical-political implications of creation order that the church must confess and guard. Since there are indeed truths of creation order that the church is called to witness to, the task of explaining and defending the natural law are necessary principles of Christian political engagement.

Preeminently, the natural law should evoke in us as human creatures to the worship of the Creator. Niels Hemmingsen sets forth one of the most important pieces of theological writing I have ever come across relating the natural law to man's ultimate end:

> For no one is so savage and void of reason that he does not determine that the things that have been created ought to be subject to the one who made them. No one is so barbaric that he does not understand that the highest gratitude ought to be rendered to those who are most deserving. Hence it follows that the knowledge of God, and the praising of God once he has become known, holds the first place in human actions. A demonstration of this fact (even if this will be the only one possible), taken from nature itself, is as follows: The supreme action of the supreme faculty in man, occupying itself with the supreme and most noble object, is the action proper to man. To know God and to worship him once he has become known is the supreme action of the supreme faculty in man, occupying itself with the supreme and most noble object. Therefore, to know God and to worship him once he has become known is the action most proper to man. Therefore man is rightly happy and blessed when he is occupied in this action; on the other hand, he is rightly wretched and unhappy when he is opposed to it.[54]

In sum, the task of natural law ethics is to bear witness to the total Christ. The Christ who redeems is the same Christ who creates and orders

---

[54] Hemmingsen, *On the Law of Nature*, 73 (see chap. 3, n. 8).

(John 1:3; Col 1:15–17). Where Christ is rejected, nature and reason are dismissed as well, which produces the very pottage of decay all around us: An anti-culture basking in the absurd and the perverse.

Perhaps the greatest non-canonical theologian of the church, Augustine, echoed such a similar refrain when he admonished his readers: "Let us attend to the real matter in debate, and let our arguments appeal to reason and to the authoritative teaching of the Divine Scriptures, dispassionately and calmly, so far as we are able."[55]

---

[55] Augustine, "Letter 23 (A.D. 392)," New Advent, https://www.newadvent .org/fathers/1102023.htm.

# PART 2

# 9.

# Interlude

## Thinking about Applied Natural Law Ethics

The previous section of this volume looked to frame how natural law should be thought about from within Christian ethics and to explain the theory of natural law on both philosophical, biblical, and theological grounds. In the last section of the book, I seek to apply the framework of natural law to a host of issues where the natural law offers definitive clarity. Before turning to the applied issues, additional comments are necessary to discuss how to go about the process of limiting the scope of issues to address within a manageable range.

The question of application raises its own set of methodological issues about what topics to address and how to organize the gamut of issues in a way that is both coherent and manageable to the task at hand. One of the infinite blessings of Christian ethics is its relevance to virtually every topic imaginable. In turn, one of the infinite curses of Christian ethics is its relevance to virtually every topic imaginable.

One of the most frustrating elements of contemporary Christian ethics is the tendency of its texts to spend an extraordinary amount of time dealing with every possible issue of ethical controversy, as though ethics is primarily undertaken to resolve conflict. Hence the unfortunate trend of ethics volumes being excessively lengthy and lacking a clear underlying organizing principle. Most ethics volumes function as a concordance of Bible verses. While it is never wrong to cite the Bible, of course, ethics-as-proof-texting sidesteps the necessary task of thinking comprehensively about morality *qua* morality.

In contrast to that approach, I have sought to explain the theory of natural law in hopes that it will provide a framework for how Christians can think about any number of issues as conflicts arise. The scandalizing element of Christian ethics is that it proposes to have an objective and definitive ethic, grounded in divine revelation, that reveals a moral order governed by universal norms accessible through reason, which all humans are accountable to obey.

Christian ethics in general, and Christian natural law ethics in particular, are concerned with discerning and safeguarding moral goods along with identifying the attendant norms that facilitate their encounter. Ethical deliberation in areas of conflict and intrigue are concerned with identifying the privations and acids in conflict with moral good. In this vein, natural law provides what I think is the most comprehensive account to evaluate what moral goods are at stake and, in turn, what goods are compromised as moral conflict arises in the culture.

One of the reasons for Protestant evangelicalism's outsized focus on applied issues to the neglect of theory, I believe, is in a criticism I made about evangelical ethics in the previous chapters. That conviction is rooted in the supposition that evangelical ethics gives disproportionate weight to applied ethics because of a truncated view of biblical sufficiency with the outcome being that theory and prolegomena are neglected. Much of this comes from the biblicist nature of much of evangelical ethics, which, of course, is no criticism about the Bible being a source for Christian ethics. Let me stress that I am not dismissing the relevance and supreme authority that the Bible provides for Christian ethics. One should never fault ethics for being biblical or appealing to the Bible as an authoritative guide. What my concern registers is a fear that absent larger textual horizons—horizons that help us understand how our ethics work in conjunction with the Bible's moral worldview, and what the true nature of moral goods are—we are left grasping for clarity about an ever-expanding number of issues that the Bible does not, on its surface, address.

For example, the Bible has no verses mentioning in vitro fertilization. The absence of direct reference to this practice could, for some, signal an embrace of the practice. After all, if there is no absolute prohibition, is it *necessarily* wrong? This, I submit, is a negligent and shortsighted approach to doing ethics and one that occurs when individuals are left without a larger field of action from which to understand how the Bible speaks ethically.

But is a "larger field of action" or "horizon" ethics-speak for dubiously importing or reading into the Bible the ethics one wants to get out of it with artificial constructs, like one sees with postmodern reader-response-driven hermeneutics? Is this an invitation for analytical tools such as critical theory or other postmodernist approaches to hermeneutics to be implanted onto the text? By no means.

I have sought to explain how the Bible's presentation of morality is grounded in natural truths—what I referred to in the previous chapter as the "ineluctability of givenness." Scripture posits a divine order imbued with moral significance. Natural law, I submit, is the mode of ethical reasoning that explains the universal, intelligible, objective, and binding nature of morality. It is the ethics of creation order. When Scripture speaks about any moral truth, it does not need to be deconstructed or reassembled with ideological lenses. Taking as our assumption the unity of reason, reality, and Scripture, we are confronted with the recognition that when Scripture speaks, it speaks truthfully about the description of creation in its pages, and all truths that comport with sound reason must comport with reality as well. Thus, owing to our belief in the perspicuity of Scripture, when we believe that Scripture speaks, we believe it can be understood as making true and rationally valid moral claims on all of creation. Scripture aligns with

the world as we know it, such that Scripture's unveiling of a moral order is
the same moral order that we find ourselves subject to as well. To quote the
powerful words of Carl F. H. Henry,

> If Truth is one, and if the Good is one, and if God is everywhere
> with a witness—and these are basic Christian assertions—then such
> a connection must be insisted upon. Christianity stresses the unity
> of Truth and the universal validity of the Good and Right, and the
> universality of rational norms, along with its emphasis on special
> revelation, because it sets special revelation against the background
> of general revelation.[1]

Thus, to offer a natural law ethics is not to foist upon Scripture any
foreign category but to allow Scripture to speak about its own system of
moral reality set forth within inscripturated truths about the very order of
creation itself.

If it sounds as though I am making the incredible claim that natural
law truthfully explains the nature of the Bible's moral order, I am indeed
making such a claim. That's not my claim as an author, but how proponents
of the natural law tradition have considered the tradition itself. It is not a
system of speculative morality. Natural law *is* divine morality given rational
expression within the creation order made known through reason. If there is
a God-given morality, that morality must be both true and knowable; true
in the sense that it is grounded in the very character of God and knowable in

the sense that the character of its being implies cognizance of its principles.
A morality that exists but is not knowable would be a fruitless enterprise to
reflect on.

But returning to my comments above concerning the organization of
applied ethics, we are confronted with the question of how to categorize
the broad swath of issues needing addressed. For example, would it be
good to moralize along such categories as creation, fall, redemption, and

---

[1] Carl F. H. Henry, *Christian Personal Ethics*, 2nd ed. (Grand Rapids: Eerdmans,
1977), 148–49.

restoration? Or what is true, good, and beautiful? Or what about ecclesial, personal, political, and kingdom ethics? All of these are fruitful approaches that have their merits, and I fault no one for choosing this approach. Discerning how the natural law could be categorized, after all, is a difficult challenge since, by design, the natural law is relevant to all activity that is understood as rational.

One of the simplest ways, and one that keeps in line with the theme of this book, is Thomas Aquinas's division of the natural law intro three primary categories. Taking as our assumption the putative correctness of his moral maxim, "Good is to be pursued and evil avoided", Aquinas goes on to categorize the natural law as grouped by its natural inclinations and implications for: (1) the preservation of bodily life; (2) the building of family life united around the conjugal union of husband and wife; and (3) knowing truths about God and acting reasonably that enables one to live with others in society.[2] Following (and slightly condensing and altering) Aquinas's typology, for our purposes, I am using (1) Life; (2) Relations; and (3) Order as the primary heuristic through which to evaluate ethical issues in light of the natural law.

That's how the following application chapters will proceed. Every issue of Christian ethics hits upon the domains of the personal, the relational, and social—how we as individuals relate to ourselves, what proper relations are necessary to continue human relations, and how to live alongside others. Once again, we see the comprehensive nature of natural law take shape: its tenets speak to the basic moral categories necessary to sustain the human life and social order.

It is worth noting that, in an albeit different way than standard ethics texts might pursue, my analysis will tend toward brevity. Moreover, all that could be said about an issue simply cannot be said without devoting book-length treatises to them individually. I am taking this approach out of the conviction that if the unreasonableness of a given issue can be demonstrated,

---

[2] *ST* IaIIae 94.2.

prolonged analysis is unnecessary. The purpose of these chapters is to set forth only the most basic elements of the natural law and not their remote applications to every possible topic. We will evaluate each area of application in view of the three following contours:

1. How or does the issue undermine, thwart, or uphold the attainment of a moral good as understood by reason's grasp of natural law principles?
2. How or does the issue undermine creation order and thus further or impede the common good?
3. How or does the issue violate or align with a moral principle of Scripture understood within the drama of redemption?

In the following chapters, we will be investigating a range of topics and assessing them under the rubric of the Christian natural law tradition. The manner in how this will be done is very intentional, and the reason these questions guide our analysis are significant.

To explain just a bit more from above, first, I will analyze the issue from the perspective of the natural law tradition and explain the underlying rationale of the issue's obligation or prohibition. Second, I will explain how Scripture speaks, directly or indirectly, about the creational component of the issue at hand and what, if any, implications there are for society. These two points are important as they will demonstrate how all rational activity comports with the order of creation described in Scripture. Third and finally, I will explain how the realm of redemption that we come to live within by virtue of our relationship with Christ illuminates our understanding of the natural order. This last step is particularly important so as not to make natural law ethics disjointed from the gospel. In this latter step, there will necessarily be elements of overlap and redundancy in how issues are explained since the domain of redemption does not license a "new" moral casuistry for each issue but is understood from within a Christotelic framework. As Carl F. H. Henry rightly observes to this same conclusion, "The ethics of redemption is not a new morality that reflects a fundamental change in the will of God regarding the essential content of the good. It preserves in full force his rule of righteousness."[3]

Fundamentally, my goal is to demonstrate how biblical morality synchronizes with principles of morality known through sound reason and vice versa. The resulting outcome is a view of ethics that sees all illicit action as not only failing to satisfy biblical criteria for moral righteousness, but which also fails the test of reason. To see biblical morality as anything less than eminently reasonable damages the integrity of Christian ethics.

I can already anticipate one major objection, perhaps, to this book in general and these last three chapters in particular, and it would be thus: What is distinctly *Christian* about natural law ethics? If natural law is sufficient, why isn't it persuasive; and if natural law ethics are not persuasive, why expend the energy on their articulation? If natural law is natural, as I say it is, it is reasonable to ask: What is revelation's interplay in the natural law enterprise? The answer is that human sin erodes (but does not extinguish) the ability for perfect knowledge and perfect consistency. We need Scripture but we must see how Scripture speaks about the ordered totality of the whole of creation itself. "Without those revelatory insights, or confirmations of insights, into our nature and potential destiny, people," John Finnis writes, have the human tendency to treat morality "as variable" and in a state of flux.[4] Revelation is authoritative and necessary in an age marked by the ravages of sin. Natural law cannot be the only argument or the main argument. God's transcendent revelation is understood in both special and general revelation modes. Henry is yet again helpful when he writes:

---

[3] Henry, *Christian Personal Ethics*, 157.

[4] John Finnis, "Telling the Truth about God and Man in a Pluralist Society: Economy or Explication," in *The Naked Public Square*, ed. Christopher Wolfe (Wilmington, DE: Intercollegiate Studies Institute, 2009), 122.

The revelation on which Christian ethics rests is not totally alien to human nature. While addressed to man from without, it is not imposed by a brutal assault upon the intellect. It is a scandal to man, not from crucifying his reason, but by driving him to his knees as sinner. It demands from him the acknowledgment that his high-sounding objections do not come from a sound morality nor sound logic, but are the rationalizations of a proud mind and rebellious will.[5]

One of the most important lessons Christians can learn about the nature of our ethics is how natural they truly are. Such a statement may be met with befuddlement. How can our ethics be natural if sin has corrupted the natural order? Is not the nature of Christian ethics one that sees an invasion of alien ethics? In other words, what hath nature to say to grace? Such a question is framed incorrectly. The better question is: How does grace better reveal to us the truth of our nature? Man, in his rebellion, has the predilection to reject both nature and grace. To understand nature correctly, we must go to grace. Grace, though, sends us back to a proper understanding of nature.

The implications for the inherent givenness of Christian ethics are dramatic. It means that Christian ethics aren't strange, weird, absurd, or eccentric. To be a Christian is to live a fully human life (Col 3:10). Christian ethics are only foreign and unfamiliar to the extent that what was once natural was lost, and, in Christ, the natural has once again been found (1 Cor 15:46). If we do not see this, there will be a temptation to divide our ethics into sectarian axioms tucked away in the privacy of our cloisters. The moral goods that comprise individual happiness and the possibility of civilization are "possible because of the Divine endowment of man-as-creature with a rational and moral nature."[6] The task of

---

[5] Henry, *Christian Personal Ethics*, 150.
[6] Henry, 149.

Christian ethics is to recall to humanity its original design as those who bear the divine image.

Ethics are Christian to the extent they align with Christ. But alignment with Christ sends us back to the original creation order. When all is said and done, the effects of sin on human nature requires a super-imposed grace to tell us, with full clarity and authority, what is true of nature.

# 10.

# Life and the Natural Law

At the forefront of the natural law is the principle of the inherent goodness of life itself. Mundane activities such as wearing a seatbelt, brushing one's teeth, or avoiding danger all reflect the moral good that it is better to exist than to not exist. Harking back to the First Principle of Practical Reason, which teaches that we should pursue good and avoid evil, acting to preserve one's own life is as intuitive and basic as principles of the natural law can be. Without the intuition to preserve and safeguard one's life, existence would cease to be intelligible. If life itself is not worthy of esteem and to be protected, any moral claims elsewhere appear arbitrary.

Underneath the claim that life should be protected is the brute fact that existence itself is a moral good. The natural law assumes there is a point to our existence as rational beings ordered by God. Thus, acting in regard for the good of one's own life is its own intelligible reason for action. Life's preservation is what allows for the experience of other moral goods. So rather than a hierarchical good, it is a sequential good in the chain of moral goods that are possible. As Richard Berquist writes, human beings "exist in order to attain their own good as an ultimate end."[1] We might also posit that the end of all persons is his or her excellence respective to the good or goods their being was meant to obtain. A person's excellence is obtained when the person reaches the fulfillment of how they were meant to live according to their Creator, who implants in them a natural inclination and longing for such fulfillment. God creates human beings in his image in order to glorify him in the attaining of virtue, the contemplation of beatific happiness, and the experience of human flourishing.

History has taught, however, that the intrinsic goodness of life has not always been valued and esteemed, to understate the matter. History is littered with tragedies done to human persons in the name of unspeakable evil. What is not in dispute, though, is the bedrock foundation that the natural law provides in offering a consistent ethic of life grounded in an inviolable principle of human dignity. Again, whether that principle is acknowledged and followed is a separate issue from whether it exists. The natural law insists that it does. A principle of human dignity means that human beings are valued with a status of their own possession and not as a composite reality or as a means to some other end. Dignity recognizes human existence is an end in itself, and thus worthy of protecting for existence to continue. Humans matter because they are humans.

What does one mean by dignity? Dignity means that by virtue of a person's sheer existence (and not some other attribute, such as skin color, height, mental acuity, etc.), there inheres within persons a profound measure of worth that calls forth acknowledgment and respect from other third parties. For a thing to possess the type of inviolable dignity it does, that dignity needs to be given by a higher authority that can assign the person with the dignity that he or she deserves in order for it to be considered inviolable. Berquist offers a helpful definition that explains the natural law relationship between dignity and God's existence:

---

[1] Richard Berquist, *From Human Dignity to Natural Law: An Introduction* (Washington, DC: Catholic University of America Press, 2019), 109.

If a thing exists for an end or purpose, therefore, it must have a cause of a different sort, a cause capable of ordering things to an end. But only intelligence can establish order. For a thing is ordered to an end by an agent who understands the end and is able to determine what is necessary to achieve it. Thus, it is because we are rational that we are able to understand the purpose of a machine we propose to build and to design it so as to achieve that purpose. Similarly, if human beings really exist for a purpose, there must exist an intelligence who has established human nature with this purpose in view. The cause of human dignity, therefore, must be the Author of nature, whom we call God.[2]

As John Finnis writes, "No reality in the universe can be, and be what it is, without God's causing it."[3] We begin our reflections about human dignity from that foundational reality. Christian ethics regards God as the foundation for human dignity. He orders existence in the first place and the ends of human nature that dignity comprises. Remove the substantive principle of human dignity grounded in the inherent dignity of the human being's *existence* (rather than, say, some *attribute*) and the same third parties that were formerly called to acknowledge and uphold said dignity, can begin to slowly chip away at dignity as a brute principle and apply other criteria to determine what level of respect the human being is owed.

In this chapter, we will focus on abortion, euthanasia, race and ethnicity, killing, assisted reproductive technology, and religious liberty. Each of these will be explored from the vantage point of the inherent dignity of human personhood and the faculties that comprise human nature and human fulfillment. Not every topic that could be addressed under the penumbra of "life" will be discussed. Limiting the scope is intentional. As I noted in the interlude, the goal of the application chapters is to explicate the

---

[2] Berquist, 17.

[3] John Finnis, *Aquinas* (Oxford: Oxford University Press, 1998), 308.

most foundational principles of natural law, not their remote application to all topics and sub-topics.

I will focus my comments at greater length on abortion since the principles undergirding the right to life are principles undergirding the protection of life elsewhere.

## Abortion: The Denial of the Good of Life

Abortion is the intentional taking of innocent preborn human life. It is accomplished by a willful act of lethal violence directed toward the unborn child. Pursued either as an elective procedure, as a last-resort method of birth control, or therapeutically as a means of ending the life of a child with a severe disability, abortion is always a moral wrong because it unjustly robs a human being of their inherent dignity and their right to life. It is important to consider who the preborn child is in the womb. The child is a human being from the moment of their conception that undergoes no change of species. It is genetically distinct, contains all the self-directing capacities to bring the person to their full development and is distinct from his or her mother.[4]

Considering the humanity of the preborn child, we should assess the taking of the preborn human's life like we would the unjust taking of any human life: as murder. Under no circumstances can the *intentional* destruction of unborn human life be morally permissible or just. Since the natural law teaches that life is an intrinsic good worthy of respect as a means to no greater end than the good of life itself, abortion is a direct assault upon the moral good of life and is therefore immoral and unjust. Opposition to abortion could be grounded in the following syllogism:

1. From the moment of conception, a human life exists.
2. It is unjust to kill innocent life.

---

[4] Hadley Arkes, *Mere Natural Law: Originalism and the Anchoring Truths of the Constitution* (Washington, DC: Regnery, 2023), 219.

3.  Abortion kills an innocent human life.

4.  Therefore, abortion is morally unjust.[5]

What cannot be debated is the fact that abortion kills an innocent human being at the earliest stages of their development, a human being whose capacities for development are self-directing and guided by processes intrinsic to their development. Who we are in the respective changes in our development does not affect our nature as human beings. As Scott Klusendorf perceptively notes, "You didn't come from an embryo. You once were an embryo. At no point in your prenatal development did you undergo a substantial change or change nature. You began as a human being and will remain so until death."[6] A pro-choice individual might contend that the biological organism lacks "personhood," but personhood understood through a pro-choice lens is an arbitrary designation applied at a time of the person's choosing whose life is not being threatened by death. "Personhood" arguments privilege the larger over the smaller. "Personhood" established by passage through the birth canal cannot explain what it is about the birth canal that magically confers "personhood" or "human rights" that did not also apply before geographically transitioning outside the womb. This is why, even as I affirm "personhood" on theological and rational grounds, it is a woefully inadequate position from which to argue for the protection of unborn life. It is safer and sturdier to argue from the essential nature of who the preborn child is: a human being.

This is how flimsy the pro-choice argument truly is: it is built on the assumption that the choice to kill by a larger human being's "right to privacy" or "bodily autonomy" supersedes the right to life of the smaller human being. The issue with both of these arguments for abortion is that they do not withstand philosophical scrutiny when put to the test. What is

---

[5] This argument is adapted from a similar argument that my friend Francis J. Beckwith makes in *Defending Life: A Moral and Legal Case Against Abortion Choice* (New York: Cambridge University Press, 200), xii.

[6] Scott Klusendorf, *The Case for Life: Equipping Christians to Engage the Culture* (Wheaton: Crossway, 2009), 36.

it about "privacy" that justifies taking life just because the decision is supposedly private? Nothing. What is it about the right to do with one's body
whatever he or she wants that justifies harm to another body? Nothing.
Both arguments are varieties of the powerful using their force against the
lesser, despite the powerful and powerless being of the same kind. Whatever
privacy or autonomy interests exist (and such interests do matter), they are
buttressed by the equal claim of another person's right to life as well. One's
claim to autonomy does not mean that the moral good of life and the moral
prohibitions against taking a lesser developed life than one's own is therefore less obligatory or non-binding just because a person wills something to
complete their satisfaction. Justifications for abortion on these grounds lead
to silly and absurd conclusions when applied elsewhere. At issue is whether,
under any circumstance, it is morally justified to apply lethal violence to
unborn life. The answer to that is no.

We should counter arguments that extend the dignity of personhood
on some stage of development or set of capacities with the undeniable truth
that a human being exists from the moment of conception. This is not a
scientifically debatable fact. The human embryo is not a potential human
being. It is a human being with the potential for further development. That
distinction is crucial. All of the essential component parts to establish the
existence of a human being occur at conception: the unborn human being
is unquestionably alive, genetically unique from its mother, and not simply
"part" of its mother. A mother's womb is simply a location for the distinct
human being to gestate. The child's dependence on the womb is no different from a born human's dependence on oxygen or water. Every human
being is dependent on some sort of external source for its continued survival. Unborn humans simply require a dependency of a different degree,
not type. The resounding philosophical truth to keep in mind is this: if you
kill a human being at any stage of their development, sound philosophy
and sound biology reveals that you have killed the same person. These are
not theological arguments any more than arguments against homicide are
grounded in theology. No, arguments against homicide are laws generally

understood by all rational persons to safeguard human life and punish those who take life.[7]

Granting the moral legitimacy of abortion introduces a categorically destabilizing principle of when life can be taken at any point of a human's existence. Echoing the Nazi regime's *lebensunwertes leben*—"life unworthy of life"—abortion codifies a principle that life is considered worthwhile only on the grounds that it meets certain thresholds or benchmarks of desirability that determine when the right to life has been achieved. Human dignity goes from being absolute to existing in degree. The natural law case for human dignity rests upon a principle of innate inviolability while the pro-abortion perspective ascribes dignity based on an arbitrary threshold that can be taken away if some attribute defined as essential to full personhood is in a diminished state. For example, Peter Singer argues that a diminished capacity for self-awareness makes a human being less of a *person*, and therefore the criteria to safeguard their life diminishes.[8] According to Singer, "The embryo, the later fetus, the profoundly intellectually disabled child, even the newborn infant—all are indisputably members of the species Homo Sapiens, but none are self-aware, have a sense of the future, or the capacity to relate to others."[9] According to Singer, degrees of self-awareness award the person with a greater right to life. Brutal as this worldview is, it is at least intellectually consistent within the pro-abortion mindset.

Abortion creates a culture of death by etching into society's thinking the metastasizing principle that life is disposable according to certain unwanted or undesirable circumstances. Were it not for abortion, other elements of the culture of death, such as euthanasia, would not be intelligible. Then again,

---

[7] For more on the question of why pro-life arguments are rational and not just theological, see Ryan T. Anderson and Andrew T. Walker, "No, Overturning Roe Would Not Establish Theocracy," *First Things*, May 23, 2022, https://www.firstthings.com/web-exclusives/2022/05/no-overturning-roe-would-not-establish-theocracy.

[8] Peter Singer, *Practical Ethics* (Cambridge: Cambridge University Press, 1997), 169–71.

[9] Singer, 86.

once life's value is determined apart from the existence of life itself, the moral principle that abortion is premised upon is simply applied elsewhere. To this end, abortion threatens the common good by subjecting all children born under its regime to the possibility that their lives could be ended for no other reason than inconvenience. That over sixty million human beings in America have had their lives ended through abortion demonstrates the aggregative threat to the common good that abortion truly is. A society that makes life's entry into this world conditioned by third-party interest is a society that has failed to grasp the dignity that naturally inheres in human persons.

As Christians think about the relationship between creation order and the common good concerning abortion, it is at its most elementary foundation to assert that were it not for the legally protected safe passage of the child from the womb into the world, there would be no common good to speak of. Abortion and the common good contradict one another as the realization "goods" held in "common" assume the existence of individuals to experience those shared goods. Abortion upends all of this, denying persons their life and cheapening the value that society places upon human beings. If abortion is moral, there is no reason murder should not be as well.

To understand what Scripture says about abortion, we must begin from the most important starting point that God is the Creator of life (Gen 1:26–28). Life is thus a creation ordinance instituted by God. There is no exception clause to where the Bible demarcates dignity inhering within persons in greater or lesser degree. God's call for human existence to perpetuate itself implies multiplication, meaning that the human species is not a dispensable feature of society, but intrinsic to its operation and fulfillment. Society requires populations brought into successive existence through generational succession. Hence, the Genesis command to be "fruitful and multiply and fill the earth and subdue it, and have dominion" is undone by abortion (Gen 1:28). Abortion is lethal inversion of the creational mandate. If Scripture speaks categorically about life in the category of fruitfulness, abortion thwarts one of the primordial foundations to existence. Abortion, scripturally speaking, is an affront to God since it gives the individual, and the culture around the individual, the false impression that the decision whether to give life or end life, begins and ends with them. That is false. Life belongs to God at all stages of life, from conception to natural death.

Both the Old Testament and New Testament support the conclusion that unborn life has moral value owed respect and protection. In Ps 139:13–16, one of the most important texts in Scripture pointing to the value of unborn life, the psalmist testifies to the intricacies and divine intentionality of prenatal human life. God's providence extends to prenatal life (Jer 1:5). Genesis 9:5–6 states an explicit warning against the unjust taking of life as a general moral norm. There is nothing in the logic of Genesis 9 that would exclude the unborn from being cabined under its canopy of protection. Common ethical consensus drawn from the Bible esteems life to be of such value that to take it unjustly can only be rectified by the person who took the life forfeiting theirs as well. Abortion violates even the minimum moral threshold for justice laid out in the Noahic covenant. Abortion should also be understood within the purview of the Sixth Commandment (Exod 20:13) which states with unequivocal clarity, "You shall not murder." Some debate persists on whether unborn life falls under this prohibition. Christians are reluctant to apply "murder" to abortion for fear of bringing shame to women who have aborted. Compassion and mercy all being equal, the need to extend both does not lessen the fact that a murder has occurred by the abortionist. Natural law helps us understand why homicide laws are valid: because life is its own intrinsic moral good established by God, law should protect life by safeguarding it by fear of retribution. Moreover, if one is against homicide, to be consistent, one should be against abortion as well.

Concerning how abortion should be understood in light of the drama of redemption, the principles supporting the intrinsic value of life remain in force in the dawning of Jesus Christ. For one, in the famous exchange between Mary and Elizabeth in Luke 1:39–44, we see that the unborn Jesus is already recognized as the Lord and that the unborn John (residing inside Elizabeth) is described as having "leaped in her womb." The infancy narratives and incarnation of Jesus Christ signifies the high value that God places upon unborn life.

It would be foolish to conclude that a high regard for the unborn life of Jesus would ever allow for disparate treatment for unborn life elsewhere.

If anything, the witness of Jesus helps us see behind the curtain, so to speak, the demonic element behind abortion and the destruction of natal life. For one, Herod's systematic mass killing of infant males in the birth narratives is depicted as a grave injustice. On what principle we would say that it is okay to take the life of *unborn* children but not of *born* children is befuddling and strikes at the heart of the irrational foundation of abortion. From the perspective of spiritual warfare, Satan is said to "steal, kill, and destroy" while Christ has come that individuals "may have life and have it abundantly" (John 10:10). In other words, satanic force is always parasitic to existing goods and seeks to destroy them. Evil seeks to destroy life whereas the gospel calls for life's flourishing. We should understand abortion as a satanic scheme to prohibit the advance of the gospel by killing its potential recipients.

Later in the New Testament, echoing the Old Testament, Jesus is referred to as the "Author of life" (Acts 3:15). Thus, abortion asserts a rival challenge to the lordship of Christ, which cannot be countenanced. Christians believe that every human being in their substance—not simply their capacities—bears God's image and as such, should not have their lives taken from them without just cause. The God who resurrects life stands opposed to all unjust takings of it.

The very "rights" and "liberty" appealed to in a secular paradigm to justify abortion stand opposed to how Christian discipleship thinks of such things. The Bible recognizes no legitimate, normative category for destroying unborn life or pitting the life of the unborn child against the life of the mother. Against autonomous self-rule, Christians understand that "we are not our own, but belong to God" as the Heidelberg Catechism states. We are not free to do anything we want by the sheer force of our existence. Of course, such statements are diametrically opposed to secular renderings of these terms. This indicates that with abortion, and practically any other topic, the Christian worldview assesses topics from what God views as good, not what humans *want* or consider good themselves. Christians thus assess not only abortion, but any moral debate, from the vantage point of what God's revelation says about a given topic. As I will write about in a later chapter, "rights" exist to facilitate access to genuine moral goods endemic to human flourishing. "Liberty" in a Christian understanding is not the liberty to do what one wants carte blanche. Liberty exists for individuals to fulfill and exercise the ability to flourish as God designs them to flourish. As Evan Lenow and Mark Liederbach both write, "God has given us free moral agency, but moral agency is truly free only when the choices made are in accord with the way in which God made the world."[10] Both "rights" and "liberty" are thus constrained by the existence of moral goods ordered by God and for God's glory. God is glorified when life at all stages is cherished and protected. Therefore, in acting for God's glory, the Christian will always extend maximal protection to all innocent persons' lives—born or unborn. Thus, no amount of liberty and rights can be appealed to in order to justify excluding an innocent human being from their own rights and liberty. Abortion is a tragic and wicked scenario where the fruits of its logic results in a denial of human goods, namely, life, but also God's glory in being the Creator.[11]

## Euthanasia

The West is currently witnessing a global revolution concerning euthanasia and physician-assisted suicide (PAS) or Medical Assistance in Dying

---

[10] Mark Liederbach and Evan Lenow, *Ethics as Worship: The Pursuit of Moral Discipleship* (Phillipsburg, NJ: P & R, 2021), 494.

[11] For three natural law defenses of the sanctity of human life, see Christopher Kaczor, *A Defense of Dignity: Creating Life, Destroying Life, and Protecting the Rights of Conscience* (South Bend, IN: University of Notre Dame Press, 2013); Christopher Kaczor, *The Ethics of Abortion: Women's Rights, Human Life, and the Question of Justice*, 3rd ed. (New York: Routledge, 2022); Francis J. Beckwith, *Defending Life: A Moral and Legal Case against Abortion Choice* (Cambridge: Cambridge University Press, 2007).

(MAiD). Terminology and correct definitions directly shape our analysis. Physician-assisted suicide involves a physician-prescribed medication being self-administered by the person that is intended to kill them. Euthanasia is the intentional taking of a human life by a third-party.[12] "Mercy killing" or "dying with dignity" are common euphemisms for these practices. For purposes of this section, we will consider any willful action undertaken to directly hasten death to be a form euthanasia.

This topic is one where modern medical categories do not find immediate scriptural reference. Scripture's immediate silence on a particular ethical challenge does not leave us, however, without sound first principles from which to consider how a practice like euthanasia squares with the worldview of the Bible. Because we have a doctrine of creation order and the natural law's principle of not taking life without justification, Christians are not left without sound moral principles in determining how to think about euthanasia. A prohibition on medically-induced suicide should fall within the general prohibition of suicide more broadly within the Christian tradition.

We can begin by deducing one fundamental principle that should inform our thinking around euthanasia and that principle begins, like it does with abortion, with respect for the inherent dignity of life as a reality of God's Creatorship and our commitment to no unjust taking of it. Euthanasia is advertised as a compassionate solution to relieve suffering and misery. Without question, one can sympathize for why, at face value, euthanasia seems plausible. After all, neither the natural law nor Christian traditions have held to the position that honoring the sacredness of life means continuing it under all circumstances. But absent a just cause that would justify taking a life under a duly-appointed authority (such as criminal prosecution for first degree murder), under no circumstance can euthanasia be considered an ethically licit option.

---

[12] O. Carter Snead, *What It Means to Be Human: The Case for the Body in Public Bioethics* (Cambridge, MA: Harvard University Press, 2020), 235.

If life is a basic moral good to be protected and the experience of life has non-instrumental value, euthanasia runs contrary to the natural law as it ends life prematurely. As Richard Berquist insightfully notes, natural law opposition to euthanasia is not based on life's "absolute value" as though biological continuity is the moral good. "Suicide and euthanasia are not wrong because life has an absolute value," writes Berquist, "but because all of our actions must be directed to our ultimate end, the life of virtue, and suicide and euthanasia cannot be so directed."[13] The moral good is the recognition of dignity that inheres within the virtue of the living person as a created being with faculties to lead them to moral excellence. Death can be a natural outcome only when life's ability to continue is surrendered to natural processes. Were biological continuity at all costs the highest good, every last measure to protect it would be called for, which the natural law tradition has never held to be the case. Because we should will what is good, in questions about death and dying, we should always act to care for life and never destroy it.

Considering that euthanasia is tied to a society's overall healthcare culture, its introduction poses an insidious impact on the moral ecology of medicine and the broader common good's understanding of the value of life. Like abortion, euthanasia cheapens life and is another manifestation of culture devaluing the dignity of the human person. Rather than beginning with the presumption that life is never to be taken, euthanasia introduces a dangerous principle that makes reversing its scale and usage virtually impossible. Once the floodgates are breached where life can be taken under certain circumstances (even, albeit, with good motives), it is inevitable that the conditions justifying its use will expand. Hence, where euthanasia regimes have taken root, the propensity to expand the criteria justifying its allowance always expands and never contracts. To my knowledge, no nation that has introduced euthanasia into law has taken steps to reverse the scope of criteria justifying it. Indeed, once a principle is introduced into law

---

[13] Berquist, *From Human Dignity to Natural Law*, 106.

that life can be taken for non-punitive reasons, it introduces into law the same principle that we saw with abortion mentioned above: putting human dignity on a sliding scale determined by third-parties or circumstances of justifiable cause.

As euthanasia and physician-assisted suicide regimes march on, the impact of these practices overturns the most fundamental principle of medicine, which is to "do no harm." It thus calls into question the vocation of medical practitioners, who turn their power of healing into killing. Moreover, once the sacred line of life's inviolability is breached, a "right to die" has no inherent safeguard against a "duty to die" once a patient's suffering is deemed sufficient or their burden on a strained healthcare system too costly.

The Christian tradition has always frowned upon euthanasia for the same reasons it has condemned abortion: it is the illicit taking of life. Seen through the prism of Scripture's concern for life's inherent dignity, euthanasia countermands dignity by redefining it apart from absolute foundations grounded in an inviolable respect for human life and apart from scriptural foundations. It is never compassionate to kill, despite whatever benevolent motives may be present. Life is not ours to give or take away. Using one's agency to end life, even for ostensibly compassionate reasons, places the sovereignty over life reserved for God into the vicissitudes of human passion. Once again, a mistaken principle of autonomy underlies the ethics of euthanasia—the idea that bodily autonomy and individual agency possesses all the requisite responsibilities for determining when life is worth living and when it can be taken.

From the perspective of redemption, a Christian's view on suffering is not like that of the world. Christianity does not make light of a person's sufferings. The Christian narrative throughout the Old and New Testaments is one where countless persons in Scripture find pronounced redemption *through* suffering. This theme culminates in the cross of Jesus Christ, where ultimate redemption was secured *through* suffering. While we can understand how the gospel's foreignness when it comes to suffering may appear to non-Christians, the experience of suffering tends to bring out some of the most humane qualities of others in responding to others' suffering. Hence, even in a world tempted by the allure of easy death devoid of pain and suffering, humanity's ability to find meaning through suffering is not altogether foreign.

Even still, the presumption of protecting life does not mean that the only solution to terminal illness is misery and suffering. Palliative care is a legitimate option to pursue to bring comfort to persons in the throes of suffering. Administering medications designed to relieve pain and suffering, insofar as they are not intended to hasten death (but could allow for death as a foreseen, but unintended consequence), is a morally legitimate option. Withdrawing extraordinary measures to allow for inevitable bodily demise is warranted insofar as it does not constitute a withdrawal of basic necessities, such as nutrition.

Moreover, protecting life does not mean that every extraordinary effort must be undertaken to further it. Prudence is required in these situations, as the determinations on whether extraordinary measures are necessary or worthwhile will be dependent on fact-specific and context-specific data (such as the age of the patient and whether there are familial dependents). For example, an eighty-nine-year-old cancer patient's determination to forgo treatment is different than that of a thirty-three-year-old husband and father with two children. Even in the latter situation, however, the unlikelihood of success in pursuing even extraordinary measures could lead to the settled and heart-breaking decision to let illness take its natural toll.

## Killing: Direct, Indirect, and Defensive

If life is a good worth protecting for its own sake, that raises the question of whether it is justified to ever take life. Are there just considerations, then, where the moral good of life's preservation can be forfeited? Obviously, this raises the question of capital punishment as well as self-defense.

We can begin with the natural law's prohibition against the intentional killing of innocent persons. Of course, "innocence" is its own freighted category. Once a person commits an unjust act, variables arise that alter considerations of a person's right to their own life. The underlying principle, however, is bedrock and without exception: taking life without justification is immoral. Killing innocent persons robs them of the very essence of the thing that makes him or her themselves and the possibility for flourishing—existence. Under no circumstance would it be moral for individuals or society to intentionally kill innocent persons.

But what about situations like an ectopic pregnancy or uterine cancer where a continued pregnancy risks both mother and child? In both instances, the procedures to save the mother's life are known to cause the death of an unborn child. Is it therefore wrong to save the life of the mother if the death of the unborn child results? In this scenario, questions of intent and motive are essential in determining the moral status of the action involved. The procedure to save the mother's life does not *intend* to kill the innocent unborn child. Rather, the action to save the mother's life has the *foreseen but unintended* consequence of the child dying. Here, the Principle of Double Effect helps us delineate actions that intend a direct harm versus actions that indirectly result in a harm. Similar instances apply in circumstances concerning euthanasia. It is never moral to intentionally hasten the death of a patient with a terminal illness. Palliative care with correct dosages used to eliminate pain and suffering that could result in a person's life being shortened is, however, impossible.

To answer whether the natural law allows for killing under any circumstance, it is necessary to consider whether killing could be warranted for the sake of the common good. This is especially relevant concerning capital punishment, a practice that divides natural law theorists. Here, questions of due process, guilt, and innocence are paramount. A murderer's actions threaten not only the individual being attacked but the well-being of society whose collective safety is harmed by unchecked violence. When a person's conduct threatens the stability of a social order, I take the view that it is within the purview of the state to kill after their guilt has been determined through a system of due process. Justice is a communal expression that the harm done to the victim endangers the equilibrium of justice for all. Thus, in a system of due process, it is not merely the "law" that is punishing the criminal; it is the community's own self-conception of justice and well-being that is tendered as well. The common good is entirely destabilized under a regime where intentional killing of innocent persons goes unsanctioned. Moreover, it a basic function of reciprocal justice that capital crimes be met with capital punishments (Gen 9:5–6). It seems clear from scriptural precedent that someone who takes a life wrongly forfeits their own life in return.

Regarding self-defense, the natural law tradition holds that one should not *intentionally* kill someone engaged in an attack, but that one may pursue defensive action that is proportionately necessary to eliminate the attacker's threat, including and up to, the possibility of death. A person can rightfully defend themselves against an injury in what is essentially a defensive posture. A defensive posture should be proportionate to the aggressive posture of the assailant, thus not employing any greater means of defense than the aggressor is on offense. The intention that resides behind the potential death of an aggressor is not the willed death, but the elimination of the threat.[14]

Thinking about these issues within the context of the gospel, the Christian Just War tradition has held that Christians may reasonably pursue defensive action for themselves and others in the face of attack. If violence is pursued for malicious ends, there is no moral principle which suggests that defensive action taken to quell injustice would itself be unjust.

Scripture places a prohibition on murder, not killing. Vengeful violence is also eschewed (Rom 12:19). Once again, questions of motive and intent factor into our consideration. Murder is the wanton and unjustified taking of human life while killing, could, in principle, be done for just ends—such as in the case of bringing a cessation to hostilities or self-defense. Indeed, under certain conditions, forfeiture of one's life seems not only justified, but obligatory (Gen 9:5–6). If there are wrongful conditions to take life, this ought to mean there are rightful conditions to take life. In other words,

---

[14] I am indebted to the thought of Richard Berquist for his views on this subject. See Berquist, *From Human Dignity to Natural Law,* 113–18.

there is not an absolute prohibition on taking life in Scripture. That is the foundation to begin any further analysis.

But how do we reconcile this with Christian pacifism and the call to turn the other cheek? While Christian pacifism is an honorable tradition within Christian ethics, it is not an approach I advocate from within the Christian natural law tradition. Quite simply: Christian pacifism fails to adequately love one's neighbor. It is an over-idealized ethic that cannot be reasonably pursued in an age marked by sin. Allowing oneself to be wantonly slaughtered or one's neighbor harmed when one has the capacity to prevent such action from occurring is theologically facile and socially irresponsible. Accepting the possibility of martyrdom does not require passivity in the face of preventing it. Accepting wanton violence for oneself or one's neighbor is a failure to rightly love oneself and one's neighbor. Society cannot be governed by an ethic of pacifism.

We should consider, however, that even as Christians may pursue an ethic of self-defense, Christians do approach life differently than do non-Christians. Christians allow the hope of the resurrection to define the ultimate horizons of their considerations around life's value. The worst outcome is not that the physical body would be killed, but that the total self would go to hell (Matt 10:28). Christians should never glory in violence even as we consider proportionate means of self-defense to be ethically justified in defense of the individual and the good of the community.[15]

## Race and Ethnicity

Questions of race and ethnicity are perennial challenges that need addressed in each age. Just as we think civilization might outgrow contempt based

---

[15] For defenses of the ethical permissibility of taking life, see John M. Frame, *The Doctrine of the Christian Life* (Phillipsburg, NJ: P & R, 2008), 701–4; Daniel R. Heimbach, *Fundamental Christian Ethics* (Nashville: B&H Academic, 2022), 431–36; Edward Feser and Joseph Bessette, *By Man Shall His Blood Be Shed: A Catholic Defense of Capital Punishment* (San Francisco: Ignatius, 2017).

on cultural difference or appearance, we're reminded of what lurks within human nature is a proclivity to see natural differences in places of origin and appearances as forces of hostility and inequality.

Regarding the natural law and questions of race and ethnicity, where we should begin our analysis is by stating that a principled account of human dignity grounded in the principles of the natural law is a categorical buttress against racial and ethnic strife. What gives the natural law such immense power in topics such as these is the natural law's focus on defining dignity in an unqualified sense—on innate attributes of *being* based not on qualities of appearance or geography, but in the very fact of existence. Since human dignity inheres simply by virtue of a person's existence, the extension of dignity applies to all, equally, across the spectrum of human cultures.

One of the best examples in learning how to confront questions of race and ethnicity is looking to Martin Luther King Jr.'s explicit reference of the natural law tradition as an antidote to racial prejudice. In his 1963 *Letter from a Birmingham Jail*, King explicitly invokes the Christian natural law tradition via Augustine and Aquinas to explain racism's injustice and offensiveness.[16] For King, a law that purposefully harms does not retain the actual power to command obedience; it is thus not true law. Justice can never entail the denial of what is owed to persons by virtue of the dignity inhering with them. That is, well, unjust. King rooted the foundation for natural justice in the eternal law.

As we saw in a previous chapter, a law is a standard or measurement that obligates individuals to obey its precepts on the basis that the precept advances some rational good. All truly sound laws will reflect an ordinance of reason that directs persons to their good. To say a law is reasonable means it accomplishes justice. But racism is an offense to justice because it seeks to degrade a person or people's inestimable worth based on irrelevant criteria. People's skin color or place of origin has no bearing on what they are owed as human beings. This does not mean, of course, that all cultures

---

[16] Martin Luther King, Jr, "Letter from a Birmingham Jail," https://www.africa.upenn.edu/Articles_Gen/Letter_Birmingham.html

are moral equals in what each respective culture values and practices. It does mean, from an ontological perspective, that human beings within those cultures are the same substance in type and kind regardless of their place of origin.

A law that obstructs or thwarts the good cannot be an actual law because it is unjust. King argues that not only are racial supremacy laws in violation of Christian theology; they violate all rational grounds for justice as well. A true law reflects the principle of justice. A law that does violence to one's neighbor is wrong because we can grasp the harm the law perpetrates. We would ourselves not want to be on the receiving end of that unjust law's application. This explains the logic behind the Golden Rule in Luke 6:31. Here Jesus assumes that any action is just toward others insofar as it is the type of action we would want applied to ourselves under the optimal conditions of right reason. No one in their right mind goes looking to harm themselves without good cause (such as self-sacrifice in the event of saving another), so likewise, any law that harms others cannot obtain the grounds of justice, either. The Golden Rule is about advancing each other's good, not reciprocal affirmation of one's wants, desires, and perceptions.

The natural law tradition views racism as odiously incompatible with the tenets of human dignity and justice. Christian figures such as Justice Clarence Thomas and Frederick Douglass have argued that absent natural law's understanding of principled equality and principled dignity, human passion and human power can easily overwhelm an ultimate authority, such as God, who has definitive say in creating standards of justice to begin with. Clarence Thomas poignantly observed how, "Those who deny the natural law cannot get me out of slavery."[17] He went on discussing his interest in the natural law: "My interest started with the notion, with a simple question: How do we end slavery? By what theory do you end slavery? After you end slavery, by what theory do you protect the right of someone who was

---

[17] Robert P. George, "The 1993 St. Ives Lecture - Natural Law and Civil Rights: From Jefferson's 'Letter to Henry Lee' to Martin Luther King's 'Letter from Birmingham Jail,'" 145.

a former slave or someone like my grandfather, for example, to enjoy the fruits of his or her labor . . . in exploring . . . a unifying theme on civil rights and on the issue of race, I was looking for a way to unify and find a way to talk about slavery and civil rights. . . ."[18]

Frederick Douglass strikes a similar theme. Douglass's comments come in the context of the Dred Scott decision from the Supreme Court that determined African American citizens were not citizens under the Constitution.

> The Supreme Court of the United States is not the only power in this world. It is very great, but the Supreme Court of the Almighty is greater. Judge Taney can do many things, but he cannot perform impossibilities. He cannot bale out the ocean, annihilate this firm old earth, or pluck the silvery star of liberty from our Northern sky. He may decide, and decide again; but he cannot reverse the decision of the Most High. He cannot change the essential nature of things—making evil good, and good evil.[19]

Douglass's comment pairs with King's statement in that both insist that human law must conform to the natural law ordered by eternal law. Not only do both quotes highlight the theistic underpinnings of the natural law, both appeal to the notion that human law cannot countermand what is true ontologically of human nature. Racism may try to degrade human worth, but it cannot truly do so. According to both King and Thomas's arguments, for justice to be achieved, the definition of what is "just" cannot be left to human courts to decide. There must be an authority outside the courts to which the courts appeal in order to gain their sense of justice. That is the role of God. It is no surprise that the Civil Rights tradition has been richly theistic in its argumentation. The movement relied upon appealing to a sense of justice and dignity that they could not find in sinful systems of human law.

---

[18] George, 145.

[19] Frederick Douglass, Speech on Dred Scott Decision, May 1857, https://www.utc.edu/sites/default/files/2021-01/fddredscottspeechexcerpt2018.pdf.

There is no greater example, at least within an American context, of damage to the common good than what transpired under the regimes of chattel slavery and systemic racism in laws that denied African Americans equal status under the law prior to 1964. Racism threatens the common good by thwarting creation order's principle of ontological equality and ontological dignity. Racism denies persons their innate dignity and what should be their corresponding equality under the law. What racism and abortion have in common is the commitment to take the substantive dignity that inheres categorically and to subject it, diminishingly, to some additional criteria, whether "bodily autonomy" or skin pigmentation. The beauty of the natural law is its simplicity in the face of racism. As the children's author Dr. Seuss wrote, "a person's a person, no matter how small." That maxim might as well read "no matter size, age, sex, economic status, productive ability, sentience, religious status, dependency, or developmental stage."

An important aspect often omitted when it comes to racism is its underlying intellectual absurdity. Skin color and geographic origin are utterly irrelevant attributes in evaluating moral worth. Biases based purely on unfamiliarity are irrational. That a culture is different than my own or that a people may look differently than me provides no *prima facie* grounds to insert animus into our evaluation of their humanity. Nothing about pigmentation or where someone lives should factor in to whether the person is anything less than a full person deserving of the same dignity as others. I'm not arguing for cultural relativism or any sort of moral relativism. Some cultures are more humane than others. But humaneness is not measured by location or pigmentation. This point highlights one of the contradictions that socio-biological views on morality cannot adequately reconcile. Naturalistic accounts of morality that view morality as some outworking of evolutionary process cannot create an inviolable principle of dignity in the same way that the natural law tradition can. Indeed, Social Darwinism that evolution is premised upon licenses the domination over an apparent lesser. Any attempt at a principled account of equality is merely an Archimedean point invented out of thin air. Honest atheists, such as Douglas Murray, will admit this. Murray writes: "The more atheists think on these things, the more we may have to accept that the concept of the sanctity of human life is a Judeo-Christian notion which might very easily not survive Judeo-Christian civilisation."[20]

Christians must begin their reflection about racism where all questions of human existence and dignity begin, with Genesis 1. There, we read that all individuals bear God's image. No exception or asterisk subtracts from the principle of dignity and equality at the heart of the creation narrative. Genesis does not envision a situation where God's image is present in degree. Humans who share in the same nature, by necessity, must possess the same degree of ontological nobility. Because God creates all people to share in an inherent equality of worth, we are enjoined to respect that worth as well. Not only does Scripture convey a principle of inviolable dignity, but it also explains the inherent goodness of diversity as a function of creation order. God did not order a monolithic culture concerning cultural diversity. God sovereignly places and oversees the variegated peoples and regions that comprise the full panoply of creation order (Acts 17:26). Sameness is not upheld as the scriptural norm. It is therefore good for Americans to be Americans, Irish to be Irish, and Zimbabweans to be Zimbabweans. It is as good that there are Bostonian accents as there are Appalachian accents. Scripture does not envision a flattening out of diversity but the ability to subject difference to an underlying horizon of equality.

The Christian message not only offers the most important conceptual framework to ground human dignity, human equality, and human justice, it also explains the sinful proclivity for human discord based on racial enmity, as well as the balm for its repair. Because of sin's introduction into the world, racial strife and cultural hostility ensure that individuals and society are prone to see difference as threatening. Racism can occur individually and

---

[20] Douglas Murray, "Would Human Life Be Sacred in an Atheist World?" *The Spectator*, April 19, 2014, https://www.spectator.co.uk/article/would-human-life-be-sacred-in-an-atheist-world-.

systemically when forces act to subjugate a class of human beings, whether intentionally or unintentionally. Far from this being a manifestation of Critical Race Theory, it is a simple reminder that sinful humans can act in concert within the cultures they inhabit. Where one or two sinners are gathered, they can create milieus that reflect sinful motives. At the same time, not every difference of outcome in a society reflected in various groups is attributable to racism. Agency is paramount in determining intentional disparate impact with racially-inflected outcomes versus outcomes that impact a particular culture because of some existing behavioral pattern that inhibits similar outcomes.

At the same time, Christianity does not overlay society with a perfect policy on what degree of cultural difference can exist within a given polity. Nor does it prescribe an ideal immigration policy that balances the desires of some humans to find new life elsewhere with the rights of native-born citizens to have their cultural identity prioritized. Extrapolations that go too far in either direction breach what can reasonably be called "biblical." In the absence of a strict policy that informs what each society's composition should look like, the Christian practice of basic virtue and prudence should inform our thinking on delicate and difficult matters, especially in public policy debates.

What the gospel of Jesus Christ teaches is that, through the redemptive work of Christ, the enmity at the heart of racist or ethnic prejudice must be crucified. Persons of all backgrounds share in the promises of redemption. Indeed, one of the most revolutionary statements of its time is found in Gal 3:28 where Paul insists that regardless of class, ethnicity, or sex, all share equally alike in the benefits of justification. Just as there are no creational hierarchies of ontological nobility, there are no soteriological hierarchies of redemptive nobility. All are created equally and saved equally. The ramifications of this truth that bear on a Christian reflection about race and ethnicity are profound and offer the world the true exemplar for ethnic harmony.

Thus, one can be a Christian or an ethnic and racial supremacist, but not both. The fact that Christianity, at least in the West, stood as one of the great incubators of racial strife—while also one of its greatest forces for abolition—will be a mark of consequence born for generations to come. Even here, the gospel is the balm for both the oppressed and the oppressor.

Those who share in the promises of redemption cannot coexist at odds. From Ephesians to Revelation, the arc of history bends toward the unification of humanity under the auspices of the united children of God. Revelation 7:9–10 envisions a future with "a great multitude that no one could number, from every nation, from all tribes and peoples and languages, standing before the throne and before the Lamb, clothed in white robes, with palm branches in their hands, and crying out with a loud voice, 'Salvation belongs to our God who sits on the throne, and to the Lamb!'" Far from obliterating creational differences established in Genesis, the fullness of redemption sees the multitudes of creation unified under the umbrella of the gospel. In Christ, then, there is radical dignity in our cultural and ethnic differences and radical unity in creational differences being subordinated to Christic reality.

The Genesis vision for a humanity united under the banner of its common humanity is the same vision that the gospel of Jesus Christ restores. The gospel then is not an alien force that diminishes the vast array of human difference but unites it under the Creatorship of God.

Race and ethnic issues continue to divide Christians into the present day. Regardless of all the complexities of how to ameliorate past wrongs and how to respond to each moment of racial controversy today, starting with the principle of innate human dignity that the natural law tradition teaches, wedded to a robust Christian anthropology, are necessary places to begin.

## Assisted Reproductive Technology: In Vitro Fertilization

Though assisted reproductive technology (ART) can take many forms (such as intrauterine insemination, gamete intrafallopian transfer, and surrogacy) the focus of this section is on in vitro fertilization (IVF). While other forms of assisted reproductive technology are worthy of further study, brevity demands that focus be given to IVF because it is a microcosm for how the natural law tradition considers illicit the pathways to family formation that require bypassing the bodily union of husband and wife and result in third parties being brought into the process of conception.

First, by way of definition, IVF involves the process of harvesting male and female gametes (sperm and egg, respectively) that are then placed in a petri dish ("in vitro" means "in glass") under optimal conditions where a pre-determined number of embryos are attempted to be conceived. The embryos most suitable for implantation are then transferred into the mother (or a surrogate) for her to naturally carry the set number of embryos to full term. Leftover embryos are destroyed, frozen, or donated to medical research. In an action I affirm as morally praiseworthy, embryos can also be adopted and implanted by the infertile couple who should be seen as rescuing these tiny members of the human race from almost-certain destruction. Embryo adoption is permissible because it tries to rectify a previous moral error. Bringing good from prior moral error is commendable.

There are several problems with IVF that should lead us to conclude that IVF is not an ethical practice. The fundamental moral good that IVF thwarts is the sacrosanct and inviolable principle of conception resulting from the bodily union of husband and wife. The nature of marriage as a generative institution of complementary sexed bodies is undermined if the role of the body can be severed from reproduction. Once this guardrail is breached, a pandora's box is opened that introduces several ethical problems. Rather than pregnancy occurring from the enfleshed love of husband and wife, pregnancy is medicalized through extraordinary intervention that poses potential risks, including the foreseeable likelihood of embryo death occurring in some form, intended or not.

First, when conception is severed from bodily union, an untold number of actors factor into conception: doctors, nurses, lab technicians, gamete donors, surrogates, and potentially lawyers when done for commercial purposes as in surrogacy. What should be the intimate union of husband and wife is opened to other parties to participate in. At this point, reproduction ceases to be a marital reality and is instead subjected to medical interventions aided by technological craft.

Concerning creation order and the common good, it is impossible to sever individual acts of IVF from the commercialization of the practice. Whole commercial industries exist to commercialize and transact human beings, in ways not totally dissimilar to chattel slavery. Individual acts must always be considered in the aggregate in order to prevent exploitative systems from occurring. IVF fails this concern spectacularly. Clinics monetize gamete donation from strangers whose traits and attributes are catalogued for parents struggling with infertility, raising the issue of manufacturing "designer babies" who are bred to embody physical or intellectual ideals. Such an approach countermands what O. Carter Snead refers to as the "tolerance of imperfection," an openness to the unchosen that embraces life on its terms rather than exerting maximal control over it.[21] Technology thus overrides the limitations of embodiment.

IVF also introduces the idea of designing parenthood without either a mother or father being present. Law and culture thus streamline the intentional denial of a child's right to a father or mother. Same-sex couples can pursue IVF treatments alongside surrogates with the intention and result of denying children the presence of either a mother or father. Singles who want children without marriage can also obtain children through IVF. IVF thus prioritizes the desires of adults, however good those desires are, over the needs of children.

All of these complications culminate in the most ethically fraught aspect of IVF, and that is the threat to the dignity of human embryos. IVF necessarily licenses a moral event where human life can be discarded at will. Life begins at conception. Treating unborn human life as discardable or expendable subjectable to human will or medical research is immoral.

---

[21] O. Carter Snead, *What It Means to Be Human: The Case for the Body in Public Bioethics* (Cambridge, MA: Harvard University Press, 2020), 9.

As we consider IVF from the drama of redemption, we begin with the truth that human embryos are made in God's image-bearers (Gen 1:26–27). Preborn human beings are our neighbors. Destroying innocent life, freezing it, or using it for further research fails to love one's neighbor (Exod 20:13; Mark 12:31).

Another issue facing IVF is that it exceeds the scriptural boundaries for where children are to be conceived. IVF bypasses the creational normativity of where God intended children to come into being: the enfleshed love of husband and wife. In that sense, IVF is deeply unbiblical since it violates the scriptural paradigm as it severs the connection between sex and procreation.

At the same time, Scripture witnesses powerfully to the experience of infertility and barrenness. Compassion and heartfelt care should be extended to all who experience infertility. Through no fault of their own, some individuals are unable to conceive, and they should not see their infertility as judgment but as a reality that stems from living in a broken creation order. And the motivation for overcoming infertility is commendable, even as we should insist that good consequences in the form of family-making does not alleviate moral responsibility in the actions we undertake to overcome infertility. All of this reminds us that the opening and closing of the womb belongs to the sovereignty of the Lord. As we consider the godly longing for children by the infertile couple, we must minister compassionately and extend the love of Christ to such persons. We must show parents who desire children the way of adoption. Children are a gift of the Lord; not a human right nor a parental right that allows for children to be begotten by any means possible (Ps 127:3–5). Christ's sufficiency is the ultimate hope of parents struggling with infertility, not pursuing extraordinary means (that may not even work) to achieve a good that cannot be accomplished without thwarting other moral goods.

Unfortunately, even conservative Protestant evangelicals debate the merits of IVF. The lack of consensus is a stinging indictment on how narrow proof-texting devoid of considerations of the natural law can lead to supporting an industry that, while no doubt resolving a godly desire for children, results in a cascading number of ethical problems.

# Religious Liberty: The Good of Knowing God and Living for God

Religious liberty might be odd to categorize under the "Life" chapter since the topic is regarded more often as an issue tied to social ethics and church-state relations. While I will say something about religious liberty in chapter 12 on "Order" as an essential component to order within a just society, my rationale for placing it in this chapter is that religious liberty, before it is thought of as a social practice, has a principally individual valence in the sense that it helps explain one of the most fundamental aspects to one's existence: pursuing, knowing, and obeying God as an expression of the total self. In Western contexts, "religious liberty," or "rights of conscience," is conceived of as the Enlightenment settlement severing the state from any established religion. While it is, it is more than that too.

The natural law tradition conceives of religious liberty as an essential component in self-constitution. Humans, to quote J. Daryl Charles, are "foremost rational, perceiving, intuiting, and conceiving."[22] For the self to be free, it must be unencumbered at its most basic level—the person's relationship to ultimate reality, that is, God. Relationship with God and ultimate reality is an architectonic moral good in the sense that one's relationship to God orders (or, in the right conditions, ought to order) all other features of a person's existence that should, in principle, lead them to the life of virtue. This is not to say that all religions are equal (the exact opposite is in fact the case) or that religious liberty is absolute. Restrictions on religious liberty are indeed legitimate insofar as rightly authorized authorities carefully delineate what harms a religion's adherents pose to society and does not arbitrarily penalize. Public health and public safety cannot countenance threats to sound order under an absolutized appeal to religious liberty.

---

[22] J. Daryl Charles, *Natural Law and Religious Freedom: The Role of Moral First Things in Grounding and Protecting the First Freedom* (New York: Routledge, 2018), 24.

Rather, the moral good of religious liberty is the protection of the faculty of conscience as it grasps what it perceives as a duty to, and harmony and alignment with, ultimate order. How a person perceives the world, the morality they subscribe to, and the ultimate horizon governing one's actions in society are consciously or unconsciously made on the basis of deeply seated worldviews that comprise human personality. Religious liberty is thus essential to individual human flourishing because it facilitates the exercise of one's duty to God.

James Madison's famous "Memorial and Remonstrance Against Religious Assessments" succinctly captures the natural law argument for religious liberty:

> The Religion then of every man must be left to the conviction and conscience of every man; and it is the right of every man to exercise it as these may dictate. This right is in its nature an unalienable right. It is unalienable, because the opinions of men, depending only on the evidence contemplated by their own minds cannot follow the dictates of other men: It is unalienable also, because what is here a right towards men, is a duty towards the Creator. It is the duty of every man to render to the Creator such homage and such only as he believes to be acceptable to him. This duty is precedent, both in order of time and in degree of obligation, to the claims of Civil Society. Before any man can be considered as a member of Civil Society, he must be considered as a subject of the Governour of the Universe: And if a member of Civil Society, who enters into any subordinate Association, must always do it with a reservation of his duty to the General Authority; much more must every man who becomes a member of any particular Civil Society, do it with a saving of his allegiance to the Universal Sovereign.[23]

---

[23] *The Papers of James Madison*, vol. 8, 10 March 1784–28 March 1786, ed. Robert A. Rutland and William M. E. Rachal (Chicago: The University of Chicago Press, 1973), 295–306.

According to Madison, humanity's relationship to God is antecedent to all other roles one occupies in society. Government voluntarily limiting itself to matters of public import only is government's rightful acknowledgement of its limited authority, limited competence, and limited jurisdiction in defining all features of a person's existence. Madison's argument follows in a similar vein of what John Henry Cardinal Newman once wrote, "Conscience has rights because it has duties."[24] The duties one perceives are not burdensome duties carried out unwillingly but obligations one must pleasingly fulfill if they perceive of themselves as rational agents who wish to live authentic lives.

Contrary to caricatures, the natural law tradition does not mean to relativize the stark differences of competing religious claims, nor grant an unhindered pathway for moral licentiousness done under the rubric of "liberty." From a natural law perspective, it is the integrity of the faculty of conscience that is owed respect, not the putative destination where the conscience arrives. The natural law tradition merely insists that individuals must be free to reach conclusions about ultimate reality on their own and to the greatest extent possible, be free to live out the implications for how one's relationship to God orders their earthly life. To protect an ecosystem of religious liberty, errors and misfires in how religion and morality are conceived of will necessarily result. The obverse of that regrettable outcome, however, is a stifling aura of religious oppression. To make the point again, religious liberty is not absolute. No society can countenance what it considers extreme threats to the common good done under the rubric of religion. Where limits on religious liberty are necessary, one must hope that legislators tasked with determining the boundaries of religious expression are possessed with the requisite virtue and prudence so as to draw appropriate boundaries, rather than capricious ones.

It may be odd to speak of religious liberty as a creation ordinance tied to the common good because Scripture does not directly speak of it in such

---

[24] John Henry Newman, *Certain Difficulties Felt by Anglicans in Catholic Teaching Considered* (London: Longmans, Green, 1897), 250.

ways. To understand religious liberty's relationship to creation order, we must go back to the Noahic covenant. There, God re-establishes a creation order constrained by the reality of sin. In stipulating what elements are necessary for the proper maintenance of society, rectifying injustice between intra-human conflict is the only form of justice within view. Nowhere outside of ancient Israel is rebellion to God placed within the government to punish and rectify. God does not delegate human authority to mediate offenses to God, but only between fellow image-bearers. Of additional note is that, according to the Noahic formula for the bare minimum of society's perpetuity to persist, correct theological belief is not listed. Of course, this statement should not be construed to minimize the importance of recognizing God's authority over creation order and within political communities. That true theological belief is not grounds for participation in civil society is a separate issue from whether society, in the aggregate, can persist when all conceptions of the divine are eliminated. Insofar as family formation and systems of justice for settling intra-human disputes are established, individuals' religious belief is not a consideration for their participation within a broader political community. A society that lacks the most fundamental freedom to constitute one's self in relationship to God is a society that cannot be called free in any sense of the term. While America's religious liberty regime is not without its flaws, the fact that religious liberty is heralded as a "First Freedom" speaks to the architectonic nature of religious freedom. Denying religious freedom is a precursor to denying all other freedoms. If the state can put itself in between citizens and God, there is no other part of life within society that the state will not see itself as apt to disrupt and intervene in, either. In that sense, religious liberty is the original buffer between the state and the state's desire to reach further and further into the lives of its citizens. At that point, the state no longer functions as a mere state, but as a form of demi-god. A statement from Evangelicals and Catholics Together, from *First Things*, rightly captures this element:

> The just state recognizes this right of persons and protects it in law.
> In doing so, the state recognizes the limits of its own capacity: It

cannot coerce consciences; it cannot compel belief. For the state that recognizes and protects religious freedom is not an omni-competent state, but rather a state that acknowledges the rights of conscience and the prerogatives of the institutions that men and women freely sustain to express and pass on their religious convictions. It recognizes its duty to serve, and not to impede, those communities of civil society. Thus the recognition of religious freedom in full is a crucial barrier to the totalitarian temptation that seems to exist in all forms of political modernity.[25]

As we think about how a natural law right to religious liberty is understood within the gospel, we can begin by stressing that religious liberty begins not with vague or generic "rights" (important as those are and worth considering in a later chapter) but with the human person made in God's image bearing the capacity for reason, deliberation, choice, and judgment. God does not program belief involuntarily. From a Christian perspective, it is the integrity of the faculty of conscience that renders individuals accountable to God.

From the fullest vantage point of redemption, however, Christians embrace a doctrine of religious liberty because we believe that God holds individual consciences to account for their rejection of him. God is the sole judge of the conscience. Because Christ is King, the domain where ultimate allegiances are sworn is his jurisdiction alone (Acts 17:31). Because the state pertains to the temporal, common, and penultimate goods only, we should understand that matters related to ultimate goods—the eternal state and the beatific vision—are outside the purview of the state's jurisdiction and competency. Government is accountable to God's moral law but it is not a direct conduit of God's covenantal redemption.

The whole program of evangelization assumes the posture of a missionary faith. According to Scripture, conversion is the result of *seeking*—an

---

[25] Evangelicals and Catholics Together, "In Defense of Religious Freedom," *First Things*, March 1, 2012, https://www.firstthings.com/article/2012/03/in-defense-of-religious-freedom.

earnest and voluntary examination of Christianity's claims about Jesus. No Christian can countenance the use of power (state or otherwise) to coerce, blackmail, or privilege belief.

## Conclusion

Many more topics, of course, could be addressed in this chapter. The limited aim of this chapter, however, has been to offer a brief survey of how the natural law tradition and a Christotelic understanding of natural law in light of the gospel informs the most basic foundations for human existence. As this chapter has intended to do, it began with a robust declaration on the innate and inviolable principle of human dignity that is best afforded in the natural law tradition and how it applies to the most rudimentary aspects of existence—the safeguarding and protecting of life from conception to natural death, the respect owed to persons across various cultures, and the self's relationship to God as the preeminent grounds for purpose and meaning.

# 11.

# Relations and the Natural Law

In the West, a general crisis of meaning looms. The crisis is readily apparent in the collapse of Christianity as an authority structure that once formerly provided civilization with a shared sense of civilizational morality and purpose. Echoing themes stated previously in the book, the crisis is a byproduct of Western culture abandoning Christian teleology. The frontiers of expressive individualism bombard persons with an unrestricted menu of ideologies and hedonisms to organize their lives around. Detached from mediating institutions that are rooted in transcendent authority, individuals now fold meaning and morality in on the self and do so with little attention to whether human nature can reasonably shoulder such existential questions without definitive answers.

The result is what some cultural critics have called the "Imperial Self,"[1] a concept born of expressive individualism and made possible by modern

---

[1] This is a phrase I have often heard Robert P. George use regarding a concept of human identity that looks to unchecked self-actualization as the fullness of being.

concepts about liberty and autonomy. Purpose is found in unencumbered selves loosening themselves from all moral traditions not sourced from their own being. No unchosen obligations are countenanced. According to one scholar,

> Modern liberalism prides itself on having secured certain rights and freedoms—to destroy one's self, one's offspring, and collectively to destroy one's culture. Built on the empty rhetoric of relativism and blind to its own de facto subservience to illicit industries, Modern Liberal Autonomy promises the good life and then drives us to individual and collective self-destruction.[2]

To define Western culture as anything less than obsessed with affixing "rights" to whatever seeks affirmation is to miss what drives modernity.

Nowhere is this more acutely evident than on the effects of rampant individualism and moral relativism in the West's shedding of its former Christian mores on gender, sexuality, marriage, and family. Scholars like Mary Eberstadt have argued convincingly that secularization is a by-product not simply of Christianity's decline, but of society rejecting the teachings of Christianity on the family. According to Eberstadt, the family is a microcosm for cosmic ordering that gives meaning and orientation to one's existence with themselves, their relationships, and with God himself. Thus, severing humanity from the natural bonds of mother and father that the Christian natural law champions produces a potent and atomizing catalyst for identity politics that reinforces secularization.[3] Emptied of any objective moral content and unguided by any fixed *telos* from which to

---

[2] Jacqueline A. Laing, "Law, Liberalism, and the Common Good," entry 4.1.3 in *The Natural Law Reader*, ed. Jacqueline A. Laing and Russell Wilcox (Malden, MA: Wiley-Blackwell, 2014), 387.

[3] See Mary Eberstadt, *Adam and Eve After the Pill: Paradoxes of the Sexual Revolution* (San Francisco: Ignatius, 2013); Mary Eberstadt, *How the West Really Lost God: A New Theory of Secularization* (West Conshohocken: Templeton, 2013); Mary Eberstadt, *Primal Screams: How the Sexual Revolution Created Identity Politics*, First edition (West Conshohocken, PA: Templeton, 2021).

order the body, the ability to do what one wants with their body without regard for consequences now serves as the animating force behind one of America's major political parties. Sex, by all accounts, is totalizing and deeply political. In this, secular progressivism is often more acutely aware of the political significance of sexual arrangements than are even Christians. Sexual anarchy, confusion, and disorder are the primary grammars of the contemporary West.

Beliefs about the definition of male and female and the proper sexual ordering between the two is a venue for a cultural tempest. As I often say to my students, no one is losing jobs or friendships over debates about Christology. Objecting to someone's identifying as transgender or refusing to affirm same-sex marriage, however, as documented instances show, can put one's livelihood at stake.[4] For issues related to sexuality and gender are the animating sources of virtually all of today's cultural conflicts related to the place of Christianity within secular society, the grammar of which was once the assumed pathway for commodious civil ordering. Abandoning a Christian teleology of transcendent order in general has had a deracinating effect on our understanding of morality, especially on the idea of the body possessing any intrinsic moral markers or moral clues about its proper use. The idea that someone should be told what to do with their body is tantamount to violating to what amounts as a Western blasphemy law. Insofar as a person consents to the practices done to or by their body, so our culture says, it is permissible. The confluence of legal "rights" tethered to psychologized understandings of sexual identity has created a postmodern revolution

---

[4] For example, see the situation involving Tanner Cross, a teacher who objected to using a student's preferred pronoun and was summarily punished for doing so. Thankfully, on appeal, Cross won and was reinstated to his position. For more on this story, see Hannah Natanson, "Va. Supreme Court affirms judge's ruling reinstating Loudon teacher who refused to use transgender pronouns," *Washington Post*, August 31, 2021, https://www.washingtonpost.com/local/education/tanner-cross -virginia-supreme-court-transgender-pronouns/2021/08/31/52f94c62-0a71-11ec -9781-07796ffb56fe_story.html#. Numerous other examples too abundant to cite could be referenced.

the likes of which could only be compared to antiquity's embrace of sexual paganism.[5] But all is not well, as even non-conservative voices are pointing to the acidic effects of sexual anarchy on social order and re-thinking their sustainability.[6]

Some have likened the West's turn toward sexual revolution as a new sort of cultural cosmology wherein persons understand themselves according to entirely different and radical reconfigurations about society's most basic underpinnings.[7] Where Christianity offered the world a vision for sexuality constrained by the good of chastity and marriage, society was flavored by Christianity's general orientation toward divine instruction and divine accountability.

On matters such as the definition of marriage, the definition of male and female, the proper composition of family, and the rightful ordering of one's sexual desires, a vast and growing chasm exists between the irreconcilable visions that Christianity and secularism each respectively stand for. Everything, as always, reduces to a conflict of material versus transcendent sources for constructing moral knowledge.

The cultural conflict is not only the result of a conflagration over the use of one's body parts. It is an architectonic debate over the vision, flourishing, and welfare of civilization. Just how far can humans go in relativizing sexual practices and family structure, and human collateral not result? How threadbare can the family be, and civil society still retain a semblance of order? That seems to be one of the underlying ironies of

---

[5] On the relationship between sexual practice and paganism in ancient antiquity, see Steven D. Smith, *Pagans & Christians in the City: Culture Wars from the Tiber to the Potomac* (Grand Rapids: Eerdmans, 2018).

[6] For two recent volumes looking suspiciously at the current sustainability of the sexual revolution, see Christine Emba, *Rethinking Sex: A Provocation* (New York: Penguin, 2022); Louise Perry, *The Case Against the Sexual Revolution* (Cambridge, UK: Polity, 2022).

[7] Rod Dreher, "Sex After Christianity," *American Conservative* 12, no. 2 (April 3, 2013): 20–23.

our predicament. At the exact moment where secular research converges on the harms of pornography, the decline of marriage rates, childhood poverty, fatherlessness, widening economic disparity, generationally high suicide rates, and the so-called "loneliness" epidemic, our society is unable or unwilling to call to account whether the indifference to the body and its natural organization toward marriage and family life is at all responsible for the malaise of Western civilization. Indeed, as of this writing, it would seem that we are terminally incapable of doing so. At the root of our challenge, then, is a conflict of purpose and meaning. Because the West no longer embraces the givenness of creation and the authority of the body's natural design, so, too, has the meaning of the body's relationship to cultural productivity and human flourishing been lost. Understanding that relationship between purpose and meaning and learning how one is tied to the other is essential for Christian witness seeing its way through the cultural tumult and cultural malaise.

Nothing short of a return to the Christian natural law's vision of sexual relations is necessary for the return of social stability and human flourishing. Like the previous chapter began with the natural law principle of human dignity as the anchor, it is important to begin this chapter's reflections with a positive vision for what the natural law tradition teaches concerning the body, gender, sexuality, marriage, and family. Again, it is important to stress that the reflections offered in this chapter are intentionally introductory as my goal in these applied chapters is to introduce *how* it is that natural law and Christianity cooperate with one another.

This chapter's organization will be different from the previous chapter. In the previous chapter, each issue was individually addressed considering its natural law foundation, relevance to creation order and the common good, and the issue's importance in light of the gospel. In the present chapter, I begin with a natural law explanation on marriage as the foundational moral good that ought to determine the proper ordering of sexual relations, its relevance to creation order and the common good, and how the gospel illuminates our understanding of marriage. It seems a better strategy to state a positive case for how Christian natural law conceives of these issues. From there, I will address the corresponding privations to the moral good of marriage and assess why these issues transgress the natural law, threaten the common good, and violate Scripture. Once again, the goal of this chapter is for the reader to understand the synchronicity between a natural law account of human relations and that of Scripture's.

## Marriage, Natural Law, and the Natural Family

Human beings are sexual creatures. The desire for sexual congress and reproductive drive are deeply knit within us. The question that follows from these truths is whether there is an arrangement or institution that most suitably organizes the facts of sexual desire and reproductive capacity intrinsic to human experience into meaningful and civilizationally productive ways. The answer that has undergirded virtually all recorded human history up until the earliest years of the twenty-first century, and the answer that the natural law tradition has similarly posited, is the comprehensive union of man and woman in marriage.

What is marriage? That question is central to the debates of our age. How one answers will reveal a number of insights about other important aspects constitutive to human flourishing. I define marriage as the conjugal union of one man and one woman united to one another within a permanent and monogamous bond that is, absent any medical problems, ordered to procreation. It is an institution that provides an outlet for safeguarding procreative potency, sexual fulfillment, and relational companionship. The consummation of a marriage is fortified by the unitive and procreative goods securing husband and wife, jointly, in a bond of mutual self-giving.

Looking beyond the good of just the individual husband and wife, marriage as an aggregative good is the building block of human society. Marriage is civilization in embryonic and microcosmic form. It is civilization's chief organizing principle, since society is nothing less and nothing more than the aggregate number of families that comprise it. Though not all marriages will produce children due to circumstances outside the control of spouses, what gives marriage its structure is the complementarity of male and female that makes procreation possible. The nature of marriage is tied to the complementarity of male and female reproductive ability. Were it not for the unique role of procreation intrinsic to male-female union, marriage would cease to be intelligible as a union distinct from other types of unions. Moreover, if the procreative primacy and uniqueness of marriage as an inherently and exclusively complementary union is denied or lessened, marriage is open to endless redefinition. Marriage, in this view, has an ontological structure that the removal of complementarity negates the ability for any relationship that strives to be marital to *actually* be marital. The reason that marriage and its orientation to family life is upheld as the moral good of the natural law tradition is that it safeguards the design for sexuality with the outcome of sexuality: children. Marriage, in other words, prevents the severing of procreation, sexual drive, and society's need for stability. It unites them all together under one canopy.

The natural law tradition upholds that the exclusive moral context for sexual activity is found within the marital union of husband and wife. It is important to note that it is not heterosexual sexual activity qua heterosexuality that is moral if and only if it is heterosexual activity. Rather, only if that activity is regulated by the bonds of a comprehensive union—a union of wills, affections, and bodies toward a coordinated end—and normed by a commitment to permanency and exclusivity within that bond is the sexual act considered moral. It is the marital union of husband and wife, through the joining together of their bodies in a coordinated action where one is in need of the other for reproductive fulfillment, that facilitates and secures the moral good of family life. The respective bodies of husband and wife make their bodily union procreative by nature and therefore open to the possibility of children. To speak of the family as a non-instrumental moral good means the experience of being in a family is a good for which no greater good, purpose, or goal can be experienced apart from the felicity of family life in itself. That a child may understand himself or herself as being in a unit linked to mother and father is a great blessing easy to gloss over.

In similar fashion, Christians understand male and female to be persons with fixed natures whose reproductive organization requires its sexual counterpart for its realization. This means, by definition, that male and female *telos* is achieved by the natural complementarity witnessed to by their bodily design. Such a definition necessarily rejects the legitimacy of "transgender" identities as an ontological category for existence.

A married man and woman engaged in intercourse are united in a comprehensive union of wills, affections, and bodies that has a potential outcome built into its design that two men, or two women, involved in same-sex sexual activity, cannot ever possibly achieve. The act that unites husband and wife is the same act that seals their union and makes possible the presence of offspring. All marriages, for it to be truly marital, must be oriented to the possibility of children even if the fulfillment is thwarted by some other circumstance. Children are therefore the perfective end of male-female embodiment. Correspondingly, the directiveness of the bodies toward a particular end informs what actions are morally justified in the use of one's body. Hence, an activity such as anal intercourse is immoral whether within a heterosexual or homosexual sex act.

A conjugal definition of marriage as described here understands that the union of husband and wife form a *comprehensive* union, the type of union of which one needs the other for the possibility of its fulfillment. Marriage is not an activity like basketball. It is a relationship unlike all others. As Melissa Moschella argues, "The relationship that unites two otherwise separate organisms into one organism is the same as that which unites the cells, organs, organ systems, etc. within an individual organism: coordination of the parts toward a single bodily end of the whole."[8] The argument is as follows: The coordination of organized parts that completes (or brings about) an end gives intelligibility to the entity in question. Thus, the coordination

---

[8] Melissa Moschella, "Sexual Ethics, Human Nature, and the 'New' and 'Old' Natural Law Theories," *National Catholic Bioethics Quarterly* 19, no. 2 (2019): 254.

of male and female toward an integrated end, namely, reproduction, is what gives intelligibility to the marriage union since coordination toward an end, generally speaking, is what gives intelligibility to a thing in question. This feature is what separates other types of human relationships in that the depth of union experienced are unparalleled in what other human relations can achieve. Marriage is thus intelligible by kind—not simply "degree"— *ultimately* by its reproductive end. To be "one flesh" as Genesis speaks of is not only a metaphor. It vividly depicts the fully organic integration of embodied persons joined together in coordinated activity. As a solitary person's circulatory system is self-enclosed and sufficient all on its own, so marriage is enclosed and sufficient only with two persons whose total persons unite at all levels of their being in gamete donation that each body is fit to contribute. As John Finnis writes,

> Marriage is a distinct fundamental human good because it enables the parties to it, the wife and husband, to flourish as individuals and as a couple, both by the most far-reaching form of togetherness possible for human beings and by the most radical and creative enabling of another person to flourish, namely, the bringing of that person into existence as conceptus, embryo, child, and eventually adult, fully able to participate in human flourishing on his or her own responsibility.[9]

What's most important to note about Finnis's observation is that the sort of union the husband and wife achieve is not merely emotional, volitional, or intellectual, but bodily. The opportunity for *comprehensive* union is what sets marriage apart from other types of relationships. Because the conjugal union of husband and wife sets the conditions for the presence of children, only a type of heightened commitment to permanency and exclusivity properly safeguards the marital union. Husband and wife bear a responsibility in the possible outcome of their union that a sacrosanct bond

---

[9] John Finnis, "Marriage: A Basic and Exigent Good," The Monist 91.3–4 (July–October 2008): 389.

of marriage helps protect. It is those grounds—complementarity, permanency, and exclusivity—that give intelligibility to marriage.

Marriage is thus inherently oriented to the common good by providing the guardrails and safe haven for the proper rearing of children. Ryan T. Anderson, Robert P. George, and Sherif Girgis are correct when they note that "marriage is ordered to family life because the act by which spouses make love also makes new life; one and the same act both seals a marriage and brings forth children. That is why marriage alone is the loving union of mind and body fulfilled by the procreation—and rearing—of whole new human beings."[10] This bringing forth of new human beings to the political community is essential to the common good's relationship to marriage, for, apart from marriage, society is robbed of the seedbed for civilization's flowering and renewal. Conversely, where marriages break down or fail to even form, incalculable damage is done to the social fabric of the political community. A society that fails to champion the primacy of marriage will cease to offer any normative vision for society's future apart from the fleeting needs of the present. Atomizing and de-populating societies, such as our own, represent the inversion of creational norms. Richard Berquist provides a helpful summary on how the natural law tradition conceives of marriage:

> The love that moves the man and woman to give themselves to each other is by nature an enduring love. For as the gift endures, so the love is meant to endure. Moreover, the love of man and woman in marriage is a fully human and honorable love, since it is rooted in their equal personal dignity. For as the woman is completed by the man, so the man is completed by the woman. And this love is meant not only to endure but to grow stronger over the years, as the couple's relationship matures.[11]

---

[10] Sherif Girgis, Ryan T. Anderson, and Robert P. George. *What Is Marriage?: Man and Woman: A Defense* (New York: Encounter Books, 2012), 30.

[11] Berquist, *From Human Dignity to Natural Law: An Introduction*, 155.

# The Biblical Testimony on Sex, Marriage, and Family

When we look at male and female reproductive design and the union of the bodies involved as set forth in Scripture, we understand the male and female body to coordinate in a particular way with a particular outcome unlike what other types of relationships can bring about, namely, children. As I want to argue, Scripture and natural law speak in concord regarding the norms and ends of marriage. The pattern for marriage and procreative relationship in Scripture is the same as that of the natural law.

The scriptural origin of the Christian tradition's understanding for sexuality and marriage begins in Genesis 1–2. In the Christian tradition, the creation narrative is the controlling motif that fundamentally shapes the biblical meta-narrative around sexuality. It begins with the creational distinctions between male and female that then forms the architectural blueprint through which sexual ethics are intelligible within the Judeo-Christian tradition. Male and female are made *for* one another to join together within the estate of marriage. Marriage's placement at the beginning of creation captures the central role that marriage and family play within the unfolding of creation. Here we see the overlapping compatibility between Christianity's relationship to the natural law concerning marriage. Normative paradigms that Scripture establishes as true of creation, as one theologian writes, "are not arbitrary decrees but correspond to the way the world is and will be."[12] The order of Scripture corresponds to the order of reality as such. This is yet another way we see Scripture speaking in natural law categories—by Scripture speaking to the correspondence of its decrees as synonymous with creation order.

When Scripture speaks of man and woman being united in "one flesh" (Gen 2:24), the metaphor Scripture employs vividly captures the depth of the natural law tradition's understanding of "comprehensive union." Central to the Christian understanding of sexuality and marriage is its inherently

---

[12] Richard Bauckham, *God and the Crisis of Freedom: Biblical and Contemporary Perspectives* (Louisville: WJK, 2002), 70.

procreational orientation. While ethicists have proposed several "goods" related to marriage, it must be said that procreation is the first among equals for marriage's intelligibility. Pleasure and relational delight stem from the fact of complementarity, the fact of which licenses procreation from the start. Were humans not procreative, there would be no future society or cultural development to speak of. Marriage thus begins, is structured, and purposed by God as an essential building block for human relations.

According to the Christian creation narrative, God created man and woman in his image to exercise dominion over the earth. A sexually differentiated species, man and woman, are told to be "fruitful and multiply" (Gen 1:28). Genesis conceptualizes marriage as a complementary (that is, relating between the two sexes) exclusive between two opposite-sexed persons, and meant to be permanent for the duration of their lives. The most basic constitutive element of marriage, however, is the physical difference that exists between men and women, which manifests itself in sexual union. Fruitfulness and multiplication require procreative capacity, which the body of man and woman are uniquely fit to fulfill. Offspring and family life are the result of sexual union. It is the reproductive difference and procreative capacity of male and female that God orders as the foundation for human flourishing and social stability. As the Genesis text intimates, the only appropriate context for sexual expression is in marriage. The covenant of marriage secures the context for these goods to occur and protects the bonds of family life.[13]

Genesis 2:24–25 illumines Gen 1:26–28 by teaching that marriage is enacted by a covenantal vow and ratified through a consummative act wherein man and woman seal their bond in a "one flesh" union. The language of "one flesh," however, is not mere metaphor as depicted above. The language suggests the natural fittedness of the male body for the female

---

[13] For more about the inherent connection to the goods of family life and sexual exclusivity, see Sherif Girgis, Ryan T. Anderson, and Robert P. George, *What Is Marriage?: Man and Woman: A Defense*, 1st ed. (New York: Encounter Books, 2012).

body and vice versa. As theologian and ethicist Wayne Grudem notes, "This unity was an essential component of marriage from the very beginning of the human race. In addition, when husband and wife come together in this 'one flesh' unity, they are a couple whom 'God has joined together.'"[14] This pattern—marriage as *conjugal, permanent,* and *exclusive*—is the archetype to evaluate Scripture's exhortations governing sexual activity.

The late professor Stanley Grenz affirms this argument stating that the Bible is unambiguous in its clarity:

> Viewed from what many see as the traditional Christian perspective, the question of the legitimate context for the sex act can yield only one conclusion. The proper context is the permanent, monogamous relationship called marriage. This perspective is the basic teaching of the Bible in both Old and New Testaments. The biblical writers do not present this sexual ethic without reason. On the contrary, as the finding of the human sciences confirm, permanent commitment plays a vital role in providing the boundaries and thus the context for the practice of the sex act.[15]

Christian ethicist Dennis P. Hollinger states Grenz's same argument in the reverse, demonstrating that nonmarital intercourse falls woefully short of the biblical ideal on the grounds that it "does not fit with God's intended purpose for this good but finite and now fallen gift."[16] The procreational, unitive, and relational goods of marriage are united within the conjugal union of husband and wife.

Marriage, then, from a Christian perspective, is an enchanted reality imbued with divine meaning and purpose. But as the drama of Scripture unfolds, sexual drive and marriage are marred—though not

---

[14] Wayne Grudem, *Christian Ethics: An Introduction to Biblical Moral Reasoning* (Wheaton: Crossway, 2018), 704.

[15] Stanley J. Grenz, *Sexual Ethics: An Evangelical Perspective* (Louisville, KY: WJK, 1997), 98–99.

[16] Dennis P. Hollinger, *The Meaning of Sex: Christian Ethics and the Moral Life* (Grand Rapids: Baker Academic, 2009), 134.

extinguished—by sin. The goods of marriage desire to be realized outside the context of marriage, leading to privations such as fornication, cohabitation, out-of-wedlock childbearing, and non-marriage as intelligible realities. Deviation from Scripture's pattern for sexuality within marriage is a severing of the goods from the totality of the marriage covenant. Such deviations from Scripture's portrayal of marriage as serving the needs of the common good come to be its detriment instead. No society can flourish when the moral ecology of its culture's sexual energies is divorced from Scripture and natural law. Society simply cannot, in the long run, work against the capacity and ends for which male, female, and child are ordered toward.

Yet, redemption tells us that the original design, pattern, and purpose of sexuality and marriage is reaffirmed and heightened as the New Testament explains its ultimate *telos*—to reflect the Christ-Church union (Eph 5:22–33). The order of redemption does not suspend, abrogate, or subsume the normative directiveness of Genesis's creation ethic. The gospel does not introduce a radically new sexual ethic. It gives pneumatological power to obey it. The gospel calls for rehabilitating the ethic begun in creation. The composition of marital goods has not changed. What is present in the life of the Christian is the Spirit's empowerment to live lives ordered to sexual obedience (1 Cor 6:12–20). The assumption that sexuality and marriage are ordered *by* God and *for* God stands in stark contrast to modernity's view that divinizes sexuality and sees marriages as little more than a self-satisfactory contract.

Jesus Christ reaffirmed the normative pattern established in Genesis. In Matt 19:4–6, Jesus states that male-female sexual exclusivity constitutes the grounds for marriage. The creational structure of marriage that Jesus defends thus parallels the natural law definition of marriage. Jesus's sexual ethics are nothing other than a ratification of the pattern of sexual ethics given at the beginning of creation. Jesus even affirms the binding obligation of the Seventh Commandment (Luke 18:20).

Owing to the reality of sexual desire, the apostle Paul states that sexual activity should be regulated within the marital context in unequivocal terms.

"But because of the temptation to sexual morality," Paul writes, "each man should have his own wife and each woman her own husband" (1 Cor 7:2). Paul sees marriage as the God-ordained outlet that addresses human sexual desire. Paul commands his listeners to "abstain from sexual immorality" (1 Thess 4:3; Col 3:5; Eph 5:3; 1 Tim 3:2). The same ethic appears in other New Testament epistles, such as in James 2:10–11, where James pronounces judgment on sexual immorality. C. S. Lewis writes in *Mere Christianity*, that "there is no getting away from it: the old Christian rule is, 'either marriage, with complete faithfulness to your partner, or else total abstinence.'"[17] Those are the stark terms put before us.

## Sexual Privations

I now turn to give attention in greater detail on why and how deviations from Scripture and natural law violate moral goods and are immoral and harmful concerning the rightful ordering of sexual relations. At its most basic, sexual privations all stem from a deviation of God's ordering for natural relations set forth in creation. By the sheer fact of creation order being undermined, the net effect to society's well-being is severely hampered as sexual deviancy becomes normalized. To put it at its most foreboding conclusion: sexual disorder necessarily metastasizes into cultural disarray. A failure to conform to God's established order means the very foundations for society's thriving is cast aside. No culture or civilization can withstand the deliberate and consistent rejection of creation order.

### Fornication and Adultery

Fornication is defined as sexual intercourse outside of marriage while adultery is defined as sexual unfaithfulness by a married person committed with someone who is not their spouse. On what grounds can we say that

---

[17] Lewis, *Mere Christianity*, 15 (see chap. 6, n. 32).

nonmarital and extramarital sex are wrong? Both fundamentally thwart the moral good of marriage as the exclusive domain of sexual activity.

At its root, fornication is wrong because it directs a person toward a one-flesh union without the intention of uniting in a comprehensive union. It is a sexual union of a particular type—one that is comprehensive in nature—that seals the bond of marriage. Reproductive ability void of the bonds of exclusivity and permanency is rife with potential for harm to both the partners and any potential offspring. Once again, we see how a privation is a severing of goods from the totality of marriage and its orientation to family life as the overarching good. Both actions sever sexual congress from the bonds of permanency. Fornication has no inherent orientation to permanency in the same way that marriage does since no guardrail of exclusivity is present. Adultery is wrong because it violates the sacred trust that a comprehensive union requires. This is to say nothing of the generally duplicitous ways in which adultery and non-monogamy is undertaken. As one scholar writes, "[I]n virtue of its comprehensiveness, the marital union requires a commitment to permanence and exclusivity (comprehensiveness over time and at every time) with regard to the act that distinctively seals it and to the open-ended coordination of all of life—including some pursuit of all human values—that characterizes family life."[18] The fact that sex is ordered to procreation speaks to the necessity of a permanent bond being present to safeguard the ideal conditions for a child's entry into the world and their development. That sex be regulated by a bond of permanency and exclusivity explains the primacy of ordering sexuality to the protection of a child's right to a safe upbringing commensurate to their needs as a human being.

As we look at Scripture, we understand that fornication and adultery violate the norms of marriage established in Genesis 1–2. The presence of polygamy in the Old Testament is never heralded as a normative good. It is

---

[18] Moschella, "Sexual Ethics, Human Nature, and the 'New' and 'Old' Natural Law Theories," 255.

merely a descriptive reality that Scripture highlights as a reality stemming from sin. We see Jesus lovingly confront a woman in a sexual relationship with a man who is not her husband (John 4:17–18). The woman recognizes this as moral wrongdoing and presumably repents of her behavior. Even still, polygamy is not a violation of the natural law in the same way that homosexual intercourse is. Polygamy is wrong because men and women are to have only one marriage, but Scripture does not depict polygamous unions as non-marriages. Polygamy is a numerical problem before it is an ontological program. Heterosexual acts sealed by a commitment to permanency but not monogamy could foreseeably still be marriages, though entered into on wrong grounds.

Elsewhere, when Jesus confronts a woman accused of adultery and facing public execution, Jesus intervenes to protect the woman's life. Contrary to some arguments, he does not loosen or suspend the prohibition on fornication but uses the standard of judgment that others were in appealing to execute her as the grounds to nullify their self-righteous judgment. Jesus is not lenient about sin; he is gracious in extending compassion to those trapped in sin. At the end of this exchange, he told the woman, "Go, and from now on sin no more" (John 8:11). Such a statement confirms that Jesus considered the woman's adulterous activity sinful.

That intercourse is both ordered and limited to the marital relationship of husband and wife explains why Scripture sets guardrails and expectations for sexual activity. For example, the Seventh Commandment ("You shall not commit adultery") in Exod 20:14 assumes that the vows made in marriage licenses sexual intercourse between spouses and governs the exclusivity of sexual activity.[19] While the text of the Seventh Commandment has only marital adultery within its purview, the Hebrew syntax (*n'p*) suggests a broader semantical domain prohibiting all forms of sexual expression outside of marriage, similar to the New Testaments concept of *porneia* (Matt 5:32). The Seventh Commandment concerns the totality of sexual

---

[19] Liederbach and Lenow, *Ethics as Worship*, 583 (see chap. 10, n. 10).

purity. This prohibition includes prostitution and sex outside of marriage (Gen 28:15 and Num 25:1).[20] It is well documented by biblical scholars that *porneia* is an all-encompassing category that condemns and prohibits all sexual activity outside of marriage.

According to ethicist Daniel Heimbach, "All sex outside of marriage is denied by the general prohibition against adultery, and no voluntary sex outside of marriage is ever moral."[21] In Deuteronomy 22, punitive action results if fornication is discovered to have occurred before marriage. Fornication is immoral and sinful, according to Lewis Smedes, because unmarried persons are engaging in a "life-uniting act without a life-uniting intent."[22] The unitive design for sexuality explains the apostle Paul's concern that joining one's body to a prostitute constitutes a marital act without the vow of marital commitment (1 Cor 6:15–20). The focus is not on prostitution as such, but on joining one's body to a person with whom there is no intention of creating a lifelong union. Hence, in this framework, as one scholar writes, "adultery and extramarital sex are opposed to the natural law because the man and woman are not in the kind of relationship appropriate for sexuality activity."[23]

## Parental and Children's Rights

While parental rights might seem odd to devote space to, this topic is nonetheless vital to draw attention to since it is increasingly likely that opposition to the state's re-definition of family and adoption of harmful sexual ideology will put Christians at odds with what the state considers routine and beneficial for child welfare. There are already instances that point to Christians

---

[20] See Mark F. Rooker, *The Ten Commandments*, NAC Studies in Bible and Theology (Nashville: B&H Academic, 2010), 135, n11.

[21] Daniel R. Heimbach, *True Sexual Morality: Recovering Biblical Standards for a Culture in Crisis* (Wheaton: Crossway, 2004), 179.

[22] Lewis Smedes, *Sex for Christians: The Limits and Liberties of Sexual Living* (Grand Rapids: Eerdmans, 1994), 101.

[23] Berquist, *From Human Dignity to Natural Law*, 152 (see chap. 10, n. 1).

being the target of the state for Christian parents' unwillingness to affirm aberrant sexual practices.

The generativity tied to the conjugal union of husband and wife entails that children have a right to their father and mother and that mother and father have a reciprocal duty to their children. The type of bond that Scripture describes as marital, being that it is inherently procreative, furnishes an indissoluble bond between parent and child. The persons who are responsible for the child's conception have a responsibility to oversee that same child's well-being.

As Christians, ultimately, the Lord is the One to whom children belong (Ps 127:3). God graciously bestows children to husband and wife as an embodied expression of their covenantal union. The act that unites man and woman as one flesh is the same act capable of bringing forth sons and daughters—populations that make possible the exercising of dominion over creation (Gen 1:26–28). The God who gives children to parents bestows on parents the earthly responsibility to care for them (1 Tim 5:8). As the Fifth Commandment instructs, children are to obey their parents (Deut 5:16). The entire pattern of family life established in Scripture recognizes parents as the authority figures over their children.

But what does it mean, exactly, for children to *belong* to their parents? Because husband and wife bear biological responsibility for their child's existence (cause), they bear a unique personal responsibility for their care (effect). While we are prone to think of "rights" as primarily possessive in nature, rights as they are conceived within the communion of parent and child entails responsibility for the child's welfare. Children are not "ours" in any selfish sense, but "ours" in the sense of bearing a unique relationship and corresponding responsibility. Said differently, there are other children I care for in a general sense (in wishing them no harm and even seeking their protection in an emergency) but there are other children—my own children—who I care for in an even deeper sense. These are the biological offspring of my wife and me, persons about whom our intimate knowledge breeds a deep familial bond unlike that of other children. The "right" I have to my children extends in proportion to the type of bond my wife and I have with them.

The relationship of parent and child is unlike any other type of biological or social relationship that could potentially lay claim to the status of being the child's guardian. As Melissa Moschella argues, parents have a unique competence that allows children "to gain important insights about their own identity through their interactions with their biological family, and, perhaps most importantly, benefit profoundly from experiencing the secure and unconditional love of those who brought them into being."[24] Offspring of a husband and wife are in a unique position to give to their children the full gamut of their origin—their ethnicity, their ancestry, and the knowledge of their genetic makeup (were genetic disorders a known concern). Parents are, simply put, the most natural and well-suited persons to care for their children.

The reverse side of this reality represents a heinous violation of the natural law: the denying, disrupting, or thwarting of the natural parent-child bond. Nothing would seem so gravely unjust than the taking of a child from the loving bond of his or her own parents. As Thomas Aquinas writes, "It would be contrary to natural justice, if a child, before coming to the use of reason, were to be taken away from its parents' custody, or anything done to it against its parents' wish."[25] Aquinas's explanation hardly needs further elaboration. His point is stunningly clear: Parents have a natural right to the children they bring forth.

The parent-child relationship arises spontaneously outside the direct auspices of the state. In other words, because the state has no natural authority over fertility, it lacks the mandate, jurisdiction, and competency to interrupt the parent-child bond. The state ought to remediate a situation of parental breakdown where abuse, divorce, death, or any other similar privation occurs—and even here, it should look to the next of biological kin to

---

[24] Melissa Moschella, "The Fundamental Case for Parental Rights," *Public Discourse*, October 6, 2014, https://www.thepublicdiscourse.com/2014/10/13635/.

[25] *ST* II-II Q. 10 A. 12.

safeguard any children. The state's role in recognizing the parent-child bond is to afford it a sacrosanct bond of unbending deference.

There is an overarching threat to the common good by the state's active efforts to redefine the very nature of family. Hence, where regimes of "same-sex marriage" have been put into place, we see the state giving tacit approval of and regulation to circumstances where children are being intentionally placed in circumstances where children are denied access to their mother and father. While society questions whether and how same-sex unions "harm" others, it is difficult not to conclude that as culture oversees and approves a proliferating number of persons parented outside the context of a married mother and father, a silent woundedness will surface as persons suffer the deleterious harms of never knowing the differentiated love of each.

## Contraception

Debates over contraception have engulfed Protestantism since the earlier twentieth-century. It is my own view that Protestants are woefully shortsighted in their understanding of contraception, often unaware of church history's negative appraisal of contraception or willfully refusing to consider the ways that contraception has led to reimagining how society—and even those inside the church—conceives of the design and purpose for sexuality. Just because Scripture may not directly speak to a particular technology like modern contraception, silence does not imply carte blanche permissibility. Rogue argumentation that relies on Scripture's apparent silence should not foreclose the need to engage in theological reasoning about contraception's consequences for understanding sexual teleology.

At the center of the debate over contraception is the question of whether each individual conjugal act of husband and wife must be open to children or whether openness to children speaks only to the totality of the marriage covenant itself, not each individual act. Somewhat controversially—and though not holding such a position with an ironclad defense of it from Scripture—I hold the position that married couples should only practice natural forms of birth control, more commonly known as "Natural Family Planning." I grant, however, that there are medical conditions that do permit the use of contraception to prevent the life of the mother from incurring harm. What is paramount in considerations as to family planning is that children are not construed as a burden or blight upon the relational and recreational predilections of couples who forgo children for the sake of some other supposed good, whether increased income, career mobility, more disposable free-time, or the ability to travel unencumbered. The Christian's first response to the question of family planning is an unambiguous declaration that "children are a gift of the LORD" (Ps 127:3–5) and that every marriage be entered into with an openness to children, regardless of whether that is ever realized due to unforeseen medical problems. And to be clear, no command is present in Scripture to have as many children as is physically possible. Wisdom and prudence are necessary ingredients in the decision to start a family. What should be resisted is what some refer to as the "contraceptive mindset," an attitude that treats children as an afterthought or addendum to the Laissez-faire freedoms of sexual entitlement.

I also grant that the moral problems tied to available methods of contraceptive devices vary from device to device. At the illicit and evil end of the spectrum are methods that terminate an embryo either through disrupting implantation or poisoning the embryo, what is commonly referred to as the "morning-after pill." These should be considered abortifacient in nature and are therefore prohibited. I consider the hormonal contraceptive pill morally dubious, meaning that questions arise as to its long-term impact on a woman's body and the general problems of disrupting natural bodily rhythms. Arguably, the least problematic form of birth control are barrier methods that are neither abortifacient nor hormonal. Still, I find their use problematic for how they license intentionally non-procreative sex and reconfigure the social imaginary around sexuality and its orientation to family life.[26]

---

[26] For representative approaches between Catholic and Protestant perspectives on contraception, see Ken Magnuson, *Invitation to Christian Ethics* (Grand Rapids: Kregel Academic, 2020), 191–94; Denny Burk, *What Is the Meaning of*

My objections to birth control are, I admit, more grounded in philosophy than they are explicitly tied to Scripture. But I will address Scripture in a moment. The underlying principle of what contraception introduces into our sexual psychology should be made very clear: once the very distinguishing characteristic that differentiates man and woman from one another is willfully nullified (i.e., their reproductive organization), the logic of such action suggests a tectonic reconfiguration of what sex is *for*. If sex is intentionally understood as no longer procreative, the likelihood of wrongly channeling one's sexual desires dramatically increases. The context where sex is understood to be reserved for—marriage—is no longer logically tied to it. If children are an afterthought to a sexual act, preserving sexual activity to the institution most suited for the care and well-being of children becomes an afterthought, too. Indeed, this has been the outcome as contraception's wholesale adoption has proceeded throughout culture.

Contraception thus damages the intelligibility of the sex act, which is understood to be procreational, as well as marriage. We come once again to the question of teleology. If anatomical design ends in reproductive possibility, then negating the reproductive end that contraception calls for signals a reconfiguring of the use and ends of our anatomical design. No longer do we conceive of sex as inherently procreative. Sexual intercourse valued primarily for its erotic end, such that its procreative end is secondary or entirely discretionary, signals that sexual intercourse need not be fundamentally reserved for the context where comprehensive union ought to occur—marriage. Hence the cascading and revolutionary effects on society where contraception is mainstreamed: no longer is marriage seen as fundamental, but only optional, since the array of benefits that were understood to have traditionally accrued in marriage, are now available outside of marriage.

---

*Sex?* (Wheaton, IL: Crossway, 2013), 139–55; William E. May, Ronald Lawler, and Joseph Boyle, *Catholic Sexual Ethics: A Summary, Explanation, & Defense, 3rd Edition* (Huntington, IN: Our Sunday Visitor, 2011), 227–43.

Once sex can be conceived as non-procreative, the bonds are loosened for where sex is believed to need to occur, namely, marriage. This all stems from the idea of a comprehensive union uniting all the goods of marriage in one synchronous act. For marriage safeguards all the goods of marriage together. But once the goods of marriage are capable of being actualized and severed apart from marriage, marriage's composition and poise retain less attractional pull. If the goods of marriage can be severed, the question will be logically raised whether the goods need the context of marriage at all for the realization. Sadly, these fears have come to fruition in the de-stigmatization of fornication, the rise of out-of-wedlock pregnancy, cohabitation, and declining marriage rates.

There is still yet one more concern raised with mainstreaming contraception, and that is the impact it has on granting intelligibility to homosexual sex acts: If heterosexual sex can be intentionally non-procreative by design or by cultural attitude, one must be very diligent to argue why it is that non-procreative sodomy is illicit. Yes, the use of body parts between homosexual and heterosexual sex acts are different as to natural fittedness for the body, but their *telos* between the two is symmetrical: pleasure sought for pleasure's own sake. The problem, however, is that pleasure, while a good within marriage, is never depicted in Scripture as something that should be sought after to the exclusion of procreative potential. Scripture conceptualizes pleasure and procreation as distinct categories within marriage, but it does not furnish a severing of them. We should avoid false dichotomies where Scripture does not permit them.

## *Sterilization*

For reasons that follow from my convictions about contraception, I argue that voluntary sterilization ought not be pursued except in cases where pregnancy can threaten the life of the mother. It is far too common in Protestant subcultures to treat sterilization procedures like vasectomies as normal and expected practices that come with later adulthood. The thoughtless routine of taking healthy body parts and surgically maiming them without justifiable grounds to do so only demonstrates so much of evangelicalism's anemic self-understanding of its sexual ethics.

I grant that my argument on these subjects lack explicit biblical warrant. What they are grounded in, however, is an understanding of the biblical text as speaking about the overall grammar of our sexual teleology, a teleology that accepts the authority of our embodiment and channels that embodiment toward personally and culturally productive outlets—marriage and the common good of all. Even the most basic reading of Scripture would suggest that procreation be maintained as the primary organizing principle of male-female embodiment. To reject that normative principle would suggest artfully tinkering with both the scriptural archetype governing sexual practices as well as casting suspicion on the natural rhythms of male-female sexuality.

## Homosexuality and Same-Sex Marriage

Homosexual desires and behavior are morally wrong. For one, though its frequency is sparse in Scripture, every mention of homosexuality is done so with vice and prohibition in mind. Some argue that the relative sparsity of homosexuality in Scripture means it is morally insignificant. This fundamentally misunderstands the underlying narrative arc that Scripture speaks in regarding sexuality. Though there are only six so-called "Clobber Passages" that speak negatively of homosexuality, we must understand the whole backdrop of Scripture's teaching on sexuality to understand the biblical prohibitions on homosexuality. In other words, when the Scripture speaks prohibitively against something, we must understand what it is speaking positively about in contrast. In the field of ethics, when we make an evaluation on whether something is moral or not, we must measure that against a standard. What does this mean? It means the biblical canon assumes a grand *a priori* principle pertaining to sexual ethics: The normative expression for sexual activity is the conjugal union of man and woman who become husband and wife through the union of their wills, affections, and, preeminently, their *bodies*. The Bible's standard for sexuality from the very first pages of Scripture assume that the complementary relationship between husband and wife is the exclusive expression of God's will for sexuality in creation. Any deviation from that explicit pattern is thus unbiblical and unreasonable due to the undermining of marriage as the moral good of Scripture.

As Scripture is the Christian's highest authority, that alone would suffice to explain the prohibition of homosexuality. Propositional claims, however, assume the existence of intelligible *reasons* for the moral illicitness of an action. We can deduce necessary and important arguments for why homosexuality is immoral according to Scripture.

First, homosexuality is an antithesis to the good of marriage and family life since it is oriented toward neither. Homosexual unions are by nature non-generative and thus nonmarital by design. It thus nullifies the procreative purpose of sexual design by disconnecting the body's form from its essential purpose, resulting in a sort of anthropological Gnosticism that views the form of embodiment as indeterminate to our nature as male and female. Homosexuality is thus sterile sex at odds with the body and sexuality's essential purpose—procreation.

Second, homosexuality dishonors the body's design by violating the organization of the body as a reproductive structure. As J. Budziszewski writes, "when a man puts the part of himself that represents new life into the cavity of another man that represents decay and expulsion, at the most basic of all possible levels he is saying 'Life, be swallowed in death.'"[27] Such a stark statement vividly captures the moral repugnance of homosexual sodomy.

Third, following from the previous statement, homosexuality is a repudiation of creation order and the generativity that is required for society's continuation. It represents the apotheosis of an inverted creation mandate, where instead of fruitful sex meant to serve creation, sex is turned back toward the service of the self alone.

---

[27] Budziszewski, *What We Can't Not Know*, 86–87 (see chap. 6, n. 21).

Fourth and relatedly, homosexuality is an idolatrous self-worship that collapses creational distinctions for the love of similarly-sexed persons instead of love being directed toward "the other."

Fifth, Scripture speaks condemningly of every instance of homosexuality within its pages. Even if reason and logic were not available to confirm the problem with homosexuality, Scripture's prohibition would be sufficient to justify its condemnation.

Concerning natural law's evaluation of homosexuality, in addition to the above statements, it is the misuse of the body and the fruitlessness of sodomy that Paul speaks of as "contrary to nature" as he does in Rom 1:26 that captures the theme of natural order. "Designedness" captures homosexuality's illicitness. Paul is speaking to the observance of a fixed created order, of a givenness to creation order that naturally reveals itself. When Scripture speaks of homosexuality being "contrary to nature," for example, it is speaking in this capacity—to use the body in ways that thwarts its design and *telos*. Paul is not conceiving of one possessing either a "homosexual" or "heterosexual" nature (though there is no reason to believe that Paul was not aware of exclusively same-sex attracted persons). Rather, his condemnation is all-encompassing in that homosexuality embodies the negation of there being a *telos* to the design of the human body being met in its sexual counterpart. Homosexuality is a rejection of the created nature of sexual design as such, regardless of the form of homosexuality being practiced. To sexually use the body in a way that does not direct it toward its fulfillment (whether realized or not) is to violate the body as some extrinsic instrument divorced from overall organization of the body's *telos*.

For this reason we must be clear: same-sex marriage does not exist in any ontological sense of the term; it is not real, but only a legal fiction. Legal licenses are issued to couples believing themselves to be in a same-sex "marriage." But a license issued by the state can no more affect the truth of marriage than it can were the state to declare that water only has one hydrogen molecule. In no way are these statements offered to be provocative, but to deal matter-of-factly with the claim on metaphysical reality that same-sex marriage tries to make. Same-sex couples cannot be married in any true ontological way since same-sex marriage is at odds with metaphysical order. Natural law attunes itself to what is true as a matter of reality. By this standard, same-sex marriage amounts to a form of imaginative wish-casting that can effectuate no true reality.

Christian moral principles and natural law theory have always defined marriage as an exclusively opposite-sexed union. Absent the principle of complementarity, marriage as an ontologically distinct union unravels. It is impossible to deny marriage to two or three persons around whatever desirable basis there is once the underlying principle is established that marriage's definition is merely based on the emotional and physical affinities of the persons in question.

Without complementarity, it becomes impossible apart from brute assertion to explain why marriage must be either permanent or monogamous. It is the case, as of this writing, that concerns about the dissolution of marriage are slowly coming to fruition in the increased presence of, and advocacy for, polyamorous unions. Marriage either is the conjugal union of husband and wife united around their offspring or else marriage as a normative institution ceases to exist apart from social construction.

### Threats Posed by Same-Sex Marriage

There are four additional threats posed by same-sex marriage. The first is that same-sex marriage, and same-sex parenting, treats mothers and fathers as indifferent to the child's needs. To see a child growing up in a same-sex household is to see a child without the differentiated love of either a mother or father. A child is owed their mother and father and to deny him or her a relationship with one or both is an injustice. Second, same-sex marriage yields tremendous authority to the state. By denying that marriage is an inherently pro-creational institution, the natural bonds of family life and the corresponding rights that interlink parent with child are called into question. Defining the boundary of the family without regard to biological kinship accedes tremendous power to the state in configuring the most basic unit of society.[28] Third, same-sex marriage is yet one additional devolution in weakening the norms around marriage, thereby weakening the need to enter marriage. Though marriage's precipitous decline is not the fault of same-sex marriage alone, same-sex marriage will only further weaken the intelligibility of marriage as a cultural standard. Fourth, same-sex marriage will and indeed *does* pose a threat to religious liberty. As same-sex marriage has gained steam culturally, along with it has been an unwillingness to accommodate the persons, business owners, and religious institutions that dissent from it.

## Transgenderism

Transgenderism is the phenomenon of an individual embracing a gender identity (a suspect category in itself) that is different than their biological sex.[29] Instead of looking to genetics (chromosomes), primary sex characteristics (reproductive anatomy), and secondary sex characteristics (mature physical differences between males and females), transgender ideology creates an entirely new foundation upon which to define human existence and human flourishing. In this, it is radically subjective and discrete, relying on the internal psychology of the person's own self-description to define their

---

[28] This comment should not be interpreted as a criticism of adoption. Adoption is a virtuous action taken to repair a familial breakdown. Same-sex marriages where children are present are, rather, intentionally designed from the start to deny the child either a mother or father. For two volumes looking at how the family is conceived of within Christian political philsophy, see Allan Carlson and Paul Mero, *The Natural Family: A Manifesto* (Dallas: Spence, 2007); Brent Waters, *The Family in Christian Social and Political Thought* (Oxford: Oxford University Press, 2007).

[29] I reject the concept of "gender identity" as a non-falsifiable category. How one can authenticate that subjective feelings or perceptions are either truly "masculine" or "feminine" is phenomenologically incoherent. Maleness and femaleness are not psychological states.

"gender identity," a concept that has no philosophical coherence to it. It also raises tremendous questions about the relationship of the body to self-conception. The transgender phenomenon, though, is not simply an ideological debate or a conflict over biological definitions. It is a question about ontology; that is, about whether male and female *exist* at all.

The question the natural law must address is whether the category of "male" and "female" are static, fixed identities that defy endless redefinition. According to the natural law tradition, human beings are categorized as either male or female. The presence of intersexed individuals does not negate the otherwise standard male-female binary. Maleness and femaleness are fixed and objective categories whose immutable nature is defined by the body's organization for acts of reproduction. Indeed, once male and female are categories severed from bodily organization, the possibilities become endless as to how to define male and female. Are male and female merely cultural stereotypes? Are they mere psychological states? The biological foundations of man and woman are what grounds our definition of them. Therefore, the natural law tradition understands transgenderism as a repudiation of nature itself. Hormone injections and surgical alterations to one's body cannot reconfigure the underlying genetic organization that attends to male and female nature.

While transgenderism may appear to be only a solitary individual matter, the fact remains that the preponderance of transgenderism is based on severing the body's design and authority in determining male and female identity. Transgenderism severs the relationship between an embodied identity and reproductive capacity. In that regard, it is a functional denial of the role of teleology in navigating issues of authority surrounding the body. The transgender worldview thus represents an active thwarting of one's nature in service to ideological forces.

Scripture teaches that male and female are biological and embodied beings with an immutable nature. Their nature reveals that the anatomical design and reproductive capacity of male and female are constitutive of their being (Gen 1:26–28). The static nature of male and female is dynamic in its capacity. Hence, the purpose of our bodies is connected to the difference of our biological sex. A male and female body bear a purpose toward a one-flesh union that unites them and which can, under regular circumstances, can lead to reproduction (Gen. 2:24). Not only does Scripture prohibit gender fluidity, but we also deduce from creation order that active attempts to suppress the gender binary are also illicit (Gen 1:27–28). While we can firmly grant that Scripture allows for differing gender expressions according to a particular culture's understanding of what constitutes male and female (e.g., men wear kilts in Scotland), the cultural variation of gender expression does not grant the premise of severing gender from biological sex, which is what modern gender theory proposes.

To embrace what Scripture says is true about male and female is to live in harmony with creation order. Accepting the limitations of our embodiment is part and parcel for accepting the order that God imposes on creation, affixing to humanity a definite nature known by its design. Scripture does not envision the distinct separation of biological sex from gender expression. The prohibition on cross-dressing (Deut 22:5), for example, is not simply about external adornment. It is about ordering one's appearance in keeping with the gendered customs of a given culture that find context-specific ways to encode male and female expression.

What transgenderism represents is a resurrected form of Gnosticism, where the "self" is severed from the authority of the body. Philosopher Robert P. George notes how, according to transgender philosophy, "the body serves as the pleasure of the conscious self, to which it is subject, and so mutilations and other procedures pose no inherent moral problem."[30] Without stable conceptions for male and female predominating within society, unspeakable damage is done to the common good. Cooperation within society requires normative scripts from which to interpret one's experiences and activities in society. Where questions of "identity" proliferate, normative scripts are destabilized and call into question the various

---

[30] Robert P. George, "Gnostic Liberalism," *First Things* 268 (December 2016): 36.

stations of life where our experiences of male and female would be otherwise unquestioned. Hence, in the modern-day West, questions surrounding gender identity are posing major disruptions to public school settings, professional medical associations, and even recreation activities like athletics.

In the new covenant, one's identity as a male or female is never negated; it is, however, subordinated to soteriological realities. Within the economy of redemption, according to Paul in Gal 3:28, there is soteriological equality amid retained creational distinctions. Men and women never cease to be men and women, even if both are "in Christ." Such an approach aligns with other teaching in the New Testament that demonstrates that in redemption, there dawns a new eschatological understanding of the significance of a creational order, not its rejection or suspension.

## Other Sexual Privations

It follows from the preceding points in the chapter that the architectonic nature of sexuality made known in Scripture and through general revelation and natural law lead to additional prohibitions on other sexual vices. Scripture's prohibitions and near-universal cultural taboos explain why deviations from the conjugal union of husband and wife are in fact wrong.

- Intentional childlessness should be understood as a denial of the marital *telos*. I am speaking only of those persons who have no underlying medical defect preventing conception. Every marriage should be open to the presence of children by virtue of what marriage *is*—a comprehensive union of man and woman joined to one another in the most intimate of ways that is organically ordered toward children. If reproductive organization is tied to the nature of what it means to be male and female, an intentional severing of reproduction from one's nature within the context of marriage is a rejection of both human nature and marriage's nature. Scripture depicts marriage as a fruitful enterprise and willfully refusing to have fruitful sex is an inversion of the Genesis mandate to be fruitful and multiply. While this may sound controversial to some, the efforts to justify child-lessness in service to career or even Christian calling poses a false dichotomy not sanctionable by Scripture. Scripture does not command maximizing one's fertility as though having as many children as one possibly can is the call of Christian faithfulness, but acting in intentional ways to permanently preclude children altogether from the institution of marriage should be regarded as sinful.

- Bestiality is condemned since sex between different animal species violates the creational boundaries demarcating the human species from non-human animals (Lev 18:23; 20:15–16).
- Rape is condemned because it forces a sex act on an unwilling partner and thus fails to love one's neighbor as a basic principle of reciprocal justice (Deut 22:23–29; Ezek 45:9; Mark 12:31). Similarly, illicit seduction as well as sexual abuse are also prohibited (Genesis 34; Prov 7:6–23; Deut 22:25–27; Mark 12:31).
- Pornography is prohibited since its use nurses prurient and lustful desires at odds with the biblical and natural good of marriage (Ps 101:3; Matt 5:28; Col 3:5).
- Non-exclusive and non-monogamous relationships of any variety are prohibited. Polyamorous relationships and marriages are forbidden for violating the principle of exclusivity and monogamy (Gen 2:24). It is important to define these two categories distinctly. Exclusivity refers to a dedication to sexual faithfulness of any type. Monogamy refers to sexual faithfulness to one person and one person only. A polyamorous couple could be exclusively non-monogamous within a sexual triad made up of the same persons who practice group sex with one another. But that is not monogamy, and thus fails to satisfy biblical criteria. For this reason, group sex or "orgies" are condemned for violating the principle of monogamy (Gal 5:19–21).

- Pedophilia is likewise prohibited for violating a child sexually on the grounds that children are not sexual beings, marriage-eligible, and whose innocence requires our uttermost protection, and thus no harm (Matt 18:5–6, 10).

- Incestuous relations are forbidden because it violates natural taboos that view sex with relatives as immoral (Lev 18:8–18; 1 Cor 5:1–5). This is one of the most universal moral customs recognizable across cultures. Relations are to be exogamous, meaning outside of themselves. While there are debates about how wide the prohibition on incest extends, Scripture seems to forbid sexual relations between children and parents, step-parents, half-siblings, relations between grandparents and grandchildren, aunts and uncles, and between immediate in-laws. Forbidding incest also protects against genetic abnormalities that occur with in-breeding.[31]

- Prostitution and the commercialization of sex is forbidden since such practices are incompatible with the boundary markers of conjugal marriage (Hos 4:14).

- Sexual acts with non-human objects are also forbidden. As of this writing, the industrialized use and acceptance of what are commonly referred to as "sex robots" is gaining acceptance. It is akin to a form of technological bestiality. For reasons that ought to be intuitive, sexual acts with non-human objects violate every threshold of the natural law's tenets. Given the procreative typology of what the sexual act represents, sex-robots should be classified as a form of masturbation.

Additional comments are necessary for discussing masturbation. This topic divides some Christian ethicists. Some believe that masturbation can be permissible as a form of sexual release to stave off greater sexual sin. While

---

[31] For an outstanding resource on the Bible's prohibition on incest, see Christopher Ash, *Marriage: Sex in the Service of God* (Vancouver: Regent College, 2003), 256–71, where analysis for this section is drawn from.

I am sympathetic with this argument, I find it unpersuasive for several reasons. First, masturbation requires prurient desire and lust for its satisfaction. Masturbation as a non-erotic activity is a contradiction to one's biological drive. Second, the act of masturbation countermands the principle of conjugality by ordering its end to the individual's pleasure alone. Masturbation is, ultimately, inherently non-procreative solo-sex. Third, masturbation reveals a lack of self-control, which is what Christians are called to exercise (Gal 5:23). Where Scripture envisions the impulses of the body being controlled by the renewing of one's mind, masturbation enlivens the passions to overwhelm the ability for one to exercise reason and self-control over their passions (Rom 12:1–2).

## Implications for a Christotelic Natural Law Approach to Sexual Ethics

All sexual ordering and sexual acts should be done with a view of the glory of Jesus Christ. It is the glory of the gospel that provides the canopy for understanding the totality of the Christian witnesses' ordering for sexuality. Below are three principles we can deduce as overarching principles for how a Christian natural law understanding approaches issues of sexual ordering.

### God's Design for Sex Is Rational and Authoritative

In Genesis 1, we see God's blueprint for males and females. Male and female are made for one another in their design. Male and female are defined by their unchangeable nature, namely, genetics and the body's ability for reproduction. Marriage was created to be the lifelong, monogamous union of a man and woman. Sexual intercourse is to occur only among a man and woman united in marriage. *Any* sexual activity outside this context is sinful. Jesus Christ affirms the pattern of this blueprint (Matt 19:4–6). We do not have the ability to change God's design for creation and thus embrace his pathway for us as best.

## God's Design for Sex Is for Our Good

Christians believe God's plan is not arbitrary or restrictive. Rather, following God's pattern is the most freeing way to live. God's plan allows us to encounter the blessings of marriage and family life. Sin distorts our desires, but exercising faith means trusting God's plan. Biblical sexuality is the only pathway that leads to true personal and cultural flourishing. Because of the gospel, sexual sinners can be reconciled to God.

## God's Design for Sex Is for His Glory

God calls us to live completely for him in glad submission. As the Bible teaches, we are not our own; we were bought with a price. The call of the Christian is to glorify God with the use of our bodies (1 Cor 6:19–20). Every sexual desire and act must be done with a view of pursuing God's honor and glory in accordance with his standards. We embrace God's pattern with joy.

# Conclusion

Few things are as controversial about Christianity in our culture than what Christians believe God's Word teaches about his design for us as males and females and the proper sexual relationship between the two in marriage. We cannot avoid clarity on this subject because culture's sexual confusion has produced profound harms that we as Christians should work to overcome. We love our neighbor by directing our neighbor in the pathway of what causes them to thrive. We embrace our created nature with the belief that, despite sin, God's design is always and forever "good."

Christians believe the Bible's teaching governing our identity and relationship as males and females offers the only pathway for true flourishing. When society rejects what Christians teach about these matters, society is not simply disagreeing with Christians, but rejecting the limits and boundaries God set for all of creation (Rom 1:18–32). We see this groaning of creation all around us when the misuse of our bodies becomes normal: Women are treated as objects, gender-confused persons misled, children aborted, men acting as sexual conquerors instead of protectors.

The call of the church in this age is to proudly declare God's standards for sexuality while recognizing the gospel is the only pathway for healing and recovery. That's because we've encountered the gospel's teaching on sexuality ourselves: Christians are not perfect in their own sexuality; we are all broken. God's grace extends to all sexual sinners (Rom 5:8; 1 Cor 6:9–11).

# 12.

# Order and the Natural Law

Where does a political community or civil society derive its purpose and shared sense of moral obligation? For however diverse and pluralist a society may be, it cannot be agnostic about the fundamental questions tied to its existence as a political community: What are we striving to achieve as a political community? Questions of basic moral truth must have consensus: How can it secure a principled basis for justice that supplies human dignity and human rights with inviolability and longevity? Morality, truth, and justice are, after all, *sine qua non* elements eminently related to public order. For apart from stable conceptions of morality and virtue, societies, and governments—to quote a biblical metaphor—are "chasing after the wind." What's currently underway in Western contexts is the extent to which social order can be achieved apart from theologically-informed foundations of each. I am not sanguine that society can construct meaningful accounts of morality, truth, and justice apart from a theistic natural law foundation.

These topics redound to one of the most important questions in ethics and public theology, namely, the "theo-political question." Questions of these varieties capture what political philosophers refer to as the Böckenförde

Dilemma: The question of whether secular liberal democracies can sustain themselves morally apart from explicit or legal attachment to religion. Framed in different ways by different voices, the question asks whether nations can persist without a high degree of religious consensus that provides the nation with moral purpose. Or, to state the matter differently: To what extent is stable political order tied to religious consensus? President John Adams's famous exhortation about how the United States' Constitution was made "only for a moral and religious people" captures the essence of the theo-political question.[1] According to Adams's argument, without morality and religion at the core of a nation's center, no governing document can withstand the excesses of human passion, what Adams referred to as "avarice, ambition, revenge, or gallantry." A nation's patrimony is secured in proportion to the degree it is religiously and morally constituted according to absolute standards of moral accountability.

According to classical conceptions of political order like we see in Adams's quote, political liberty requires a trust in a self-governing people to possess the necessary virtues that restrain human vice. Religion was valued as beneficial to public order in providing moral training and a source of virtue for the citizenry. Liberal democracies, such as our own, still require animating forces beneath it to give it substantive moral vision and social consensus. Justice, truth, and morality robbed of transcendent foundation cannot sustain a vision for human flourishing and civic justice.

What follows the theo-political question is another question relevant to Christian ethics: How can Christian faithfulness in the public arena and in the church's relationship to the state not devolve into equal and opposite errors of either: (1) a withdrawal and sectarianism that views political engagement as irrelevant, futile, or corrupting; or (2) modes of establishment that can end up instrumentalizing faith for political ends, thus deadening conversionary Christianity?

---

[1] "From John Adams to Massachusetts Militia, 11 October 1798," *Founders Online*, National Archives, https://founders.archives.gov/documents/Adams/99-02 -02-3102.

The answer to all the above questions demonstrates how relevant Christian natural law is to questions of political order. At its root, theo-political dilemmas focus on whether religion ought to factor into society's needs and how it would do so if it were agreed that it was necessary. The natural law allows for religiously grounded viewpoints to find rational expression and public relevance.[2] It also offers a foundation for society to reason together about the source and substance of morality even as citizens and legislators disagree about the identity of who that God is or whether God exists. But debates over morality stem from the reality that humans and human community are plagued by deep moral questions. We must assert out of transparent honesty that apart from a transcendent basis for public order's self-conception of itself being rooted in the natural law, societies are confronted with a nihilistic abyss. In other words, a materialist society lacks the necessary limitations from preventing moral anarchy to engulf it. One of the ironies of this book is that while natural law is a mode of moral reasoning that non-Christians can, in principle, have access to, the Christian must always assert the natural law's reliance upon divine transcendence for its ultimate intelligibility. The Christian can never, then, cloak their natural law maxims in pure reason alone but must use the means of deliberation to direct society toward a transcendent God.

In the previous two chapters, I looked at how the Christian natural law tradition evaluates areas integral to the protection of human life and the proper ordering of human life as regards its sexual *telos*. In this final chapter of applied ethics, I will examine what the Christian natural law tradition requires as the necessary elements for social cooperation that allows individuals, families, and the voluntary associations they form to flourish. Our analysis has thus had three movements to its organization: (1) from an examination of the human being with a definite nature intrinsic to itself; (2)

---

[2] Once again, I wish to clearly state that the use of the natural law should not be to the neglect of religious arguments or to disguise or cloak the religious foundation of one's argument. The issue at hand, rather, is how the natural law translates and harmonizes the intelligibility of Christian ethics for public debate.

to an investigation of human relationships and what, as beings with a reproductive nature, are uniquely suited to fulfill, namely, family life; (3) and finally, in this chapter, to considerations about how individuals that form families are to flourish alongside others in society under properly constituted authorities. I am labeling this third sequence "order" because the label captures what is necessary for individuals and families to thrive together within a broader communal setting. The focus on this chapter, however, is not simply on individuals or families, but political order more broadly.

There is a concentric pattern to my analysis, beginning with the protection and preservation of a person's life, their relationships, and, finally, their participation and cooperation within society as a whole. The approach I've taken is intentional in hoping to demonstrate the integrated totality through which the Christian natural law tradition does its analysis. While the natural law tradition does not presume to give exacting detail over every area of life, at its foundation, the Christian natural law tradition affords a powerful mode of analysis that foregrounds all the essential components of earthly life while ordering life to its ultimate, beatific good.[3] Because we believe that all moral realities have the providential and mediatorial Christ as their origin and end, we should never foreclose the ways that natural law opens individuals, families, and societies to deeper questions of ultimate reality. To go about this task, it will be essential to reflect upon the constitutive elements that go into the proper ordering of society.

## The Nature of Order

Before I discuss the particular elements that comprise a sound *public* order—meaning, what principles are necessary for social cooperation—I

---

[3] For example, natural law theory does not specify what an ideal public policy should be regarding gun ownership. At its foundation, the natural law could be deployed for an argument that one has a right to self-defense of their own life and in defense of others, but even there, the natural law does not specify what types of guns, how many guns, or what reasonable actions a political community may take to regulate the presence of guns in society.

want to briefly comment on the very *nature* of order itself. Order is a theological species. The insistence that order is required for social coordination and social cooperation stands as a bulwark against a materialist understanding of the cosmos. From the start of Scripture, God acts according to his sovereignty to bring order into existence as a reflection of the divine mind communicated through an eternal law. Were it not for the presence of God bringing order to the cosmos, there would be no moral law to speak of nor any society to properly organize.

One of the organizing principles of the natural law is the very idea of eternal law: that God is a law unto himself and from which all intelligibility emanates in its promulgation. Law in this sense is not simply referring to conformity to a standard; it is the existence of the standard itself. Albert Wolters is correct in noting that "law" in the broadest sense of the word refers to "the manifestation of God's sovereignty in creation."[4] This is not an unreasoned sovereignty where God acts according to sheer will but a sovereignty that accords with God's own reasonableness within the Godhead. Order is thus the by-product of God's providential action in creation. Once again, I stress the importance of John Webster's observation from an earlier chapter in laying a foundation for why order of any type exists at all: "[T]heological apprehension of Christ and his dominion is at once metaphysical and moral—only moral because metaphysical, and because metaphysical necessarily moral."[5] As our study into the natural law has sought to be Christotelic, we are reminded once again that the structure of created reality is upheld by the person of Jesus Christ. We thus begin our analysis from the perspective that order exists because of God—and because God exists, there is order. The task, then, is to evaluate what a society must do to conform itself with the order God has imposed on it. In practical terms, we will refer to these issues related to political ethics.

---

[4] Albert M. Wolters, *Creation Regained: Biblical Basics for a Reformational Worldview*, 2nd ed. (Grand Rapids: Eerdmans, 2005), 15.

[5] John Webster, *God Without Measure: Working Papers in Christian Theology*, 2:6 (see chap. 3, n. 16).

The reason that Christians insist upon the correct ordering of society springs from our belief that society must conform itself to the principles that align with the nature of reality itself. Life in society requires a commitment to order one's actions to the simultaneous benefit of oneself, one's neighbor, and one's nation. Thus, in this chapter I will focus only the broadest contours necessary for sound public order.

In this chapter, I will explore the facets of order necessary for social cooperation and human flourishing. They include no less than: *Recognizing order* (God's existence), *administering order* (political authority and law), the *conditions for order* (the common good), and the *realization of order* (a respect for persons and the natural family, truth-seeking, and justice).

## Recognizing Order: The Recognition of God's Authority in Public Order

Why is it, when national tragedy strikes, the first impulse of individuals—whether legislators or media—is to respond with, "Our thoughts and prayers are with X during this situation"? It is because when individuals go searching for how to explain and understand tragedy, they need an explanation that human finitude alone cannot offer. Grief and tragedy draw us into the depths of the human condition and so we naturally resort to a source for interpreting events outside the events themselves.

Or consider how "One Nation Under God" is on American currency; and why the Declaration of Independence refers to a "Creator" as the source for inalienable rights. The search for deep meaning, ultimate reality, and public order are inextricably tied. All require an acceptance of God's existence for their intelligibility. Some will, of course, deny this, insisting that public life is meant to be "secular" and that all mentions of transcendence violate the conditions for civic pluralism and social agreeableness. Try as societies' secular elites might, the human impulse to seek after the divine is hardwired into human nature. In view of this impulse that inevitably directs people to seek divine explanation for the vicissitudes and sundries of human existence, it is good that society and even government foster conditions conducive to contemplating, acting upon, and realizing the higher ends that human nature naturally directs itself to.

These reflexive actions that humanity adverts to remind us that a sound order cannot persist without the recognition of God as the ultimate source for explaining existence, truth, and morality. Granted, inhabitants within a society will disagree on the identity of this God, but they cannot persist in totally denying God's existence. Without God, public order is subject to, at best, endless relativism and subjectivism, and, in its intellectually honest permutation, nihilism. Apart from a transcendent account of the universe, there is no sure foundation for law and justice; it collapses solely into convention, consensus, and majoritarianism. The question becomes one of scale as we consider what costs there are to society as it abandons belief in God. Marginal disbelief can be socially tolerated insofar as its tenets are not mainstreamed. It is very important in broader considerations about public order to conceive of how God's existence could be understood in a broadly pluralistic culture. But belief in God is a requirement for social order. Societies will come to this with glad acceptance and accommodate such a necessity as a function of human nature, or else it will learn this lesson in regret as the pitfalls of unbelief create conditions conducive to human ferocity.

In my view, the natural law naturally lends itself to recognizing God as the ultimate force for public order. I arrive at this conclusion by what I refer to as "Civic Theism."[6] Civic theism is different than the category of "Ceremonial Deism" that has been invoked in legal opinions. Ceremonial Deism is impersonal in that it trivializes and defenestrates dogmatic religion to functionary and nominalist ends. Rather, owing to my belief that God has inscribed evidence of himself in creation, in every human's heart,

---

[6] I'm indebted to my student and friend Michael Carlino for helping me develop my thinking around Civic theism.

and every human's conscience (Psalm 19; Eccl 3:11; Rom 1:18–32; 2:14–16), the natural law assumes that even despite willful self-deception, every human being possesses an awareness of God's existence. Theologian Stephen Charnock observed centuries ago that despite professed atheism by some, "No people were so untamed that absolute, perfect atheism had gained a footing."[7] No regime can withstand the constant assault, active negation, and eventual extinction of truth from its boundaries.

This I find to be true. No person or society practices pure atheism or else individuals and societies would cease to exist. Pure atheism eviscerates moral accountability and flowers into genocidal totalitarianism or anarchical nihilism. Some form of public acknowledgment of God, then, is a basic moral minimum to restrain the government's self-understanding of itself as totalizing. Depriving public order of acknowledging God's existence also fails to explain why societies constitute themselves under government to begin with: It is the God-given, indemonstrable, and felt sense of securing one's own good that best accounts for public order that is seen as both necessary and legitimate. Government provides the justified authority to secure this good by what it determines as fitting to prudentially bring about this end.

Civil religion becomes necessary to some degree for the natural law to have effect. Civil religion is civic theism expressed in concrete form. Civil religion refers to the cultural utility and accommodation of religious doctrine, religious tradition, and religious symbols that legitimizes and services the identity and social cohesion of a given political community. Though civil religion can be abused, the general category of a nation anchoring itself to a theistic tradition is not extraneous to sound public order. It requires it. United States' President Calvin Coolidge captured the necessity of civic theism for sound political order:

> Our government rests upon religion. It is from that source that we derive our reverence for truth and justice, for equality and liberty,

---

[7] Charnock, *The Existence and Attributes of God*, 1:50 (see chap. 4, n. 23).

and for the rights of mankind. Unless the people believe in these principles they cannot believe in our government. There are only two main theories of government in the world. One rests on righteousness, the other rests on force. One appeals to reason, the other appeals to the sword. One is exemplified in a republic, the other is represented by a despotism.[8]

Coolidge's statement captures how a sentiment of theism is essential without going to the lengths of full church-state establishment. Civic theism and civil religion speak to a mood and ethos of the commonweal and as a leavening effect to allow religion's influence over public morality to proliferate.

This raises an important question of whether there is biblical warrant for civic theism. I hold the position that a doctrine of civic theism builds from John Calvin's *duplex cognito Dei* and *sensus divinitatis* doctrines to argue that human beings have an innate, non-salvific awareness of God's existence. Humans are naturally oriented to the divine and a natural knowledge of God the Creator is a legitimate knowledge of God as Creator, but not knowledge of God as redeemer. One will recall from a previous chapter that for individuals to be held culpable for their guilt against God, they must actually *know* the God they are disobeying. This fact reinforces the principle that there exists a natural-though-wounded knowledge of God that is common to human nature. A natural revelation metaphysic and epistemology differs from that of a special revelation metaphysic and epistemology by virtue of conversion. Civic theism, in contrast to the redemptive covenant offered through Christ, affirms knowledge of God the Creator. It provides a platform by which creation order persists and which allows for individuals to make sense of morality, even if they cannot perfectly explain why that is so. Civic theism is supported by the Noahic covenant's preservative function to uphold the most basic standards

---

[8] Calvin Coolidge, "Religion and the Republic," Washington, DC, October 15, 1924, https://coolidgefoundation.org/resources/religion-and-the-republic/.

necessary for creation order's continuity. Maintaining the providential rule of Christ as the upholder of the cosmos from the mediatorial rule of Christ as the Savior of the church are paramount to maintain the intelligibility of this approach.

Civic theism *doctrinally* looks to explain and commend the public recognition of God even as Christians press for greater persuasive clarity and explanation into God as triune. Since the Noahic covenant encompasses all of creation, it implies that even government has a duty to recognize God as Creator in order to sufficiently ground morality. Thus, the United States' "In God We Trust" language is a prime example of civic theism in action. The language suggests that America, as a nation, understands itself as accountable to a God, but it does not go so far as to put America in covenant with God the redeemer (a principle left for ecclesial authorities to determine). Regimes will establish their own prudential ways for determining how to acknowledge God within the apparatus of government and the broader public order but acknowledge him they must.

## The Government's Accountability to God

A correct church-state relationship will have the relationship between the order of creation and redemption properly calibrated and foregrounded. The state is a creation order institution tasked with upholding justice. Nowhere in Scripture is the state assigned a directly redemptive role, even if it remains accountable to God. Scripture witnesses to the existence of government and its duty to obey God but not its formalization as a vehicle through which the message of redemption is transmitted. But, when a state plays within the narrow confines of the jurisdiction it is equipped for, it aids in allowing the transmission of the gospel by not impeding the church's mission. The church is a redemption order institution tasked with proclaiming the gospel that can necessarily create craters of impact within the political order.

These spheres are occupied by people with overlapping creational and redemptive identities. Thus, while church and state should be kept institutionally distinct, religion will rightly infuse the body politic, including the consciences of those who occupy governmental office.

None of this implies that being religious has no bearing on the life of the magistrate; it means only that the Christian magistrate, as they rule, is not ruling *exclusively* on the basis of the ultimate order of redemption that would over-realize what is possible within the penultimate order of creation.

To argue for disestablishment is not to argue for public atheism. There is no logical entailment that says disestablishment cordons off religion from influencing the moral judgments of those tasked to rule.

There is no problem for a magistrate to appeal to their biblically-shaped conscience in arguing for a particular policy. The magistrate, for example, should feel free to believe that marriage represents the Christ-Church union but also relates why the biblical definition of marriage translates to a natural law principle and public policy commensurate with creation order. Additionally, legislators may make religious arguments when arguing for a particular public policy, but should not make religious arguments alone. As Matthew Franck writes,

> There is no compelling reason in principle for religious citizens to refrain from employing religious discourse in the public square. They must, of course, reason together with their fellow citizens in order to persuade others of their policy views. But if their major premises, so to speak, are theological, there is no harm done, so long as their policy conclusions can be reasonably embraced by others who have different commitments.[9]

Governments and charter documents like constitutions are accountable to a natural revelation metaphysic, not a special revelation metaphysic.

---

[9] Matthew J. Franck, "The Unreasonableness of Secular Public Reason," *Public Discourse*, August 28, 2015, http://www.thepublicdiscourse.com/2015/08/14619/.

Proponents of establishmentarian arguments fail to distinguish between whether government is accountable to God's creational law and God's redemptive law in the same way to the same effect. It assumes that redemptive law (life in the Spirit) is symmetrical in the type of obligation the state has to creational moral law (natural law). In other words, the state is indeed accountable to God's law, but God's law is expressed in different forms that must be institutionally respected in the forms consistent with what are able to be carried out, respectively. Which is why the state is never assigned a directly redemptive role in Scripture, even if it is tasked to execute Noahic justice.

Legislators have metaphysical commitments and so can government in a way unique to what government is designed to do—which is preservative justice, not redemptive glorification. Because of it being a mixed body, government *qua* government will be agnostic about absolute metaphysical foundations, but cannot be on moral ends. A government will have legislators who differ about God, but they cannot be indifferent about basic creation order requirements: life, the identity of male-female, natural marriage, justice. That government *qua* government does not legislate according to one specific religion does not elide the reality that those making judgments within government are relying upon ultimate metaphysical foundations within the operations of their internal faculties. Government cannot violate the natural law, which presumes a natural revelation metaphysic, but without the particular manifestations of that metaphysic being comprehensively codified.

## Administering Order: Political Authority and Political Judgment

Order requires an authority suitable to the task of overseeing its fulfillment. An authority of this nature must be appropriately recognized as possessing the type of authority to organize public order to desirable ends. Political authority resolves the question of how individuals, families, and institutions can coordinate their activity under a centralized authority in reasonable ways respective to their proper ends. President Abraham Lincoln aptly

*Roads, bridges, armies, etc.*

observed to similar effect, "The legitimate object of government is to do for a community of people whatever they need to have done, but cannot do at all, or cannot so well do, for themselves—in their separate, and individual capacities. In all that the people can individually do as well for themselves, government ought not to interfere."[10] Government is centrally fixated on the coordination of disparate persons toward meaningful action in society. Individuals and even families are unable to competently administer a society without a centralizing authority to establish norms of obedience and punishment. Political authority thus arises out of a need for order to disseminate itself in reasonable and just ways for the benefit of all.

Society has a duty to organize itself according to scriptural realities that optimize human flourishing—the establishing of public justice and public morality. Failing to uphold the distinctiveness of those realities under the canopy of an attenuated pluralism is not a principle that Scripture recognizes as compatible with flourishing. Public authority must execute judgment in order to carry out its commission of establishing the rightly-ordered society. Without a trust in the reliability of public authority to provide reasonable grounds for securely entering into public life for the sake of commerce and mutual exchange, no person or family can be expected to thrive.

Political authority is justified to the extent that its judgments are conducive to, and not contrary of, moral goods. Just political order, then, requires a self-limiting political authority with rightly recognized power to oversee the directiveness of society to its proper end through the administration of civil law. By self-limiting, I mean merely the idea that political authority best legitimizes its authority when it respects and recognizes the moral goods that are pre-political. Before speaking about government's responsibility to sound political order, it is important to consider the nature of power itself. Power, correctly understood, is the channeling of one's agency

---

[10] Paul McClelland Angle and Earl Schenck Miers, *The Living Lincoln: The Man and His Times, in His Own Words* (New York: Barnes & Noble, 1992), 155. The quote is excerpted from remarks written by Abraham Lincoln in 1854.

to an end that is just and good. Political power, then, is the use of political power for the aggregative benefit of those under its authority. Power in itself is neither problematic nor corrupting. Power is simply intrinsic to the nature of government in order for government to possess the capacity to do what it is designed to do—to direct society to its true end, which is flourishing and social harmony. Baptist ethicist Foy Valentine's reflections on the nature of power and government are doubtlessly true:

> There could be no politics at all without power. To speak disparagingly, therefore, of "power politics" is to reveal a serious lack of understanding of political realities. Political power is the ability to put a policy into effect and to fit that policy into a concrete program. The government of a nation maintains the preponderance of political power. It cannot tolerate any group within the state with more power than that of itself. The moment such a group emerges with more power than the government, it immediately becomes the government. As all ice is cold ice, so all politics is power politics. Basically, politics has power as its chief ingredient, compromise as its primary method of getting things done, and the public good as its main purpose.[11]

The *telos* of the justly ordered society is the flourishing of individuals, families, and institutions each with their own end by attaining the common good. Think of this as the First Principle of Political Authorization: a government is legitimately constituted to the degree that it pursues the good of society and avoids the privation of society. The logic of government's authority and legitimacy is tied to its execution of just laws stemming from sound moral principles.

In this regard, it is understood that the levers of political authority are controlled by individuals whose faculty of reason can properly discern right from wrong and order society accordingly. A government that knowingly

---

[11] Foy Valentine, *Citizenship for Christians* (Nashville: Broadman, 1965), 9.

inflicts evil upon its citizenry is illegitimately constituted and subject to regime change. Similarly, a wicked magistrate that inflicts evil on its citizens can be duly toppled even while those engaging in seditious or rebellious acts seek to restore to the office of magistrate one who can rule in justice. Hence, we must understand the task of politics as the ordering of life together for the purpose of flourishing, felicity, and civil tranquility. But flourishing, especially in a world bombarded by the reality of human self-interest and evil, requires an authority to arbitrate disputes, hold contracts accountable to their terms, and protect society from evildoers. Trust in the reliability of society's administration is what restrains the ferocity of human nature.

Without a duly recognized authority that can administer society to just ends, society cannot persist. As Robert P. George rightfully notes, "Where there is no reliable system of the administration of justice—no confidence that the courts will hold people to their obligations under the law—business will not flourish, and everyone in the society will suffer."[12] While the natural law tradition does not specify the best *form* of government, what animates its reflections is the insistence that government is necessary to oversee society's direction with reliability and trustworthiness.[13]

## The Importance of Civil Law

This raises another issue: law. Why is civil law so important to political authority? Political authority uses the power of law for the just exercise of

---

[12] Robert P. George, "Five Pillars of a Decent and Dynamic Society," in *The Thriving Society: On the Social Conditions of Human Flourishing*, ed. James Stoner and Harold James (Princeton, NJ: Witherspoon Institute, 2015), 3.

[13] As natural law philosophers Ryan T. Anderson and Robert P. George write, "And so, from the natural-law perspective, there is no single uniquely correct political arrangement—no 'ideal regime.' There is simply no one best legal system of regulating speech or property. These can take a variety of morally appropriate forms given the particularities of culture, of a people's circumstances, history, traditions, needs, and challenges." Robert P. George and Ryan T. Anderson, "The Baby and the Bathwater," *National Affairs*, no. 53 (Fall 2019): 177.

power. Civil law is natural law in statutory operation. Law is the formalized application of political judgment for advancing justice and redressing injustice. We come back to Thomas Aquinas's famous definition that law is an "ordinance of reason for the common good, made by him who has care of the community, and promulgated."[14] Aquinas's definition of law brings our discussion into greater focus, since we see in his definition the idea that all law follows a principle of practical rationality and administered by a competent and recognized authority who seeks the proper end of society: its common good. All political authority is legitimate to the extent that its legal determinations issue from the natural law, thus commanding our obedience. A sound law will rest upon reasonable claims to regulate behavior in the furtherance of justice.

As Christians consider what role government has in promoting public order, we must turn to Scripture to see what God's design for the state entails. A Christian account of political authority parallels the natural law tradition's view since it understands the state as a creational ordinance that reflects the Creator's general will for justice and society's welfare (Rom 13:1–7; 1 Pet 2:13–14). Scripture does not speak in exacting detail about government's calling. I take this to mean that government's authority is modest in comparison to regimes that are more materialist in origin and prone to greater accounts of its own authority and competence.

Looking at the above verses, it is reasonable to conclude that political authority is primarily preservative in nature in that it seeks to restrain the effects of wrongdoing in society. Government, in Scripture, is an authority tasked with upholding (maintaining its continuous rule) and overseeing (executing its rule) the conditions for justice (i.e., deterring and ameliorating injustice). To what degree government can commend the good is a prudential determination that Christian political thought has wrestled with for millennia, but needless to say, it is called to "praise those who do good," meaning that its legitimate calling entails some degree of moral

---

[14] *ST* I-II.90.4.

vision. Government cannot be morally agnostic. It must draw moral boundaries where moral infractions and threats to sound order necessitate them. Of course, much of these considerations will be left to prudential determinations about how to safeguard liberty while securing the public moral good. Surely it must be assumed that the authority of the state is to recognize, preserve, and defend institutions of creation order necessary to society's own continuity. No one of seriousness argues for total moral agnosticism on the part of the state. How the state adjudicates moral disputes will always be subject to context-specific and fact-specific realities. The limited calling of government in Scripture speaks to the potential harms that come when government seeks to implement overly burdensome regulations in society.

## *The Christian as a Political Leader*

Taking up positions of power to oversee this possibility is legitimate for the life of the Christian. Otherwise, desiring just enactments while forfeiting or rejecting the means to achieve them is incoherent. One cannot long for social reclamation while rejecting one of the most important vehicles—political authority—*for* reclamation. Christians should understand political power as an entirely legitimate domain for Christian involvement if pursued for rightful ends and with rightful motives and should unapologetically defend the use of political power in the direction of righteousness and order. The furtherance of justice is inseparable from a positive vision for statecraft; and statecraft entails the responsible stewarding of power in the direction of truth and the common good and the disempowering of falsehood. As Carl F. H. Henry wrote,

> Although the New Testament places a temporary "hold" on the forced messianic overthrow of world-powers during the Church age, it places no "hold" whatever on the divine demand for justice in the public order. Christ's followers are to exemplify the standards of God's kingdom, and they are to be "light" and "salt" in a dark

and rotting society where God intends civil government to promote justice and restrain disorder.[15]

Political power wielded by Christians for just ends is never the instal-
lation or an imposition of an alien morality upon the world. Christians do
not conceive of "Christian morality" as something distinct from general
morality. All morality emanates from the eternal law of God, meaning the
bifurcation of morality into "Christian" and "secular" erects a false division
giving a false presumption to secularism.

If Christian morality is the very nature of order itself and is ordered to
what is true, good, and beautiful (and it is), then Christians should be insis-
tent that true morality be reflected in law. Christians do this not out of self-
interest or to the neglect of others, but because Christians believe that human
flourishing is inseparable from alignment with what is ontologically true.
This, understandably, is no small source for today's so-called "culture wars."
The intractable nature of moral conflicts, however, means that some moral
vision will attain dominance. We should hope and indeed work toward the
end of seeing that it is a morality ordered toward truth. Any moral system
that tears apart the fabric of human flourishing, human society, and human
nature ought to be disempowered. This is the case not because Christians
want power as an end in itself, but because organizing society against the
grain of the universe will lead to misery (Rom 1:18–32). Societies cannot
organize themselves in opposition to God's design for culture and hope to
thrive. Institutions of creation order necessary for sound political community and human flourishing cannot be negotiated away under the canopy of
pluralism. Law will either conform to the truth or work to suppress it.

From the perspective of a Christotelic understanding of authority and
judgment, we understand that Christ possesses all authority under heaven
and earth (Matthew 28; Psalm 2). All earthly authority is derived from and

---

[15] Carl F. H. Henry, "Jesus and Political Justice," *Christianity Today*, December
6, 1974, 35.

finds it legitimacy in the authority of Jesus Christ, whether recognized by the magistrate or not. Such a recognition does not imply any sort of formal church-state establishment inasmuch as it calls for magistrates to have the interior recognition that their judgments will be held accountable for the degree of justice or injustice they mete out on society. Christians must insist that all earthly political judgments are shadows of a coming heavenly judgment. They should remind public officials of their obligation to justice, the common good, and ultimately to Jesus Christ. They work to order the affairs of their political society so as to differentiate the temporal from the eternal even as they declare the criteria by which temporal affairs are founded, ordered, and eventually judged.

## The Conditions for Order: The Common Good

Though the concept has been invoked countless times already, it is important to precisely define what the common good is, its origins in the natural law, and its relevance to a Christian view of public order.

As for a natural law definition, the common good is a principle of social organization that refers to a set of conditions and a state of affairs where the individuals and institutions of society are able to fulfill their respective callings or "ends." At its most basic, the common good insists that society should be organized to allow individuals, families, and institutions to flourish. The common good allows individuals, families, and institutions to experience what befits their nature, natural aptitudes, and vocation-specific callings. Persons are equally protected by law; families are allowed the ability to be families; teaching institutions are allowed to go about the task of teaching; and businesses are free to be able to pursue entrepreneurship. The whole notion of society attaining an end due to itself speaks to the teleological foundations at the heart of the common good. The common good understands that civil order is required for human flourishing. Government has power at its disposal to competently oversee the administration of the common good. As the very idea of "common" suggests, every person and every institution within society has an equal stake in seeing the common good realized—everyone benefits equally: my ability to reach my proper end should pose no degradation or subtraction to someone else's ability to reach their due end.

The natural law component of the common good insists that it is the innate knowledge of right and wrong and the directiveness of persons toward moral goods that allows for the capacities of mutuality and cooperation that the common good requires. The common good is the conditions where public justice and public order promote human flourishing. Ideally, it is the pursuit of the common good that creates just political societies where oppression and injustice are not intended realities. Where society robs or thwarts the justice denied to people, the common good is undermined. The common good does not tell us every policy or procedure for its realization. Fundamentally, it is itself a moral vision that a society has for what defines its own flourishing. For example, what program of waste collection is the best for society that the common good does not supply? It tells us only that waste collection is necessary for the sake of the community's public health and that garbage strewn about streets is a blight to a community's aesthetic appreciation.

### Common Good as a Communal Reality

The common good is a communal reality that recognizes that humans are not solitary units left to fend only for their own interest, nor can society be directed toward its proper end without the proper authorities being present to secure them. The belief that goods can be held in common means the experience of those individuals and institutions flourishing each to their natural end does not deprive any other person or institution of their ability to thrive, either. They are goods, so to speak, able to be held in "common" simultaneously by different parties without deprivation.

The common good is thus the delicate balancing of political authority reaching a proper equilibrium between individual and social flourishing. Political authority helps secure these realities. As John Finnis observes,

"There are human goods that can be secured only through the institutions of human law, and requirements of practical reasonableness that only those institutions can satisfy."[16] What Finnis's phrase captures is that legal authority is necessary to bring about the ends that people of sound mind identify as beneficial to their and society's flourishing. We thus need political authority to direct us toward the fulfillment of public order. Far from the common good letting the state engorge itself with increasing power to administer more capacious understandings of the common good, the common good requires a pre-political commitment to the human good, which the state is not sovereign in determining, only recognizing. For example, when considering the sanctity of unborn human life and the natural family, the common good requires that government simply acknowledges these pre-political realities that allow for the prudential tailoring of policy to secure and protect their fulfillment.

The common good is the fulfillment of being not only for individuals and families but the totality of society itself. Its connection to the natural law stems from the generic "oughtness" to which society is believed to need to conform itself to for society to thrive.[17] It further assumes the existence of "goods" that promote human flourishing. Kentucky, where I live, is actually called a "commonwealth" rather than a state. "Commonwealth" is a term that vividly captures the common good—that government should oversee the administration of a society where the respective elements of society's interests are realized: Where laws are obeyed and roads are paved (for example) and society can engage in meaningful cooperation. The common good reminds us that "apart from political communities—and its local form of authority, law—we cannot reasonably attain our end."[18] The common good

---

[16] Finnis, *Natural Law and Natural Rights*, 3 (see chap. 3, n. 6).

[17] Brian Matz, *Introducing Protestant Social Ethics* (Grand Rapids: Baker Academic, 2017), 171.

[18] Ryan T. Anderson, "The Promise and Peril of the Political Common Good," *The New Criterion*, January 2022, 29.

should inform our evaluations about society and laws by considering what conditions are most conducive to human flourishing.

Is there a biblical warrant for the common good? I believe so.[19] The most obvious place to locate an embryonic understanding of the common good is in the cultural mandate of Genesis. Genesis paints a picture of a teleological order where the individuals and families are assigned the task of stewarding the resources of earth toward the end of human flourishing that is creational in scope. Genesis does not envision a social order where individuals or families are denied what is owed to them for their flourishing—the bare elements of creation order: family, law, and cultivating one's habitat for productive living. The shared beneficence common to humanity can only be achieved by family formation and a respect for coordination among the institutions of creation order. Jeremiah 29:4–7 also furnishes an understanding of the common good by YHWH's call for exilic Israel to engage in communal participation for the benefit of all.

> "Thus says the LORD of hosts, the God of Israel, to all the exiles whom I have sent into exile from Jerusalem to Babylon: Build houses and live in them; plant gardens and eat their produce. Take wives and have sons and daughters; take wives for your sons, and give your daughters in marriage, that they may bear sons and daughters; multiply there, and do not decrease. But seek the welfare of the city where I have sent you into exile, and pray to the LORD on its behalf, for in its welfare you will find your welfare."

At least two observations are worth making. First, YHWH's concern is for the exiles to participate within the social order where they presently are. In other words, their care of society was not based on a perfected

---

[19] For more on the common good and its relationship to natural law, see Andrew T. Walker and Casey Hough, "Toward a Baptist Natural Law Conception of the Common Good," *Southwestern Journal of Theology* 63, no. 1 (Fall 2020): 153–74.

eschatological vision, but in a shared creational platform. Second, there is also a principle of reciprocity that shows how regard for one's context is meant to be mutually beneficial for all. These verses can thus be seen as recapitulating the cultural mandate established in Genesis 1–2. Romans 13:1–7 indicates that governments "are God's servants for your good." Government possesses a unique authority in exercising the power to command obedience, enabling the common good. That Romans 13 is spoken of a non-Christian government seems to confirm that the common good, though finding its origin in God, is not exclusive only to "Christian" governments. First Timothy 2:1–7, 1 Thess 4:10–12, and 1 Pet 2:13–17 suggest that one of the primary goals for Christians in society is to live peaceably alongside their neighbors with due reverence and obedience for public authority.

Likewise, the institution of government seems intended to oversee the common good. Though the above section spoke of justice and retribution as necessary conditions for just government, we should also see that the proper execution of political judgment, whether negative in the form of retribution or positively in the form of commending that which is good, is done with a view toward directing society toward its proper end.

Prudential determinations are always at the heart of discerning what can be complex discussions around how best to order society toward the common good. The natural law does not give every last explanation for how to resolve every tension in a political community; it rather insists upon basic moral fundaments required for society's well-being. For example, anything that transgresses the natural law does not have a natural right to be legal. But permitting certain immoralities to occur in society may be prudentially allowable in order to not create a stifling moral authoritarianism. What degree of immorality a political community can absorb without upending it is the sum and substance of prudential statecraft. Resolving those disputes is beyond the scope of this chapter. It is important to lay bare the claim that a justly constituted government will see the fulfillment of the common good as its chief aim.

# Realizing Order: A Respect for Persons, Family, Truth-Seeking, and Justice

We now turn to what public order as such must value as moral goods in themselves, if public orders are to thrive, as well as the norms that help actualize them. Additional categories could hypothetically be conceived, but since space prevents an exhaustive catalogue of moral goods from being offered here, let us mention what are at least bare minimum necessities: (1) a respect for the dignity of the human person to pursue a life of virtue and purpose, including the ability to use one's agency to provide for their well-being; (2) the recognition, respect, and preservation of the natural family as the pre-political origins of public order that give rise to just order; (3) an allowance for truth-seeking and that we will concisely refer to as the liberty of self-constitution through speech, religion, and education; (4) the promotion of these realities through a regime of legal protections (i.e., "rights"); and (5) a communal (though not necessarily governmental) recognition and appreciation for God's providential order.

Though elements of the following items have been discussed in the previous two chapters, it is important to set the value of the individual, natural family, and truth-seeking within the context of political communities and as ordering principles necessary for the common good.

## A Respect for Persons

Sound public order will recognize the common dignity shared by all persons and take no action to willfully do violence to citizens of a political community. Sound order will also respect the ability for persons to experience virtue and happiness. A respect for human beings is a baseline requirement for the just society. A failure to extend recognition of the right to life that persons possess by virtue of their existence is the seedbed for totalitarianism. Indeed, a regime that tolerates or promotes the taking of innocent life—whether unborn or born—is sowing a dangerous discord that strikes at the very notion of order itself. The protection and securing of the human person's flourishing—both individually and in the aggregate—is why governments exist.

Refraining from killing citizens, however, as a baseline expectation, is not all that a regime must do. It must not treat citizens as slaves whose servitude is secured or permitted by the state. Both a human being's existence and agency must be respected as constitutive elements comprising human personality. Respecting the human person means just that—acknowledging and respecting the inherent pre-political realities inhering within persons and granting to them reasonable protections to secure their protection and livelihood, which necessarily includes respecting vocational agency. The just political order will foster conditions where the human person will have their pre-political and political attachments (whether to tradition, property, or religion) secured as reflective of the goods that lead to fulfillment and virtue.

Likewise, citizens must recognize the dignity of their fellow citizens. Such recognition does not imply moral approval of any person's life choices or refraining from moral judgment about a person's choice, but only the recognition of an equal place in society owing to the fact of their existence.

## Respect for the Natural Family

The rightly ordered political community will recognize the primacy of the natural family as the original foundation for fostering civic virtue. Rather than narrowly focusing on protecting the sanctity of the individual to the exclusion of the context in which the individual was begotten, the natural law views the natural family as the irreplaceable and uniquely suited social unit from which individuals learn restraint and virtue under the naturally arising authority of father and mother.

Seen from this vantage point, the primacy and supremacy of the natural family does not arise due to any willingness to extend harm or injury to other nonmarital relationships. Rather, the just order recognizes how marriage organically arises as an institution to resolve the question of a child's welfare stemming from the reality of procreative potential. Sound social order thus requires the natural family as it affords society the most efficient and least cumbersome way of resolving the possibility of procreation with the reality of procreation. A society that devalues the natural family, whether statutorily or culturally, is a society that does not possess the internal rectitude to order itself into perpetuity.

## *Respect for Truth-Seeking*

As we have argued thus far: (i) individuals should be respected by the sheer fact of their existence; (ii) their moral agency, as far as the use of their skills to secure their livelihood should be respected; and (iii) in the pursuit of truth-seeking ends in what they grasp—even erringly—as true. Human beings should thus have the integrity of their authentic convictions respected within the bounds of rightly ordered civil law. An allowance of this nature is not meant to sanction relativism; it is to recognize that in large and diverse societies, individuals will disagree on many things pertaining to what is true. In acknowledging the wide array of opinions on deeply entrenched matters in society, it is wise for government to have a capacious account for human error and, in turn, deliberative systems of government and due process in place to make determinations on what expressions of truth-seeking are detrimental or subversive to sound order. The orientation of individuals to seek after ends that meaningfully define them, however, requires that societies respect the ability or *faculty* for truth-seeking. Putting all three of these components together, we can argue that individuals should have the totality of their self-constitution respected by society. Truth-seeking necessarily implies the freedom to search after truth, educate oneself in what they believe is true, and to live authentically in response to their grasp of what is true.

Upon granting a respect for truth-seeking, we immediately run the risk of accusations that the natural law endorses moral relativism under the guise of truth-seeking. Honesty requires clarifying that this is not so. A respect for truth-seeking understands that individuals possessed with minds, wills, and affections will naturally disagree about a whole host of important moral debates. A respect for self-constitution is not a respect for moral indifference. What a respect for self-constitution *is* is a recognition of the fact of pluralism and the harm done to society when an entrenched viewpoint seeks to eliminate difference. By providing a pathway for truth-seeking to occur, a sound order allows for degrees of error to persist in full knowledge that the cure for eliminating error could potentially be worse than the disease of error itself. Hence, the natural law tradition has never called for the exhaustive elimination of erring persons.

The natural law tradition rightfully argues that prudential determinations must be made about the degree of liberty a nation can extend to various expressions of deep-seated conviction. A respect for truth-seeking does not entail that threats to the common good can go unchecked under the banner of truth-seeking. No, legislatures are tasked to make determinations on the scope of legal protections afforded to the truth-seeking enterprise. Legislators and governments must make measured delineations between conduct that threatens the common good in egregious ways versus conduct or convictions that that could be in error but are benign and not necessarily subject to criminal prosecution. Public order thus requires not only a commitment to liberty, but a correct understanding of liberty by those tasked with securing it. A broad liberty regime will be faced with scenarios where even its presumption toward liberty reaches its outer limits. Such action is justified because liberty is not a basic moral good but is an instrumental good that helps procure access to basic moral goods. Liberty is not the license to do whatever one wishes and expect that there will not be accountability. Rather, rightly secured, liberty is essential for sound order for individuals and families to experience the fullness of being that accords with their nature.

Melissa Moschella writes to similar effect, arguing that "the natural law account recognizes that liberty is an essential instrumental good that governments must respect precisely because the political common good—which includes the goods of the individuals and smaller communities that make up the political community—cannot be achieved without it."[20]

## Legal Securing of Goods: Rights and Justice

Human beings have a duty to God and themselves to experience the full range of activities and goods that comprise the fullness of their being. If God has ordered human nature to such ends, such that there are aspects of human well-being that need secured in order for persons to fulfill—by way of obligation to themselves and their Creator—the fullness of their being, protections become necessary for society to ensure such outcomes. Legal codification becomes a necessary mechanism to safeguard such realities for the sake of public order. Law, then, as a principle, should always act to secure what is true of human nature and its thriving. If we have a natural duty to ourselves and our family, law should recognize our duty to ensure our own and our family's well-being. Of course, prolonged debate exists about the extent to which "positive" rights versus "negative" rights are in view. In my view, a regime of negative rights is preferable since it does not require distributing scarce goods, instead only setting apt conditions for human flourishing.

At the level of political authority and the common good, respecting individuals and the natural family requires the issuing of legal protections around the sanctity of the individual and familial institutions they form. Thus, human rights are legal protections that protect human flourishing. A belief in human rights relies on the assumption that there are moral goods intrinsic to human fulfillment that humans are duty-bound to procure as a measure of their own creatureliness. Political "rights" exist to recognize and protect the duties that comprise human flourishing. They result from the

---

[20] Melissa Moschella, "Natural Law, the Common Good, and Limited Government: Friends, Not Foes," Public Discourse, August 10, 2022, https://www .thepublicdiscourse.com/2022/08/83850/.

reality of natural truths about human nature and that measures should be taken to protect access to them.

A legal reality that aims to secure the moral goods necessary to human flourishing is thus a "right" since humans are owed by right of their sheer existence the ability to exercise their agency consistent with their being. Human rights as a civil matter are simply codified natural rights. A more precise definition of a "right" is a legal enactment that recognizes the need to secure and facilitate access to human goods, for example, the right to secure and protect one's life. This means, *prima facie*, that rights exist for something beyond endless speculation—but chiefly for protecting access to the fulfilling of moral goods. Rights lay a claim to duty on both the claimant and their fellow citizen. The claimant has a duty to fulfill the goods necessary to their human excellence while their fellow citizen has a duty to not obstruct their neighbor's duty to obtain moral excellence. Law then codifies this moral transaction in the form of rights. As Robert P. George states, "Human rights exist (or obtain) if it is the case that there are principles of practical reason directing us to act or abstain from acting in certain ways out of respect for the well-being and the dignity of persons whose legitimate interests may be affected by what we do."[21]

Rights protect the moral faculties and the duties they come to grasp in response to a God-given conscience. Rights are ultimately directed toward the protection and fulfillment of moral goods commensurate with reasoned reflection about human nature and human nature's fulfillment. Rights merely make explicit the protections needed a human being to fulfill human excellence. They are a buttress against authorities that style themselves as self-sovereign or totalitarian. As Steve Berquist puts it on the relationship between natural law, rights, and social order, "we have a natural right to the social conditions that enable us to achieve the

---

[21] Robert P. George, "Natural Law, God and Human Dignity," in *The Cambridge Companion to Natural Law Jurisprudence*, ed. George Duke and Robert P. George (Cambridge: Cambridge University Press, 2017), 60–61.

life of virtue."[22] Human rights are legal protections that recognize there are moral duties necessary for human goods to be realized. As Jacques Maritain writes,

> There are things which are owed to man because of the very fact that he is man. The notion of right and the notion of moral obligation are correlative. They are both founded on the freedom proper to spiritual agents. If man is morally bound to the things which are necessary to the fulfillment of his destiny, obviously, then, he has the right to fulfill his destiny; and if he has the right to fulfill his destiny, he has the right to the things necessary for this purpose. The notion of right is even more profound than that of moral obligation, for God has sovereign right over creatures and he has no moral obligation toward them (although he owes it to himself to give them that which is required by their nature). The true philosophy of the rights of the human person is therefore based upon the idea of natural law. The same natural law which lays down our most fundamental duties, and by virtue of which every law is binding, is the very law which assigns to us our fundamental rights.[23]

Rights are at once a sword used to proactively wield one's agency but also a shield to find protection from autocratic regimes. Robert Kraynak writes that "rights" are "claims for protections and immunities or for entitlements that put authority on the defensive."[24] Hence, humans have a "right" to worship since it is alignment with divine order that is architectonic and duty-shaping in a person's whole outlook. Or humans have a right to free speech under the belief that humans have an obligation to search after the truth and order their lives in response to it.

---

[22] Berquist, *From Human Dignity to Natural Law: An Introduction*, 188 (see chap. 10. n. 1).

[23] Jacques Maritain, *Christianity and Democracy, and The Rights of Man and Natural Law* (San Francisco: Ignatius, 2011), 107.

[24] Robert P. Kraynak, *Christian Faith and Modern Democracy: God and Politics in the Fallen World* (Notre Dame, IN: University of Notre Dame Press, 2016), 22.

As we consider how Christianity informs our understanding of respecting persons, family, truth-seeking, and the formulation of legal protections, we do so from the beginning point of acknowledging that the more intricate details for public order are oftentimes deducements that stem from our theological anthropology. The Christian tradition is considered by many the intellectual storehouse for human rights. Apart from a grounding in certain anthropological truths that result from Christian anthropology, human rights are merely an Archimedean invention with no sure foundation. That's why a rights regime untethered from a broadly theistic tradition will always run the risk of rights being endlessly re-evaluated, denied by evil regimes, or expanded under the canopy of human passion that do violence to other moral goods (i.e., "rights" to sexuality autonomy, reproductive freedom, "rights" to same-sex marriage).

The assertion of human rights does not, in itself, mean that all that falls under "rights" are, in fact, rights or even moral. A rights regime requires a moral vision underneath it for it to have meaningful structure and purpose to it. The ever-expanding and pliable use of "rights" to justify moral evil in our day is all the proof necessary to show how "rights" left unattached to a deeper moral vision becomes, rather than a catalyst for true human good, a catalyst for moral chaos and even evil. A duty-bound vision for rights that assumes the existence of moral goods humans have a right to experience by virtue of their existence are "confined to the purposes for the sake of which they had been endowed by their Creator."[25] As Harry Jaffa notes about the Declaration of Independence, it was this vision that animated its drafter Thomas Jefferson. As Jaffa notes, "When the signers of the Declaration appealed to the 'supreme judge of the world' for the 'rectitude of [their] intentions' they had acknowledged the divine government of the world as the framework within which their rights might be exercised."[26]

---

[25] Harry V. Jaffa, "Thomas Aquinas Meets Thomas Jefferson," *Interpretation: A Journal of Political Philosophy* 33, no. 2 (Spring 2006): 181.

[26] Jaffa, 181.

It is Christianity's value on the human person from whence a regime of "rights" is most securely anchored. Without that sure foundation provided by a divine guarantor, the value, responsibilities, and duties that attend to individuals are mere contrivances; they need to be secured to a divine ontology not subject to the vicissitudes of human passions. In other words, Christianity provides the social order with what someone like the non-Christian political theorist Vàclav Havel longed for but could not find—a "Cosmic Anchoring," the notion of a foundation that orders existence and which political orders hostile to God cannot supply on their own. Christian anthropology and its emphasis on the human person bearing God's image forever changed the equation for the significance of the individual—the human became definitively suffused with moral meaning. With Christianity, as historian Larry Siedentop writes, "Individual agency acquires roots in divine agency."[27]

## A Communal Respect for God and Sacred Order

If there is a God, then there is a divine incumbency upon persons and the institutions of society to acknowledge God's existence and to obey God's moral commands. Having an awareness of where one originates and what destiny awaits is vital to possessing deep meaning. A failure, in other words, to honor the efficient and first cause of a person and society's end will impale the recognition of the formal and final cause of one's existence. No attainment of social happiness is possible apart from the mass of society recognizing the due end of all persons toward their flourishing as both a moral and spiritual creature.

Though obviously desirable, this need not require the total conversion of society for its realization, only the due recognition of God the Creator's existence. Apart from a recognition of transcendent realities that secures objective moral norms, no society can perpetuate itself. The most brutal of societies are those that define a social imaginary according to the

---

[27] Larry Siedentop, *Inventing the Individual: The Origins of Western Liberalism* (Cambridge, MA: Belknap, 2014), 65.

predilections of power and conquest for their own sake. Individual and social happiness is thus found in knowing God and living truly in response to the knowledge of God's law and his design for the universe.

While this last category may be difficult to pin down, what it looks to propose are the conditions themselves that make respect for God's existence as the divine Creator possible. It is doubtlessly complex to determine which sort of public arrangement best promotes the conditions for belief in God. Surely, though, even if committed to a principle of disestablishment, as I am, we can recognize appropriate ways for public order, and even government itself, to be more conducive to accepting God's authority. In 1790, when Rhode Island ratified the United States' Constitution, it included a declaration for religious liberty based on a principle of natural rights. Crucially, the declaration suggests a "duty" of persons to their Creator and does so without a formal religious establishment:

> That religion, or the duty which we owe to our Creator, and the manner of discharging it, can be directed only by reason and conviction, and not by force and violence; and therefore all men have a natural, equal, and unalienable right to the exercise of religion according to the dictates of conscience; and that no particular religious sect or society ought to be favored or established, by law, in preference to others.[28]

The state, in other words, need not be agnostic about the good of religious truth, even as it remains committed to temporal authority only. The state should not set itself against religion, even if it does not establish one formally, either. A capacious appreciation and respect for the role of religion in society is thus incumbent on legal regimes.

---

[28] Jonathan Elliot, *The Debates in the Several State Conventions on the Adoption of the Federal Constitution, as Recommended by the General Convention at Philadelphia, in 1787,* 2nd edition (Washington: Taylor and Maury, 1836), 1:334, quoted in Vincent Phillip Muñoz, *Religious Liberty and the American Founding: Natural Rights and the Original Meaning of the First Amendment Religion Clauses* (Chicago: University of Chicago Press, 2022), 39.

Nor does a state merely observe the ceremonial register of religion; it appreciates the values-forming mechanism that religion plays in cultivating citizenly virtue. Indeed, between "religion" and "politics" is a missing middle: ethics, which is often formulated by religious sentiment. As Finnis rightly notes, "It must be accepted that individual voters and legislators can rightly and should take into account the firm moral teachings of a religion if it is the true religion, so far as its teachings are relevant to issues of law and government."[29]

The religious foundation of public ethics merely requires citizens to communicate those truths in publicly accessible ways. If the natural law speaks in categories that seek to explain the intelligibility and reason for a religion's moral axiom relating to political debate, it is entirely legitimate to see how religion itself provides a sure foundation for moral reform. John Finnis echoes the sentiment that the common good include appreciation for the role of divine order,

> Taking the common good in its widest extension, it is for the common good of the members of a political community that they find the truth about divine creation and redemption, live in accordance with that truth, and so enter and remain forever in the altogether fulfilling fellowship of the divine family extending from this world into eternity. But the state is responsible only for temporal common good, and correspondingly the coercive jurisdiction of state government and law has as its defining objective not the widest common good which might include salvation itself, but what the Council calls a (or the) "basic component of the common good," namely public order.[30]

How particular regimes will arrange themselves pertaining to the promotion of religion is a matter of prudence. My own position is that

---

[29] John Finnis, *Religion and Public Reasons*, vol. 5, Collected Essays (Oxford: Oxford University Press, 2011), 101.

[30] Finnis, 94.

a principle of disestablishment that allows for robust public expression of religion is the most fortuitous to bring about this goal.[31] One can think of government promoting national holidays with a religious bent such as what George Washington did in his 1789 Thanksgiving Proclamation:

> Whereas it is the duty of all Nations to acknowledge the providence of Almighty God, to obey his will, to be grateful for his benefits, and humbly to implore his protection and favor—and whereas both Houses of Congress have by their joint Committee requested me to recommend to the People of the United States a day of public thanksgiving and prayer to be observed by acknowledging with grateful hearts the many signal favors of Almighty God especially by affording them an opportunity peaceably to establish a form of government for their safety and happiness.[32]

## Conclusion

We come to the end of this chapter asking what Jesus Christ has to do with public order. We can answer this question by reiterating that from the Christian perspective, the reason that nature has nature is because Jesus Christ is alive. It is the centrality of the gospel that Christians believe that the structures of creation are not only real, but *knowable.* What we also must insist is that, regardless of whether such claims are admitted as such, every claim by every individual is made on the basis of faith. The test is whether the claim of faith posits truths that are culturally beneficial at large. Ironically, it is historian Tom Holland who understands this. In public remarks from 2021, Holland was asked how Christians should position

---

[31] For my defense of disestablishment and a broader defense of my views on church-state relations, see Andrew T. Walker, *Liberty for All: Defending Everyone's Religious Freedom in a Pluralistic Age* (Grand Rapids: Brazos, 2021).

[32] George Washington, Thanksgiving Proclamation, November 26, 1789, https://www.mountvernon.org/education/primary-source-collections/primary-source-collections/article/thanksgiving-proclamation-of-1789/.

themselves in a culture that is growing less Christian and more secular. His answer is nothing short of stunning as it concerns the Christian's self-understanding of their duties to public order and how the gospel can promote the common good:

> Because the West has been so hegemonic for so long, it's been in a position to assume its concept of human rights is universal. They don't need to think about it. Of course, human rights exist. But what the rise of China and other civilizational powers is doing is to remind us that the concept of human rights is one that has emerged in a very specific cultural matrix, which is a Christian one. Therefore, if you want to believe in human rights, you have to believe. It takes a leap of faith to believe that there are things called human rights just as much as it takes a leap of faith to believe that the Lord Jesus Christ rose from the dead. They're both beliefs. And the fact that most people in the West sign up to the fact that human rights exist and they're important and that they should determine public policy. Actually, it's as rooted in theology and myth and metaphysics as all the teachings of Christianity. And, I think once people are reminded of that, I think it becomes impossible not to feel a greater sense of what Christianity is about. If you believe in human rights, why not believe that Jesus rose from the dead? . . .[33]

---

[33] "Tom Holland Christianity, Persecution, and the Meaning of the Cross," YouTube, December 31, 2021, https://www.youtube.com/watch?v=p6w7qw9kJ9k; starting with 42:26.

# Conclusion

# Christian Mission in the Post-Rational Society

"You live in a deranged age—more deranged than usual, because despite great scientific and technological advances, man has not the faintest idea of who he is or what he is doing."

—WALKER PERCY, *LOST IN THE COSMOS: THE LAST SELF-HELP BOOK*[1]

The goals of this book have been as simple as they have been audacious. First, I have sought to *frame* how natural law ought to be conceived among Protestant evangelicals. This was done against a backdrop of concern for how Protestant and evangelical reluctance around the natural law is built largely upon strawmen, caricature, and general misunderstanding. Secondly, I have attempted to explain what the natural law is—its origins, its knowability, its content, and its utility. Lastly, I have tried to apply the

---

[1] Walker Percy, *Lost in the Cosmos: The Last Self-Help Book* (New York: St. Martin's, 2000), 76.

363

natural law to a number of issues, thereby offering an applied theory of natural law in the broadest categories of its relevance.

Overall, what I hope this book accomplishes from an academic perspective is advancing the discussion of contemporary Christian ethics and natural law's relationship to Christology. I have done that by trying to argue that it is Jesus Christ who explains the origins, substance, and goal of the natural law. We must not, and indeed cannot, excise or abstract Jesus from considerations of natural law. The natural law is preparatory to the gospel. It indicts our guilt, and exposes our need for cosmic reconciliation.

Human nature, human action, and human goods are not impersonal. Each finds its *telos* in Jesus Christ, the One who is fully God and fully man. It is in Jesus where creation is fused to redemption. It is Jesus who unveils true humanity. The Christ of grace is not opposed to the Jesus of nature—in him, they are mystically fused into one divine-human substance. To proclaim "Jesus Christ," then, is to tell of maximal human fulfillment and divine endowment conjoined in one person. It is looking to Christ that we understand the *telos* of our nature. It is in Jesus Christ where we see the embodiment of just action mediated by love. It is through our obedience to Christ that we understand what "good" in both the natural and heavenly domains means. Our ethics are not merely veiled propositions about axiology. If this book aims to propose a theory upon which its thesis is based, it is this: *We understand the integrity of the natural order as an expression of Christ's sovereignty and goodness to us in the world he has ordered for our good and for his glory. It is by seeking Christ's glory that we experience the fulfillment of our being and know and exult in the good.* This is what "Christotelic natural law" ethics means as I've tried to argue. A thoroughgoing "theory" requires an explanation of its origins, its prescriptivity, and the reason or choiceworthiness for the ends it sees as fulfilling. Or, to state it more clearly: a theory needs to explain where it came from, why it is obligatory, and the purposiveness of its directives. Natural law provides all of these elements. Grounded in theism, it provides an account for morality's origins, the substance and intelligibility of moral standards themselves, and how moral standards hold people accountable to their norms. In contrast to most discussions of natural law theory, I have sought to explain each of these aspects in reference to Jesus Christ. To go against the grain of the universe is to go against God's Word and God's own Christ because all affirm, each in its own way, the same reality of givenness ordered by a holy God.

In this last and much shorter chapter, I want to conclude by asking: What now? After all, if the goal of this book is to equip Christians to understand the rational coherence of their ethics, to encourage them in their engagement with the world, what value is the natural law in a world that is increasingly not only post-religious, but also post-rational? Much of the modern world rejects not only divine explanation for our most pressing questions; it rejects any concept of nature as well, the combination of which results in intellectual squalor and human misery.

What, then, are we to do as Christians with our knowledge of the natural law in the world right now? I would argue that regardless of what cultural context Christians find themselves in and regardless of persuasive success, the mission always stays the same: Christians witness to the truth for the sake of the truth as its own moral good. The Christian does not measure faithfulness to Christ by the outcome of our witness but rather by the faithful witness of our testimony. A society that does not reason will not be persuaded by reason. Considering that secularism cordons itself off from the transcendent, it is even more urgent that Christians speak not only in the dialect of natural law but fulsomely in the language of special revelation— that through the static and white noise of secularism that Christians speak not merely with a natural dialect but a Christic dialect.

## The Limits of Pluralism

Pluralism as its own end cannot absorb the shocks that come from undermining creation order. When we destroy life at all stages, a stable gender binary, and marriage, no culture can persist in health. It just cannot. Hence the epidemic of "despair" in our society. Our culture is deeply unwell.

Some Christians have let pluralism become an end unto itself, permitting harmful ideologies to gain footing instead of treating pluralism as an instrumental good for negotiating the relationship between private vice and public harm. Our inoffensiveness is thus servicing social decay. The natural law reminds us that society can practice pluralism when accompanied by a meaningful moral ontology. Pluralism is durable only when creation order is respected. Pluralism without ontology is relativism. Pluralism is no safe harbor against a society that devalues and rejects the truth.

The command to love our neighbor as they truly deserve to be loved commands us to faithfully steward the conditions for their thriving. A disordered commitment to pluralism provides an output where basic goods become at first unattainable, then unrecognizable, and in a perverse degradation evidencing severe moral devolution, as betrayals to what society considers decent morals.

Liberal democracy cannot have a meaningful future apart from Christianity. It will eventually peel off into barbarism. Rights only work where the duties that rights protect are grounded in objective moral goods. Attempting to ground morality apart from transcendence is futile. As always, the pluralism that liberal democracy seeks to protect, without a coherent ontology underneath it, breeds relativism. If the Christian faith teaches that there are objective moral obligations (and it does), then it will have cultural and political implications. When we downplay the real-world implications of proclaiming an objective moral order that promotes human flourishing and serves the common good, we do not pledge ourselves to a "pure church," not seeking to impose an alien ethics upon the world. All we do is abdicate the responsibility to tell the truth to the world. To understand the need for natural law anew is to situate it within a broader evangelical political framework, one that understands that political power is not the ultimate end of Christian ethics. Rather, the function of the natural law is to bear witness to the logic of the gospel's moral demands by giving it the categories for public pronouncement. The political nature of the church's mission is to "declare the criteria by which nations will ultimately be judged, and the divine standards to which man and society must conform if civilization is to endure."[2]

## Christian Witness in the Post-Rational Society

I want to end this book with exhortation. I do not live my life for the sake of the academy alone. What I have written in this volume is not merely an academic exercise. I teach and write for the sake of Jesus's kingdom and the building up of his church.

Christians right now, at least in the West, find themselves in an often dispirited fashion. It is doubtlessly true that we are living in one of the most revolutionary times. Though I run the risk of falling prey to what C. S. Lewis called "Chronological Snobbery," I do believe that the moment before us is a revolutionary one where settled norms that provided the seedbed for stable order are being torn asunder. The task of Christian public ethics has never been more urgent. One of the ways we are to love our neighbor is by being truthful with our neighbor. This means truthfulness as to the norms and goods befitting their nature. The Christian desires happiness for themselves and for their neighbors, and insists that ultimate happiness is impossible apart from knowing the one true and living God and Jesus Christ, who lives faithfully in response to the knowledge of God's law.

The goal of Christian cultural engagement or cultural criticism right now is the same as what it has always been: witnessing to the truth. It is to this we are called to "not grow weary" (Gal 6:9). The apostle Paul promises that in due time, we will reap a harvest. That may be a harvest none of us will live to see, which is as thrilling as it is committal. Martin Luther was once asked what he would do if he knew the world was ending tomorrow. He replied that he would plant an apple tree. Though subject to various

---

[2] Carl F. H. Henry. "An Ecumenical Bombshell," *Christianity Today*, September 15, 1967, https://www.christianitytoday.com/ct/1967/september-15/editorials-ecumenical-bombshell.html.

interpretations, I think Luther's quip is relevant to us today: The Christian is called to preserving and cultivating the created order according to God's timetable, not ours. We may not be around to taste the tree's fruit, but the presence of the tree is a commitment to our trust in the goodness of the world God has created and upholds.

This has profound implications at a moment where fraying cultural division leaves one tempted to despair. Christians are called to witness to the truth for the sake of the truth as its own end. This is what this book has called a "self-evident good." Truth is a good for us to live by. We are to live by it regardless of whether others are or not. The gospel of Jesus Christ is true. Witnessing to the truth has no greater justification for its purpose than its own end. We are to share it with reckless abandon. For that, I am thankful. The message of the gospel is purposeful truth to share. We are called to this regardless of outcome or consequences. We have an obligation to do it. We are to speak what is true, defend what is true, walk in justice, to protect the weak and the vulnerable.

Witnessing to the truth for its own sake is the call of the Christian. Refuse to surrender what the Bible refers to as a divine creation order, what the philosophers and theologians call the "natural law," and what everyone else is bound to, regardless of whether they recognize it or not: reality and truth—all of which are not up for a vote. What a beautiful truth that allows us as believers to unlock the fullness and beauty of a life ordered to, patterned after, and fulfilled in, Christ—the Logos of Creation. I end with where this book began: With a call to the gospel. A call that harmonizes us with the way God created the world and the cosmos: "Only when the Gospel has penetrated to the very depth of human substance will natural law appear in its flower and its perfection."[3]

The culture wars that besiege us are little else than a shorthand expression for the conflict that persons in society have over the deepest questions about our existence, truth, and ultimate reality. Christians understand

---

[3] Maritain, *Christianity and Democracy, and The Rights of Man and Natural Law*, 106 (see chap. 12, n. 23).

the culture war to be a debate over objective truth, moral goodness, and aesthetic beauty—what we call the unity of transcendentals. Though we should caution the use of military metaphors to describe our contending for such truths, a concern for their recognition at the highest levels of society invites one to engage in a protracted struggle in the arenas where conflicts are most urgent. Christians should not and must not bristle at having to make hard declarations in defense of God's sacred order. Even so, while the Christian must have those necessary debates, we should never let our love for the transcendentals be eclipsed by a pursuit of conflicts as its own means. Seen through this lens, the Christian is less motivated by a reflexive defensiveness, fears of marginalization, belittlement, or forlorn nostalgia about better times and more concerned that our neighbors—whom Christians are called to genuinely love as persons made in God's image—are better acquainted with conditions that impart to them life-giving and joy-giving truth.

The object isn't to win or cultural conquest for its own sake. Vanquishment is a mere means to a greater end—the witness and triumph of truth. To witness assures us that victory has already been won; that the victory belongs to Christ, not to us. Christians are not promised absolute victory this side of heaven. What we are called to do is to witness to the truth of the gospel, regardless of outcome or consequence. That does not take us off the battlefield, but to wage a battle in a particular way.

# Appendix 1

# Responding to Natural Law Objections

The place of the natural law within contemporary Protestantism has a tenuous status. Originally heralded by theologians of the Reformation (contrary to the caricatures that say otherwise), natural law's role in Protestant ethics is one of decline and, thanks to recent efforts, recovery.[1] Despite natural law's predominance throughout Christian history, in the twentieth century, natural law fell out of favor within Protestantism. For reasons that go beyond the full scope of this appendix, this rejection of the natural law was biblically unwarranted, over-extended in its claims, led to a major lacuna in Protestant social ethics in the latter half of the twentieth

---

[1] For two volumes that explain the Reformers' attitudes toward the natural law, see J. V. Fesko's introduction in Geerhardus Vos, *Natural Theology*, trans. Albert Gootjes (Grand Rapids: Reformation Heritage Books, 2022), xvii–lxx; Grabill, *Rediscovering the Natural Law in Reformed Theological Ethics* (see chap. 4, n. 2). A well-known article by John T. McNeill also makes the argument for the essential continuity of the natural law for Reformed thinking; see John T. McNeill, "Natural Law in the Teaching of the Reformers," *The Journal of Religion* 26, no. 3 (1946): 168–82.

century, and exhibits a fractious discontinuity with the Reformation's acceptance of natural law theory.[2]

Within the last twenty years, however, a resurgence of openness to
natural law thought has emerged from such Protestant scholars as J. Daryl
Charles, David VanDrunen, Jordan Ballor, Brad Littlejohn, Carl Trueman,
Bryan McGraw, David Haines, Denny Burk, Paul DeHart, Kevin DeYoung,
Jonathan Leeman, Stephen Grabill, and Micah Watson. This is a welcome
development as it signals a maturing recovery of Protestantism's own ethical
heritage and a rejection of caricatures foisted upon the natural law by its
detractors. It is the opinion of this author that the most significant factor
in the renaissance of Protestant natural law theory has had to do with its
necessity as a tool to combat cultural decline within the broader culture.
Caught flat-footed in response to decades-long cultural decline, criticisms
made from such titanic figures as Karl Barth and Carl F. H. Henry, alongside the so-called "culture wars" of the latter twentieth century, have created
a vacuum left by natural law's absence and helped bring forth its ongoing
resuscitation and retrieval within Protestantism.

Such is the case that a culture that rejects special revelation is not without accountability to the morality of general revelation, both given by God.
Culture only pretends epistemological ignorance in its self-deception, trying, whether stealthily or vocally, to evade a law that it cannot truly jettison.
The best use of the natural law tradition, then, never content to leave moral
considerations to the bare contemplation of "nature" alone, should direct
culture to the originating gaze of the natural law, which is God.

In contrast to the preceding chapters, which have been primarily constructive in nature from the categories of philosophy and theology, this
appendix seeks to synthesize and categorize the broad types of arguments

---

[2] J. Daryl Charles, "Protestants and Natural Law," *First Things*, no. 168
(December 1, 2006): 33–38; J. Daryl Charles, "Burying the Wrong Corpse: Second
Thoughts on the Protestant Prejudice toward Natural Law Thinking," in *Natural
Law Today: The Present State of the Perennial Philosophy*, ed. Christopher Wolfe and
Steven Brust (Lanham, MD: Lexington Books, n.d.), 87–109.

used to reject the natural law and, in turn, respond to them. Thus, this appendix serves as a brief apologetical capstone to much of the volume's preceding chapters.

Given that the purpose of this appendix is to respond to theological objections to the natural law arising within even conservative Protestantism, the bulk of this chapter will focus on protests, caricatures, and criticisms of the natural law from within Protestantism's own ranks.

## Theological Antipathy to the Natural Law

If natural law has been so embedded within Christian moral thought throughout church history, why is it then that the central tradition of Christian ethics has fallen out of favor with the bulk of Protestantism? There is no one single answer to this vexing question. But the answer, I think, can be decisively located in the mid-twentieth century. Prior to the twentieth century, there was broad consensus on the centrality of the natural law to Christian ethics in general, and protestant ethics, in particular.

Some would answer that evangelical Protestantism's strong tendency toward "the devotional and interior" never forced it to develop sophisticated canons of social thought that one sees in Catholicism.[3] The pietistic nature of evangelicalism coupled with the recognition that American public life shared, at least to some degree, the moral consensus of Christian thought meant that sophisticated defenses of Christian ethics' rational superiority never had to be materially developed. Second, owing to its intellectual embattlement leading to a fundamentalist retreat in the twentieth century, it is arguable that the retreat from public life created a Christian ethics accented by fideism. If Christianity is not seen as able to compete with the towering heights of secular intellectualism, retreating to the safety of "belief" to the neglect of reason can create intellectual ghettos suspicious of intellectual explanations for Christian faith. As a response to rationalist

---

[3] Charles, *Retrieving the Natural Law*, 21 (see chap. 2, n. 14).

attacks on Christianity, it is easy to sympathize with a quick reversion to Christian ethics as built upon a fideistic foundation, unaccountable to the test of reason. Third, the devotional and fideistic criticism parallels with a criticism I made earlier in that Protestant ethics tends toward biblicism, a reading of Scripture that unnecessarily narrows its sufficiency to what can be left to proof-texting alone.

But the fallout from Protestantism's abandonment of natural law has had consequences into the present. As I will argue below, many objections to the natural law are flawed by misunderstood definitions, strawmen arguments, and unrealistic expectations as to its utility. The proceeding rebuttals against natural law are intended to follow sequentially.

### Argument #1: Natural law places too high a view on human reason and fails to adequately account for sin's impact on human reason and human will.

It is doubtlessly the case that the most popular and perhaps most effective argument against the natural law is that it treats human reason with too much optimism and fails to duly reckon with the impact of sin upon reason and the human will.

What can be said about a line of critique that seems so patently obvious? Looking through history it is clear that sin has indeed warped and wounded both human reason and the human will. But I find this argument grounded in a caricature of the natural law. First, no natural law proponent I am aware of discounts the impact of sin on human reason or believes that humans have exhaustive knowledge of the natural law or can consistently obey the natural law. Natural law is never salvific and evaluated against the realm of redemption, natural law is inferior as to the mode of ethics made crystalline from divine revelation. Natural law is not the culmination of ethics; Jesus Christ is. But we can and should allow for natural law to have an integrity consistent with its design as a mode of moral argument for non-redeemed humanity. I hold the position that while man's spiritual relationship to God was obliterated after the fall and putting enmity between God and rebellious humanity, man's knowledge of God's law and capacity to obey it was not altogether extinguished, but severely hampered. Our wills and intellects are darkened, but they subsist constrained by the pull of fallen human nature.

The natural law has a three-fold integrity to its structure. First, it has an integrity of its own by serving as a guide for matters pertaining to fallen life within the civic arena. Natural law is nothing less than the modus operandi for fallen society's continued existence. We can call this, for argument's purposes, the civil integrity of the natural law. Secondly, natural law has a preparatory integrity owing to the biblical injunction that knowledge of violating God's holy law is what renders humans culpable before a divine judge. Third, natural law has a pedagogical integrity in helping Christians understand the origins, substance, and end of God's natural order as upheld by Jesus Christ.

As I have argued, the natural law simply holds that certain foundational truths cannot be blotted out, namely, the First Principle of Practical Reason—that all persons seek after ends they believe will benefit them. The First Principle of Practical Reason does not imply a perfect seeking of the correct ends. Natural law theory has ample resources to explain why people err in the ends that they seek (which were written about in an earlier chapter): Genuine ignorance of certain entailments of the natural law, evil disposition, inconsistent application, bad habit, and cowardice. Knowledge of God's moral law, of ourselves, and of the world is gained through practical insights into our everyday interactions with the world, and it is those interactions that provoke questions about ultimate existence, the origins of morality, and the deepest mystery of the universe.

There may be a debate about the severity of sin's impact on reason and the will, but even granting a spectrum of views about the severity of sin's impact, this line of argument cannot be worked out consistently. Scripture portrays humanity's primary problem as a volitional suppression of an inextinguishable natural law, not a comprehensive ignorance of the natural law. Furthermore, it is theologically untenable that the natural law could be blotted out entirely. That would mean moral nihilism is the operative condition of the world and that the world would have no ability to govern itself with any degree of moral order. Total ignorance of the natural law and absolute rebellion against it would mean the repudiation of common grace. While humanity may be unable to account for its own moral intuitions, the fact that longings for justice and meaning persist testifies to the natural law. If humans were completely void of the natural law, they would not go about the great efforts they do to try to find meaning within the universe. But they do to great fanfare. Humanity cannot be so depraved that it is unaware of a moral law that it is not following. The fact that fallen humanity has knowledge of its own moral error assumes a backdrop of correct moral order and correct moral action.

If acceptance of the gospel and divine revelation—rather than just theism—is what is necessary for morality to have coherence for the unregenerate in society, then ethics as a discipline is a moot discipline. It also means that trying to have fruitful discussion with non-believers about how best to order civil arrangements is futile. If the Christian response to the natural law is that only divine revelation can account for human morality, there can be no meaningful moral common ground whatsoever. Of course, we can and should confess that ethics are *ultimately* and *definitively* derived as a matter of divine revelation, but owing to our belief in general revelation as a medium of God's revelation, we can insist that non-Christians have true moral knowledge despite lacking a coherent foundation. Positing the need for a public ethics as Christians insist upon, but denying the possibility for public ethics to have any coherence to it, makes Christian interaction with the world a futile enterprise. Public justice and statecraft would be unintelligible were acceptance of the gospel and divine revelation the only way for there to be a modicum of civil tranquility. Christian ethics is thus a sectarian project cocooned off from relevance to our neighbor and the common good.

If it were the case that humanity's reason was beyond hope for providing any ground for morality even in a state of sin, humanity could not be held accountable to a moral law that it has no knowledge of violating.

Without a knowledge of the moral law, it would be unjust for God to hold people to a law that they are accountable to but have no knowledge of. Human reason must have some minimal knowledge of the moral law for God to hold humanity accountable and for society to have even a modicum of moral sanity.

### Argument #2: Natural law is not persuasive to non-Christians.

Among the most important questions of sin's impact on reason is the natural law's continued usefulness considering sin's impact on reason and human will. According to this line of argument, even if it is granted that a remnant morality persists after the fall, it is so minimal and marred that whatever morality exists is insufficient to the task of providing any sort of exhaustive moral content to build the just society. Therefore, ethics is primarily, and by necessity, a revelatory enterprise.

There are several replies to this line of thinking, not least of which is the false dichotomy in pitting special and natural revelation against one another, as though the use of one negates the legitimacy of the other. It is also a mistake to believe that people could not be convinced of a reasonable truth. The whole fact of Western society's turn away from racial strife is a testament to the possibility of moral reformation. The question in moral conflict is whether someone would admit to themselves the reasonableness of the truth claim they have been confronted with and whether they would turn to live in light of it. Willed self-deception is a category we must allow for in our conceptions for why people flout the natural law.

At the deepest level, natural law grounds its existence in the God who reveals, whether in nature and attested to in reason, or in inscripturated form. Natural law is simultaneously natural in that it speaks to a moral order that is truly there but finds its existence within the eternal law of God's own reason and promulgation to rational creatures. Someone accepting the theistic underpinnings of natural law is irrelevant to whether the claims of the natural law itself are both intelligible and persuasive. If the natural law is what it says it is, then elements of its reasonableness must be self-evident, regardless of whether verbal assent to said reasonableness is uttered. The unregenerate cannot argue that 2+2=5 because that argument eclipses reason, not special revelation. Now, the reason that 2+2=4 is because God has ordered mathematical formulae to align with rational and logical order. A non-Christian can know 2+2=4 as true knowledge even if they do not know it is *real* knowledge imparted by a rational God.

Second, when Scripture is understood properly, we will see it speaking of natural law as one form of God's revelation. Thus, natural law ethics *are* revelatory ethics under the supposition that the reason anything exists—including morality itself—are the products of divine will, reason, and design. The question is the type of revelation natural law is. That it is revelatory issuing from God's ordering of creation, however, is never to imply that its ultimate point of origin separates it from the domain of reason. Not at all. To clear away confusion about the natural law requires rebutting the false dichotomies erected against it and clarifying the proper use of reason in Christian ethics.

Protestant objections to the natural law fail to observe that natural law *will* inevitably become the grounds upon which moral communication depends upon within a fallen creation order. Natural law is a moral reality constrained by the era of redemption that we are in. Until the dawning of the *eschaton*, natural law will most certainly be the grounds for moral cooperation within society apart from society becoming comprehensively regenerate. Attempts to bypass the natural law simply end up reaffirming it, ratifying it by different names. This, to me, captures the essence of the natural law being truly natural: we cannot avoid it. Even the faintest admission that non-Christians can understand moral goods at any level is to play on the natural law's terms.

Another response to this line of objection is, "So what?" Objection to the natural law no more disproves the natural law than a wrong answer to a mathematical equation disproves the existence and operation of mathematics. The persuasiveness of the natural law is not a measure of its enduring truthfulness. Humanity in a state of error will always resist the natural law. Evasion is no excuse for discounting its relevance. If the natural law is true as an ontological account of morality, the Christian has reality and not mere consensus as the grounds for their moral claims. Moreover, society cannot run headlong against the natural law without self-destructing. So, a culture's confrontation with the natural law will be to learn to live within its contours as wisdom and self-correction avails, or else run the risk of cultural suicide. One way or another, God's natural law as an authoritative moral account will be vindicated by either flourishing or futility.

## Argument #3: Nature is not self-interpreting.

The argument is formulated like this: if one accepts "nature" as a self-attesting category, reason is elevated as an authority over God's Word. Because of sin, "nature" is not self-interpreting and therefore, nature has no objective moral content to it and only the Bible can properly interpret nature for us. It is a common argument made by adherents to the presuppositionalist camp of apologetics, an approach to apologetics that I find value in, but not as a stand-alone approach to apologetics.

This argument is rife with false dichotomies, pitting faith against reason, and misunderstands how the natural law tradition understands "nature." We should recognize, as we have already throughout this book, how this line of argument misunderstands the proper relationship between faith and reason. All genuine truths of reason align with faith and truths we grasp from faith are not incompatible with reason, even if reason cannot get to those claims perfectly on their own. But secondly, just because human reason may fail to grasp the moral directives inherent with nature does not nullify nature's intelligibility.

Second, this argument is particularly pernicious because its reliance upon special revelation as the only lens to interpret the world ends up eviscerating the natural order of intelligible moral content. How so? It ends up creating a Christian version of the fact-value dichotomy and accepts the underlying critique of the is-ought dilemma by granting it legitimacy.

These are two philosophical modes of attack that have sought to undermine Christian ethics by (1) assuming that knowledge consists only of empirically verifiable facts and any "value" we assign to these facts are illusory expressions of emotion; (2) that nature has no in-built moral direction inherent with it. Reality and nature are simply an "is" and no objective "ought" can be derived from it. Both lines of criticism taken together result in nature having no objective moral content or moral direction built into it. All moral claims are just expressions of emotion, and words are little else than linguistic constructions that reveal nothing else than the logic of language to express our emotion.

Practically speaking, if this argument is true—that nature has no moral clues within itself—then we are left with granting the legitimacy to emotivism as a construct. We are left concluding that the atheist is just as equally justified in their moral skepticism as we are in our moral objectivity. Because, after all, if nature is just a blank page for us to impute meaning onto, who can say who is right or wrong since the plane of our natural existence has no brute moral content?

This is devastating for Christian public ethics. Making nature dependent exclusively, rather than ultimately, on Scripture means the ardent same-sex marriage proponent has just as much credibility at disputing marriage's nature because nature exhibits no natural truths of marriage on its own. If nature has no morally intelligible content of its own integrity, the transgender activist has just as much plausibility at the idea of denying the body's authority in identifying gender.

Lastly, this line of argument assumes the Bible is simply self-interpreting. As a divinely inspired document, the Bible is inspired but its inspiration requires understanding through interpretive investigation made available by cognition's inquiry and insights. If we do not grant validity and authority to some degree of nature (including our own minds as a faculty that can grasp truth), even the ability to correctly interpret biblical passages over and against bad interpretations that dishonor the text, we are left admitting that the LGBT revisionist has just as much credibility in their interpretation as we do in ours. After all, if nature has no fixed meaning, interpretations themselves are just expressions of emotions we impute on or from the text. All interpretive acts require reason, which is a product of nature. The Bible is self-interpreting, but it also rests upon the nature of our cognitive abilities to interpret it. Human reason vis-à-vis nature is inevitably brought into the interpretive exercise. Christians cannot implicitly accept the fact-value and is-ought fallacy by denying that nature has any self-evident claims about itself.

To summarize: If unbelievers are robbed of any common foundation of reasons to believe that the world has any comprehensible order to it as such, then the secular person's interpretation of "nature" is just as valid as the presuppositionalist's insistence that "nature"—apart from regeneration—means nothing. Presuppositionalists downplay creation as a stable medium of revelation that communicates common notions because it means that actors within creation would have to be able to grasp comprehensible truths and deducements from it apart from special revelation, which is entirely at odds with presuppositionalist axioms.

It should be pointed out, additionally, that the is-ought dilemma is itself self-defeating as a rubric for how to do ethics. The is-ought and fact-value dilemmas used to deny moral obligation in Christian ethics by secular critics is the same dilemma that renders claims of secular progressivism moot as well. One cannot reject Christian ethics and remain unscathed from the consequences of dispensing with objective accounts of morality for ethics. We fail to understand how thoroughly nihilistic modern moral philosophy is. Sound moral reason, again, is going to require God's existence, and God's existence known through some form of revelation. Christianity affirms both, which is why Christianity offers a far more superior way to do ethics in any capacity we'd call meaningful and truly reasonable.

A similar argument tied to this broad category is the collapse of "nature" down to what is "natural." The argument goes as follows: If the natural law commands to do what is natural, that must mean that any thwarting of a natural inclination is wrong. This argument confuses "natural" with "what naturally arises" with "therefore, do it." No one consistently lives this way. We all recognize—even the unfallen—that desires, perceptions, and feelings well up within us that cannot be acted upon. We must consider the assault of sin upon our nature. What the natural inclinations that arise within us require is investigation into whether the inclination to do X is a good inclination or a fallen inclination. We can grasp by way of practical reason the virtue or vice of an inclination based on whether the inclination lets us complete ourselves commensurate with our nature or whether it leads us toward a privation of our nature. As Joseph Koterski writes, "The intellect must then investigate the natural inclinations to discern which will, in fact, bring about the natural end of happiness and which are somehow excessive, insufficient, or disordered in a way that would lead to frustrating the natural end. We must remember that some of our inclinations are subject to passion."[4]

A final way that "nature" pertaining to the natural law is dismissed is by observing that non-Christians dispute the concept of "nature" to begin with. To that, we must simply reply that if we are to validate that a non-Christian has good reason to question the very concept of nature itself, we have unwittingly given ourselves over to moral nihilism. Some underlying notion of "nature" will be present at the heart of our moral debates, even a denial of "nature" is to posit a truth about "nature"—that there is no nature to nature. Again, this leads back to a chain of circular reasoning that is vapid and unsustainable as a moral code for society.

According to Scripture, nature itself is a form of revelation (Psalm 19). This means, regardless of whether the unbeliever has exhaustive understanding of why nature exhibits order, or why they have moral perception in whatever degree, that nature does exhibit order that indicates some actions to be right and some actions to be wrong. Nature must have some degree of self-authenticating and self-attesting objectivity to its design or else nature is just a blank canvas that one derives whatever they want from.

---

[4] Joseph Koterski, *Natural Law and Human Nature* (Chantilly, VA: Great Courses, 2002), 57.

It seems to me that if our opposition to natural theology and natural law leaves us in the position of saying that a non-Christian would have no good reason NOT to murder or no good reason to be able to identify marriage as a complementary union of man and woman, we have gone further in rejecting the validity of natural theology than what the Bible allows for. This belies human experience in a thousand ways, too. Of course humans err and sin. But human civilization throughout all of history has arrived at certain moral truths (marriage among them). Certain actions, like murder and sodomy, are contrary to nature, because they thwart what nature directs us to as good: life and procreation. If nature exhibits no moral significance on its own integrity, Christians should vacate the public square.

### Argument #4: Natural law grants a sphere of autonomous reason.

Another familiar objection is that natural law theory not only overvalues the role of reason but makes reason its own autonomous authority. This is a caricature of what the natural law teaches. No less than the architect of classical natural law theory, Thomas Aquinas, held that human reason is endowed by divine reason. According to Aquinas:

> For this reason, since all things subject to Divine providence are ruled and measured by the eternal law, as was stated above. It is evident that all things partake somewhat of the eternal law, in so far as, namely, from its being imprinted on them, they derive their respective inclinations to their proper acts and ends. Now among all others, the rational creature is subject to Divine providence in the most excellent way, in so far as it partakes of a share of providence, by being provident both for itself and for others. For this reason it has a share of the Eternal Reason, whereby it has a natural inclination to its proper act and end. This participation of the eternal law in the rational creature is called the natural law. Hence the Psalmist after saying (Psalms 4:6): "Offer up the sacrifice of justice," as though someone asked what the works of justice are, adds:

"Many say, Who showeth us good things?" in answer to which question he says: "The light of Thy countenance, O Lord, is signed upon us": thus implying that the light of natural reason, whereby we discern what is good and what is evil, which is the function of the natural law, is nothing else than an imprint on us of the Divine light. It is therefore evident that the natural law is nothing else than the rational creature's participation in the eternal law.[5]

As we can see from Aquinas's own words, construing reason as anything else than a divine endowment of the rational creature's participation in the eternal law is false and misleading.

### Argument #5: Natural law is insufficiently Christological and cheapens the radical demands of Jesus's kingdom.

This is a common argument made against the natural law by prominent narrative theologians who believe that natural law trades the uniqueness and radicality of Jesus's commands for the staid offerings of universal morality based on general abstractions.

In a famous exchange with Emil Brunner, Barth famously answered with "Nein!" (no) to the question of natural theology and natural law.[6] Undoubtedly the most influential theologian of the last one hundred years, Barth's influence led to the near abandonment of natural law among Protestant theologians. This happened for several reasons: Barth rejected the natural theology that had dominated German theological liberalism since Friedrich Schleiermacher. Too anthropocentric in nature, he believed natural theology and natural law had been misappropriated by the likes of Nazism. The remedy is to make God "wholly other" and to make revelation entirely disclosed in Jesus Christ, to the negation of nature and natural

---

[5] *ST* 1a2ae.91.2.

[6] For this debate, see Emil Brunner and Karl Barth, *Natural Theology* (1946; repr., Eugene, OR: Wipf & Stock, 2002).

religion. While one can appreciate the historical setting that led to Barth's disavowals, his rejection of natural law went too far. Rejecting the legitimacy of natural law for fear of its abuse can have disastrous implications for public ethics. "The dilemma for Barthian Christians," writes Lutheran theologian Carl Braaten, "is how it is possible to engage in public ethical discourse in a pluralistic world, when the majority, who are non-Christian, do not accept the Christian source of revelation."[7] Barth's approach to public ethics makes Christianity's relationship to the broader social order unbridgeable.

In contemporary theology, anabaptist theologians such as Stanley Hauerwas have emphasized narrative theology and counter-imperial readings of Scripture over and against natural law. In this framework, natural law's universalized moral principles are at odds with the peculiar and radical ethics of Jesus, preeminently demonstrated by the tradition's commitment to non-violence. According to the narrative critique, the radical nature of discipleship cannot be known or relayed as a universal norm since non-violence upends earthly political communities. Christian incorporation of non-Christian morality is seen as defiling and diluting the uniqueness of Jesus.[8] Such "anti-Constantinian" ethical schemes view natural law as an ethic of compromise.

Responding to these objections have less to do with logic than with the approach one takes to the natural law itself. If natural law is used to the neglect of mentioning the radical demands of Jesus's kingdom, natural law is indeed in error. We can countenance no ethical tradition that is reluctant to mention, bring, or insist upon the authority of Jesus to the task of ethical obligation in the public square.

But secondly, as I have been at pains to do in previous sections of this volume, my concern around natural law has been to tether it more closely to Christology, positing what I am calling a "Christotelic" reading of the natural law where natural law is understood as originating, upheld, and culminating in the person and work of Jesus Christ.

---

[7] Braaten, "Protestants and Natural Law," 21.
[8] Hays, *The Moral Vision of the New Testament*, 294.

## *Argument #6: Natural law diminishes the need for revelation.*

According to this strain of thinking, if human reason is sufficient as an authority for moral guidance, special revelation is superfluous. Again, this is a caricature and misreading of the natural law tradition. According to Aquinas, humanity has a supernatural end that it is in need of divine revelation to grasp:

> First, because it is by law that man is directed how to perform his proper acts in view of his last end. And indeed if man were ordained to no other end than that which is proportionate to his natural faculty, there would be no need for man to have any further direction of the part of his reason, besides the natural law and human law which is derived from it. But since man is ordained to an end of eternal happiness which is inproportionate to man's natural faculty . . . therefore it was necessary that, besides the natural and the human law, man should be directed to his end by a law given by God.[9]

Natural faculties alone, though they direct us to transcendent wonder and speculation, do not tell us the finite and comprehensive details of man's supernatural end. Man's natural faculties are incomplete and, due to sin, wounded in its knowledge of God. Thus, divine revelation was necessary for natural-though-fallen man to gain clarity about himself. This is not the only reason that supernatural revelation was necessary according to Aquinas. Human judgment can err or be uncertain, so divine and supernatural revelation is necessary to bring clarifying authority on matters that humanity can get wrong. Third, for Aquinas, natural law concerns exterior acts that can be judged by competent authorities as either right or wrong, but interior movements of the soul need an authority to judge them that human laws are not able to competently adjudicate. So divine revelation is necessary to judge the internal desires of humanity. Lastly, Aquinas argues that because human

---

[9] *ST* 1a2ae.91.4.

law cannot prohibit all human evil because a government of such exacting authority would also do damage to the common good overall, there is the need for divine revelation to clarify matters that are wrong or evil but still not within the purview of government to exercise authority over.[10]

# Conclusion

Without a thoroughgoing natural law doctrine, Protestant social ethics were robbed not only of an external-facing apologetic necessary to ground its engagement in the public square, but it also led to the deracination of Christian ethics as an internally facing project for how Christians understood the coherence of their own ethical commitments. Seen in this light, natural law offers a centrifugal force for engagement in the civic agenda and a centripetal force for gaining insights into the intelligibility of Christian ethics.

In the absence of decisive arguments that render the natural law a futile enterprise, Protestants should accept the natural law as a teleological ethic ordered to God's glory, but also the human good. Moral goods are never at odds with God's glory or human flourishing. They are, rather, correlates to both.

---

[10] *ST* 1a2ae.91.4.

# Appendix 2

# Deploying the Natural Law in Public Apologetics

Naturally, the question about the use of the natural law when engaged in public apologetics necessarily arises given the topic's relevance to matters of public concern. So, how should the natural law be used? When I'm asked this question in classes, I often use the following example to demonstrate an approach to the natural law that both (1) honors the natural law tradition itself; and (2) shows how its relationship to Christology can and should be used in public apologetics. As the example below demonstrates, the nature of argumentation in public apologetics should be likened to a bag of golf clubs. As there are different types of clubs for different types of swings, so there are different modes of argument to be contextualized as each type of argument is called for. As the clubs by no means contradict each other, neither does deploying different-though-complementary arguments cancel each other.

For the sake of the example that follows, imagine that a bill to legalize same-sex marriage is being debated and a Christian legislator is being asked to argue from the floor of the legislative chamber for why he or she is opposed to same-sex marriage. Of course, much more could be said below than what will be said. The example that follows is merely a sampling of how argumentation from the paradigm I've explained in this book would proceed. The legislator's floor speech in this hypothetical example is as follows:

> My fellow legislators, I rise to speak against the proposed legislation to legalize same-sex marriage. I have four arguments I would like to make.
>
> First, I would like to speak to you about the very nature of marriage itself. Marriage is not simply any relationship. It is unlike all other relationships. It has a uniquely comprehensive feature to it that other relationships cannot fulfill. Conjugal marriage is not merely an emotional union built on companionship or romance. It is an embodied union capable, and indeed oriented, to bringing forth from its enfleshed nature what no other relationship can bring forth—children.
>
> Marriage as the union of man and woman by no means discriminates against same-sex persons since same-sex relationships lack the reproductive fullness that a conjugal marriage possesses. If marriage were not reproductive *by nature*, society would have no vested interest in granting it legal recognition since there would be nothing publicly oriented about it. Words and terms matter: same-sex marriage is not a marital institution since reproduction has no association with it. If we attempt to legally redefine marriage, we are only continuing down the path of making the norms of marriage more difficult to perceive and enter. Law should duly recognize marriage as a distinct union for what it affords society that other relationships cannot.
>
> Second, I would like to make a sociological argument about the needs and welfare of children. Children enter this world as the result of male-female sexual union. It follows, logically, that in ideal situations, the individuals responsible for creating the child also bear

the unique responsibility—and, inherent to their callings as mother and father, the capability—to care for this child in unique ways. Children, in other words, need both a mom and dad. Studies too numerous to count testify to the reality that children fare best when cared for in a married household with a mother and father. A mother and father's respective differences provide them with complementary gifts that cannot be replaced by two moms or two dads. To legalize same-sex marriage is to intentionally sever the connection between a child's well-being and marriage's unique offerings to provide that well-being. By legalizing same-sex marriage, we would be licensing and regulating unions that would be welcoming children through adoption or assisted reproductive technology that knowingly denies a child either a mother or father. Marriage is not about the desires of adults, but the needs of children. Law should not confuse persons as to the type of relationship that a child needs to prosper.

Third, I would like to make an argument from the perspective of political philosophy that follows from my previous argument. At its most bedrock foundation, a political community requires that people inhabit it. The perpetuity of a political community is tied to fertility and demographic replenishment. It follows, then, that political communities have a vested stake in reproduction and the well-being of those who are brought to life and reared within the political community. We need not only people in our country, but virtuous people capable for self-government and meaningful production within society. As same-sex relationships are not generative, they offer the political community nothing outside of the relationship's own existence. It is right and fitting that law honor and recognize the irreplaceable foundation that marriage plays in the bringing forth of new citizenry.

While the three previous arguments are arguments that I believe someone of goodwill could agree with without sharing my same religion, my fourth and final argument comes from my religious background. It is well known by many that I am a Christian. But as I have been at pains to explain why marriage retains its own essence apart from appeals to revelation, and why marriage matters to a child's welfare and the political community's need of future citizens, it is also incumbent upon me to explain why, at the deepest level, I hold the position that I do. Truth and conviction require that I be honest with you about the deepest wellsprings of my conviction—about the foundation for what I believe is responsible for there being an institution like marriage in the first place: my Christian faith.

I believe marriage is a creational ordinance given by God for the prosperity of humankind. I believe that it is a creation ethic given from a benevolent Creator who wishes to see his creation not only reproduce but thrive. I believe, fundamentally, that since marriage is an institution given by God, government is powerless to redefine it. We cannot redefine what we did not create. I believe that this august body of legislators must honor God the Creator's will for creation. But let me conclude with even one deeper level of explanation: I believe that the marriage of man and woman reflects the most profound reality of the universe—the gospel of Jesus Christ. As the apostle Paul makes explicit in Ephesians 5, marriage is no mere contrivance or contract. No, marriage reflects the Christ-Church union. We read in that same chapter that as Christ laid his life down for the church, so the church honors and respects its Bridegroom, Christ. I believe that in attempting to legally redefine marriage, we are trafficking in matters that offend a Holy God.

Our nation will not be blessed if we transgress God's created order and natural law. I do believe that homosexuality is a sin. I believe its practice goes against the very fabric of nature. I understand that many of you will disagree with me on this latter point. But my religious convictions and religious liberty requires me to be honest with you and to call you to a sober recognition of the terms of offense before us.

My fellow legislators, we are dealing here in weighty matters. I know many of you do not share my faith, but I do believe you share in the same rational capacity I do to see the difference of conjugal marriage from rival conceptions and definitions, and I would plead with you in goodwill to retain our centuries-long understanding of marriage as the conjugal relationship of husband and wife.

# NAME INDEX

# SUBJECT INDEX

# SCRIPTURE INDEX